'It is surely a marvel that death is washed away in a bath.' So Tertullian saw in baptism a striking example of the paradox central to the Christian idea. Ambrose, a very different spirit, showed how this tension between mere water and salvation is very close to the desire which forms belief. This book makes a number of studies of different interpretations of baptism, as a way of showing how the force of sacrament comes less from its formal authority than from the understanding it calls upon. Indeed, it suggests that baptism was one of the central acts by which men and women in the Middle Ages perceived the world in which they lived.

But the variety of understandings is also the variety conferred by change; so there is a story to tell, too, of the beginnings of baptism in the 'crisis' of Late Antiquity through the long period up to the eleventh century when the baptism of a small child became one of the great moments at which the infinite is brought into a fragment of the finite, to the time, in the mid-eleventh century, when the sense of so dramatic an operation begins to become puzzling. In the puzzlement, most clearly expressed in the debate over the whereabouts of the body in the eucharist, there is a loss of innocence: the innocence of the sacramental symbol. In the tentative theology of Abelard we can see some of the anxiety which comes of loss. It is akin to the anxiety of 'not quite getting there' which Abelard finds in the pagan philosophers of Antiquity, whose knowledge was not yet made good by revelation; whose wish to be baptized was, as it were, not yet accomplished by baptism itself.

Cambridge studies in medieval life and thought

BAPTISM AND CHANGE IN THE EARLY MIDDLE AGES, *c.* 200 – *c.* 1150

Cambridge studies in medieval life and thought
Fourth series

General Editor:
D. E. LUSCOMBE
Professor of Medieval History, University of Sheffield

Advisory Editors:
R. B. DOBSON
Professor of Medieval History, University of Cambridge, and Fellow of Christ's College

ROSAMOND MCKITTERICK
Reader in Early Medieval European History, University of Cambridge, and Fellow of Newnham College

The series Cambridge Studies in Medieval Life and Thought was inaugurated by G. G. Coulton in 1921. Professor D. E. Luscombe now acts as General Editor of the Fourth Series, with Professor R. B. Dobson and Dr Rosamond McKitterick as Advisory Editors. The series brings together outstanding work by medieval scholars over a wide range of human endeavour extending from political economy to the history of ideas.

For a list of titles in the series, see end of book.

BAPTISM AND CHANGE
IN THE
EARLY MIDDLE AGES,
c. 200 – c. 1150

PETER CRAMER
Research Fellow, Wolfson College, Oxford

CAMBRIDGE
UNIVERSITY PRESS

Published by the Press Syndicate of the University of Cambridge
The Pitt Building, Trumpington Street, Cambridge CB2, IRP
40 West 20th Street, New York, NY 10011–4211, USA
10 Stamford Road, Oakleigh, Melbourne 3166, Australia

First published 1993

Printed in Great Britain at the University Press, Cambridge

A catalogue record for this book is available from the British Library

Library of Congress cataloguing in publication data

Cramer, Peter.
Baptism and change in the early Middle Ages, *c.* 200–*c.* 1150/ Peter
Cramer.
p.   cm. – (Cambridge studies in medieval life and thought)
Includes bibliographical references and index.
ISBN 0 521 35163 4 (hard)
1. Baptism – History – Early church, *c.* 30–600.   2. Baptism –
History – Middle Ages, 600–1500.   I. Title.   II. Series.
BV803.C73 1993
234′.161′09–dc20   92-17489 CIP

ISBN 0 521 35163 4 hardback

For my mother and father,
and for Sammy

For from what could we weave the boundary
Between within and without, light and abyss,
If not from ourselves, our own warm breath,
And lipstick and gauze and muslin,
From the heartbeat whose silence makes the world die?
(From Czeslaw Milosz, Tidings)

CONTENTS

Contents

ILLUSTRATIONS

PREFACE

I made a first study of baptism in the early Middle Ages in my doctoral thesis. After putting the thesis aside for two years or so, I went back to it and quickly came to feel that it must be re-written entirely. This book is the result of the re-writing, which could only be done by a thorough-going return to the documents. In the process of going back over old research, and adding new inquiries, I have altered my view of the liturgy's place in the early Middle Ages, and in particular I have become very much aware of the dangers of using liturgical texts in any simple way as evidence of social practice. If I have changed my views, the problem around which the book is built is the same problem I have had in mind – in one form or another, more or less precisely formulated – since I was made aware of the difficulty experienced by eleventh- and twelfth-century thinkers over the nature of sacrament; the difficulty of the reasoning mind in its attempt to understand the myth which it inherits from its own past, the myth, that is, of sacrament, of liturgy in general, and of the whole received content of faith. It is the fascination of this difficulty, a thing of the present as much as of the past, which has continued to make the subject compelling to me, even if I have tended to put my energies less into the discourse of the reasoners than into its pre-history, the genesis of sacrament. The compulsion has grown with the inquiry, as I have begun to see the complexity, on one side, of liturgy, and on the other, of the theological account of liturgy, and have begun to understand that what I first saw simply as a conflict between minds and periods, reason against sacrament, was in fact a historical dialogue of much greater richness.

Where I have succeeded in being clear at all, this is to be explained by the mid-wifely influence of Christopher Brooke, who, earnest and amusing in just the right places, has pulled many ideas which would otherwise have led only a fumbling, underground kind of existence out into the light of day. I am deeply grateful to him for this and for the great patience with which he has gone about it. I owe another big debt to David Luscombe, who supervised my thesis, cutting away deftly at the knots produced by early research, and balancing himself like a funambulist in order to deal out that kind of criticism which makes things more possible.

It is to Martin Brett's highly suggestive teaching that I owe my first interest in sacrament and debate about sacrament in the eleventh and twelfth centuries; Henry Mayr-Harting I would like to thank for the great help he has given me over the history of conversion in the early Middle Ages; and Giles Constable for some most useful criticism of earlier drafts of chapter 2 and the two Excursuses on the baptistery. Père Pierre-Marie Gy, in the Convent of Le Saulchoir in Paris, has time and again demonstrated to me, with his enormous subtlety, the many-layered thing which liturgy is, and the intricate possibilities it offers to the historian and theologian. I have always been grateful to him for his searching questions.

To the President, the members and fellows of Wolfson College, Oxford, I owe the vast debt of having been given a near-perfect place of work, a place of invaluable talk and friendship, and surely the only place in Oxford where one can write to the sound of a woodpecker pecking. The President and his wife, Sir Raymond and Lady Hoffenberg, I would like to thank especially for the kindness they have shown me, and for their hospitality.

It is a pleasure to be able to thank the British Academy for providing the wherewithal for much of the later research on the book, in the welcome form of a Postdoctoral Fellowship; the British School at Rome for three months spent in Rome and in the Apostolic Library in the Vatican; and my friends at the Max-Planck-Institut für Geschichte in Göttingen, for two months of discussion and reading in the illuminated expanse of their library.

Much in the book comes from *conuersatio*, the swapping of thoughts which are themselves forms of life. It would be impossible to name all those with whom I have had such conversation, or to give more than a hint of what it has meant, and I will let this short list stand for them all: Sara Cramer, Burcht Pranger, Margaret Raymond, Kristian Jensen, Simon Saunders.

Preface

To my family, to my mother and father especially, after all their help with typing, their constant support and patience, and to Kate, I feel a gratitude which falls into no class I know of.

ABBREVIATIONS

CCCM	*Corpus christianorum continuatio mediaeualis* (Turnhout, 1953ff)
CCSL	*Corpus christianorum series latina* (Turnhout, 1966ff)
Councils and Synods	*Councils and Synods with Other Documents Relating to the English Church*, I, ed. D. Whitelock, M. Brett and C. N. L. Brooke, 2 vols. (Oxford 1981) (pt I: *871–1066*; pt II: *1066–1204*)
CSEL	*Corpus scriptorum ecclesiasticorum latinorum* (Vienna 1866–)
DACL	*Dictionnaire d'archéologie chrétienne et de liturgie*, ed. F. Cabrol, H. Leclercq and others, 15 vols. (Paris 1907–53)
EHR	*English Historical Review* (London 1886–)
Hastings	*Encyclopaedia of Religion and Ethics*, ed. J. Hastings and others, 12 vols. and indexes (Edinburgh 1908–26)
Hefele–Leclercq	C. J. Hefele, transl. into Fr. by J. Leclercq, *Histoire des conciles d'après les documents originaux*, 11 vols. (Paris 1907–52)
Hennecke–Schneemelcher	E. Hennecke, *New Testament Apocrypha*, ed. W. Schneemelcher, Eng. transl., ed. by R. M. Wilson, 2 vols. (London 1963 and 1965)
HBS	Henry Bradshaw Society (1891–)
JEH	*Journal of Ecclesiastical History* (London and Cambridge 1956–)
JLW	*Jahrbuch für Liturgiewissenschaft* (Münster-in-Westfalen 1921–41)
JTS	*Journal of Theological Studies* (London

	1900–5; Oxford 1906–49; n.s., Oxford 1950–)
Lewis and Short	C. T. Lewis and C. Short, *A Latin Dictionary Founded on Andrews' edition of Freund's Latin Dictionary* (edn of Oxford 1975)
Mansi	*Sacrorum conciliorum noua et amplissima collectio*, ed. J.-D. Mansi, 53 vols. (Florence etc., 1759–1927)
ODCC	*The Oxford Dictionary of the Christian Church*, ed. F. L. Cross and E. A. Livingstone (2nd edn, Oxford 1974)
MGH	*Monumenta Germaniae Historica*
Capit. reg. Franc. I	*Leges* II: *Capitularia regum Francorum* I, ed. A. Boretius (Hanover 1883)
Capit. reg. Franc. II	*Leges* II: *Capitularia regum Francorum* II, part 3 (Appendix), ed. A. Boretius and V. Krause (Hanover, 1897)
Conc. aevi Karol. I	*Leges* III: *Concilia aevi Karolini* I, ed. A. Werminghoff (Hanover and Leipzig 1906)
Epist. Karol. aevi II	*Epistolae* IV: *Epistolae Karolini aevi* II, ed. E. Dümmler (Berlin 1895)
Epist. Karol. aevi III	*Epistolae* V: *Epistolae Karolini aevi* III, part 1, ed. E. Dümmler and K. Hampe (Berlin 1899)
Epist. Mer. et Kar. aevi	*Epistolae* III: *Epistolae Merowingicae et Karoli aevi* I ed. W. Grundlach and others (Berlin 1892)
Pass. Vitaeque Sanct. aevi Merov.	*Scriptores rerum Merovingicarum* V: *Passiones Vitaeque Sanctorum aevi Merovingici*, ed. B. Krusch and W. Levison (Hanover and Leipzig 1910)
Poet. lat. aevi Carol.	*Poetae latini medii aevi* I: *Poetae Patini aevi Carolini*, ed. E. Dümmler (Berlin 1880–1)
Script.	*Scriptores* XII: ed. R. Wilmans and others (Hanover 1856)
PG	*Patrologiae Cursus Completus, series graeca*, ed. J. P. Migne, 162 vols. (Paris 1857–66)
PL	*Patrologiae Cursus Completus, series latina*, ed. J. P. Migne, 221 vols. (Paris 1844–64)
RB	*Revue Bénédictine* (Lille and Bruges 1884; Maredsous 1885–)

RTAM	*Recherches de théologie ancienne et médiévale* (Abbaye du Mont César, Louvain 1929–)
SC	*Sources chrétiennes* (Paris 1940–)
TRHS	*Transactions of the Royal Historical Society*, 5th ser. (1951–)

INTRODUCTION

Very soon after beginning work on the history of baptism in the Middle Ages, I found myself going backwards. Struck with the difficulties encountered by Berengar of Tours and Lanfranc of Bec over what happened in sacrament – they were concerned with the eucharist first, but with baptism too – I started out by studying the history of sacrament and ideas about sacrament in the eleventh and twelfth centuries. But the habit, so typical of this period, of 'standing like dwarves on the shoulders of giants' – in other words grounding all opinion on a thorough knowledge of ancient authorities – made it necessary to know at least something about the authorities themselves. Trying to see what Hugh of St Victor or Peter the Lombard, or Berengar himself, had in mind, without some familiarity with Ambrose and Augustine, felt like walking across an attic floor with faulty floor-boards.[1] It was important to see not just what they said, but how they had shaped their material.

Equally, I felt that the debate carried on in the twelfth century, although it might seem to have sprung out of nowhere with the strained, perhaps slightly eccentric, account of sacrament in Berengar in the mid-eleventh century, would be better understood as a debate which had begun among the Carolingians, in the ninth century, not only with the controversy over the eucharist between the two monks of the Abbey of Corbie, Paschasius Radbertus and Ratramnus, but perhaps even with the attempt by Benedict of Aniane, Alcuin and others to give the liturgy a semblance of intellectual consistency, to make it answerable to reason. From this time, sacrament, and liturgy generally, had come under scrutiny; questions had begun to be asked about what we would call its apparent irrationality. What did it mean to say that the bread and wine turned into the body and blood of Christ?

[1] Or like going for a walk with a giant carrying a dwarf on his shoulders, and only talking to the dwarf, which might be just as risky.

How did baptism save a child too young to have any conception of what he or she was undergoing?

Periods in history are epistemological skittles, made to be bowled over; and no period is in reality shut off from the period before and the period after. But the twelfth century began to take on a curious aspect. It seemed both more and less divided from what preceded it: more divided because with great self-consciousness, it questioned the tradition it inherited, and doing this it took its distance from the tradition: and it seemed less divided, because to understand this questioning, the material questioned – the nature of liturgy and sacrament – had also to be understood.

It was for these reasons that I went backwards, to the Carolingians, and to the time of Augustine, Ambrose and – perhaps overdoing it a bit in a book about 'the early Middle Ages' – Tertullian and Hippolytus of Rome. My idea was to find out something not only about the interrogation of sacrament which grew from the ninth to the twelfth centuries, but about the genesis and nature of sacrament itself. Since the period dealt with thus turned out to be a long one – about a thousand years – and since the problem of what sacrament really is, what its effect is, is something of a quagmire, the book has, at times, a deliberately tentative quality.

Over this long period of the growth and decline of sacrament – for the interrogation of sacrament by theology is in a sense its decline – I found that liturgy itself, to an important degree, resisted time and change and period. It remained relatively unchanged over very long periods.[2] It remained unchanged in itself but, perhaps more significantly, in that it was always *thought* to have been instituted by Christ, and so to be essentially a repeat performance if not of the events of Christ's life in the Gospels, at least of their significance and saving effect. More obviously than any other activity in early medieval life, liturgy was subject to the power of memory to forget change, or to ignore it, and so to make all time appear to stand still. Baptism was not a recollection *that* Christ once died and returned to life; it was a death and

---

[2] The very fact that the liturgy was in Latin, the language associated with the time of Christ, gave it a character of permanence against the background of the vernaculars: Mohrmann 1957, p. 87 and *passim*. I am not saying here that there is *no* change in the liturgy: it has been one of the accomplishments of Père Pierre-Marie Gy to show, with great art, how the texts of the liturgies can be made to yield evidence of changes in religious sensibility. In Gy 1987, for example, he shows how the Roman rite expresses developments in Christology.

resurrection. The history of liturgy is in this sense the history of a *permanence*, of a phenomenon from which change is absent. Thus one of the great questions raised by the history of baptism is how it was that even after the habit of infant baptism had become widespread in the churches of Latin Christendom, the *form* of adult baptism – of a rite of conversion celebrated either at Easter or Pentecost, and not just of passive or magical exorcism – continued largely to prevail. On the other hand, this example shows how ambiguous is the permanence of liturgy. For if the forms of liturgy remained much the same, its sense, the meaning it had in a particular place at a particular time, or refracted in different minds, or subject to different moods, could never be the same. So, infant baptism puts the dramatic stress of the old rite of conversion in a quite different place, and would have drawn under the umbrella of the little-changed forms the manifold associations carried by the child. Indeed, the child, and the small body of the child with its vulnerable nakedness and its suggestions of uncertainties and precariousness, perhaps replaced water as the central symbol of baptism. Can we detect the same shift in the ivory relief of the Baptism of Christ, carved in the late tenth century in Winchester? It shows a childish Christ – not the Immanuel youth, the God-with-us, but a plump child – awestruck by the bigger, over-arching figure of the Baptist.[3] There is an infinite number of possible senses of baptism, even at a given time, let alone over a thousand years, and we have been warned about the chances of being sure what *any* of them was. How can we know? But I have tried, in a series of essays – I have thought of each chapter as an essay – to give an impression of possible senses, or rather to translate into words the immediate impression of sense that came to me in each case. Tertullian's sacrament is not Ambrose's; Ambrose's or Cyprian's is not Augustine's, and so on. If I think of Ambrose's urgent addresses to those baptized a few days before, I remember what he says about the fish, struggling through the stormy sea, buried in water and yet alive, a humble image which carries effortlessly the whole weight of the theology of death and resurrection and of rebirth. Tertullian's baptism conjures up a quite different picture, the Spirit at the beginning of Creation, not plunging into the water as it did elsewhere – and in the later baptismal *epiclesis* – but carried over it, and imparting to

[3] Ambrose, *De sac.* 3.1, p. 69; Tertullian, *De baptismo* 4.1, p. 279; Beckwith 1972, no. 14, pl. 35.

it its quality, a scene held in place by the habitual restraint of Tertullian's mind. Thinking of the rite of the eleventh or twelfth centuries, one might be reminded of many things – perhaps, for example, one of the Exultet Rolls from south Italy, a twelfth-century manuscript now in the John Rylands Library in Manchester. These rolls contained the text of the Exultet prayer, which was part of the blessing of the Easter candle on the vigil of Easter Saturday, shortly before baptism; but they also give depictions of the images used by the prayer. The rolls were unfurled from a pulpit by a deacon, in such a way that he could read the blessing, while the congregation could see the pictures of what he was saying. The prayer itself makes of the bees, who were thought to give birth without sexual contact, a metaphor of the Virgin Birth of Christ; and this roll follows the spoken blessing by juxtaposing, in two interlinear drawings only three lines apart, the two scenes of the Nativity above and bees in their hive below. But in the artist's contemplation of the liturgical image, the hive has become the stable of the Nativity, and the stable is a hive. The apparent oddness of the metaphor is effaced, as all the figures take on a bee-like aspect: the diminutive mother and child, both the same size, lying down, and the animals above them; to the left of the Nativity an enigmatic onlooker, sitting on the ground with his hand over his cheek; and the small Christ-child crammed into a basin in a Purification scene to the right; all are bees. There is no difficulty now in seeing the Nativity as a bee-hive.[4]

To some extent, the essays are independent of one another. I have let the bucket down into the river as it flows past, to see what might come up; it would in any case have been impossible to dredge the river systematically. Each chapter, or essay, is an attempt to make sense of a bucketful, to say how its contents got there. Lying between the chapters, there remain, consequently, some important unanswered questions. I have tried to give some explanation of the relation of the thinking of Augustine to the liturgical practice, and the unarticulated thought behind it, of the Middle Ages. But I have left dangling the question of how Augustine's tendency to see liturgy, or the *cultus dei* as he called it, as principally a return to the understanding of God by man through language and memory, becomes – or perhaps gives way to – the liturgical preference for the understanding which is

---

[4] John Rylands Library, MS 2; Avery 1936, pl. LV, 6–7.

4

awakened by and which passes through Nature: through the brute matter of salt, water, oil, ashes and body. For the medieval liturgy is a transfiguration of the physical from which Augustine shied away. Again, I have not put together the various representations of time in the liturgy: I have let the 'instant' which seems to be depicted in the wall-paintings of the baptistery of Concordia Sagittaria, and the notions of history and repetition which emerge from the poetic reconstruction of the benediction of the waters by Leidrad of Lyon (*c.* 812), and which are so important in the liturgical concept of time, remain separate (see pp. 291ff; 167ff).

In leaving these themes a little in suspense, I am following in the steps of liturgy itself, which, however much it aspires to the perfection of clear, regular, repetitious forms, often achieves its effect by juxtapositions where the relation between the parts is only implicit, and where each part is open to the impact of the others, so that the congregation is constantly invited to make its own connections. In this way, liturgical celebration is like the performance of a mime-artist, who does not *copy*, but suggests all the more forcibly the personality he mimes by picking out one or two typical gestures or habits of speech or dress. When this is done, the audience – or congregation – is not passive; it must make the mime true to its object.[5] The series of readings for Holy Saturday, one of the preludes to baptism, in the *Gelasian Sacramentary* is a fine example of how this happens in the Roman liturgy: one after the other, the stories of Creation, Noah's Flood, the sacrifice of Abraham, the crossing of the Red Sea, the three boys in the fiery furnace, the thirsting deer of Psalm 41 (42), and other stories, are read out from the Bible.[6] Biblical history has thus become a group of juxtaposed scenes rather than a succession over time.

But I have also tried to give a narrative account of baptism in the early middle Ages; to show the development of symbol in baptism, through the early Western Church and into the time after Augustine, until its questioning by theology in the eleventh and twelfth centuries. The centre of this account is the attempt I have made, in chapter 4, to describe the working of sacrament in the period, roughly, from the death of Augustine to the eleventh century. Since there is little theological commentary on liturgy in these centuries, it is only possible, on the whole, to work from the

[5] See Warnock 1976, pp. 169ff, for an analysis of what goes on in a mime of this kind.
[6] *Gelasian*, nos. 431ff, pp. 70–2.

documents of the liturgies themselves – the *Gelasian Sacramentary*, the different versions of the Gregorian rite, the Gallican, Mozarabic and Italian rites, the Irish and so on[7] – and from texts which do not (usually) talk directly about liturgy, but, running parallel with the liturgy, throw an oblique light on it. The capitularies of the Carolingians are an example (they also sometimes speak directly); then the saints' lives; and vernacular literature when it echoes liturgical themes (*Beowulf*, perhaps, and *Andreas*, an account in Anglo-Saxon of the life of the apostle Andrew, more definitely); Bede's commentary on the Song of Songs, whose rhythms, and whose theme of aspiration to beauty, I have taken to be those of the liturgy; and, sometimes more illuminating than any other source, painting, both miniature painting in manuscripts and wall-paintings, like the ones in Concordia Sagittaria in northeast Italy. The problem of how liturgy stands to what lies outside it is a rich one which could never be exhausted. This will always be true because liturgy is a concentration of society, and in that sense contains society itself. This is eminently so in the early Middle Ages, from Augustine to the eleventh century, say, when almost everything was made to keep time with the pulse of liturgy; the idea of the past (in Gregory of Tours, for example, who took the history of the Franks back not only to Adam and Eve but to the Creation, with an intense remembering akin to that of baptism or the eucharist); the judgement of guilt or innocence in the ritual of ordeal; illness, death, birth, the possession of land and the tilling of it; eating, fighting, sex, going on journeys (of which the apotheosis is pilgrimage), and so on.[8] It would never be possible to give a full account of this reflex of benediction in medieval society, because there was nothing which was not potentially included in it. The pictures of St George and the dragon and Mary Magdalene in the baptistery of Concordia raise, tantalizingly, the question of the relation between the cult of the saint; the life of the saint by which the cult is carried; the representation, or even 'real presence', of the saint in a painting; and liturgy. I have said very little about this, but the question might be put here: how far is the saint himself a sacrament, a kind of ambulant conjunction of heaven and earth, a perfect union of spirit and body which overflows in the expressionism of miracle?

---

[7] For brief notes on these rites, see Vogel 1983.

[8] See Marett 1933 for an account of ritual and sacrament along these lines. Dupront 1987 evokes the relation between pilgrimage and liturgy.

Sources such as the saint's life throw an oblique light. Their connection with liturgy is partly, or sometimes wholly, beneath the conscious level. In chapter 4, using the indirect sources as well as the documents of the liturgies, I have tried to describe what liturgy does, against the historical background of the increasing prevalence of infant baptism. I have considered both the formal aspect of the rite – its regularity, its fixedness, its repetitions, and, especially in the Roman rite, its austerity – and its symbolic aspect, by which I mean the power it has to make the physical world open to the infinite, and even to show that if looked at with the right kind of eye, it contains the infinite. Symbol, as I have used it here, is just this: the endless expressiveness of things in the world, despite their limitedness in themselves; so that it is also the *tension* between the sense that something in the world – water, say – *is* all the possible meanings it suggests (and these have no end); and the sense that it is 'really' only water. With symbol, we are making the crossing of the Red Sea with the Israelites, from captivity to the Promised Land. But in the symbol, the tension of trying to get to the Promised Land is never relieved. Unable to enter it once and for all, we must always, and repeatedly, aspire to it; always be in a state of 'crossing over' to it. This is the *transitus* (crossing over) within symbol, which is also the *transitus* of conversion and repentance, which Ambrose was so keenly aware of, and which is the rhythm of medieval liturgy. It is never just a spectacle, a priestly act observed by a detached congregation; but only happens at all because the congregation recognizes in the tension of symbol its own aspiration to be saved. It sees there the same mixture of the difficulty of attaining to truth, and the possibility of doing so. The story I have told is how, in baptism, this perception of symbol grows out of the background of the conversion to Christianity of the Greek, Latin and Hebrew worlds, how it rises to a pitch in the Middle Ages with the remarkable imagery of the baptism of infants, and then how, from the ninth century (but with real effect from the mid-eleventh) the tension in symbol is, in a sense, betrayed, or misunderstood, and lost sight of, by the theologies of sacrament. It is retrieved momentarily, perhaps, by the introversion of symbol which is one of the things that can happen when it is transposed into commentary (thus Rupert of Deutz), and which can also be an effect of visionary theology, as in Hildegard of Bingen. But I have ended with the perception by Abelard that to see symbol in the light of intention, as though intention were something outside it and not generated by it, is to see above all – and with all the anxiousness and playfulness characteristic of Abelard – the difficulty of symbol, and in this sense to lose confidence in it.

Although I have been interested in the social context of liturgy, I have been concerned not to reduce liturgy to the poverty of social theory. I have wished to understand something about what liturgy itself was, not how effective it was as a means of social control, nor how exactly it manifested systems of classification; and the attempt to see something of what it was has convinced me that the explanation of liturgy as mere ideology – besides suggesting a very low opinion both of the priest who used it and the peasant or knight who was (supposedly) subjected to it – is indeed impoverished. To be persuaded that the social in the early Middle Ages was ever an end in itself, and thus to speak of authority without understanding its relation to belief, is, I think, to do the job of a theoretician rather than that of an historian, and instead of looking at the Middle Ages, to look through them at the present. To guard against this, we might keep in mind Augustine's observation, that everything short of God is a sign or symbol.[9] Seen like this, everything demands a search for meaning, rather than dictating meaning; and the search for meaning far better characterizes medieval liturgy than the view that it was just the instrument of authority.

---

[9] *De doctrina christiana* 1.2ff, pp. 7ff.

Chapter 1

HIPPOLYTUS OF ROME: RIGHT AND WRONG AND THE UNKNOWN GOD

BAPTISM AS *CRISIS*

In the early third century, Hippolytus, a priest of Rome during the pontificates of Zephyrinus and Callixtus (i.e. 217–22), wrote the *Apostolic Tradition* which, after being incorporated into the so-called *Egyptian Church Order*, was only recovered from it in the early years of this century.[1] In the *Tradition*, a work in three parts describing the more important aspects of church organization and liturgy, Hippolytus gives a lengthy account of baptism (cc. 15–21). It is the first explicit witness to the institutional, ecclesial baptism which followed on the more or less spontaneous 'baptisms of faith' in the Acts of the Apostles.[2] This is how Hippolytus sets the scene.

At the moment when the cock crows, first a prayer is said over the water. It should be water flowing into a font or flowing from above, unless this is impossible. If it is impossible for some reason which is permanent and pressing, use what water you can find. They are to remove their clothes; and you must baptize the children first. All those who can speak for themselves should do so; and those who are unable to speak for themselves; their parents should speak for them, or someone from their family. After this baptize the men, and lastly the women after they have loosed their hair and put aside jewellery of gold and silver that they are wearing. None is to take anything unsuitable into the water.[3]

The dryness, the juridical restraint with which Hippolytus describes the rite, veils a far greater intensity; his matter-of-fact realism, which is also a quality of the prayers he sets down, is the

---

[1] The contents of the *Tradition* were first established by E. Schwartz (Schwartz 1910); and independently by R. H. Connolly (Connolly 1916). Important treatments of early Christian baptism, which include discussions of its antecedents in the Old Testament and in Judaism, are Beasley-Murray 1962; Ysebaert 1962, this last a study based in philological analysis.

[2] Capelle 1933, p. 129.

[3] *Tradition* 21, p. 44 (references are to the edition by Dom Bernard Botte).

basis for an encounter with the holy: the awesome transition of the individual from profane to sacred is conveyed here not by open emotion, but by the very modesty of what is said; and it is implied in the potent idea of 'tradition' or *paradosis*: the handing down intact of a teaching which has been given. Baptism is to be at a certain time, at dawn on Sunday after an all-night vigil;[4] it is to be done if possible in running water, or 'living water' as the *Didache* had called it more than a hundred years before;[5] sponsorship of some kind, already apparent in the Acts,[6] is suggested here by the baptism of children who are spoken for; and the sequence of the rite is meticulously laid down: children are to be washed first, then men, then women – an order which recalls traces of Judaic taboo elsewhere in this Roman baptism.

Hippolytus' liturgy is at once artificial and concrete: it employs the natural symbolism of water, nakedness, loosed hair; but there is never any doubt that these symbols are set apart from the ordinary by the prescribed circumstances in which they are used; and raised above the ordinary by the formal – though still practical – language of prayer. Liturgy is therefore a place where the ordinary and the sacred meet; and, because it has this ambiguity as a part of its make-up, it is able to become the meeting-place of the personal, human will, on one side, and, on the other, the otherness of divinity. It is a place and a time of crisis, in all the senses that word would have had in the Greek: a decision, a judgement, a resolution, a climax embracing all the anxiety which goes before conversion.[7] But as in the Roman liturgy of the Middle Ages, the crisis of ritual already takes its power from a measured quality, from a tone of legalistic understatement.

Much of what Hippolytus describes is a movement towards crisis, and a preparation for the conditions in which it can happen. Baptism begins with a preliminary interrogation of the person who has come forward together with witnesses who will vouch for him; this is followed by a period of catechesis, usually three years; when the time for baptism draws near, there is a second

---

4 It is probable, though not certain, that this is Easter Sunday: see Hippolytus, *Commentary on Daniel* 1.16.1–3, pp. 100–1, where the Pasch is given as a suitable time for baptism; and see the discussion in Talley 1986, pp. 33–7.

5 *Didache* 7.1, p. 19 (and see note).

6 Dujarier 1962.

7 For the various meanings, see the entry under *krisis* in Lampe's lexicon of Patristic Greek: Lampe 1961, p. 779.

interrogation, again with witnesses present, of those who are chosen (*eliguntur*) from among the catechumens; and as the approach to the new status of holiness gains impetus, the candidates are now paradoxically more carefully and deliberately separated from the body of believers, and the rules governing their conduct are stiffened; accordingly, they are exorcised several times and then subjected to a crucial episcopal exorcism. This acts as a test of the possible presence at this late stage of a persistent impurity: 'the bishop exorcises each one of them, so that he might know whether they are pure. If any is not good or is not pure, he is to be put to one side, because he has not heard the word in faith.' Uncleanness at this juncture is considered a blameworthy fault, 'because it is not possible for the stranger to hide himself always'.[8] The implication is that the devil cannot have survived this far in the rite, so that the individual must be held responsible. There is now a growing nervousness; precautions are taken against the contamination of the *electi*, and against that of the *fideles* by the dangerous condition of those who will be baptized – dangerous because they are neither wholly pagan nor wholly Christian. They are unclear. On Holy Thursday, the candidates are to bathe and wash, a practice which is perhaps taken from Jewish proselyte baptism, or perhaps borrowed from the Levitical regulations concerning cleansing and ritual ablutions (Lev. 15; Numb. 19);[9] the corollary of this, that a woman in menstruation is to be baptized another day, certainly has a Levitical air (Lev. 15:19–33). On Friday, they are to fast; on Saturday they are to come together in one place, where the bishop will lay his hand on them one by one, as another gesture of exorcism, blow on their faces and sign them on forehead, ears and nostrils. After a night of receiving instruction and hearing readings, they will go to the water, carrying with them only what they will give as an offering at the post-baptismal eucharist. In the immediate prelude to baptism, the tension now higher than ever, the emphasis is on simplicity, bareness, nakedness. The water-rite at the heart of the sequence is presented as a natural symbol, self-evident in meaning and effect.

---

[8] *Tradition* 20, p. 42.
[9] Ibid. On proselyte baptism, Ysebaert 1962, pp. 32–4. It seems that if proselyte baptism influenced early Christian baptism, it did so as one of a number of Judaic rites of ablution; the first documentary evidence of a proselyte baptism is in fact from the first century AD. See also on this connection, Zwi Werblowsky 1975; and Zwi Werblowsky 1957: in this earlier article the author denies that any purification is expressed in Judaic baptismal rites, a view revised in the second article.

Again, this content of natural purification no doubt owes much to Judaism. Something like it is in the Essene initiation of the Qumran sect, in the baptism of John the Baptist, and then reappears in the various Jewish–Christian documents.[10] This natural metaphor of bodily cleansing as spiritual, although it becomes less striking with the growth of imposed allegorical meanings, is kept up in Late Antique art. The depictions of the baptism of Christ in the Orthodox and Arian baptisteries at Ravenna, rich as they are in abstract symbols, still aspire to the classical style of both naturalism and idealism: the mosaics show Christ and the Baptist in the running water of the Jordan, against a rocky landscape.[11]

In connection with purification, it is worth considering a moment longer the comparison with Judaism. As always, there is between Christianity and Judaism a relation both of continuity and change. In this case, while the context of stain, purification, washing is provided by the Old Testament and the contemporary Jewish law, the interpretation given these categories by emerging Christianity is quite distinct. The Jewish concern with cleanness and uncleanness in the time of Christ is ritualistic to an elaborate

---

[10] For the Essenes, see the *Community Rule* 3, p. 75; cf. *Didache* 7.1, p. 19; *Clementine Homilies* 11.26; *Clementine Recognitions* 3.67, 4.32, 6.15. As Bigg and Maclean point out (p. 19n, in their edition of the *Didache*), this 'living water' is to be distinguished from the 'sign' of the living water in John 4:10, etc. On the living water in baptism, see Klauser 1939.

[11] Deichmann 1958, pls. 39–41, 251–3. Much later, in *c.* 1100, the Baptism of Christ in the nave of the church at Daphni has some of the same effect of clarity and purity in running water (illustration in Grabar 1953, p. 116; on the coincidence in Late Antique art of naturalism and ritual abstraction, Grabar 1969, pp. 8ff). In *c.* 1000, the illumination of the Baptism of Christ in the *Fulda Sacramentary* (accompanying the feast of Epiphany) depicts Christ in a dark blue stream of water which rushes across his body from the upper right of the frame to the lower left: fo. 19r (pl. 16 of the edition). On the use of the motif of the four rivers of paradise in Carolingian art, and its possible theological senses, see the rich discussion in Underwood 1950. On the association made by the Latin of early Christians, and then by the liturgies – particularly the Mozarabic – between *refrigerium* as refreshment (by water or shade) and as eternal *pax* and *quies*, see Mohrmann in Botte and Mohrmann 1953, pp. 123–32 (*locus refrigerii*); and on the naturalism of the image: 'Je ne crois donc pas que les Chrétiens ont adopté le ψυχρὸν ὕδωρ des Osiriens, ni que leur *refrigerium* est une version latine du *Ḳbḥw* des Egyptiens, mais il me semble extrêmement probable qu'ils sont restés fidèles dans leur langue à une conception inspirée par des données naturelles et qui est si généralement et foncièrement humaine qu'aucun culte ou conception religieuse n'en a la possession exclusive' (at pp. 130–1). The themes of running water, coolness and the slaking of thirst are brought together by the Spanish poet Prudentius (d. 410) in one of the verses of his *Peristephanon*: 'Pastor oues alit ipse illic gelidi rigore fontis, / uidet sitire quas fluenta Christi' (12.43–4). On the Good Shepherd and his association with baptism, Quasten 1939 and 1947.

degree. The Mishnah distinguished six kinds of water-supply, three of them varieties of flowing water. Each had its own greater or lesser power to cleanse; beyond this, legal discussion turned mainly on the problem of deciding at what point flowing water was rendered ineffectual by additions of drawn water.[12] If we set against this meticulousness, and against the pervasive ritualism of Judaism in this period, the almost offhand instructions of Hippolytus, the *Didache* or especially Tertullian, who allowed baptism in any water that could be found,[13] we see how 'natural' the Christian symbol of baptism was; and being natural, it motivated the subject of the rite – the *electus* – and therefore provided the grounds for a moral approach. Through baptism he converted himself, as well as submitting himself to conversion. When Jewish washings and baths brought to bear on their subject a cultic system, Christian baptism invited a moral approach expressed in the medium of cult. A difference which on first acquaintance seems to be one of emphasis turns out also to be one of kind – although this ignores other powerful elements in Jewish piety from which Christianity was able to draw much of its accent on personal conversion. I will try to say later how this is important to the development of baptism in particular.

The natural metaphor of water is, however, only one aspect of the crisis of baptism. It is one point – possibly the most important – at which forces aroused in the rite are brought together. A physical washing, because it is done in a manner heightened by circumstance, gesture, words spoken, awareness, is made a metamorphosis of the soul. Not only water, but wine, bread, milk, honey, oil, the body itself, all become ambiguous in this way. The same is true for every other physical substance and action. The application of oil to parts of the body is a sensual metaphor; it may mean exorcism, or it may mean an irruption of the Trinity. So, just before the descent into water, the bishop gives thanks over what now becomes the *oleum gratiarum actionis*; with the usual attention to symmetry, one deacon holds this oil and stands to the right of the priest, while another holds the *oleum exorcismi* and

[12] Schürer, Vermes, Millar and Black 1979, pp. 475ff; cf. Ysebaert 1962, pp. 21–39.
[13] Tertullian, *De baptismo* 4.3, p. 280: 'ideoque nulla distinctio est, mari quis an stagno, flumine an fonte, lacu an alueo, diluatur, nec quicquam refert inter eos quos Iohannes in Iordanem et quos Petrus in Tiberim tinxit; nisi si et ille spado quem Philippus inter uias fortuita aqua tinxit plus salutis aut minus retulit.' None of this is to say that in the Judaism of this time there was no notion of a baptism which washed sins: Ysebaert 1962, pp. 35ff.

stands to his left. Before he goes down into the water, each candidate is given an anointing-exorcism; after he has come up from the water, and before putting on clothes again, he is anointed with the *oleum gratiarum actionis*, once by the priest 'in the name of Jesus Christ', again by the bishop 'in God the Father the Almighty and in Christ Jesus and in the Holy Spirit'.[14] The ambiguity of meaning in every word, gesture, object is partly the general result of their dramatic and unusual context, and partly that of the specific meanings attached to them in the context.

These two confused senses of physical and metaphysical are the texture of the performance: what is said and done. Against this background, there takes place a moral and social encounter with metaphysical values; and in each case – moral and social – we find that the rite of baptism is a crisis: a point – or at least a sequence of points – where ambiguities meet. It is this meeting or resolution which brings about the transformation of the person which is baptism.

Is it the rite, though, which makes this change happen, or is it something which the person does to himself? Morally, he or she is expected to be at one moment autonomous, at the next subjugated to an absolute moral truth – or even sometimes both at once. In the presence of witnesses, he answers for himself when examined: 'Have they lived honestly while catechumens? Have they honoured widows, visited the sick, done all kinds of good?'[15] In the first examination, each must give his reason for coming forward: 'They are asked to give the reason why they are coming to the faith.'[16] On the other hand, the candidates are subject to repeated exorcisms, laying-on of hands, anointings, ritual and social taboos, to a dramatic system of gestures and words which is immutable and outside. The final exorcism is accordingly both an operation of external power on the individual and a personal commitment by him: it is at once exorcism and renunciation: 'I renounce you, Satan, I renounce all service to you and all your works.'[17] Exorcism itself could often mean one thing or another in this manner. Was it a moral exorcism, or demonic? The line between the two became even harder to discern with

[14] *Tradition* 21, pp. 50–4.
[15] Ibid. 20, p. 42. On the origins of this interrogation in the New Testament, and its bearing on the institution of godparenthood, Dujarier 1962.
[16] *Tradition* 15, p. 32.
[17] Ibid. 21, p. 46: 'Renuntio tibi, Satana, et omni seruitio tuo et omnibus operibus tuis.'

time. A Milanese exorcism found in an eleventh-century manuscript, but no doubt much older in fact, shows the devil not just as an embodiment of evil, but as a character, almost as if in a farce. The abjuration begins with a doxology which includes the story of Satan's fall, then turns to a steady rhythm of *anamnesis*: the devil and Job, the devil and Pharaoh and his army, and so on to the devil condemned in Judas; but then the devil changes into a caricature of all the wicked and unruly: he is the *sacrilegorum caput*, the heresiarch, the pornographer, the magician, the murderer. He is reprimanded: 'But why are you still here?' 'This is no time for delay.' After a recapitulation, the end comes with a vision of the judging Christ, appearing with the double-edged sword of the Apocalypse in his mouth. The whole thing is in one breath a battle between gods and a fable about the fate of bad people. Despite the serious intent, there is already some sense of the devil as a fool, which will be a theme of the Mystery Cycles.[18]

Hippolytus' baptismal exorcisms, which as we have seen are closely bound up with renunciation, show the same indecisiveness. They treat the person as a moral subject and a ritual object. The only hint he gives about the content of catechesis is in his chapter on professions (c. 16: *De operibus et occupationibus*). There are certain things a Christian can do, others he cannot. Becoming a Christian is a choice, but if compared with, say, the Aristotelian notion of ethics as a matter of discernment of what is good and bad according to circumstance, and as a continuous development of this discernment through habit and knowledge, then it is a very limited kind of moral choice.[19] Hippolytus says nothing about a sacrament of penance, and it seems that he meant that in principle the choice should be made once only; certainly, evidence from other texts would indicate this, and the idea of baptism as an isolated, unrepeatable moment is the reason for 'clinical' or

---

[18] *Manuale Ambrosianum*, pp. 469ff (cited by Dölger 1909, pp. 59–60): ' . . . Tibi enim impie et angelis tuis est vermis, qui nunquam moritur, tibi et angelis tuis inextinguibile praeparatur incendium; quia tu es maledicte homicidii princeps, tu auctor incaesti, tu sacrilegorum caput, tu artium pessimarum magister, tu haereticorum doctor, tu totius obscoenitatis inuentor. Exi ergo, impie; exi, scelerate; exi cum omni fallacia tua; qui hominem templum suum uoluit esse deus. Sed quid diutius moraris? . . . '.

[19] Aristotle, *Nicomachean Ethics* 2.5–9, pp. 27–33. In the *Eudemian Ethics* Aristotle argues (against Plato and Socrates) that the virtues are not kinds of knowledge, for knowledge can be used wrongly and virtues cannot. Virtue is a consistent *ability* to choose what is right.

deathbed baptism – the practice of taking baptism as late as possible before dying, so as to void the arduous task of keeping to the baptismal vow.[20] And this was a choice not between many possible interpretations, but between two simplified orders of existence: the pagan and the Christian; the bad and the good. To a great extent, these two possibilities are represented in the *Tradition* as social. In this the *Tradition* is evidently inspired by the Judaic literature of the Two Ways (cf. Jer. 31:8; Deut. 30:15, 19; Prov. 12:28; Ecclus. 15:17; Matt.7:13ff), but borrows from this literature only the small part of it which has to do with occupations. It is likely for this reason that the rest of the catechism, left unde-scribed by Hippolytus, also uses the Two Ways, but in more detail. There is an echo of the motif in the fourth century in Athanasius' letter on the lections to be used at Easter; and again in Augustine's *De catechizandis rudibus*.[21] The choice made by the convert thus represents a radical reduction of the moral universe to two paths; and – ideally at any rate – can only be made once.

What Hippolytus says about the licit and illicit professions goes some way towards making Christianity a collection of social taboos; certainly, it invests Christianity with a vigorous simplic-ity: on one side is the subject, on the other a series of alternatives which, because they are inflexible, come close to being abstract principles of good and evil. The categories of the *Tradition* tumble out inexorably in an assault on profanity, but also on society:

If anyone manages a house of ill-fame or keeps prostitutes, he must cease or will be rejected. If anyone is a sculptor or maker of pictures, they must be taught not to make idols: either they cease or will be rejected. If anyone is a player or puts on shows in the theatre, either he must cease or be rejected.

And a schoolmaster, because he would have to teach the pagan authors, should if possible give up his work; the charioteer, the gladiator, the man who hunts animals in the arena, the idol-priest, all must give up their occupations. The common soldier may not kill; the city magistrate may not govern; the prostitute, the homosexual, the eunuch, magicians, astrologers, charlatans of various descriptions, will be turned away from the preliminary

[20] The story of Constantine's clinical baptism is told by Eusebius, *De uita Const.* 4.62, col. 1216A.
[21] *Ep. festalis* 39–41, cols. 1437–40.

examination.[22] Where the Levitical law of purity was ethnocentric, that of early Christianity was social and cultural. Although the gist of what Hippolytus says about occupations, as well as the form, is Jewish, there is some small precedent for it in the moral approach of a few Hellenistic religious associations: a stone inscription from Lydia (Asia Minor) of the late second century BC, tells us about a group who made a not dissimilar attempt at fixing and separating the good and the bad. Here too we find the hybrid notion of pollution of the group by a moral offence, in this case adultery.[23] All this could scarcely be further from the Aristotelian concept of a reasoned course between excess and deficiency, a constant re-discovery of the middle way. But it is just as far away

[22] *Tradition* 16, pp. 34–8: 'Si quis est πορνοβοσκός uel qui nutrit meretrices, uel cesset uel reiciatur. Si quis est sculptor uel pictor, doceantur ne faciant idola; uel cessent uel reiciantur. Si quis est scenicus uel qui facit demonstrationem in theatro, uel cesset uel reiciatur. Qui docet pueros, bonum est ut cesset; si non habet artem, permittatur ei. Auriga similiter qui certat et uadit ad agonem, uel cesset uel reiciatur. Qui est gladiator uel docet eos qui sunt inter gladiatores pugnare, uel uenator qui est in uenatione, uel publicus qui est in re gladiatoria, uel cesset uel reiciatur. Qui est sacerdos idolorum, uel custos idolorum cesset uel reiciatur. Miles qui est in potestate non occidet hominem. Si iubetur, non exequetur rem, neque faciet iuramentum. Si autem non uult, reiciatur. Qui habet potestatem gladii, uel magistratus ciuitatis qui induitur purpura, uel cesset uel reiciatur. Catechumenus uel fidelis qui uolunt fieri milites reiciantur, quia contempserunt deum. Meretrix uel homo luxuriosus uel qui se abscidit, et si quis alius facit rem quam non decet dicere, reiciantur; impuri enim sunt. Neque adducatur magus in iudicium. Incantator uel astrologus uel diuinator uel interpretes somniorum, uel qui turbat populum, uel qui abscindit oram uestium, uel qui facit phylacteria, uel cessent uel reiciantur.'

[23] The inscription is edited by Barton and Horsley 1981, pp. 8–9. On Greek cults generally, see Nock 1925; Nock 1928; Cumont 1929; and Rice and Stambaugh 1979, esp. pp. 184ff on cult regulations. There is in Greco-Roman culture a theme similar to that of the Two Ways: Xenophon (*Memorabilia* 2.1.21–34) tells the story of Heracles, midway between boyhood and youth, finding himself before two female figures, vice and virtue. He must decide which of them to follow in life. The way of virtue is hard, that of vice easy and immediately pleasurable. But this is not entirely the objective morality of the Jewish and Christian Two Ways: in Xenophon's account, the emphasis is on the debate between virtue and vice which appeals to Heracles' reasoned judgement; moreover, the two paths are not the opposite of one another – both aim at pleasure and happiness, virtue through restraint and toil, and vice through laziness, indulgence, lust. In the story, Heracles is persuaded by the debate that virtue gives a greater happiness than vice, and not just in the next world, but in this moral existence. And, because it is a debate between two relative approaches in this way, the story is better understood as an allegory of the debate which goes on in the mind of the moral agent than as a mythical personification of good and evil. The same philosophic idea of choice between alternatives appears in Stoicism, e.g. Diogenes Laertius, *Lives of the Philosophers*, in which the lives of the philosophers are recounted for the moral standards they show; there are several cases of conversion to philosophy and thus to moral truthfulness: 2.31 (I, pp. 162–3); 4.47 (I, pp. 424–5); 6.49 (II, pp. 50–1); 7.3 (II, pp. 112–13); 10.2 (II, pp. 528–9). But again the crux is in persuasion and judgement according to circumstance, not in conversion from one set of rules to another (*ibid.* 7.24; 9.21, 112).

from the New Testament ethics of Paul, with its emphasis on the right-seeing of the inner man, or – for that matter – from the immediacy and eschatological urgency of Jesus' teaching.[24]

The theme of the Two Ways occurs frequently in Jewish and Jewish-Christian literature. The Scrolls from the caves at Qumran, and the *Letter of Barnabas* (mid-second century) and the *Didache*, are impregnated with it. Whether or not it has its source in a lost treatise is unclear. In *Barnabas*, the Two Ways seems to be an afterthought, perhaps added some years later, and at any rate bears little relation to what goes before.[25] But both the *Community Rule* found at Qumran and the *Didache*, place the moral dualism of the Two Ways in apposition to initiation into the group – in the first case to that of the 'Community', almost certainly the Essene community, in the second to some form of Jewish-Christianity.[26] The relevant passage in the *Community Rule* of the Essenes runs:

He shall be cleansed from all his sins by the spirit of holiness uniting him to His truth, and his iniquity shall be expiated by the spirit of uprightness and humility. And when his flesh is sprinkled with purifying water and sanctified by cleansing water, it shall be made clean by humble submission of his soul to all the precepts of God.[27]

The elements are very similar to those of the *Didache*: admission to this higher order of Essenism is preceded by several years of instruction in the Two Ways, here as in *Barnabas* expressed not in the traditional antithesis of life and death, but as light and darkness; the postulant is evidently examined, and then undergoes some kind of water-rite. There is a consistency of spirit between

---

[24] See Vermes 1973.

[25] On *Barnabas*, Quasten 1950, pp. 90–1: 'a date later than this (138) cannot possibly be defended'; but Prigent in the introduction to his edition (1971), pp. 25–7, considers AD 200 a plausible *terminus ad quem*. Quasten argues that the allegorical tendency in the author of *Barnabas* betrays an Alexandrian; Prigent that a Syro-Palestinian is just as likely (Prigent 1971, pp. 20–4).

[26] *Community Rule* 1–3, pp. 72–5; *Didache* 1–7, pp. 1–21. On the identification of the Qumran sect with the Essenes, Dupont-Sommer 1961; further literature in Schürer, Vermes, Millar and Black 1979, pp. 583ff; and the dissenting view of Golb 1985, who argues that the identity is based on the order in which the Scrolls were found; and that the documents should be taken to represent the literature of a number of groups of Palestinian Judaism rather than a single one. With regard to the *Didache*, Audet 1958, pp. 187–200, believes the Two Ways section to be an interpolation; against this view, however, see the strong arguments of Rordorf 1972; Giet 1970 for acceptance, though cautious, of the use of the Two Ways as catechesis in early Christianity.

[27] *Community Rule* 3, p. 75.

18

the unorthodox Jewish version (Essene) and the Jewish-Christian (*Didache*) and the Christian: they all tend to reduce moral choice to a dualist simplicity of purity against impurity.

The ablution, for Hippolytus as for the *Community Rule*, is a making clean 'by the humble submission of his soul to all the precepts of God'. The moral disposition of the individual is apparently eclipsed and yet nothing can be done without it: 'all those who freely devote themselves to His truth shall bring all their knowledge, powers and possessions into the Community of God, that they may purify their knowledge in the truth of God's precepts and order their powers according to His ways of perfection'.[28] This is what the *Community Rule* says; and the *Didache*: 'Thou shalt not forsake the commandments of the Lord, but shalt keep what thou didst receive, neither adding thereto nor taking aught away.'[29] This paradox of a way to follow which is somehow at the same time a yoke, a principle given in fulness, is perhaps best put in the imagery of repentance in the hymn at the end of the *Community Rule*, where the righteous man is the one who 'stumbles' and 'staggers' and 'steps' uncertainly towards a justification which is at once his only strength, and without which he would be confined interminably to the Pit.[30] This same combination of a journey from one status to another, and hesitancy as to whether the will to make the journey is personal or determinate, occurs in the *Tradition*. Here, though, it is carried not in poetic imagery, but in the motion of the drama, from a negative condition of exorcism/renunciation before baptism, to a positive one of acquiescence/wilful acceptance afterwards.

The hesitation between will and determinism is implicit in every gesture, metaphor, prayer; it is inevitable because all ritual is by nature a prescribed and necessary expression, and yet a deliberate act of conversion. Just after the first post-baptismal unction, Hippolytus has this rubric: 'The bishop, laying his hand on them, says the following invocation: Lord God, who has made these people deserving of the remission of sins through the washing of rebirth of the Holy Spirit, send into them your grace that they might serve you according to their will . . .'[31] They have been made deserving; their will to serve him is God's will invoked, brought down by an imposition of hands.

---

[28] Ibid. 1, p. 72.   [29] *Didache* 4. 13, p. 14.
[30] *Community Rule* 10–11, pp. 89–94.   [31] *Tradition* 21, p. 52.

In one of the Qumran hymns, the 'staggering' of the would-be righteous man becomes the battle of the sailor against 'furious seas'. He encounters the whirlwind, and finds no path over the waters in his journey towards death. Here is the old theme of the threatening water which enters into Christian baptism as the association of baptism of water and baptism of fire, and in the carrying over of the conflict of exorcism into the water-baptism itself.[32] But in the next verse, the righteous hero of the hymn is 'as one who enters a fortified city, as one who seeks refuge behind a high wall . . . '. It is a commonplace of the Scrolls that the moral struggle to keep to the right path is somehow – theologically this is never made clear – relieved by the certainty of an eschatological refuge. The refuge is a 'foundation on rock', a city where 'no enemy shall ever invade', and where 'no man shall stagger'.[33] This state of repose is more a product of the moral imagination than of reflection: it is a time and a place of apocalyptic judgement and emotional release. On the other hand, there is evident in the Scrolls a temptation to develop these emotional and imaginative efforts into an abstract theology of dualism which comes close to the Gnostic conception. The Ways thus become the principles of light and dark: 'Truth abhors the works of falsehood, and falsehood hates all the ways of truth. And their struggle is fierce in all their arguments for they do not walk together.'[34] And often the approach to the refuge is seen not only as the observance of covenant, but also as a matter of knowledge; 'the vision of Knowledge', and 'the drink of Knowledge', as the hymns put it.[35]

GNOSTICISM AND THE SICK SOUL

Gnosticism was formed by the encounter of the Greek philosophical spirit with currents of religious enthusiasm coming from further East. The many Gnostic sects diverge in their teachings, but they are all, broadly, characterized by an intellectualist and, at heart, elitist, belief which may be expressed as three stages.

1 Gnosticism begins from a 'dualist' account of God and creation: the universe is divided between good and evil powers, which are in constant conflict; in the individual and in the universe at

[32] Edsman 1940.   [33] *Hymns Scroll* 6, pp. 171 and 162.
[34] *Community Rule* 4, p. 77.   [35] *Hymns Scroll* 4, p. 161.

large, this conflict takes the form of an opposition between *hylē* or the physical, bodily principle, and pneuma or spirit. The soul, *psychē*, is in the grip of one or other of these powers, or of both at once. Gnostic myth usually relates that despite its predominantly physical condition (*heimarmenē*), the soul, and the universe, has in it a spark of divinity, the good, of light, and from this the possibility of redemption arises.

2 Redemption is by attachment to the principle of good, detachment from that of evil; that is, effectively, by the destruction of the principle of evil, in favour of the good.

3 Within the individual soul, as in the cosmos, salvation and the good which saves are reducible to knowledge (*gnosis*). This means that to know the truth (i.e. the good) is to be the truth. Salvation is therefore absolute and indubitable, and amounts to a form of deification.

The diversity of the Gnostic groups is the result of the different ways in which these absolute terms – knowledge, salvation, the good, evil – were given practical, this-worldly expression. The diversity is most obvious in the many myths which were the objects of *gnosis*; and in the differing attitudes to morality: some groups, though by no means all, held moral rules to be worthless, since they involved bodily action, which was of no consequence, because evil. Many other anomalies would have to be taken into account by a full definition: it is debatable, for example, whether Marcion should be counted a Gnostic. Instead of the principles of good and evil, he set against one another those of mercy and justice; the alien God of the Old Testament against the saving God of the New.[36] The very difficulty of defining Gnosticism indicates something about its nature; and the second-century Neoplatonist Plotinus condemned Gnosticism as a false philosophy. These judgements are apt. Gnosticism in this sectarian, religious form – rather than as a vein in Neoplatonic and neo-Pythagorean philosophy – is best understood as an extreme moral position, either antinomian or ascetic, which in its zeal pushes moral belief beyond itself into belief in metaphysical absolutes: good and evil. In Marcion we can see this transition in the making, but the issue remains for him a moral one. I want to argue that the tension between the moral and the metaphysical has the same psychologi-

[36] Harnack 1924.

cal roots as the 'crisis' which we have already seen in the Roman baptism of Hippolytus.

For Tertullian, Gnosticism was an extreme metaphysical reaction to the moral problems of the origin of evil. The Gnostic mistake, he said, comes of asking the question *unde malum?*[37] Evil cannot be from God, who is good, so it must come from a contrary force. Salvation is in the knowledge (*gnosis*) of this metaphysical division, and in identification through knowledge with the good principle, that of light as against dark. The discoveries in 1945 at Nag-Hammadi (Upper Egypt) of what is evidently the library of a Gnostic sect or possibly of a Pachomian monastery has shown once and for all that Gnosticism was not simply the product of Hellenistic philosophy.[38] It was protean, syncretic, subtle, and in many forms, including those closest to orthodox Christianity (Marcionites, Valentinians), had a highly developed mythology.[39] And yet it is still possible to see at its heart this conviction that a moral dilemma could be solved by a metaphysical abstraction. Manichaeism, for example, looks from the outside almost like a job-lot of mythological systems fitted together into an unwieldy whole. Buddhist, Zoroastrian, Mandaean, as well as Christian and Jewish influences have been argued to explain Mani's inspiration in the third century. But Gilles Quispel has argued that the only thing Mani would have needed for his basic vision of good and evil principles was his confrontation with the Judaic ethic he would have heard during his own upbringing as an Elkesaite, an ethic which praised the Lord for creating both good and evil, but stopped short of asking why he should have done so. This Jewish-Christian sect attributed both good and evil to the one God, making a tension and an obscurity in the divinity which Mani – and Gnosticism generally – was

---

[37] *Adu. Marc.* 1.2, p. 6: 'Languens enim (quod et nunc multi, et maxime haeretici), circa mali quaestionem, unde malum, et obtunsis sensibus ipsa enormitate curiositatis, inueniens creatorem pronuntiantem, Ego sum qui condo mala, quanto ipsum praesumpserat mali auctorem et ex aliis argumentis, quae ita persuadent peruersoque cuique, tanto in creatorem interpretatus malam arborem malos fructus condentem, scilicet mala, alium deum praesumpsit esse debere in partem bonae arboris bonos fructus.' On the psychological and philosophical origins of Gnostic belief, Puech 1949b, pp. 59–92; Puech 1979, pp. 5–101; Festugière 1932; Festugière 1967, esp. pp. 13–27: 'Cadre de la mystique héllénistique'; and Jonas 1958.

[38] Doresse 1960. For the possibility that the library belonged to a Pachomian cell, J. M. Robinson in his introduction to *The Nag-Hammadi Library*, pp. 16ff.

[39] On the Marcionites, Tertullian, *Adu. Marc.*, is the most informative Patristic source; and see Harnack 1924. On the Valentinians, Sagnard 1947; Laynton 1980.

unable to bear. The practice of asceticism and the absorption of mythologies of fall and resurrection, of battles between light and dark, spirit and flesh, could follow naturally from this initial response.[40] Myth, in the Gnostic usage, gives body – and tangibility – to the austere teaching of salvation by knowing, *gnosis*.[41]

When the Qumran Scrolls speak of knowledge, it is obvious they do not have in mind a full metaphysical dualism of the Gnostic kind. Essene 'knowledge' is too bound up with the stumbling movement towards fulfilment; with failures to keep covenant; with the existential difficulties of being truthful. Moreover, the spirits of truth and falsehood are creations of one God. And yet there is enough in the Scrolls to suggest a shift already in sectarian Judaism of the second century BC, towards a more abstract understanding of salvation. I will try to show from the *Tradition* and elsewhere that the 'crisis' of baptism reflects this leaning to the abstract, and is partially a crisis about what it is to know the divine.

Into its discourse on the Two Ways, the *Didache* inserts a version of the Sermon on the Mount in which Matt. 5:39–42 and Luke 6:27–30;32–5 are combined. The rhythm of contradictions and exaggerations makes of ethics something absolute, something cut off from the everyday and the social and the flesh by what is in practice its absurdity: 'Bless them which curse you . . . love them which hate you', and: 'If anyone give thee a blow on the right cheek, turn to him the other also, and thou shalt be perfect. If any compel thee to go one mile, go with him two; if any take thy cloak, give him also thy tunic; if any take from thee what is thine, ask for it not again . . .'.[42] This spirit of the morally absurd, which is nonetheless the practical basis of the ascetic life, tells us how close the moral and the metaphysical could be. The principle is taken a step further by the *Gospel of Thomas*, one of the texts found at Nag-Hammadi, and evidently a Gnostic re-writing of what had been an orthodox Apocryphon.[43]

---

[40] See his essay on 'The Birth of the Child' in Quispel 1974, pp. 221–39.

[41] Puech 1979, p. 13: 'Si l'expérience affective se formule en problèmes intellectuels, ceux-ci ne trouvent finalement que des réponses mythiques.'

[42] *Didache* 1.3–4, pp. 3–4.

[43] Cf. Puech 1978, suggesting Edessa as a possible place of composition. Vermes 1983, p. 53, makes it clear that the Jesus of the Synoptic Gospels – and the historical Jesus – would have meant nothing absurd by these remarks. He was deliberately exaggerating in order to bring home his point, and especially the teaching of love freely given.

Jesus said; Blessed are the poor, for yours is the Kingdom of Heaven. Jesus said: Whoever does not hate his father and his mother will not be able to be a disciple to Me, and (whoever does not) hate his brethren and his sisters and (does not) take up his cross in My way will not be worthy of Me. Jesus said: Whoever has known the world has found a corpse, and whoever has found a corpse, of him the world is not worthy.[44]

There is even a note of mockery: 'His disciples said to Him: Is circumcision profitable or not? He said to them: If it were profitable, their father would beget them circumcised from their mother.'[45]

Considerable stress is laid in some Gnostic teaching traditions on perplexity; the resolution of all the paradoxes, the meaning behind all the symbols, would seem to be in an enigma, an aporia. When, in the *Gospel of Thomas*, Jesus asks his disciples to say whom he is like, only Thomas admits he is not capable of it. Withdrawing Thomas, Jesus 'spoke three words to him. Now when Thomas came to his companions, they asked him: What did Jesus say to thee? Thomas said to them: If I tell you one of the words which He said to me, you will take up stones and throw them at me; and fire will come from the stones and burn you up.'[46] One might suppose that there is here some kind of nihilism, a recourse to the refuge of meaninglessness and futility. Hans Jonas, a pupil of Heidegger, has compared modern existentialist disillusionment with Gnosticism; and some Gnostic groups – though fewer than the contemporary heresiologists would have us believe – appear to have been antinomian, on the grounds that action belongs to the flesh and is therefore irrelevant to salvation.[47] The use of allegory in Gnostic writings, however, makes it quite clear that aporia is only temporary; the *nous* might lose its way – as does the youth who has gone down to Egypt in search of the pearl in the *Hymn of the Pearl* – but the possibility always exists of grasping the pearl, of knowing what is true. Puzzlement, lack of clarity, is the youth's dangerous mingling with the men of Egypt;

---

[44] *Logia* 54–6, pp. 30–1.   [45] *Logion* 53, pp. 30–1.
[46] *Logion* 13, pp. 8–11.
[47] Jonas 1958, pp. 320–40: 'Gnosticism, Nihilism and Existentialism'; and see ch. 11 of the same work, on Gnostic morality. Against the view that Gnosticism was generally antinomian, Chadwick 1980. The powerful ascetic tradition of fast and repression of sexual desire leaves little room for doubt, at least for the Gnostic elements in these texts, that Gnosticism was far from moral nihilism.

embroilment with the world. Gnostic images of the release of the soul are thus images of consummation; of objects grasped wholly, despite whatever monstrous obstacles have lain in the way: the dragon in the lake in the Valentinian *Hymn of the Pearl*, or the archons of Gnostic mythology generally.[48] The images may be more conceptual, like that of the beginning which is the end, or 'the inner as the outer ... the outer as the inner ... the above as the below' and 'the male and the female [made] into a single one' (all from the *Gospel of Thomas*).[49] Or they may be concrete, even sacramental. The *Odes of Solomon*, a collection of poems (second-third century), of which the original language may have been either Greek or Syriac, expresses knowledge by the Gnostic *topos* of the meeting with the self:[50]

Behold, the Lord is our mirror: open the eyes and see them in Him: and learn the manner of your face: and tell forth praise to His spirit: and wipe off the filth from your face: and love His holiness, and clothe yourselves therewith: and be without stain at all times before Him. Hallelujah. (Ode 13)

Ephrem Syrus adapted this, giving it a baptismal interpretation by making the mirror the water of the font.[51] Whether or not the hymns themselves were composed as baptismal songs is a vexed question. It is not easy to argue from the flexible imagery of the poet to the necessity of the ritual symbols. Ode 24, for example, is about the extinction of the 'chasms' of untruth and the triumph of the true word in the baptism of Christ; but whether it is also about baptism after Christ is harder to say. The thread of ideas would suggest that it is; the descent of the dove in Christ's baptism is the singing of the dove's voice, and thus apparently the 'word' and the 'thought' of later verses; the baptism of Christ is also, it would seem, a descent into hell, depicted again as the work of wisdom against 'the devices of all those who had not the truth with them'; ' ... the chasms were submerged in the submersion of the Lord,/And they perished in the thought with which they had

[48] The *Hymn of the Pearl* has come down in Greek and Syriac versions; it is included in the *Acts of Thomas* (Hennecke–Schneemelcher 1965, pp. 498–504; and see comments, pp. 433ff).

[49] *Logion* 22, pp. 16–17; cf. *logion* 18, pp. 12–13.

[50] Translation from J. H. Bernard's 1912 edition, p. 76.

[51] Cited by Harris and Mingana 1920, pp. 18ff.

remained from the beginning.'[52] (In a similar way, 1 Peter 3:19 –
itself probably a paraenetic framed around baptism – talks of
baptism, though not the baptism of Christ, in connection with the
descensus.)[53] This, and the last two verses, in which the baptism of
Christ is a revealing of the way to 'those who understood it',
make Ode 24 a thematic whole, held together in such a way that it
would almost be odd if the poet had not had the ritual of baptism
somewhere in his mind.

This is, of course, tentative, and pertains only to one poem out
of forty-two – although it should be said, following J. H.
Bernard,[54] that imagery which would be given coherence by
baptism, images of sealing, water, birth, and death, is pervasive
throughout the *Odes*. But again, whether or not the *Odes* are
related to baptism, however tenuously, and whether or not they
show a tendency to use Semitic references in a Gnostic mode,
there is something in them too veiled and supple to be Gnostic in a
plain sense. In other words, the knowledge of truth in the *Odes* is
more a knowing towards the divine than an accomplished, finite,
cognition of it. It is true that the songs abound with symbols of
ecstasy and fulfilment such as the meeting with self, the entry into
paradise and so on; yet their bent is for the desire reaching towards
these symbols; and the succession of symbolic ideas is a drawing of
moral righteousness towards consummation. In Ode 20 the
'thought of the Lord' is 'an offering of righteousness':

[52] Bernard 1912, p. 42, maintains that the *Odes* are directly related to baptism; Harris and
Mingana 1920 believe the references to baptism to be 'occasional not structural' (I, p.
197), on the grounds that the 'illuminated one' is Christ, not the baptized; but now see
Pierce 1984, pp. 35–59, giving a useful summary of the *status quaestionis* and pointing out
that neither the date (early second – late third century) nor the original language (Greek
or Syriac) has been clearly established (pp. 37–8). On the baptismal question, he wishes
to avoid Bernard's view that the *Odes* are describing particular rites in the Syrian
baptism, but feels that the recurrence of certain themes is explained by a baptismal
inspiration in the odist. The baptism he would have had in mind, however, was not the
Pauline baptism of identity with the death/resurrection of Christ familiar in the West
(and, after the late third century, in the East too), but the Messianic and pneumatic
baptism typical of early Syrian liturgy, in which the candidate was assimilated to the
Messiah-hood and Sonship of Christ by the ritual repetition of the descent of the Spirit
in Christ's own baptism. This notion of baptism as participation in Christ's wisdom
answers Harris and Mingana's objection that the *Odes* are non-sacramental because they
contain no clear idea of the *logos* incarnate. Daniélou 1964, pp. 325ff, takes the *Odes* as
evidence of Jewish-Christian sacrament.

[53] 1 Peter is also problematic: Boismard 1956 considers this letter originally a group of
pieces from the liturgy of baptism. Kümmel 1975, pp. 416ff, surveys the literature and
comes down against a direct connection between 1 Peter and the liturgy of baptism.

[54] See n. 52.

and to Him I do priestly service: and to Him I offer the sacrifice of His thought. For His thought is not like [the thought of] the world, nor the thought of the flesh, nor like them that serve carnally. The sacrifice of the Lord is righteousness, and purity of heart and lips.[55]

Elsewhere, though, there are more definite signs of Gnostic sacraments, and of a kind that correspond exactly to the Gnostic understanding of knowledge as having a finite object.[56] In these traces of sacrament it is no longer the quest for knowledge which is emphasized, but the appropriation of it in such a way that the act of knowing by *nous*, is identified with the knowledge of *gnosis* which is its end. Knowing is swallowed up by what is known. So, the myth of salvation told by the late second-century Valentinian text, the *Exegesis on the Soul*, is a myth of return: the soul has a female name, and is a woman, but, so long as she is with the Father, she is a virgin and has a bisexual appearance; when she fell into a body, she was abused and was a harlot, the victim of 'faithless adulterers'; she was abandoned and cried out to the Lord in pain; the Father took pity on her and turned her womb from inside to outside so that she became androgynous as before; this change is accompanied by a water-baptism of purification, and by a rite of the bridal chamber in which she prepared herself for marriage. That these passages in the *Exegesis* refer to performed rites is attested by the closely related *Gospel of Philip* and by other material. The marriage which then takes place is the final joining of male and female, from which comes the birth of 'children who are good', 'For it is fitting that the soul should give birth again to itself.' This, and what follows, circles around the central ideas of deliverance from imprisonment and a marriage – rebirth – resurrection – ascent, all of it in a baptismal context. Interestingly, the *Exegesis* ends on the need for repentance, in a passage which shows some of the eclecticism of Gnosticism by weaving together quotations from the New Testament, Isaiah, the sixth psalm and the *Odyssey*. Despite this last note of grief and sorrow, however, in which the soul is warned to repent of itself, the apotheosis of the soul is not something primarily aspired to, but is accessible.[57] Repentance is a condition of finite knowing, which will duly take

[55] Bernard 1912, p. 89.

[56] Puech 1979, pp. 235–394: 'Liturgie et pratiques rituelles'; Quispel 1974, 221–39; Quispel 1951; Segelberg 1962; and see the Valentinian treatise on baptism edited by E. H. Pagels and J. D. Turner in *The Nag-Hammadi Library*, pp. 435–42.

[57] *Exegesis on the Soul*, pp. 102–9; cf. *Gospel of Philip*, pp. 76–101.

its place. Gnosticism abounds with expressions of this completeness: the meeting with the self; the conception of the universe as a
pharmacy, to use Puech's image (a chemical process of separation
and purification); and the motif of the Twin. In the *Acts of
Thomas*, the apostle Thomas is thus the twin of Christ, bound to
him by resemblance, and therefore in a position to hear his secret
teaching. In Manichaeism, which appears to have made use of the
Acts, this is taken further with the idea of mankind as both saviour
and saved, both alienated from his own nature and accommo-
dated to it.[58]

William James described the religious experience based on this
kind of enlightenment as a journey of the 'sick soul'.[59] In the
post-Reformation religious pathology which provides his material, James finds a similar condition, where the drives to moral
asceticism, physical self-denial and metaphysical escape lie very
close to one another, even shape one another. The 'sickness' might
take many forms – in John of the Cross it is a transformation of
painful desire into the joy of union: *con ansias en amores inflamada*.
Gnosticism, instead of seeking to resolve the tension between
body and spirit in this way, entrenches it in a division and makes
its object the flight from one into the other. But the psychological
impulse is the same: the initial wound which exposes the body's
rottenness and awakens the desire to pass beyond it.

The drives of the sick soul – to moral and physical discipline
on the one hand and to metaphysical escape on the other – exist
side by side, in different combinations, in Essenism, in orthodox
Christianity, in ascetic Gnosticism. This psychological combination bears out Quispel's historical theory that both Gnosticism
and Christianity are more than anything else developments of
Judaism. The shared strain is an antagonism towards the self and
the situation in which it finds itself (*heimarmenē*), causing a critical
break within the self, usually expressed as body against spirit,
which is finally translated into the metaphysical values of dark and
light. The important thing in all of this is that the moral and social
dualism of Essenism or of Hippolytus and his pagan and Christian
professions is not qualitatively different from the full-blown
metaphysical dualism of the Gnostics. They are different degrees
in the same religion of disaffection; different degrees of turning,

[58] On the meeting with the self, Quispel 1974, pp. 140–57. For dualism as pharmacy,
Puech 1949b, p. 83. For Thomas and Christ as twins, *Acts of Thomas*, pp. 442–531,
passim.
[59] James 1960: on John of the Cross, pp. 300ff.

away from self and world and towards God. 'He who does not hate his soul will not be able to follow me', reads the *Exegesis*. The obstinate demand for an answer to the question, *unde malum?*, is what brings on the metaphysical certainty of Gnosticism. The cosmos is now seen as divided between the forces of good and evil. The strength of the Gnostic system is in its fixity: the present flux in which light and dark are mingled, is – in the majority of Gnostic myths – a temporary aberration. It will be resolved by a return to the original static condition of things. It is significant that despite its reduction of theodicy to abstract principles, Gnosticism is able to put its thought in the language of a story. The intellectual impulse of Gnosticism leads it to 'fix' values thus making them finite objects of the mind, and then allowing the mind to become one or other of those objects. The objects are as accessible as the events of a story; but at the same time the story-teller is the protagonist of the story he tells. Whether he ends up in the upper or lower regions at the dénouement of the story is a matter of whether he 'knows' the story, and acts on it. Throughout, what is sought, and, if possible, achieved, is a return to the static condition of the break within self and cosmos: a fixity. Gnosis is not a coming-to-know, but an act of the mind in reaching out and taking up an object; it is a knowing *that* rather than a knowing *how*.[60]

Gnosis makes of divinity an object of the intellect. If we follow James, or, on Gnosticism itself, Festugière and Puech, we can surmise that it comes to this stance in the first place not because of an intellectual vision, but because it attempts to express logically the meaning of repentance, or turning from *heimarmenē* to God. Given this original motive of moral distress, it is not surprising that the major Gnostic groups were rigorously ascetic, stressing fast and poverty and chastity. If we move our attention from Gnosticism to Essenism, or to Jewish-Christian ascetic sects such as Encratism, we find them in a hesitant position on the verge of metaphysical dualism, but not quite there. The main stress is still on action and therefore on will to do rather than on knowledge. The setting of the will is social and moral and in large part it is so precise as to be juridical. But at the same time, the determinate quality of the will, and of the two paths it might follow – truth and falsehood – give it at least some of the 'fixity' of *gnosis*.

[60] This distinction is developed by Ryle 1949, pp. 26–60.

Although there does not seem to be in Essenism any possibility of the identity of will with its object, the rigidity of its rule and institutions go some of the way towards such an identity. It remains true, however, that life cannot be made a static certainty; it is always a struggle:

the spirits of truth and falsehood struggle in the hearts of men and they walk in both wisdom and folly. According to his portion of truth, so does a man hate falsehood, and according to his inheritance in the realm of falsehood so is he wicked and so hates truth, for God has established the two spirits in equal measure until the determined end . . .[61]

If we then look for traces of these possible relationships with the divine in the baptism of the *Tradition*, we find that Christianity, like Essenism, but more evasively, is ambiguous. It shifts back and forth between perspectives, now a repentance in which the will is the active force, now a knowing which engages the intellect; on one side an existential and thoroughly Jewish relation to the divine, on the other an approach more metaphysical. The complexity of the crisis of becoming Christian is a result of these different perspectives. If, broadly, Judaism expresses religious truth through experience racial and historical, and if late Hellenism offers the possibility of self-identity through metaphysical knowledge, then Christianity of this early period keeps both these dimensions. In the *Tradition*, the layer of repentance and experience is obvious enough. It is in the questioning: 'Have they lived honest lives as catechumens? Have they honoured widows? Visited the sick? Have they done all kinds of good?' It is suggested by the metaphor of the naked unencumbered bodies, by the ability of the water to clean; and it is in the exorcisms and renunciations, and the pre-baptismal fast and vigil. All these are ritual interpretations of Old Testament themes, and are no doubt borrowed from sectarian Judaism. But even these passages are ambiguous. The way in which symbols are used in the rite – water, oil, milk and honey, bread and wine – requires a cognitive perception of abstract meaning. It requires intellectual knowledge. So, Hippolytus tells us in an earlier chapter that oil means kingship, prophecy and priesthood; and now he says that the milk and honey, which are associated with the eucharist, refer to the Promised Land; that the bread is the *antitypum* of the body of

[61] *Community Rule* 4, p. 78.

Christ, the wine of his blood.[62] Through symbol, but also because the rite is itself a metaphor, the illusion of something other than merely physical is sustained. At the centre of this is the discourse of the baptismal formula: the candidate responds *Credo* three times to the Apostolic Creed cut into three sections, and at each *Credo* he is immersed, the priest's hand laid on his head.

When he who is to be baptized goes down into the water he who baptizes, laying his hand on him, should say this to him: Do you believe in God the Father Almighty? And he who is baptized should say: I believe. And straightaway, with his hand laid on his head, he should baptize him once, and then say: Do you believe in Christ Jesus the Son of God, who was born of the Holy Spirit and from the Virgin Mary, was crucified under Pontius Pilate, died and on the third day rose again from the dead to the living, who ascended to the heavens, and sits at the right hand of the Father, and who will come again to judge the living and the dead? And when he has said, I believe, he is baptized again. And then he says: Do⁀ you believe in the Holy Spirit and the holy church and the resurrection of the flesh? And the one who is baptized now says: I believe. And so he is baptized a third time.'[63]

To believe is at once to participate in and to have knowledge of. The medieval sacramentaries will speak of the *traditio symboli* and the *redditio symboli* to describe a ritual in which the Creed is recited first by the priest and then by the candidate. This later language shows what is already true in Hippolytus, that the Creed is a myth to be recounted, a story to be known. In this it is akin to myth in Gnosticism, however much its contents, and the story itself, are unquestionably the products of Jewish ideas of God revealed in history, of monotheism and, according to Gregory Dix, of the Messianism of the 'living God'.[64]

---

[62] *Tradition* 5, p. 18: 'Ut oleum hoc sanctificans das, deus, sanitatem utentibus et percipientibus, unde uncxisti reges, sacerdotes et profetas, sic et omnibus gustantibus confortationem et sanitatem utentibus illud praebeat.' And c. 21, pp. 54–6: 'Et tunc iam offeratur oblatio a diaconibus episcopo et gratias agat panem quidem in exemplum, quod dicit graecus antitypum, corporis Christi; calicem uino mixtum propter antity-pum, quod dicit graecus similitudinem, sanguinis quod effusum est pro omnibus qui crediderunt in eum; lac et melle mixta simul ad plenitudinem promissionis quae ad patres fuit, quam dixit terram fluentem lac et mel, quam et dedit carnem suam Christus, per quam sicut paruuli nutriuntur qui credunt, in suauitate uerbi amara cordis dulcia efficiens; aquam uero in oblationem in indicium lauacri, ut interior homo, quod est animale, similia consequantur sicut et corpus.'

[63] Ibid., pp. 48–50. On Hippolytus' Creed, generally thought to be the earliest known, Connolly 1924; Ghellinck 1949; and Botte 1951, arguing that the phrase *resurrectio carnis* was not in the original, but was added later, perhaps against Gnostic teachings.

[64] Dix 1953, pp. 90 and 97ff.

There is no direct evidence that Hippolytus is consciously using the baptismal theology of John or Paul. He never says with Paul that the water-rite is a moral and ritual burial with Christ and an entry into his death/resurrection; and he does not say as does John that baptism expresses the passing of belief through the palpable symbol of water to the *logos*, in such a way that the believer is reborn from the birth of the flesh to the birth of the spirit. The *Tradition* is reticent about theology and only uses the phrase *lauacrum regenerationis* once.[65] On the other hand, it is impossible to say what is implied in this reticence: there is no reason why these theologies should not have been an unrecorded part of its catechesis, perhaps of a post-baptismal catechesis, as they are in Ambrose of Milan later on. The general problem is the same, though, whatever the subtleties: how is it possible to approach the hidden thing which is God? The existential approach offered by Judaism was not enough, because the God of the Christians, being a fulfilment and embodiment of the history of man from Adam to Christ, could not be a part of psychological or ethnic experience in the way he had been in the Old Testament; because he was the Messiah, because he was the son of God and the son of Man, because – according to John – he was the *logos*, he could no longer be familiar in the same way. He could not be historical or apocalyptic except in the sense of taking up into himself the past and the future and therefore standing outside their contingency. Being a man who was also God, who had died but also risen, he was utterly remote from simple experience: 'the unknown God' (*agnostos theos*), as Paul put it to the Athenians (Acts 17:23).[66] In this, he is quite distinct from the God of the Old Testament, who although distanced from his people, either by fear or as the object of pious love, was always implicated in their life by repeated covenant, by his activity as a law-giver, and in later Judaism by prophecy.

John's strategy towards this hiddenness is a faith-knowledge which perceives the *logos* in the sign (*semeion*):

---

[65] *Tradition* 21, p. 52.

[66] By *agnostos theos* I have understood Paul to mean not just that he could tell the Athenians the name and nature of a god until then unknown to them, but that in imparting this knowledge, he is proclaiming to them the God who cannot be known; in other words, a God who remains unknown. If this is right, the Stoic and broadly Hellenic sense of the divine as known from the order of the cosmos, and the idea associated with the Mystery religions that divinity is beyond rational cognition, would be combined in Paul's speech on the Areopagus. See Norden 1913 on these themes; and Dibelius 1956, pp. 26–77.

There was one of the Pharisees called Nicodemus, a leading Jew, who came to Jesus by night and said, 'Rabbi, we know that you are a teacher who comes from God; for no one could perform the signs that you do unless God were with him'. Jesus answered 'I tell you most solemnly, unless a man is born from above, he cannot see the Kingdom of God.' Nicodemus said 'How can a grown man be born again?' Jesus replied: 'I tell you most solemnly, unless a man is born through water and the spirit, he cannot enter the Kingdom of God: what is born of the flesh is flesh; what is born of the spirit is spirit. Do not be surprised when I say: You must be born from above. The wind [i.e. spirit] blows wherever it pleases; you hear its sound, but you cannot tell where it comes from or where it is going. That is how it is with all those who are born of the spirit.' (John 3:1–8)

John goes on to use the image of the brazen serpent in the desert to complement the sign of water. Moses raised the serpent before the Israelites, and those who had been bitten and had died now looked on the serpent and lived (Numb. 21:4–9). Baptism, then, is a transition to life by virtue of 'seeing' God. C. H. Dodd has shown how this makes use of the Old Testament theme of the two serpents, one of the Fall, the other its antithesis, a sign of life; the language and the context, however, make the 'lifting up' of the serpent equally the upward motion of the Ascension, so that to look on the serpent is to look on and believe in the rising up of the Son of Man. John ends the night-dialogue with Nicodemus on a moral note. A man's belief can be read in his actions, and on them he will be judged. But the metaphysical origin of his action is apparent in the phrase used: 'he that does the truth (ὁ δε ποιῶν τὴν ἀλήθειαν) comes into the light'. And – to follow Dodd again – belief is a raising of the spirit through water to *logos*: Jesus is at once the witness of *logos*, and *logos* itself. This process of lifting from flesh to spirit is therefore a knowledge of God through the son of Man, and of *logos* through water.[67]

In this play of perspectives within baptism, John is thus inclined towards a metaphysical account of faith. As Dodd says, he is close to the Hellenistic theory of knowledge, even if he does not depart from the thought-world of rabbinic Judaism. Paul's notion of baptism is perhaps more difficult to capture. The threads which are in it are not so easy to undo. As a result, there has been much discussion of whether his ideas, particularly that of baptism 'into Christ' (*eis Christon*), were founded mainly on Judaism or on

[67] Dodd 1953, pp. 303–8 and *passim*.

Hellenistic sources. Per Lundberg has shown how the imagery of death and resurrection can be found in the Old Testament and its Apocrypha.[68] Paul may have been inspired by the myth of *descensus* as a return from the meeting with death, seen for example in the story of Jonah; in rabbinic circles, moreover, occurs the teaching of death as the ultimate expiation of sin; on the other hand, the idea of a life-giving celebration of the death of a god is reminiscent of the Greek mysteries. It is in Apuleius and in Ovid's description of the death of Adonis, where Cytherea sees the young god lying dead, and promises that the 'image of his death' will be repeated every year in a mourning which will bring with it rebirth. These are mere fragments, though, beside Paul's unified and radical conception: he is not simply pillaging images, but establishing a whole ritual theology.[69] Paul's approach to the hidden God is through a faith in the justification of man, and a moral turning which enables the believer to imitate the righteousness of the just man who dies for the unjust. This imitation reaches the pitch where the imitator becomes the death of the just man in baptism and therefore becomes his resurrection too. The theology passes from moral imitation to ritual identification by way of the one moral act which absorbs into itself, but in the same moment transcends, all possible moral acts, and all moral history from Adam to Christ: the death of Christ. By taking the moral condition of man to its most extreme expression – the death of a just man for the unjust race of men – an event is made both moral and metaphysical. Baptism is a repeat of this event. It is true that Paul's theology of baptism had little influence throughout the second century, and does not appear explicitly in Hippolytus; but the depiction of baptism as a meeting of forces and a crisis is equally present in both writers.[70]

In Hippolytus, the Pauline concentration of forces in an event is largely absent. There does exist in the *Tradition*, though, a sense of

---

[68] Lundberg 1942, pp. 221ff; Ysebaert 1962, pp. 53ff.

[69] Wedderburn 1987 emphasizes that the Mystery religions do not teach identity with the death/resurrection of the god. A god – Isis, Osiris, Dionysius, Demeter, Cybele – may die and rise, but the initiate beholds this event and takes hope from the proof it gives of divine power; he does not participate in it. Wedderburn argues that Paul develops his theology of participation out of the Judaic concept of the solidarity of the nation from one generation to the next: when Christ dies, the generation of Adam dies; when he rises again, the generation of the new Adam rises with him. See more generally on Paul's relation to rabbinic Judaism, Davies 1955 (pp. 102ff on the solidarity of the generation).

[70] On the scarcity of Paul's theology of baptism in the second century, Benoit 1953, p. 228 and *passim*.

participation by the person being baptized in the myth of Christ and Christianity. This is present first in the very nature of ritual: it proceeds by metaphor. Each part of it is a sign of what is beyond it; the whole rite is a dramatic sign of spiritual truth. To be converted by baptism, or by the periodic 'conversion' of the eucharist, is to take part in this metaphor, to pass with the metaphor from physical to spiritual being. But this metaphorical function, which is variously enacted in gesture, physical symbols, prescribed circumstances, has its centre of gravity in the *Tradition* in language. More than anything, it is the word which is ambivalent. At intervals throughout the rite, and most intensively in the interrogatory creed, we can see how the word which states the myth – Trinity, Virgin Birth, historical Christ, death/resurrection, Last Judgement, resurrection of the flesh – is also the word from which it originates. Again, this is not an explicit theology as it is in John's *logos*, but remains implicit in the texture of the performance.[71]

BAPTISM, CREATION FROM NOTHING, AND THE REJECTION OF SOCIETY

I have suggested that the ethical dualism of late Judaism and early Christianity, and the metaphysical dualism of Gnosticism, are linked closely by the labours of the 'sick soul'; by its movement from a repentance of the will to a repentance of knowledge. Hippolytus expresses, although in the oblique manner of the liturgy, both these attitudes to divinity: what he describes is a 'turning' after the style of John the Baptist, a baptism of repentance (*baptisma metanoias*) to the remission of sins and to the kingdom of heaven which is at hand, (see Matt. 3:1–11; Mark 1:4). If we are to understand more fully the connection between the turning and the obscure kingdom which is turned to, we should also see that the condition of the 'sick soul' is social as well as individual. The repudiation made by Christians of their social milieu – witness Hippolytus on taboo occupations – is the source, but also the continuing expression, of the remoteness of their God. The paradoxes of the Creed – Virgin Birth, death/resurrection, man/God – behind which lies the unspeakableness of God are the

---

[71] Steiner 1975, ch. 3 ('Word against Object'), discusses from many angles the ambiguous content of freedom and determinism in language.

immediate result of a conversion by rejection, denial, exorcism, renunciation.

Again and again the texts speak of disenchantment and transcendence in the same breath. In the *Letter to Diognetus* (early second century), the beginning of conversion is a 'purifying of the mind from prejudices', a *catharsis* from the gods of the Greeks, which are no more than pots and pans, from 'the blood and fat and burnt-offerings' of the Jews, who should know better than to give such things to a God who has no need of them. When he has finished pouring scorn on Jew and Greek, the author paints his well-known picture of the Christian community, transient, alien, as the soul to the body, living in cities but not of them, quickened by suffering and persecution, straining with knowledge towards the incorruptible, the just and sinless Christ. There is a pastoral quietude here which will not always be achieved.[72] Tatian, a Christian convert born in Assyria in the late second century, is more strident. He delivers, in his *Oratio ad Graecos*, a wholesale assault on Greek culture. Its rhetoric, he says, is no more than the prostitution of free speech; its poetry a mere description of embattled and amorous gods; the philosophers he caricatures, telling the old tales of Plato sold as a slave and the 'fawning' Aristotle shut up in a cave by Alexander. The centre – textually and psychologically – of this polemic is the metaphysical apartness of God from his own creation: 'he is not visible to human eyes nor in any way to be comprehended ... Our God has no origin in time, since he alone is without beginning and himself is the beginning of all things ... How can I proclaim sticks and stones as gods?'[73] There is a shrill note in Tatian, and a suggestion that he aspires to Greek sophistication as he damns it, but there is also an intrinsic strength of conviction in his feeling that the values and ambitions of Greco-Roman society are empty through and through. The equation is made between the delusion of contemporary social conditions and the reality of the Christian god which is their opposite. The anger which in Tatian leads to the unknown God shares much with the sceptical withdrawal of Marcus Aurelius. In both cases, the beginning is a scorn of mere human emotion and value. The difference is between the world-weariness of Marcus, who retreats from ambition and grief and turbulence as such, and the Christian apologist, whose contempt is

[72] *Letter to Diognetus* 2–4 etc.
[73] *Oratio ad Graecos* esp. 1–4 and 22ff, pp. 1–11 and 45ff.

itself a passion, a certitude, and whose object is not mankind in general but the particular excesses of Hellenistic culture. Marcus can only be tentative in his withdrawal; Tatian, having a definite object against which to strive, can be more decisive. His *Oratio* finishes with an effort to show that the Biblical account of the life of Moses is more ancient than the Homeric stories and their Greek heroes.[74] But the belief that one culture is better than another is derived from and part of the basis of, the belief in the transcendent divinity.

In Tertullian, the same themes find a more exacting exponent. Once more, Christianity is a renunciation of other possible forms of life; and the Christian divinity is that which other gods are not. In his *De spectaculis* and elsewhere he chastises pagan society, while in his work *Against Hermogenes* he maintains against Hermogenes the doctrine of *creatio ex nihilo*. Hermogenes, whose writings have not survived, evidently held a view like that of Plato's *Timaeus*, that God brought matter into being from unborn plasma co-eternal with himself. By rejecting this view, Tertullian was insisting on the separateness of God from all created things.[75] In this, the formula *creatio ex nihilo* is in a line of philosophic thought stretching from the Platonic idea of *chorismos* to the discursive mysticism of Nicholas of Cusa.[76] Early in the fourth century, Lactantius, another North African, condemns the religious statues of Phidias and other Greek sculptors, calling them 'over-sized dolls' in the hands of foolish men: 'No wonder Seneca ridiculed old men's folly, saying not that we have a second childhood, (as the saying goes), but that we are always children.'[77] 'Ubi ergo ueritas?' demands Lactantius. The mistake, he feels, and here he is close to Tertullian, is the Stoic mistake of confusing God with his creation, abstract energy with matter. The distinctiveness of Christianity, then, is in a philosophic aesthetic. It is one thing to wonder at the works of God, but an immeasurably greater to see

---

[74] Ibid. 31–41, pp. 56–77. Cf. Marcus Aurelius, *Meditations* (for example 2.17).

[75] *Adu. Hermog.*, pp. 395–435.

[76] Cassirer 1963. According to Louth 1981, the creation from nothing is the mainspring of Christian, as against Platonic, mysticism. Rather than a Platonic merging of the soul with ideas (*syngeneia*), Christian theologians as early as Philo talk of God as unknowable and other. Cf. Stroumsa 1982; Norris 1979: Irenaeus, argues Norris, is quarrelling above all with the role of the demiurge in Gnostic teaching. The Platonic demiurge, Irenaeus holds in his *Aduersus Haereses*, does not mediate divinity in such a way as to limit it to Nature and deprive it of freedom. See also Schoedel 1979.

[77] *Diu. inst.* 2.4, cols. 271–2. On Lactantius, Jerome, *De uiris illustribus* 80, col. 687.

that they were made from nothing.[78] In this way, the otherness of what Ovid had already called 'Ille opifex rerum, mundi melioris origo' ('the artificer of all things, source of the better world', *Met.*I.79) was affirmed. Perception of truth could therefore not be founded in a vision of man's implication in the material forces of the cosmos, in the Stoic concept of fate, but in the realization that he was capable of standing aside from material necessity. For the old Stoic harmony, Lactantius substituted another: man is a composition of the four elements, but also of earth and heaven. If he shows himself capable of perceiving this, he raises himself towards heaven; if not, he returns to the source of sin, and all that he sees is illusion and idol. Sin is ignorance of, or denial of, the new harmony, above all the harmony of subjugation of body to soul.[79] The Stoic act of perception which enables man to see what he is and where he stands, now becomes his ability both to see what he is and to raise himself above this position. Lactantius has turned the Stoic idea of harmony on its head: obedience to harmony has been made into the possibility of transcending it.

However much these writers may express themselves within the forms of the culture they are attacking – and all of them are doing this – the crux of their thought is in a repudiation of that culture. Their rejection of it is also an escape from it. We can see from their contempt of civilization how this refusal is as much social as personal, and how the hiddenness of God is as much a function of social malaise as of the individual 'sick soul'. Festugière has described the general despair in a few words: 'ensuite des changements politiques, sociaux, moraux, ... l'homme héllénistique se sent seul, perdu dans une cité terrestre qui n'est plus à sa mesure'.[80] The substitution of *romanitas* in its territorial immensity and its legal abstraction, for the definiteness of the Greek *polis*, was a source of deep disquiet. Stoicism, with its vision of the harmony of man and cosmos, teaches a difficult equilibrium of acceptance of the world and withdrawal from it: it was an answer only for the high melancholic spirit of a man like Marcus

---

[78] *Diu. inst.* 2.5, col. 277: 'Unde quidam hebetis obtusique cordis, elementa, quae et facta sunt et carent sensu, tamquam deos adorant. Qui cum dei opera mirarentur, id est coelum cum uariis luminibus, terram cum campis et montibus, maria cum fluminibus et stagnis et fontibus, earum rerum admiratione obstupefacti, et ipsius artificis obliti, quem uidere non poterant, eius opera uenerari et colere coeperunt; nec umquam intelligere quiuerunt, quanto maior quantoque mirabilior sit, qui illa fecit ex nihilo.'

[79] Ibid. 2.12, cols. 316–25; and 7.4, cols. 746–9.

[80] Festugière 1967, p. 25.

Aurelius. The majority were inclined to something more gratifying, both spiritually and socially; and to turn from a strategy of restrained contemplation and contingent action to the relief and drama of apotheosis of the self. The tendency in Stoicism to allegorize the Homeric gods, and of Alexandrian Judaism to do the same with the Old Testament, helped make divinity more remote; the desire, and the practical need, against the background of so far-flung an empire, to establish the principle of universal justice over that of territorial immunities; the further desire in these times to feel in some way chosen, which could be borrowed from Judaism, but which was also an aspect of the Gnostic groups; together these were compulsions not only towards monotheism, but to the *deus ignotus*.[81] Disillusionment made it preferable to see divine power as the negation of all other power. And yet, unlike Gnosticism, Christianity perceives monotheism not as a simple negative. For all his hiddenness, the God of the Christians has penetrated the world, the will, the mind.

Baptism in Hippolytus, like the eucharist, or the church with its part-charismatic, part-institutional character, provides circumscribed time and space in which this penetration can take place. In this respect, early Christian sacrament has the same purpose as the early Christian holy man or saint or martyr. It represents the infinite in the finite: as Peter Brown has made clear, the holy man of Late Antiquity is all the better defined for being grafted on to the Roman idea of friendship.[82] On the other hand, the holy man and the martyr were more obviously manifestations, more theophanic, than was a sacrament. A ritual, typically baptism or the eucharist, was an apparatus of subtle ideas demanding interpretation, whereas the holy man and martyr made their meaning quite plain in what were seen as outlandish actions: shunning social intercourse, and seeking death.

Baptism, as we have seen, is no mere theophany, but an interpretation of theophany by will and intellect. The dialectic emerges from a simple reading of the Acts, where the story of *kerygma*, of progressive proclamation of faith, is interspersed with accounts of baptism. In each account there is a different emphasis.

---

[81] Ibid.; and Festugière 1932, on the 'wound' which breaks apart the careful poise of Late Antique ethics and metaphysics, and makes possible the entry of the Christian *hubris*. The cause of the wound was an aspiration to a consistent, transcendent justice: 'C'est ici le point sensible, la blessure d'où va jaillir ce qu'il y eut de plus profondément religieux dans la pensée grecque' (at p. 38).

[82] Brown 1981.

Sometimes baptism is more a manifestation of power, sometimes more the result of teaching.

When Lydia was baptized, it was after the Lord had 'opened her heart' to the words spoken by Paul (Acts 16:14–16); Paul's conversion is a blindness and a healing from blindness (Acts 9:17ff); when Philip meets the Kandake's eunuch on the road from Jerusalem to Gaza, he finds him perplexed by a passage from Isaiah: 'How can I understand unless someone will guide me?' Beginning from the passage, Philip teaches him 'the glad tidings' (Acts 8:27ff) Elsewhere, baptism is an acquiescence to *charis*, to divine power working through the apostles, as in the baptizing which follows the descent of the Pentecostal fire (Acts 2:37–8 etc.). Repeatedly, these aspects of understanding and power are put together, so that the active coming-to-truth and the passive reception of it are made to coincide. On hearing that Jesus is the anointed one of God, the Jews listening to Peter at Pentecost are stricken, and do not know what to do. Peter tells them they are to repent and be baptized in the name of Jesus Christ (Acts 2:38: Μετανοήσατε, καὶ βαπτισθήτω ... ἐπὶ τῷ ὀνόματι Ἰησοῦ Χριστοῦ). In Judaism, the name has profound significance based on the idea that it is inseparable from the person or object which bears it. Personal names have in them in varying degrees the authority, the power and the inner character or quality of the person. For this reason, God is spoken of as 'the Name' (Lev. 24:11; Prov. 18:10; Isa. 30:27). The particular mental habit of attributing religious force or *mana* to the name, and the more general association of *mana* with language, is a commonplace of ancient religion, and, some would say, of modern societies. It has a clear relevance to the concept of revelation, but equally, as modern literary criticism has shown, to the nature of poetry. In the Bible, however, and more than anywhere in the New Testament theology of baptism, the act of naming has a precise transformative effect. The sense given it in this passage of the Acts is that a person is baptized in the authority of Jesus Christ; by using a different preposition (*eis*, with accusative, instead of *epi*, with dative), and by saying simply *eis Christon*, Paul, in Romans 6:3, makes the relationship with Christ direct and without mediation. The possibilities suggested by these idioms are taken up and developed by Jewish-Christianity and Gnosticism. Quispel has argued that Valentinian baptism takes its effect from the belief that the Name of God descended on Christ at the moment of his own baptism by John; there is a possible echo of this in the appeal to 'put on the name of the Most High' in the *Odes of Solomon*.[83] The form of this myth of the Name is reproduced in a complex of Jewish–Christian notions about the baptism of Christ as the source of all subsequent baptism. Christ's baptism is at once the descent of the Holy Spirit and the moment of anointing (see Acts 10:38: at the baptism 'God anointed Jesus of Nazareth with the Holy Spirit and with power'). Some Gnostic groups held the rite of unction in higher esteem than that of water-baptism, a preference already suggested by the affinity of oil with kingship, prophecy and priesthood in the Old Testament.[84] Baptism is therefore the act by which Christ is named, by which he receives the Spirit and becomes the 'anointed one' – the Messiah or the Christ. This complex of descending power, emphasized in certain interpretations of baptism, is brought out liturgically in the motif of sealing or *sphragis*.[85] Although Lampe has made the case that this term means baptism as a whole, Cardinal Daniélou has conjectured that it may have referred in Jewish–Christian circles both to the whole rite and to the particular gesture of signing on the forehead.[86] Whether or not this is so the term, carried over from the Septuagint and taken up repeatedly by Paul, has again this sense of arbitrary divine intervention. For Hermas in the second century it is a 'bearing the name' of Christ and thus a choosing of the servants of God after the manner of the Tau-sign at Passover (cf. Apoc. 7:3);[87] and Paul shows characteristic ability to entangle the meanings of sealing in a fashion which somehow also gives them an internal logic: 'Remember it is God himself who assures us all, and you, of our standing in Christ (*eis Christon*), and has anointed us (*chrisas*), marking us with the seal (*sphragisamenos*), and giving us the pledge of the spirit (*tou pneumatos*) in our hearts' (2 Cor. 1:21–2). The

[83] See Quispel 1974, pp. 196–212, quoting the *Gospel of Philip* 12; *Excerpta ex Theodoto* 22.6; *Odes of Solomon* 39.
[84] For the sacramental value of oil over water in Gnosticism, *Acts of Thomas* 27.157, and Bornkamm's commentary in Hennecke–Schneemelcher 1965, pp. 437ff.
[85] Dölger 1911; and Quasten 1939, suggesting that the theme of the Good Shepherd, found in the baptisteries of Dura-Europos (second century) and Naples (fifth century) and elsewhere in relation to baptism, may have developed partly from the particular sense of *sphragis* as the mark of possession and protection put on an animal. Also Lampe 1967; and for a detailed semantic inquiry, Ysebaert 1962, pp. 181–426 (on imposition of hands, anointing, sealing). Lampe and Ysebaert stress the application of *sphragis* to all three rites of unction, water-immersion, laying-on of hands in early Christianity.
[86] Daniélou 1964, pp. 330–1.
[87] Hermas, *Sim.* 9.13.2–3, cited Daniélou 1964, p. 330.

associations are compressed into a few phrases: Christ the anointed and the chrism, a sealing which is also a promise of the Spirit. Again the dominant themes are those of choosing and possession.

Sphragis, the Name, anointing, are all devices used by the liturgy of baptism to express the aspect of manifestation or theophany. A person who comes to baptism is as if possessed. Where the rite is able to reconcile this aspect with that of personal will and understanding by its dramatic sequence and by the notion of the symbol as something which should be understood, the baptismal episodes of the Acts do the same thing by the use of narrative. The most elaborate example is in the account of the conversion of Cornelius and his baptism by Peter (Acts 10:1–48). The structure of the narrative has been broken down by M. Dujarier.[88] It is a story about the meeting between two men and two groups: Cornelius the Roman centurion, a Gentile, and Peter, the apostle. The meeting is also a communication of messages: Cornelius in Caesarea and Peter in Joppa each have a vision, Cornelius of an angel who tells him to send for Peter, Peter of a great sheet coming down from heaven and holding in it the unclean flesh of 'creeping things and birds of the air'. He is told to kill and eat, and refuses because the flesh is not pure; but the voice tells him that what the Lord has made clean should not be called profane (*koinou*). When the messengers from Cornelius arrive at Peter's place of lodging in Joppa, they recount their master's vision, and Peter allows them to enter his door. His hospitality looks forward to Acts 15, the so-called council of Jerusalem, where Peter lays it down that Gentiles coming to Christianity are not to be circumcised and do not need to stand by the Mosaic law.

The vision of the unclean beasts, and the baptism of Cornelius which comes of it, is therefore a turning-point in the unfolding of *kerygma*. Baptism is now placed in precise relation to circumcision and the law. It can no longer be seen as a mere development of circumcision, and indeed of Judaism, but supersedes it. It remains a purification, but of a different kind, based not on a legal and ritual system, but on a personal, self-conscious perception. It grows from the capacity to 'fear' God, to offer prayer to God, to give alms. Luke thus describes the qualities which make Cornelius eligible for baptism in the same words used of the sacrifice which is acceptable to the Lord: baptism is the new offering.[89] The story

88 Dujarier 1962, pp. 136–48, 391–3.
89 See Brown and others 1968, II, no. 45.55–6, pp. 187–8.

goes on to tell how Peter makes his way to Caesarea, accepts hospitality from Cornelius, and asks him what he intends. Cornelius explains his vision again, and Peter replies, by now understanding what is required of him, with a pre-baptismal teaching which is also a Creed. It is in what he says here that we can see very clearly how the first Christians made the step from the objective content of the Creed to personal acceptance of it. The connection which Gnosticism makes an act of cognition, and which Christianity from Paul to Ambrose makes a process both of will and intellect, is in the Acts a question of witness. The 'myth' of Christianity is composed of events which have happened and have been witnessed by the apostles (they are *martyres*), who are now charged to testify (*diamartyrasthai*). In their testimony, and in the Creed which Peter recites to Cornelius, it is the baptism of Christ, the moment when he was 'anointed by the Holy Spirit', which stands at the beginning of the account. The *charisma* given the apostles by their mission, their chosenness as witnesses of the word, is itself a manifestation, and in the Cornelius episode the centurion and his household receive the gift of the Spirit, the gift of tongues, before being baptized in water. The historical continuum between Christ and the apostles through witness is underwritten by the interpretation of baptism as both evolution of, and rejection of, circumcision and the law. The structure of the narrative meanwhile mimes the sense of the story. In the comings and goings between Joppa and Caesarea, the apparent arbitrariness of the two visions is progressively clarified. Cornelius' vision occurs once and is told twice; Peter's occurs three times, and even then its meaning, that he must accept the Gentiles, seems not to be quite clear to him. The link between vision and understanding, the exegesis, is the recital of the Creed; and this explanation is made good by the descent of the Spirit and baptism. By repetition and symmetry, the distance between divine vision and human seeing is cut down.[90]

The intensity of the crisis which baptism marks is evoked by all the early references to it. It is this which makes the baptism of Hippolytus comparable with entry into Gnosticism. Baptism is a single moment of judgment between two moral and metaphysical orders. Much could already be found in the Old Testament idea of repentance which would tend to break down this intensity, and

[90] On the resolution of dilemmas by symmetry in the Bible, see Edmund Leach's essay on 'Genesis as Myth', Leach 1967.

thus make the turning towards God an attitude of mind rather than an act accomplished once and for all. In other words, Hippolytus' idea of baptism as a black-and-white contrast between denial of the past and adherence to truth is later softened by the possibility of doing penance for sins after baptism. As penance becomes more important, baptism takes on more the sense of a preparation of the mind and will for what will come afterwards. More and more it will be seen as the beginning of spiritual development, not the end.

I have singled out one aspect of the thought-world of Christianity in its emergent form, that of the relationsip between moral and metaphysical radicalism. This relationship offers some coherence to the problem of how Christianity stands to Judaism and Gnosticism, a difficulty which has been the cause of argument. Some have held that each system of thought is to be regarded as independent; others that, historically, the connections between them are undeniably present in any number of borrowings and shared motifs. Once the dividing-line between historical fact and religious expression is discarded, however, the problem, though less exact, becomes less awkward and more realistic. Certainly, Gnosticism or Christianity or Judaism are independent visions; yet at the same time, they not only borrow from one another, but even grow from the same psychological roots. They learn from one another not just the elements of the architecture of religion, but also religious sentiment itself. Circumcision is not 'borrowed' by baptism, but some of the ideas expressed in circumcision become baptismal ideas: thus, the baptism of infants which leans on the practice of circumcision on the eighth day; the association of initiation with purification; the proximity of sacrificial ideas and initiation; and the link between deliverance, exodus and initiation.

In this sense, Christianity begins as interpretation of Judaism, Hellenism and Gnosticism. It is worthwhile pointing to this early on, because Christianity continues to interpret as it develops. This habit of using old forms in another context, and therefore to mean something different, should become more evident as we follow the place of baptism in society and thinking. I have tried to show how the Jewish exorcism which is primarily ethnocentric, becomes the Christian which is social, cultural and moral. There are periods when the Jewish theme of a chosen people will seep back into Christianity, and will be implicit in Christian exorcism, as though Christianity had been re-judaized. Again, to know what is meant by resurrection, rebirth, renewal, in baptism would require a full understanding of Jewish Apocalyptic, of the Jewish ideas of the renewal of Jerusalem and of the heavenly Jerusalem, of the renewal of the world and its connection with the coming of the Messiah.[91] This in turn raises the Jewish and Christian attitudes to time: the Jewish sense of incomplete time looking forward to completion in Messiah and eschatology; the Christian, which does not entirely supersede this, of a finished time in which the final event has already happened, and can only be repeated, in sacrament or in some form of mysticism.

In the meeting of Gnosticism with Christianity, the principal issue is a very wide one. Gnosticism is a myth about knowledge. The myth is that the vision of the divine reality as a whole, the fruit of a mystical, emotional and moral experience, can be translated into the language of objective knowing. The feeling of divinity is therefore the same as the cognition of it as an external state, and both are complete. It is as though a person could be known absolutely, in a set of principles. In practice, of course, this central position of the Gnostics is not always borne out. It is diffused and obscured by the wealth of mythology and legend, so that the lines between Gnostic and Christian are not easily drawn. Christianity is also about knowing God and experiencing him. But instead of supposing that 'seeing' God by experience and by objective knowing are equivalent, the Christian maintains that in passing from one to the other – from faith to philosophy – there is a shift in perspective. To keep both perspectives is to allow that the approach to God will always be tentative, never replete. Christian baptism, I have suggested, bears the traces of a constantly shifting perspective.

[91] Schürer, Vermes, Millar and Black 1979, pp. 529ff, for an outline of these themes and further references; and see Ysebaert 1962, pp. 89–154.

Chapter 2

TERTULLIAN AND AMBROSE: REASON AND DESIRE

fiunt, non nascuntur Christiani   (Tertullian, *Apologeticum* 18.4)

CONVERSION

If, until the fifth century, the act of becoming a Christian implied an attitude of contempt for the paganism which was left behind, it should also be kept in mind that the 'turning' to Christianity was not always in practice so dramatic. To the conversion of the 'sick soul' we should add the common experience of a progression into Christianity; the absorption, more or less gradual, into the Christ-centred vision, into its ethics, into the apparent paradoxes of its doctrine, into its highly emotive Apocalypticism and, not least important in the Latin world, into its language, the language of the Vulgate and the various earlier versions, with their solecisms and loose syntax, so unlike anything which would have been heard in the mouth of the most ordinary orator.[1] Conversion, and therefore baptism as the statement of conversion, was a rejection of the past but at the same time, and in the same man or woman, a development of the past. This is as true of the individual as it is of whole cultures: the history of early Christianity is the history of how Christianity was brought out from Judaism; from Hellenism; from Latin civilization; and conversion is the process in which individuals and groups absorbed this transition.[2]

In its early form, Christianity was not a state of being but a state of becoming; a transition and, literally, a translation. It follows from this that the identity of the Christian is in the sense he has of his own becoming: he has become what he was not before; and, except in certain extreme communities of Montanists and Nova-tianists, who allowed no penance after the first, all-consuming

---

[1] Mohrmann 1961, p. 148; Mohrmann 1965, pp. 171–96; Löfstedt 1959, pp. 68–87.
[2] Harnack 1904; Daniélou 1964; Jaeger 1962.

penance of baptism,[3] he will, paradoxically, continue to become; he will go on seeking proximity to God, the *similitudo* which he has acquired ritually, but not finally, in baptism. This is apparent in the words of Ambrose to those who have just been baptized: 'you were marked with the image (*forma*) of his cross, with the image of his passion; you received the sign (*signaculum*) that you might bear his likeness (*similitudo*), that you might rise up in his image (*forma*), that you might live out the symbol (*figura*) of him who was crucified for sin and lived for God'.[4] *Viva figuram*: the ritual sign of baptism (*signaculum* here means both post-baptismal 'sealing' with the sign of the cross, and the water-baptism),[5] however complete in itself, can only be fulfilled outside ritual by the moral life which follows. This is the Pauline theology of the baptism which makes men 'alive with a life which looks towards God' (Rom. 6:11). The Christian, then, was not like the Jew, whose belief bound him to the land and to Jahweh through a divine history, through the law, through blood and family and through the bodily sign of covenant in circumcision; he was not like the Greek, who in this 'decadent' period of Hellenism, regarded himself, even if he was compelled to live in the furthest reaches of Syria, as the peripatetic, self-sufficient embodiment of *paideia*, and of all the intellectual and moral virtues of the Greek *polis* which that suggested; and he was equally unlike the Roman with his attachment to *gens*, to his ancestors, to *urbanitas* and *romanitas*. It is as though the Christian takes up any or all of these states, and infuses it with movement.[6] The point can be made from Augustine's *Confessions* and his *City of God*, the first an account of how the individual moves from pagan rhetoric to philosophy and finally to Christianity in a drawn-out process of self-purification; the second, of how a civilization has done the same.[7]

---

[3] A tendency to this extremism already exists in Tertullian before his encounter with Montanism: *De baptismo* 15.3: 'Ceterum Israel cotidie lauat quia cotidie inquinatur. Quod ne in nobis quoque factitaretur propterea de uno lauacro definitum est. Felix aqua quae semel abluit, quae ludibrio peccatoribus non est, quae non adsiduitate sordium infecta rursus quos diluit inquinat.' Novatian himself never denied the value of penance, but it seems that some of his later followers, probably influenced by Montanism, did so: Theodoret, *Haeret. fab. comp.*, col. 408B.

[4] *De sac.* 6.7, p. 99.

[5] Cf. ibid. 3.8–9, pp. 74–5.

[6] Harnack 1904, I, pp. 300ff, on the *tertium genus*; Marrou 1956, pp. 314ff ('Christianity and Classical Education').

[7] Marrou 1938, pp. 121ff

Here, though, I want to concentrate on the earlier history of the transition into Christian belief, by commenting on three texts: Tertullian's homily on baptism (*De baptismo*), a polemical work written, like much of what Tertullian wrote, against various heretical interpretations, and a work which gives sacrament a profoundly *rational* appearance, because of the accent its author places on argument; the *De sacramentis* of Ambrose of Milan, a series of sermons delivered to the recently baptized in Milan, giving a symbolic, highly sensual and emotional account of sacrament, and thus standing in marked contrast – almost conflict – with Tertullian. Lastly, with a view to pushing Ambrose's approach back to its origins, I will argue from the *Passion of Perpetua and Felicitas* that baptism is in a sense a martyrdom put into ritual, and, conversely, that martyrdom is sacrament – above all baptism – acted out in its physical extreme. Sacrament and martyrdom, in other words, are different expressions of the same *desire*. From these texts, I hope to show something of the motivation involved in becoming Christian through baptism: to underline its various content of cold reasoning and passionate desire, of self-examination and change in the will, and of acquiescence to truth.

It is perhaps too easy to take for granted that because baptism is initiation, it is also conversion, and in some sense contains all that is meant by becoming and being a Christian. With the development of penitence and of the 'higher' forms of the holy life in monasticism and martyrdom, the priority of baptism was made less obvious. A sentiment of Christian heroism grew up, as well as its corollary, the realization that not all Christians could be heroes, so that baptism was seen more and more as the beginning of a life of aspiration.[8] And yet, there is no doubt that until about the time of Augustine it remained the image of what distinguished the Christian; it contained, doctrinally, morally, eschatologically, symbolically, all that a Christian *could* be, and in that sense defined what a Christian was. This is most apparent in the Creed, which concentrated within a few words not only the statement of Christian doctrine, but by implication the movement within conversion: P. T. Camelot has pointed out how the Trinitarian structure of the Creed corresponds to the Trinitarian rhythm of revelation and salvation as it is found in Irenaeus: the word is

[8] For the background to this, de Labriolle 1913; Cyprian, *De lapsis*; and the letter by an unknown author (thought by Harnack to be Sixtus II), *Ad Nouationem*.

revealed, and the race of man saved, in a sequence which passes historically from Father to Son to Spirit; elsewhere, Irenaeus observes how, in each convert, the sequence usually runs the other way, from knowlege of the Spirit who is active in the church, to that of the Son and finally to the Father.[9] The Creed, then, like the rite of baptism to which it was central (as we have seen from Hippolytus), 'contains' Christianity.[10] It unifies (hence *symbolum*, and the Latin translation of it given by Ambrose, *collatio*, i.e. a bringing together)[11] the eternal truth of doctrine with the aspiration to truth; the history of salvation with the personal perception and assimilation of it. That the words of the Creed should not be written but only said, and never said in the hearing of catechumens or the infidel, gives a practical turn to this taking within of what had been worked out in historical acts of God. An utterance was made a 'meditation within the heart' (*meditatio cordis*), an 'inward chamber of treasure' (*thesaurus pectoris nostri*), a 'protection' (*magnum tutamen*);[12] and, in the very direct expression of Ambrose, the greatest of all the articles of faith, the seminal Christ-event of resurrection, is placed inside the speaker as he says the words of the Creed: 'This whole sacrament is concerned with your resurrection. If Christ rose not again, our faith is vain (1 Cor. 15:17), but because he did rise again, our faith stands firm.'[13]

In the progression to belief through revelation which is implied in the Apostles' Creed, the identity of the Christian is still an identity through transition. This transition is visible again, in the same dialogue between history and personal faith in the narrative of the mission to the Gentiles told by the Acts of the Apostles, where it is the 'God-fearing' Gentiles, in other words those who have already acquiesced to the Biblical account of God in history, who turn to baptism;[14] and it is in chapter 11 of Hebrews, where faith is shown to run like an unbroken thread through the 'illustrious men of Israel' (cf. Ecclus. 44:1), from Abel's offering, to Enoch who 'walked in the Lord' and vanished upward to God (Gen. 5:24; Ecclus. 44:16), to Noah and his Ark, to Abraham,

9 Camelot 1978, pp. 19–30.
10 On the liturgical origins of the Apostles' Creed, Capelle 1930, pp. 5–20.
11 Ambrose, *Explanatio symboli* 1, p. 7.   12 Ibid., *passim*.
13 Ibid. 9, p. 10: 'Quid enim opus fuit ut Christus carnem susciperet: quid opus fuit ut Christus crucem ascenderet? Quid opus fuit ut Christus mortem gustaret, sepulturam et resurgeret, nisi propter tuam resurrectionem? Totum hoc sacramentum tuae est resurrectionis. Si Christus non resurrexit, vana est fides nostra; sed quia resurrexit, ideo firma est fides nostra' (Connolly's translation).
14 Acts 2:14–41, 8:26–39, 10:1–48.

Isaac and Jacob and then to Moses and so on. But what was an extension of history for the born Jew or the 'God-fearing' Gentile was a more difficult leap for the pagan convert whose background was in the Hellenistic or Roman world. For those unversed, the *meaning* of this history was alien, difficult to understand both intellectually and morally. It had to be grasped; faith only came after a time of learning, and it was in this that the catechumenate had its origins.[15] In the writings of Augustine or Jerome we can see how agonizing the process of change might be; and Cyprian of Carthage described in a letter to Donatus how astonishing, even unthinkable, conversion had seemed before it came (I quote from the anonymous translation of 1830 which preserves much of the rhetorical force):

For me, while I yet lay in darkness and bewildering night, and was tossed to and fro on the billows of this troublesome world, ignorant of my true life, and outcast from light and truth, I used to think that second birth, which Divine Mercy promised for my salvation, a hard saying according to the life I then led: as if a man could be so quickened to a new life in the laver of healing water, as to put off his natural self; and keep his former tabernacle, yet be changed in heart and soul! How is it possible, said I, for so great a conversion to be accomplished, so that both the obstinate defilement of our natural substance, and old and ingrained habits, should suddenly and rapidly be put off; evils, whose roots are deeply seated within? Where does he learn frugality, to whom fine feasts and rich banquets have become a habit? Or he who in gay sumptuous robes glisters with gold and purple, when does he reduce himself to ordinary and simple raiment? Another, whose bent is among public distinction and honours, cannot bear to become a private and unnoticed man; while one who is thronged by a phalanx of dependents, and retinued by the overflowing attendance of an obsequious host, thinks it punishment to be alone. The temptation still unrelaxed, need is it that, as before, wine should entice, pride inflame, covetousness disquiet, cruelty stimulate, ambition delight, and lust lead headlong.

Such were my frequent musings: for whereas I was encumbered with many sins of my past life, which it seemed impossible to be rid of, so I had used myself to give way to my clinging infirmities, and from despair of better things, to humour the evils of my heart, as slaves born in my house, and my proper offspring. But after that life-giving Water succoured me, washing away the stain of former years, and pouring into my cleansed and hallowed breast the light which comes from heaven, after that I drank in the Heavenly Spirit, and was created into a new man

[15] Capelle 1933.

by a second birth, – then marvellously what before was doubtful became plain to me, – what was hidden was revealed, – what was dark began to shine, – what was before difficult now had a way and means, – what had seemed impossible now could be achieved, – and what was quickened in me by the Holy Ghost now had a growth according to God. Thou knowest well, thou canst recollect as well as I, what was then taken from me, and what was given by that death of sin, that quickening power of holiness. Thou knowest I name it not, over my own praises it were unwelcome to boast; though that is ground, never for boasting but for gratitude, what is not ascribed to man's virtue, but is confessed to be God's bounty; so that to sin no more has come of faith, as heretofore to sin had come of human error. From God, I say, from God is all we can be; from Him we grow, and by that strength which is from Him accepted and ingathered, we learn beforehand, even in this present state, the foretokens of what is yet to be. Let only fear be a guard upon innocency, that the Lord, who by the influence of this heavenly mercy has graciously shone into our hearts, may be detained by righteous obedience in the hostelry of a mind that pleases Him; that the security imparted to us may not beget slothfulness, nor the former enemy steal upon us anew.[16]

The beginning of this experience is the painful, desperate self-consciousness of the sinner who knows he has sinned; but although the sinner has come to know his condition he cannot break out of it. It is the sum of what he is, the involuntary centre of his being.[17] The only possible escape from this finitude is apparently arbitrary. Cyprian represents it as assimilation to a group of images: when the confinement of sin is broken down by the water-washing, a new order stands revealed, an order of light instead of darkness; of Holy Spirit instead of the demons of ambition, pride, anger, lust, covetousness, cruelty: and of a second birth which is the death of sin, and brings on the 'quickening power of holiness' (*mors ista criminum, uita uirtutum*). And just as the release through water is arbitrary in the sense of being *given*, so it is without limit, since it is given of God and pertains to the life to come: 'From God I say, from God is all we can be; from Him we live, from Him we grow, and by that strength which is from Him accepted and ingathered, we learn beforehand, even in this present state, the foretokens of what is yet to be (*futurorum indicia*).' The neophyte has passed from knowledge of his incapacity to faith in being raised up to God. This is the movement of

---

[16] *Ad Donatum* 3–4, translated in *Treatises of Cyprian* 2–3.
[17] On what follows, Ricoeur 1960.

salvation, from consciousness of the finitude which is sin to the negation of the same finitude.

Like salvation, symbol provokes a movement from the concrete and limited to what has no bounds. Rebirth is birth again, and only takes on its spiritual sense because it is at once a repetition of the creaturely birth *and* a cancellation of it. It cannot do without its material origin. These feeling words of Cyprian make it clear enough that the movement of desire towards salvation is the same as the movement which happens within symbol: indeed, on his account, the experience of salvation is an experience of symbol. He passes from physical darkness to spiritual light and from birth to rebirth just as he passes from self-knowledge to faith.

TERTULLIAN

The writing of Cyprian is inclined to *pathos*, to the rhetorical appeal to emotion. Tertullian, writing some fifty years earlier (*c.* AD200), offers a sharp contrast:[18] he has the more abrasive style of the forensic orator, no doubt largely because he was concerned to demonstrate, as though in a court of law, the ineptitude of the pagan, Jewish and heretical opposition to Christianity. By those who have commented on his life and writings he has been both praised and blamed, and with vehemence on both sides. Ronald Knox, who takes a more measured view, judged him the only one among the Fathers with 'the makings of a journalist', a man whose genius lay less in thinking than in talking, and who talked himself 'into extreme positions, and [was] too dazzled by his own eloquence to recede from them'.[19] Certainly, he was sometimes given to trivial reasoning and to small-minded sarcasms, to a kind of dyspeptic moralism which runs over large tracts of his apologetic; but behind the jibes lies a man who is using his powers to an end inestimably more serious. And although the truth of Jerome's report that he was a professional orator has long been doubted, the critical study of Tertullian's use of language has shown him to be far more than just a loose talker.[20] His enthusiasm – the trait which was to lead him to Montanism and its ecstatic doctrine of

[18] On the dating of Tertullian's life and writings, Barnes 1971, where a number of inaccuracies originating in Jerome's *De uiris illustribus* are identified: Tertullian was not the son of a soldier, nor a professional lawyer, nor did he live to great old age.
[19] Knox 1950, p. 45.   [20] Michaélides 1970; Fredouille 1972.

the New prophecy – was not merely the brittle product of a 'nagging' logician, as Knox puts it; at the bottom of it was something much more considerable: a sustained effort to confront the issue of belief and reason as it was inherited from the Christian-Hellenistic debate; and to translate this debate into a language and a pattern of thinking which would be understood by Latin Christians.[21]

In Tertullian's character, just as in the Pascal of the *Pensées*, there is a logic of enthusiasm; the emotional power of belief is born of rigour, and in such a way that the belief and the logic penetrate one another. They make a common substance. What is true of the character is true of the thought, and it is eminently true of Tertullian's account of baptism (*De baptismo*): he begins, in the midst of the debate, by confronting the peculiar difficulty of a religion whose first rite, and in fact whose very belief, was evidently based in an attachment to the material symbol of water: Catholicism, as he gladly admits, is *religio aquae*.[22] Where Cyprian expressed his sinful frustration through symbol, Tertullian concentrates on its apparent absurdity, in a manner which possibly echoes the Platonic contempt for physical representation:

Nothing does more to harden men's minds than the simplicity of divine action as it appears to the eye, and the magnificence promised of its effect! Here too, the complete simplicity with which a man is sent down into the water, dipped (*tinctus*) with one or two words and then gets out (*resurgit*) hardly even cleaner, if at all; the lack of pomp and new-fangled machinations, the absence of a fee – at least in most cases – all this makes it incredible that there should be any eternal repercussion (*consecutio aeternitatis*).[23]

It is the *distance* between the element of water and the power of divinity which makes the symbol work, not any similarity or fittingness. The natural symbol of washing, which was in the *Didache* and is the axis of Thomas Aquinas' theology of sacrament,

[21] Tertullian wrote a treatise on baptism in Greek (now lost): *De baptismo* 15.2, p. 290; on the importance of the Greek language for Christianity in second- to third-century Carthage, Mohrmann 1961, pp. 236–7.

[22] Cf. Cyprian, *ep.* 63.8: 'Quotiescumque autem aqua sola in scripturis sanctis nominatur, baptisma praedicatur.'

[23] *De baptismo* 2.1, p. 277; cf. Firmicus Maternus, *De errore prof. rel.* 1–2, pp. 3–7 (thus esp. 2, pp. 4–5, on the religious beliefs connected with the Nile: 'Frustra tibi hanc aquam quam colis, putas aliquando prodesse. Alia est aqua qua renovati homines renascuntur').

is reversed, and, by the same stroke, the Platonic scruple about the separation of matter from idea is appeased. In this first instance, it is the impossibility of mere water effecting an act of God which makes it believable. Baptism, Tertullian implies with the contempt that came easily to him, has nothing to do with the indulgent sensuality of the pagan mysteries, which 'build their authority and their faith on intimation and on elaborate surrounds and on the payment of fees'.[24] The complexities of Mithras, or the description by Apuleius of his initiation into the mystery of Isis, give an impression of what Tertullian had in mind. In another passage, disgusted by the resemblance borne by some mystery-rites to water-baptism, he dismisses all such parodies as operations of the devil.[25]

The movement within symbol, then, is couched by Tertullian in a paradox: 'It is surely a thing of wonder that death should be washed away in a bath? If, because it is a thing of wonder, it is all the more to be disbelieved, equally, for the same reason, it is all the more to be believed.'[26] Spiritual belief has its grounds in natural disbelief: elsewhere, talking about the Virgin Birth, he goes further and says that the sign (*signum*) is known to be from God precisely because it is preternatural;[27] and in this homily on baptism he continues by emphasizing the principle of antithesis, of the soteriological gap between matter and God which the symbol is required to traverse: 'If God is wise and powerful, which even those who deny him will allow, it is consistent that he should have founded the physical processes of his work in what is contrary to wisdom and power, in other words in folly and impossibility, since there is a necessary connection between all forces and their origins.'[28]

The premise appears to be one of scepticism, and in this it suggests the influence of Cicero's attitude to religion as well as that of the more diehard sceptics of Tertullian's own day; critical reason can reduce all religion to superstition, and so religion, to the educated man, has no more than the moral function –

[24] *De baptismo* 2.2, p. 277.   [25] Ibid. 5.3, p. 281

[26] Ibid. 2.2, p. 277; cf. Porphyry's attack on Christian baptism in *Macarius Magnes* 4.19: 'We must feel amazed and concerned about our souls, if a man thus shamed and polluted is to stand out clean after a single immersion, ... if such a creature, I say, is lightly set free from it all, throwing off the whole guilt as a snake sheds its old scales, merely because he has been baptized and has invoked the name of Christ' (cited by Harnack 1904, I, p. 484).

[27] *Aduersus Iudaeos* 9.7–8, p. 1366.   [28] *De baptismo* 2.3, p. 278.

important enough in itself – of maintaining the principles of tradition and authority. It is a political-cum-historical piety. Something like it can be seen in the arguments against Christianity used by Caecilius in the *Octavius* of Minucius Felix.[29] It seems that Tertullian has done no more than appropriate this scepticism to Christian apologetic and, into the breach which it opens to the enthusiast, has thrown all the irrationality of faith. And yet the very language he uses, and the fact that this entire corpus – whether or not ,he practised as a jurisconsult – is set quite deliberately within the intricate canon of formal rhetoric, should be enough to tell us that there is more here than a clever man's ecstasy.[30]

In an important sense, the debate about whether Tertullian was a rationalist or an anti-rationalist is redundant; and he was not in any straightforward way a sceptic.[31] The critical stance, which made him such an acid opponent of paganism and heresy, is drawn from the same perception of order with which he constructs Christianity. There are two paradoxes in his theology, not one: the first is the incredibility of faith ('Credo quia ineptum'); the second is that despite its incredibility, true belief is the highest form of reason. The entire conception can be put as one: precisely that which demands the greatest leap of faith is that which is most rational. Scepticism, then, is not superseded by faith: it is the content of faith. Tertullian's believer looks upon his faith with a kind of double-vision: since the *potentia* and *simplicitas* of divinity can only be represented in the world of matter by the distance they cross, by the reconciliation of opposites, faith

---

[29] Minucius Felix, *Octavius* 6.1, p. 7: 'Cum igitur aut fortuna certa aut incerta natura sit, quanto venerabilius ac melius antistites veritatis maiorum excipere disciplinam, religiones traditos colere, deos, quos a parentibus ante inbutus es timere quam nosse familiarius, adorare, nec de numinibus ferre sententiam, sed prioribus credere.'

[30] Sider 1971.

[31] Jung 1923, pp. 15–30, suggests that what he takes to be Tertullian's irrationalism was the greatest sacrifice he could have made, given his naturally *rational* disposition or 'type': such sacrifice, literally a sacrifice of self, was the result of Tertullian's desire to be Christ-like; Origen was a like case, but the self he destroyed was predominantly sensuous, while the writings of the new self were profoundly rational. Given the Pauline doctrine of the 'new man', which plays so big a part in Christian conversion, and in view of the ambiguous personalities which show through the writings of both Tertullian and Origen, Jung's inversion has strong intuitive force; but the evidence does indicate that at least in his pre-Montanist writings, Tertullian was quite conscious of his own powers of reason, and used them with conviction, not only as a polemical weapon, but as a sign of the transfiguration of reason. This was his conversion, not the repression within himself of the intellect.

in such a divinity is equally and simultaneously logic and illogic. Here again, in more analytic form, is the dynamic of conversion.

The 'logic of baptism' (*ratio baptismi*),[32] which Tertullian can consider now that he has established its *stultitia*, interweaves two strands, and in fact the two quite different cultures of the Bible and Stoicism. With a mixture of sarcasm, polemic, suggestion, imagery, erudition and sheer precision in the use of language, he is able to make the sacrament look compellingly real when compared with the pathetic illusion of pagan rites. One is *sacramentum*, the other perjury; both may be *religio*, with the sense of a binding together, but one binds in 'knowledge of the living God' (*agnitio dei uiui*), the other by mere medication.[33] Isis and Mithra 'weave deception in the widowed waters' (*uiduis aquis*), he says,[34] with a disdain which conjures up the neurotic figure of Aelius Aristides, forlornly seeking bodily and sacred health, but never able to come to rest with a single cure.[35]

In some degree, the fusion of Stoicism and the Bible, or more generally, the stringent exegesis of Biblical extensiveness by means of a forensic discipline, mimes the rhythm of logic and illogic. The centre of the argument is that there is no distinction between cosmos and sacrament: 'it cannot be doubted that the matter which God has ordered in all things and in all that he has made, he has caused to appear also in his own sacraments; and that what governs the life of this earth also procures the life which is in heaven'.[36] It is a part of this disposition of things that water is the 'authoritative' element, imbued with a grace higher than that of other elements; it has the power to create, and Tertullian makes this creativity something which is all at once Biblical, scientific and poetic. When the world was all 'formless shadow and sad abyss and untilled earth and shapeless sky, only water, an element always perfect, joyful, simple, and pure of its own nature, was

[32] *De baptismo* 4.1, p. 279: 'Sed ad ea satis erit praecerpsisse – in quibus et ratio baptismi recognoscitur – prima illa, qui iam tunc ipso habitu praenotabatur baptismi figurandi, spiritum qui ab initio super aquas uectabatur, super aquas instinctorem moraturum.' *Ratio* is often in Tertullian a translation of Greek *logos*, and its use here may suggest that in Tertullian's mind sacrament works on the pattern of *logos*, i.e. of the word made flesh. Thus, *De oratione* 1.1, p. 257: 'Dei spiritus et Dei sermo et Dei ratio, sermo rationis et ratio sermonis et spiritus utriusque, Iesus Christus, Dominus noster, nouis discipulis noui testamenti nouam orationis formam determinauit.'

[33] Ibid. 5.2, pp. 280–1.   [34] Ibid. 5.1, p. 280.
[35] *Sacred Tales I*, pp. 278ff.   [36] *De baptismo* 3.6, p. 279.

adequate to become vehicle to God'.[37] In this first state of things, water created souls, gave life, and it did this by imparting the spirit which it had received into itself.[38] It is now, with this mutual penetration of spirit and matter, that Stoicism rises almost to the surface: Tertullian has adapted to the Biblical account of Creation the Stoic theory that water plays a nutritive, 'tonic' role in the universe.[39] The notion of water as principle of all life is already borrowed by Melito of Sardis (d.180), evidently from Posidonius who in turn was interpreting for Stoicism a passage in Homer.[40] In Melito too, water has a power, a *tonos*, which is its natural property both as element and as sacramental symbol. The ocean is thus the 'baptistery of the sun', and of the stars and moon; the setting sun, like Christ, sun of the East, when he went down into the Jordan, is bathed in a mystic baptism of the sea, and receives a new *tonos*.[41] Tertullian lacks the aesthetic rapture of this Greek vision, but he keeps the basic idea of a 'physics' of sacrament, applying to it his habitual, Latinizing word-artistry. Here he is speaking of the spirit over the waters in Genesis 1:2 as a figure of baptism:

A holy thing was in fact carried upon a holy thing, or rather, that which carried acquired holiness from that which was carried upon it. Any matter placed beneath another is bound to take up to itself the quality of that which is suspended over it: and especially must corporal matter take up spiritual quality, which because of the subtlety of the substance it belongs to finds it easy to penetrate and inhere. And so, made holy by the holy, the nature of water has itself taken up the power to make holy.[42]

---

[37] Ibid. 3.2, p. 278: 'Nam et tenebrae totae adhuc sine cultu siderum informes et tristis abyssus et terra inparata et caelum rude: solus liquor, semper materia perfecta laeta simplex, de suo pura dignum uectaculum deo subiciebat.'

[38] Ibid. 3.3, p. 278: water the *antiqua substantia* and *diuini spiritus sedes*: 'Quid quod exinde dispositio mundi modulatricibus quodammodo aquis deo constitit? Nam ut firmamentum caeleste suspenderet in medietate distinctis aquis fecit, ut terram aridam expanderet segregatis aquis expediit. Ordinato per hinc per elementum mundo cum incolae darentur, primis aquis praeceptum est animas producere, primus liquor quod uiueret edidit, ne mirum sit in baptismo si aquae animare nouerunt.'

[39] For what follows, Spanneut 1957, pp. 354ff.

[40] Grant 1949.   [41] *Fragment on Baptism*.

[42] *De baptismo* 4.1, p. 279 (translation by Evans 1964, pp. 9–11): 'Sanctum autem utique super sanctum ferebatur, id quod ferebat sanctitatem mutuabatur, quoniam subiecta quaeque materia eius quae desuper imminet qualitatem rapiat necesse est, maxime corporalis spiritualem et penetrare et insidere facilem per substantiae suae subtilitatem. Ita de sancto sanctificata natura aquarum et ipsa sanctificare concepit.' A similar continuity between science and worship, based on the composite nature of man (spirit and matter, *animus* and *corpus*), is in the Hermetic text, *Asclepius* I 8–9, in Scott 1924, pp. 299–303 (the text dates from *c.* 190).

For Stoicism, spirit was not the contrary of matter but a kind of matter.[43] Tertullian draws on this to demonstrate the rationalism of what he had begun by calling impossible; what he has done is to 'explain' through a conjunction of science and poetry, the descent of spirit into matter, the epiclesis. The waters, in receiving into themselves the spirit, are 'drinking in the power to make holy' (*uim sanctificandi conbibunt*).[44] In the more modern idiom, he has made myth the very essence of reason. If the initial 'saving movement' had been between logic and illogic, the second is rather in the style of Augustine's conversion by way of the philosophy he read in the *Hortensius*: a transfiguration of paganism.[45]

What Tertullian and Melito of Sardis had thus shown from liturgical imagery – that the religion of Christ was a higher reason, a transfigured cosmology – was more commonly conceived as a general shift in philosophy and ethics. It was particularly the Alexandrians, Clement and Origen, and later the Cappadocian Fathers, Basil, Gregory of Nyssa and Gregory Nazianzen, who propagated Christianity as the culmination of philosophy. The *paideia* of catechesis was preceded by the *propaideia*[46] of Greek education: the *morphosis* which shaped the Greek ideal of an infinitely adaptable, and infinitely repeatable, individuality was made the grounds for the reception of other-worldly wisdom.[47] And for all the theological insistence that education or human knowledge was not enough on its own – Origen for example makes this point very clearly against the Neoplatonism of Celsus[48] – it is hard not to feel that many would have been conveyed with the minimum of torment from the old *paideia* to the new knowledge. Among Latin Christian authors, perhaps the most obviously philosophical in this sense is Minucius Felix, apparently a North African and probably writing some years later than Tertullian. In his *Octavius*, an *apologia* for Christianity in the form of a dialogue, (of which Minucius himself is arbiter, Octavius the apologist), the protagonists are roused to argument as they stroll in leisure along the beach at Ostia. While boys play ducks and drakes, Caecilius kisses an effigy of Serapis and challenges Octavius to defend his faith.[49] The discussion on both sides remains

---

[43] Spanneut 1957, esp. pp. 288–91.   [44] *De baptismo* 4.4, p. 280.
[45] Augustine, *Confessions* 3.4 (7–8), pp. 29–30.   [46] Jaeger 1962.
[47] Marrou 1956, pp. 314ff.   [48] Origen, *Contra Celsum* 7.42, pp. 430–1.
[49] *Octauius* 1, pp. 1–2.

true to the classicism of this opening scene, and in what Octavius says, there is not a word of Christology and only one mention of Christ – to defend him against charges of criminality.[50] The most powerful strain in Octavius' answer is all lucidity and simplicity. There is no secret, he says, for God is in man himself, and man in God's image; and God is in the universe. It follows from this anthropological view that the only right sacrifice is a moral sacrifice, made within, and with a lapidary phrase, he renders all the fuss of altars and statues and temples obsolete: *sic apud nos religiosior est ille qui iustior*: 'for us the more religious man is the one who is more just'.[51] Adolf von Harnack, whose theme is the remarkable oscillation in the Christian mission between an endlessly absorptive syncretism and an impregnable simplicity, points to a more dramatic instance of the same principle: when the proconsul of Africa tried to persuade the martyrs of Scillium with the human simplicity of imperial religion (*simplex est religio nostra*), the martyrs' spokesman, Speratus, replied that if the proconsul will only listen for a moment, he will tell him 'the very mystery of simplicity'.[52] It is this *mysterium simplicitatis*, whether in the refined spirit of Minucius Felix, or in the *sermo humilis* indicated by the Scillitan Acts, that carries the case for Christianity, even when it is set within Tertullian's obstinate paradoxes.

We can get some idea from Minucius Felix's *Octavius*, or from Origen's writings, of how Christianity gave to *paideia* a new object on which to work; and it requires little imagination to see how the ethical doctrines of Christianity, particularly the theme of *enkrateia* or restraint which it had drawn from sectarian Judaism, answered to the moral sadness of a Tacitus, or to Juvenal's bitter tongue. What is less easy to explain is how self-restraint turns from scepticism into the passion of martyrdom.

The daring of Tertullian's rationalism, which allows him to speak in such antitheses as *ratio baptismi* or *argumentum figurae*,[53] seems a cold-blooded thing if put next to Cyprian's effusive, impressionistic prose, or, as we shall see, if it is compared with the warmth with which St Ambrose approaches the sacraments. Tertullian's power is analytic, and comes from a breaking down into parts and a forcing together into new wholes.

---

[50] Ibid. 29.2, p. 28.
[51] Ibid. 32.3, p. 30.
[52] Cited Harnack 1904, I, p. 103.
[53] *De baptismo* 8.4, p. 283.

The technique is something like what Eliot recommended for the poet in his essay on 'Tradition and the Individual Talent': 'For it is not the "greatness", the intensity, of the emotions, the components, but the intensity of the artistic process, the pressure, so to speak, under which the fusion takes place, that counts.'[54] It might be objected that Eliot's suppression of personality in favour of tradition is a far cry from Tertullian's heated engagement with state-paganism or the Marcionite heretics; from the Tertullian whose moral enthusiasm seems with hindsight to converge inevitably on Montanism. Yet the very fact that he conducts the discussion of liturgical imagery here in the homily on baptism, and of Biblical imagery generally throughout his work, strictly within the bounds of apologetic, is an indication of his intellectualism. The homily on baptism itself begins as polemic against the anti-baptismal teaching of the 'dried-up and waterless' sect of the Cainites; and from chs. 10–15, Tertullian answers a number of questions about baptism, which had been the cause of dissent and confusion: were the apostles baptized, and if so, when? What is the status of John the Baptist's baptism? Is baptism unnecessary to those who already have faith? And so on.[55] As Knox says, he is always against someone; and it was passionate lack of imagination rather than a passionate excess of it which brought him to the New Prophecy of Priscilla. The effect of bringing such intellectual 'pressure' to bear on the liturgy is to contain diffuse and disparate episodes in the Old and New Testaments within an idealist logic of symbol. The Bible, instead of giving rise to different *possible* interpretations as it did for Origen or Augustine, is treated as a tissue of *necessary* connections which exist ideally, in other words outside their origins in the Biblical narrative. Water, as Tertullian shows, is the principle of such a matrix of connections. There is in the Bible, an 'ideal water', a *genus* in which the difference of *species* is irrelevant;[56] it is the water of the Red Sea; the water of Mara 'healed by the wood of Moses', which is itself the 'healing Christ'

---

[54] Eliot 1934, pp. 13–22.

[55] For the Cainite heresy, *De baptismo* 1.2, p. 277; cf. Evans 1964, pp. 47–8.

[56] *De baptismo* 4.2–3, pp. 279–80: 'Ne quis ergo dicat: "Numquid ipsis [enim] aquis tinguimur quae tunc in primordio fuerunt?" Non utique ipsis, si non ex ea parte ipsis qua genus quidem unum, species uero complures; quod autem generi adtributum est etiam in species redundat, ideo nulla distinctio est, mari quis an stagno, flumine an fonte, lacu an alueo diluatur, nec quicquam refert inter eos quos Iohannes in Iordanem et quos Petrus in Tiberim tinxit; nisi et [ille] spado quem Philippus inter uias fortuita aqua tinxit plus salutis aut minus retulit.'

(*Christus remedians*); it is the water gushing from the stone accompanying the Israelites in the desert, and the stone is again Christ; it is Christ's baptism; the miracle at Cana; the water taken from the Samaritan at Jacob's well; the water given to little children; Jacob's well again, where the weary Jesus rested; the walking on water and the storm which followed; the washing of the disciples' feet; it is the water from Christ's side: *scit lancea militis* ('the soldier's spear knows of it').[57] Tertullian's style owes much to the Second Sophistic, the highly self-conscious, almost mannerist, school of rhetoric of the second and third centuries, of which the best-known exponents were Aelius Aristides in Asia Minor and in North Africa Apuleius and Tertullian himself.[58] This is a formal speech which promotes idealism through the artifice of language. Its adoption by Tertullian, the virtuosity of his linguistic performance, makes the Christian liturgy appear an exercise in erudition, rather than the simplistic thing he had begun by calling it. The prayer of *anamnesis* has been subsumed to rhetoric: the prolixity of narrative, the digressiveness of Old Testament history and the differences within the New Testament, have been subjected to definition, to system, gathered into the ideal order.

Although the principle of typological unity in the Bible, and particularly the unity linking Old and New Testament, is attested already in Paul (1 Cor. 10), and in I Peter 3:18–21, it had never before been erected into a systematic principle like this.[59] It had never been so obviously put forward as the source of *efficacia baptismi*.[60] When Melito of Sardis in his *Homily on the Incarnation* talks about Israel being 'baptized in the shed blood', he is not reducing the infinite complexity of relations in and between New and Old Testaments to a rigid idealism, but rather coaxing his listeners – who are mourning Christ's death on Good Friday – to participate emotionally in the sense of these relations: that is, to participate in the story of salvation as it breaks through in typology.

O strange and ineffable mystery! The sacrifice of the sheep was found to be the salvation of Israel, and the death of the sheep became the life of the people, and the blood abashed the angel. Tell me angel, what stayed thy hand, the sacrifice of the sheep or the life of the Lord? The death of

---

[57] Ibid. 9.1–4, pp. 283–4. [58] Sider 1971.
[59] On typology and baptism, Daniélou 1950. [60] *De baptismo* 11.4, p. 286.

the sheep or the Spirit of the Lord? Show me that whereat thou wast confounded. Thou sawest the mystery of the Lord enacted in the sheep, the life of the Lord in the sacrifice of the sheep, the type of the Lord in the death of the sheep.[61]

Like Cyprian, Melito is using a quite different rhetoric, epideictic rather than forensic. The *Homily* as a whole is worked around the overtly emotional themes of the suffering of Christ and the ingratitude of the Jews: the sacrifice of the Paschal lamb and the crucifixion of Christ have in common the suffering of innocence; and as Cyprian makes his reader feel the frustration of the sinner and the relief of the neophyte, so Melito makes the Good Friday assembly feel the pain of suffering, heightened by the iniquity of Judaism and of mankind. The doctrinal message about redemption from sin and death, and the more or less technical distinction between type and reality, are almost incidental to this vein of sympathy, in its deliberately sensual contemplation of Passion.

The movement of salvation occurs within symbol. In Cyprian or Melito, the movement is sensual and emotional. In Tertullian it is more a process of discipline, as though the historical and prophetic and evangelical aspirations of the Bible come to rest in the closed order of rhetoric. There are other approaches, too: the fourth-century homilist Zeno of Verona tended to concentrate groups of images in a few words, in a way which suggests their Biblical origins, and which causes the mind to leap back and forth from the brevity of the expression to the openness of the Biblical past.[62] Reading him, we feel that instead of defining the Bible as Tertullian had done, he is releasing its possibilities.

Tertullian's was a philosophical, even a sceptical, faith; a dry passion. Time and again we see in his writings a need to give shape to brute matter, whether this was Hebrew revelation, the moral decadence of the Empire, or, in his later years, the rural pro-

---

[61] Melito of Sardis, *Homily on the Passion*, p. 171.
[62] Thus Zeno of Verona, *Tractatus* 2.23, p. 197: 'Exsultate, fratres, quos sua parturit fides, qui mundi huius fugientes insidias, reatum, uulnera ac mortem paternae inplorastis auxilium maiestatis omnique non pedum uelocitate, sed mentis, pii fontis ad gurgitem conuolate. Vos constanter inmergite, saluo salutis statu "ueteris hominis" uestri felici morte uicturi.' Among the many allusions of this passage is that of the stag of Psalm 41 (42), thirsting for the water of the living God, a scene depicted in the baptisteries of Naples and Spalato: on the use of this theme in baptismal liturgy and art, Puech 1949a; Maier 1964, pp. 132ff.

phecies of the Montanists. To this passive material he brought his organizing intellect, and built an ideal order which compelled belief. Belief was therefore an acquiescence to truth, the recognition of something necessary. It is against this background that Tertullian used the expression *sacramentum*.[63] He used it in its original, juridical, sense of an oath, and often for the oath of baptism; but he also used it, after the example of earlier translators of the Bible, for the Greek *mysterion*. What matters here is how the two senses meet. The first is political: it carried the idea of a vow made under formal law, and resulting obligation. The oath could be the military oath made by a soldier to his legion. The second, the Biblical and Greek sense, is theological, meaning, broadly, revealed truth, although also, sometimes, referring to the books containing the truth, the Old and New Testaments. The distinction was, however, made less clear by its content of *sacer*. The idea of the sacred had already coloured the Roman sense of legal oath, and at the same time had made *sacramentum* a suitable term of entry into religious societies. It was evidently these connotations which allowed the translators of the Bible to employ *sacramentum* for the Greek *mysterion*, and, up to a point, to translate a theological concept by a predominantly political one.

It is difficult to know how much Tertullian was responsible for the Christian use of the word. It is clear, though, that he was quite at home with – even if he did not invent – the use of a juridical word to describe a mystery.[64] Like many Christian authors writing in Latin, he gave theology a political cast; the approach to truth was not divided in his mind from adherence to a society of believers. The notion of an adherence to clearly established forms, which pervades his moral teaching, is also the message he preaches about the particular 'sacrament' of baptism. We will rediscover some of the same 'formalism' in the juridically inspired baptism of the twelfth century.

[63] On Tertullian and *sacramentum*, Mohrmann 1958, pp. 233–44; Michaélides 1970; and Mohrmann 1973 for a critique of Michaélides' book: much of the debate has to do with how much the sense of *sacramentum* as military oath was original (Michaélides), and how much it was a particular usage of Tertullian, which then entered the mainstream of Christianity (Mohrmann). For the possibility that the Latin translators of the Bible took into account the Hebrew behind the Greek *mysterion*, Verheijen 1957.
[64] See *De corona* 11.1, p. 1056. On the tendency of Latin to render concepts by concrete expressions, Marouzeau 1949.

AMBROSE

For Tertullian the shift in perspective involved in becoming a Christian, came of intellectual discipline. The same shift is represented by Ambrose, in his discourses *On the Sacraments*, as a movement of the imagination. Where Tertullian describes, Ambrose evokes; where Tertullian appeals to the mind, Ambrose appeals directly to the emotions.

Ambrose delivered his addresses to the neophytes of Milan during the octave of Easter, and thus after they had received baptism on Easter day, probably in the 370s or 380s. There are six sermons, spoken day by day, presumably from the Easter Monday to the Saturday following. The doubts which used to be expressed about their authenticity have abated considerably since Dom Bernard Botte argued in favour of Ambrose's authorship in the edition he published in 1949, proposing that if the bishop did not write them himself, the *De sacramentis* and perhaps also the more carefully composed *De mysteriis* on the same subject-matter, might have been drawn up from notes taken by someone in the audience. The virtue of this suggestion is obvious to anyone who reads the *De sacramentis* straight through: it has the urgency and spontaneity characteristic of a speaker who is sufficiently confident to adapt his speech to his audience as he goes on, something Ambrose would no doubt have been well able to do after his long experience in secular politics before being elected (much to his distress) to the see of Milan. In their immediacy, his words display exactly that quality of *charitas*, of the 'love' binding the catechist to his hearers, which Augustine was to stress in his *De catechizandis rudibus*.[65] In all this, and in much more, Ambrose differed radically from the formalities of Tertullian. Christianity, for Ambrose, is a feeling for Christ, a right-seeing. His sermons are filled with bodily images: hearing, touching, smelling, seeing. To see right, to desire right, is to pass from fault to grace, like the blind man in the Gospel of John, whose eyes were opened when he went to the pool of Siloam and washed off the mud Christ had put on them:

With the eyes of your body you saw bodily things but you were still unable to see what sacrament held within it. So when you gave your name at the beginning of Lent, the priest took mud and spread it over

---

[65] Botte, in introduction to *De sac.*, pp. 12–24. On Augustine's *De cat. rud.*, see below, pp. 98ff.

your eyes. What does this mean? That you should recognize your sin, search your conscience, do penance for faults, in other words, recognize the condition of the race of man. It is true that he who comes to baptism does not make confession of his sins, and yet he does make confession of all his sins in the sense that he desires baptism so as to be saved, to pass from blame to grace.[66]

Responsibility for seeing right, for 'feeling God' in the phrase of Minucius Felix, is with the one who sees; it is no longer an intellectual acquiescence and adherence. It begins with the right knowledge of self and of self-limitedness, and ends with the greater self, the self which has been placed under the aegis of grace, and whose knowledge is in prayer. The sixth and last book of Ambrose's addresses is therefore largely about prayer, about the quiet condition of the purged soul in its recital of the *Pater noster*: '"When you pray, go into your inner room and shut the door to yourself, and so pray to the Father" [Matt.6:6] ... Give the attention of your whole mind, go within the retreat of your heart, go wholly within.'[67]

There is, then, a note of repose at the end of Ambrose's lectures, a satisfaction of the desire for God found in prayer. Yet prayer itself implies a motion towards God. It is not a simple, crude demand, but must begin – like any piece of good oratory – with praise, and go on to supplication, then to the request itself, and end with a thanksgiving. In the main body of his exposition, though, Ambrose is talking of the far more radical transition to grace which occurs within liturgical symbol, and which is the matter of the passage quoted above. What is said here is typical of Ambrose's approach. Being inextricably bound up with the sensual attributes of symbol, with the concrete sign, conversion to 'seeing-in-faith' is itself never dissociated from sense, and therefore from a kind of aesthetics.[68] The 'eyes of the body' (*oculi*

---

66 *De sac.* 3.12, p. 76.
67 Ibid. 6.13, p. 101; cf. Weil 1951: 'Si pendant la récitation [du Pater] mon attention s'égare ou s'endort, fût-ce d'une manière infinitésimale, je recommence jusqu'à ce que j'aie obtenu une fois une attention absolument pure ... Parfois les premiers mots déjà arrachent ma pensée à mon corps et la transportent en un lieu hors de l'espace d'où il n'y a ni perspective ni point de vue. L'espace s'ouvre ... Parfois, aussi, pendant cette récitation ou à d'autres moments, le Christ est présent en personne.'
68 Cf. Cyril of Jerusalem, *Mystagogic Catecheses* 2.7, p. 7: 'It was in fact a true death which touched Christ: his soul was taken from his body. His burial too was a true burial: his holy body was wrapped in a pure shroud. Everything in him happened in truth. For us now death and suffering are likenesses; yet in the matter of salvation, there is no longer salvation, there is no longer likeness, but reality.' Against the argument that Ambrose based his *De sac.* on Cyril's *Catecheses*, see introduction by Botte to *De sac.* pp. 36–7.

corporales) see or do not see; and the mud – glutinous, earth bound matter – is the means of passing beyond blindness and seeing, to a 'confessional' vision. Ambrose never shirks the corporality of salvation, and so, between the first seeing, which is no more than a kind of blindness, and the second, 'confessional' seeing, which is absolute vision, there is the impulsion of appetite, of desire (*baptizari petit ut justificaretur*), which leads from one to the other. We shall see some of the ramifications of this sensual desire for salvation, both in Ambrose and elsewhere.

Since he is talking to those who have been baptized, the intention of Ambrose is to deepen the perception in his hearers of what they have already gone through. This is what he means in his opening remark to them, when he says that only now can he begin to give them the *ratio* of the sacraments (of baptism and eucharist), since only now do they have faith: 'accepistis baptismum, credidistis'.[69] Without faith there can be no explanation (*ratio*); but he is not interested in historical or philosophical explanation, or in the *ratio baptismi* Tertullian spoke of. What he has in mind is a mystical exploration: in its breadth and suppleness, Ambrose's *ratio* is nearer to the *logos* of Origen, or even of the Gospel of John.[70]

By making the neophytes *remember* what has been said, done, felt over Lent and Easter, Ambrose is able to make them imagine all the better the *sense* of their experience. He makes every use of the proximity of memory and imagination: it allows him to pass without obstacle from the physical enactment of the rite and its elements and spoken words to their non-physical meaning: and in this way to reproduce more compellingly the movement of the soul from the limitedness of the captive self to limitless release, from gravity to grace. In the emergence of truth from the signs and figures of the Old Testament past, Ambrose finds this movement of release. To see by faith is to see reality not shadows, to see *non signa sed fide*; 'the sign is for the unbeliever, faith for the believer', 'in the beginning was the sign, ... afterwards came perfection'. Limitedness, though, is not only a

---

[69] *De sac.* 1.1, p. 54.
[70] Cf. Mohrmann 1958, pp. 179–87, showing how Ambrose would have known *rationabilis* as a translation of *logikos*, e.g. in Rom 12:1, and would have been aware of the original Greek spiritual and philosophical sense of *logos, logikos*, but also used *ratio, rationabilis* in the more restricted, often juridical sense given them by Latin. And see above, n. 32.

quality of matter and the human condition, it is the property of history, time. The two aspects are put together, in a passage from the first book of the *De Sacramentis*:

Then you came nearer, you saw the font, you saw the priest standing by. And I do not doubt that there entered into your mind what entered into the mind of the Syrian Naaman: he was purified, but beforehand he doubted. Why? Listen, I will tell you. You entered in, you saw the water, you saw the priest, you saw the Levite. No doubt one of you said: is that all? Yes, it is all, truly all, where is all innocence, all piety, all grace, all making holy. You saw what you were able to see with bodily eyes and human sight, you saw not what is done, but what is seen. Much greater are the things unseen than those seen, 'since what is seen is of this world, what is unseen is eternal' [2 Cor.4:18]

Let us say this before going on: you are to hold fast to the pledge I speak and demand its fulfilment. We stand in awe of the mysteries (*mysteria*) of the Jews given to our fathers; they excel in the antiquity of their sacraments (*sacramentorum*), and in holiness. But this I promise, that the sacraments of the Christians are more divine and more ancient than those of the Jews.

What surpasses the crossing by the Jewish people through the sea (as we are talking about baptism)? Yet all the Jews who made this crossing died in the desert. And he who passes through this font, who passes from the things of this world to those of heaven – for this is a passage, a Passover, his passage, the passage from sin to life, from blame to grace, from impurity to holiness – he who passes through this font does not die but rises again.

So Naaman was a leper [2 Kings 5:1–14]. A slave-girl said to his wife: My lord, if he wants to be purified, must go into the land of Israel and there he will find a man able to rid him of leprosy. The slave-girl told her mistress, the mistress told her husband, Naaman told the King of Syria: the King, holding Naaman in high regard, sent him to the King of Israel. The King of Israel heard that a man had been sent to him and that he was to rid him of leprosy, and he tore his garments. Then Elisha sent word to him: why have you torn your garments as if there were no god powerful enough to purify leprosy? send him to me. He sent him, and the prophet said to the man who had come: go down into the Jordan, bathe and you will be healed.

He began to ponder and to say to himself: is that all? I have come from Syria to Judaea and I am told: go to the Jordan, bathe and you will be healed? As if there were no better river in my own country! But his servants said to him, Lord, why do you not obey the word of the prophet? Why not obey it and see what happens? Then he went down into the Jordan, bathed and got up healed.

What does this mean? You saw the water. Water does not always heal though. Water heals if it has the grace of Christ. The element is one thing, the consecration another; one thing, what is done (*opus*), another, what is brought about (*operatio*). What is done is done in water; what is effected is in the Holy Spirit.[71]

Ambrose faces the same question as Tertullian: why believe that the water has spiritual efficacy? But his response is very different. He seeks no inner logic in Biblical narrative, but rather confuses the sensual memory of baptism with the memory of the Biblical past. Accordingly, in the same imaginative gesture, the elemental water and the historical, Old Testament event, are raised up. History and element are 'saved'. Water is not just water, or not always, and history is not just event. The ritual act is not the same as the ritual effect; and the sacraments of the Christians are prior to and more holy than those of the Jews. The peculiar skill of Ambrose is, by stimulating the sensual memory, and pushing it beyond itself into the Biblical past, to give his audience of neophytes the sensation of being *inside* the transfiguration which makes figure, or similitude or sign, into reality (*figura, similitudo, signum: veritas*).[72] What the Jewish people was blind to in its own history is revealed to the eye of the *fidelis*; and where before there was *creatura aquae*, now is *presentia trinitatis aeternae*.[73] The eternal difference between figure and truth, event and effect, is also the vital inward difference between plain-seeing and faith-seeing: or, more radically, it is the conversion from blindness to vision. The change in the object is the change in the person.

This absence of a subject–object distinction is the crux to Ambrose's notion of sacrament. The reality of liturgy is both in the self, with its capacity to remember and imagine sensually, *and* in the *sermo Christi*, not in one or the other alone. It comes of what Martin Buber called the 'I – Thou' relationship, as against the relation of I and It. The Biblical narratives of Noah, Naaman, Elias and the priests of Baal, of Elijah's axe, Moses and the bitter

---

[71] *De sac.* 1.1, p. 54.
[72] Ibid. 4.10ff, pp. 80ff; cf. Ambrose, *Exameron* 1.4.14, p. 12: 'simul illud aduertere licet, quia iure concurrit, ut eo tempore uideatur in hanc generationem atque in hos usus ingressus tributus, quo tempore ex hac generatione in regenerationem legitimus est transitus, siquidem uerno tempore filii Istrahel Aegyptum reliquerunt et per mare transierunt, baptizati in nube et in mari, ut apostolus dixit, et eo tempore domini quodannis Iesu Christi pascha celebratur, hoc est animarum transitus a uitiis ad uirtutem, a passionibus carnis ad gratiam sobrietatemque mentis, a malitiae nequitiaeque fermento ad ueritatem et sinceritatem.'
[73] *De sac.* 1.18, p. 60.

water, Jesus at Bethsaida; and the *sermo Christi*[74] which embraces all these; and the revealed fact of salvation; and the physical structure of the liturgy; all of them take effect only insofar as the imaginative power is raised to belief in their Christian meaning. It is to rouse up this power that Ambrose addresses his listeners as though individually, using the second person singular; and forces his way into their memories, their doubts and worries: 'You came to the altar, you stood in wait for the sacraments lying on the altar, and you were struck with wonder at them . . . Listen . . . Understand . . . Listen . . . Listen again.'[75] His mastery of simple narrative, and of the natural symbol, serves the same end; as does the almost crude physicality he gives to the death and resurrection which is in baptism, and the equivalence he sees between water and the grave which brings to mind the gaping and unmistakably sepulchral *piscinae* found in some baptisteries of this period.[76]

There is a heaviness of word and a frankness in Ambrose which addresses the intellectual faculties *through* the emotional: the symbol comes before theology, as it did in Cyril of Jerusalem a little earlier, or in Cyprian with his image of the one church as a *hortus conclusus* embracing a central fountain.[77] It is the image of the fish which stands out in Ambrose in this respect:

We read, 'Let the earth yield fruit and seeds which grow' [Gen. 1:11]; and likewise you have read concerning the waters: 'Let the waters produce living things, and living things were born' [Gen. 1:20]. That was at the beginning of creation, but for you it has been reserved that water should regenerate you to grace, just as it generated those other things to life. Imitate the fish which has received a lesser grace, but which to you should appear as a miracle. He is in the sea and he is on the waves, he is in the sea and he swims with the swell of the water. On the sea the storm rages, the winds scream out, but the fish swims; he is not swallowed up because he is used to swimming. To you, this world is the sea. Its currents uncertain, its waves deep, its storms fierce. And you must be this fish, that the waves of the world do not swallow you. There is beauty in what the Father said to the Son: 'I have begotten thee this day' (*te genui*) [Ps. 2:7], which means: when you redeemed my people, when

[74] Ibid. 2.1–13, pp. 62–6.   [75] Ibid. 4.8–18 *passim*, pp. 80–3.

[76] Ibid. 2.19, p. 68; and see, for example, the baptistery at Djemila (fifth century): *DACL* XIV col. 1089 and pl. 1031.

[77] Cyril of Jerusalem, *Mystagogical Catecheses*; Cyprian, *ep.* 69.2, pp. 750–1 (using the imagery of the Song of Songs 4.12 and 6.8).

you called my people back to the kingdom of heaven, when you fulfilled my will, you proved yourself to be my son.[78]

Behind its apparent simplicity, its 'humility', the progression of ideas within this passage is uncommonly powerful. As was his habit, Ambrose carried his listener from one image to another, and from one meaning to another, by an appeal made almost entirely to sensation.[79] There is no argument, no conduct from one point to another in a given direction, but rather a series of imaginative leaps, each of which colours the last, affects it and re-forms it, so that a group of idea-images comes into being; but already, besides the animation, there is a resonance here (and Ambrose has spoken of this in the preceding paragraph) of the immersion and burial and death which is in earth and in water, and above all in the *similitudo mortis*[80] of baptismal water. That which gives life also gives death; but what gives rebirth also gives resurrection from death. The fish stands for Christ (the five letters making up the Greek word for fish are the first letters of the words for 'Jesus Christ Son of God Saviour' in that language), but here it is used as a natural as well as a theological symbol, and through it Ambrose is able to bring together his various meanings. The fish is one of the living things (*animantia*) of creation; and yet it lives in submersion; its burial is its life, as the burial of the baptized is their resurrection. The fish is indeed miraculous: miraculous in the more obvious sense that it lives beneath water, undisturbed by the tempest; and miraculous in a peculiar sense to the neophyte (*debet tibi esse miraculo*) because of that other, higher 'grace' with which it is endowed, the grace of ritual meaning. It is seen by the neophyte in faith.

The freedom of the sensual imagination evident here and throughout Ambrose's addresses takes strength, however, from its limitation: to see in faith is not to see with complete freedom. It is tempered by theological orthodoxy. Ambrose reveals to the senses the possibility of their own apotheosis into faith; the possibility that they can perceive the true and miraculous nature of things. Accordingly, his words have an aesthetic and not an intellectual force in the first place. They have a gravity, a downward motion which is in contrast with Tertullian's use of language

[78] *De sac.* 3.1, p. 69.
[79] Ambrose's language here is very close to that of the Latin *Physiologus B:* see Carmody's introduction, p. 8.
[80] *De sac.* 3.2, p. 71.

as an elevated nexus of relations. But all this comes to nothing if it is not understood that the progression between earthly, humble symbols is at the same time a theological progression, and controlled by theological ideas. The fish is thus the meeting-place of Johannine and Pauline theologies of baptism: like Christ of whom it is the figure, the fish is at once 'engendered' (*generatus*) and raised from the dead: *generatus* because it has grown to life from the water; and *resurrectus* because buried in water. The context of birth and death means also that the sea suggests both womb and tomb. The connection made through the fish is also made in an exegesis borrowed from the Acts of the Apostles (13:30ff), and which is itself part of a catechetical homily made by Paul in the synagogue in Antioch: the Psalmist's verse, 'Thou art my son; I have begotten thee this day' (Ps. 2:7.), is taken by Paul, and Ambrose following him, to refer to the recognition by God of the saving work of the son by means of death to sin and the resurrection which results from it. In this way, Christ was born of the Father at the moment of his death and resurrection; and equally, the death and resurrection in baptism is again a birth, or rebirth.[81] The rebirth-idea and the death/resurrection-idea are brought together, made into the same idea, by the lowly figure of the fish. Meaning, and with it salvation, is a creation of the sensual understanding.

This idea of the liturgy as the place where God is felt as well as thought will persist (just as Tertullian's 'sophistic' version of ritual will persist): it is in Augustine's Paschal sermons, in the liturgy itself, and it will recur, for example, in the visions of Hildegard of Bingen.

The sensation of faith which Ambrose brings out from symbol does not go so far as mystical assimilation: the truth which the symbol points to cannot be grasped in the hand, but remains a thing *desired*. Earlier in his lectures, Ambrose had said that to seek to be justified is to seek baptism (*petere baptizari*); in the fifth lecture, he characterizes the desiring soul, about to receive the post-baptismal eucharist, by way of the erotic symbolism of the Song of Songs. It is here, and in book IV when he describes the accession of the purified soul to the Holy of Holies, to the burgeoning rod of Aaron which lies inside it with the manna and the altar of perfumes, that Ambrose dwells most on the aspect of

---

[81] Ibid. 3.1, p. 69.

desire in sacrament. Approaching the altar 'full of desire', the baptized soul seeks *sacramenta mirabilia*, and, knowing its own purity and worthiness, asks to be kissed by Christ. Baptism – of which the eucharist is an integral part for Ambrose – is a nuptial bath; it is the consummation of love in the Song of Songs: 'And the King took me into his bedchamber (S. of S. 1:3)'.[82] In the sensual imagination, it is true, and within the bounds of the sacrament itself, desire does find its fulfilment: the baptismal eucharist is a heavenly feast; those attending it, clothed in white, are themselves the fruit, the vine, the myrrh and perfumes, taken up into Christ who reaps this sinless harvest like the lover in the garden in the Song of Songs; and yet they too are drunk with the sober drunkenness of the spirit and thus 'rooted in Christ'.[83] But the feast and the consummation remain in the imagination; faith itself was *made* by desire and imagination, and in this sense could never be replete: it was caught between physical finitude and imaginary – though nonetheless real – infinity. When the liturgy or the prayer is finished, the moment of fulfilment recedes,and desire returns. This is the impossibility of satisfaction expressed by Dante in Canto 21 of the *Purgatorio*:

> La sete natural che mai non sazia
> se non con l'acqua onde la femminetta
> sammaritana dimandò la grazia . . .

The natural thirst which is never slaked save with the water the little Samaritan woman asked for . . .[84]

It was natural that in times of insecurity for the church, when its members were called on to demonstrate the reality of faith, to be 'witnesses' (*martyres*) of it, some of them should have sought the consummation of desire in the physical death of martyrdom, and thus to drag all the strain of imagining into the 'proof' of pain: 'What if you have trials of many sorts to sadden your hearts in this brief interval? That must needs happen, so that you may give proof of your faith' (1 Peter 1:7). Much later, in sixteenth-century Holland and Germany, the various Anabaptist groups have the same tendency to 'prove' their baptismal conviction by willingly – or wilfully – accepting martyrdom. In martyrdom, the imagined reality of ritual becomes a physical reality through death.

[82] Ibid. 5.11, p. 90.   [83] Ibid. 5.14, pp. 91–2.
[84] Cited and translated Foster 1977, p. 77.

THE DEATH OF PERPETUA: BAPTISM, VISION, MARTRYDOM

In what follows, I will use the *Passion of Perpetua* to show how the tension of desire which is momentarily released in Ambrose's baptism is more radically undone in the death of a martyr, and in the visions which precede and prepare for this death. In other words, I will make a brief study of the psychological connection between baptism, martyrdom and dream.

Vibia Perpetua, 'a married mother of good birth and with a good education', was imprisoned in a suburb of Carthage together with a number of other catechumens, after Septimius Severus had forbidden conversion to Christianity in 202. She was about twenty-two years old, and had a son still on the breast. After being baptized in prison, and refusing to offer sacrifice to the pagan gods, she was condemned and executed in the arena at Carthage on 7 March 203.[85] The *Passion* which records her imprisonment and martyrdom is a composite document. It opens with a prologue whose author – very likely Tertullian in his later Montanist period – defends with obvious feeling the validity of 'new witnesses to the grace of God' against those who place credence only with the canon of 'old examples'.[86] In an Apocalyptic spirit almost certainly inspired by Montanism – a sect originating in Phrygia and fired by a number of woman prophets – the prologue stresses the force of Perpetua's passion as a revelation 'of the last days'; as an act of the Spirit 'which we have heard and touched' (cf. 1 John 1:3).[87] That is, it emphasizes the prophetic immediacy of Perpetua's experience. The remainder of the *Passion* is made up of two pieces, easily told apart by difference of style and content. First, Perpetua's own account of the time of imprisonment, apparently authentic although perhaps written up from her notes; and then the account by Saturus,

---

[85] *Pass. Perp.* 2, p. 108. On the date, Barnes 1971. On the historical background of the visions, Dölger 1930, pp. 1–40. Dodds 1965; Dronke 1984. On the question of the original language of the *Passio* (which exists in both Greek and Latin versions), Fridh 1968, who concludes that the diary section was written in Latin and translated into Greek. The text does not mention Perpetua's husband.

[86] *Pass. Perp.* 1.1–16, pp. 106–8. De Labriolle, the historian of Montanism, argued that the prologue (cc. 1–2) was by Tertullian, as well as some phrases in c. 3; but that Perpetua herself was not a Montanist: de Labriolle 1913, pp. 345–51; cf. Franz 1951, pp. 397ff. De Labriolle is equally against the idea that she was a 'Cheese-Eater', i.e. a member of the Artotyrites (pp. 340–5).

[87] *Pass. Perp.* 1.6, p. 106: 'et nos itaque quod audiuimus et contrectauimus, annuntiamus et uobis, fratres et filioli'.

another of the martyrs, of his own vision of combat with the beasts and the entry of the band of martyrs into heaven.[88] Saturus speaks with a quite different voice, with a mawkish combination of almost brutal realism and stylized ecstasy; and yet the *Passion* as a whole, with its various content of *apologia*, diary, and visionary intensity, gives unusual insight into the drives which led to the martyr's death. In a sense, the three parts are not so far apart. With this in mind, I will concentrate on Perpetua's account, allowing its simplicity to stand as the best argument that she wrote it herself.

Perpetua reports the physical circumstances of imprisonment, baptism, her father's pathetic attempts to dissuade her from what he sees as the insanity of martyrdom – he was the only member of the family not a catechumen or Christian – trial, concern for her baby, movement between prisons; she reports her fears and the gathering momentum of her conviction; and she reports her four visions. It is a matter-of-fact account of agony; not just the agony of death anticipated, but that of reconciling herself to the full strength of her own desire for death. The medium of her struggle, I shall argue – the means by which she represents it to herself and so at each stage gains control in it – is in the first place vision, but then sacrament and finally death itself. Vision, sacrament and death cross over one another in Perpetua's psychology; through each of them she makes real and present what would otherwise be imagined in faith.

The first vision comes in the difficult days of early imprisonment. Afflicted by her father's efforts to turn her from her destiny, pained by the thought of her family's pity, not yet certain of herself, she asks for a vision.[89] Her brother has suggested she do this, knowing she is privileged, and she herself knows that she can 'talk with the Lord': *fabulari cum domino*.[90] The word *fabulari* and the context suggest an exchange, and in her visions Perpetua – unlike those passive Homeric dreamers who did not even get out of bed[91] – is always an active figure. On this occasion, she climbs a ladder, high, narrow, and made of bronze. To its sides are attached spikes, hooks, daggers and other instruments of torture, a thinly veiled reference to the ordeal of death. Saturus climbs ahead of her on the ladder, and looks back from the top to warn

---

[88] Dodds 1965, pp. 47ff, suggests the text may have originated in notes; see Auerbach 1965 on the question of authenticity. For Saturus' account, cc. 11ff, pp. 118ff.

[89] *Pass. Perp.* 4.1, p. 110.

[90] Ibid. 4.2, p. 110.   [91] Dodds 1951, p. 105.

her of the dragon below; Perpetua responds by using the dragon's head as her first step upward. Arriving at the top, she sees a shepherd with white hair, milking sheep, and standing round him many thousands of people in white. The shepherd greets her, and gives her 'a kind of lump of the cheese he was milking'.[92] In waking life, a shepherd milking cheese would be strange enough, but a dream is at liberty to conflate in this way: the milking of cheese expresses (it seems) the two ingredients of the eucharist as they are found in the *Apostolic Tradition*, the drink of milk and honey, carrying with it a sense of rebirth (milk being the food of the newly born), and then the food of bread and wine.[93] Perpetua's first vision is a dream about the struggle to reach the apex of martyrdom. After the test of the ladder and dragon, she reaches the garden of an other-worldly paradise, where she receives food from the Good Shepherd or Christ. The death which this vision anticipates and symbolizes is therefore also a eucharist. After the vision, she knows that she and her brother and the others should hold no hope 'for the present life' (*in saeculo*).[94]

The second and third visions occur when the prisoners have been condemned.[95] Perpetua's father has again tried to dissuade her from her course, appealing to her pity and her family feelings. He is abject, afraid for his reputation, throwing himself down before his daughter in tears, and at the hearing causing such a scene that the proconsul has him beaten publicly:

'I felt grief for his sorry old age', writes Perpetua, 'I grieved for my father's humiliation as if the rod had beaten my own back.'

Earlier she had given her baby over to her father, and now when she asks for him back, her father refuses. But:

'By God's will, the boy no longer hankered after the breast, and my breasts no longer gave me pain.'

[92] '. . . de caseo quod mulgebat dedit mihi quasi buccellam' (ibid. 4.9, pp. 110–12).
[93] *Tradition* 21, pp. 54–6. Cf. Franz 1951, pp. 440ff. And *Tradition* 6, p. 18, where Hippolytus sets down a prayer for the blessing of the milk which uses the metaphor of curdling – after Job 10:10 – to express the shaping of man by God's hand: 'Sanctifica lac hoc quod quoagulatum est, et nos conquaglans tuae caritati.' Dronke sees this shaping in Perpetua's reference to cheese: Dronke 1984, p. 9. Quodvultdeus of Carthage in the fourth century saw an opposition between the cheese (which he also calls milk without distinguishing) received by Perpetua, and the milk produced by her for her child: her milk is the milk of suffering, the other that of solace (*De temp. barbarico* 5.3, pp. 430–1).
[94] *Pass. Perp.* 4.10, p. 112.
[95] Ibid. 7–8, pp. 114–16.

She is distancing herself from the emotions of fear and pity which hold her back.

The two visions which follow, however, are experiences of compassion. While the condemned prisoners are at prayer one day, Perpetua finds she has uttered the name of her younger brother, Dinocrates. He had died at the age of seven from a cancer which had covered his face with sores and made him an object of loathing to all who saw him. Until this moment in the prison, Perpetua had never thought about this brother, but now she was suddenly struck with his memory. She understands that she has the power to pray for him and that night when she has already begun her prayers, she sees him coming out of a dark place. He is hot and thirsty, his clothes dirty and his skin pale:

There was a wound on his face, the one he had when he died ... Between me and him was a great chasm, so that each was unable to reach the other. In the place where Dinocrates was, there was a pool (*piscina*) full of water, its rim too high for the height of the boy. Dinocrates stretched up in an effort to drink. I grieved that the pool held water and yet he was unable to drink because of the height of the rim. I woke up and knew my brother was suffering. I prayed for him every night until we were transferred to the military prison. We were to fight at the military games on the birthday of the emperor Geta. Day and night I moaned and wept in prayer that what I asked be given.[96]

Augustine, some two hundred years later, thought that Dinocrates must have sinned after baptism; if the boy had not been baptized, he argued, Perpetua's prayers could not have helped him.[97] But Augustine had his own reasons for saying this, being wedded to the view (by the time of writing, in *c.* 419) that the child who died without baptism would remain unsaved.[98] In Perpetua's time, no clear statement of this kind had been made, and it seems that the two visions of Dinocrates make up a kind of baptism through dream. It is as though Perpetua not only prays for the boy, but also – as it were – sees him through a posthumous baptism. There is nothing in such flexibility which does not fit in with the general currents of thinking about the after-life in the early centuries of Christianity, all of which are based in the belief that between

---

[96] Ibid. 7.4–10, pp. 114–16.   [97] *De nat. et orig. animae* 1.12, p. 312.
[98] See below, pp. 125ff.

death and final judgement at the end of all time, the souls of the departed spend a period of waiting, or sleeping.[99] The third vision recounts the quenching of Dinocrates' thirst:

One day, when we were left in chains, the following was shown to me: I saw the place I had seen before, and in it Dinocrates, refreshed, well-clothed, and clean in body. Where there had been a wound, I saw a scar; and the pool I had seen before now had its rim lowered to the boy's waist. He took water from it endlessly. Above the rim was a golden bowl full of water. Dinocrates went up to it and began to drink from it; and the bowl never ran dry. When his thirst was slaked he started to play with childish abandon. I woke up then, and understood that he had been taken from his pain.[100]

Perpetua perhaps saw in Dinocrates that childish part of herself which was as yet unreconciled to what she felt she must do; the part which was still divided against herself by a chasm, and still unable to drink from the 'endless water'. So goes the psychological interpretation offered by Marie-Louise von Franz.[101] But we should not let it obscure another element which is less purely internal: Perpetua's compassion for her brother, and the striking contrast it makes with the refusal of compassion for her father and even for her child. There is throughout Perpetua's diary an experience of suffering which goes beyond the inwardly psychological.

The fourth and last vision, seen on the day before death in the arena, is of the *agon* itself.[102] Pomponius the deacon, in a white tunic, leads Perpetua through narrow windy paths to the amphitheatre, where they arrive out of breath. He takes her to the middle of the arena, reassures her that he will be with her, and leaves. Instead of the beast she expects, an Egyptian is sent against her, accompanied by his helpers. Stripped down to be oiled by her own helpers, Perpetua finds she has become a man. Into the theatre comes the giant figure of the *lanista*, the athletic trainer and umpire, holding a rod and a green branch from which hang golden apples. He announces to the enormous crowd the rules of the contest: if the Egyptian wins, he will kill his opponent; if Perpetua wins, she will have the branch. Battle commences, and after a brief struggle Perpetua fells the Egyptian and crushes his head with

99 Angenendt 1984.
100 *Pass. Perp.* 8, p. 116.
101 Franz 1951, pp. 444ff.
102 *Pass. Perp.* 10, pp. 116–18.

her heel: *calcaui illi caput.* The words recall her stepping on the dragon's head (*calcaui illi caput et ascendi*), and just as in the first vision she took a mouthful of cheese from the shepherd, so now she takes the branch of victory from the *lanista*, and walks through the Porta Sanavivaria, the gate of the victorious gladiators. Her own interpretation of the dream is simple as always:

And I understood that I was to fight against the devil, not with beasts; but I knew the fight was mine. This is what happened up to the day before the games. If someone wants to write about what happened at the games, let him do so.[103]

With this the diary ends.

Commenting on her baptism, which takes place a few days after her arrest, Perpetua binds it closely with her death:

In those days, we were baptized, and the Spirit told me I should seek nothing from the water other than the suffering of the flesh.[104]

On the face of it, this might mean only that in the circumstances, baptism was the final act of defiance which would make punishment by death inevitable. However, that baptism was itself a kind of death, or a suffering towards death, was in early Christianity almost a commonplace. It was expressed in the original Greek sense of baptism as a 'going-down', and by implication a going down into the earth, a burial – an etymology that was no doubt in Paul's mind when he spoke of baptism as death and resurrection with Christ (Rom. 6:3);[105] it is consonant with the notion of baptism as the ultimate repentance through death, which evidently passed into Christianity from rabbinic thinking;[106] and it is sustained by the dominant images of baptism as a passage through the Red Sea (and thus involving the death of the Egyptians), as Passover (including the coming of the avenging angel), and as Flood (see 1 Cor. 10:2; 1 Peter 3:17-21).[107] Water in these episodes, as in the Apocalypse (22:14–17) is as much threat as release; or rather in them, release cannot be dissociated from threat. The same coincidence of death-as-suffering and yet as

---

[103] Ibid., p. 118.
[104] Ibid. 3.5, p. 108: 'in ipso spatio paucorum dierum baptizati sumus, et mihi spiritus dictauit non aliud petendum ab aqua nisi sufferentiam carnis'.
[105] Ysebaert 1962, pp. 53ff.
[106] Edsman 1940.   [107] Daniélou 1950.

release is in Origen's 'baptism of fire';[108] so that the martyr who has not previously been baptized is baptized in his own blood.[109]

Throughout all this there is a curious double value. In both sacrament and death (death generally but most forcibly death by martyrdom), death itself and the pain, punishment, threat and suffering associated with it is at once an annihilation of life and an increase of life. With this we have come to what is perhaps the axis on which psychology turns, the dialectic between two competing drives, one towards life and the other towards death; a dialectic which lies at the centre of the modern interpretation of the *psyche*, but which is – as I will suggest – more subtly and more fully stated in the drama of baptism-and-martyrdom, and, in Perpetua's case at least, in the visions which come between baptism and martyrdom. We can if we wish here speak openly with the language of Freud and Jung, all the more since the disagreement between the two men seems to be most precisely situated in the question of the death wish. Freud came to believe, with some misgiving, that a desire to return to the quiescence of the inorganic was a force in human psychology even stronger than the desire to turn 'unpleasure' into pleasure and to pursue life; that *thanatos* was more insistent than *eros*.[110] Jung took the more sanguine view that death was an enrichment of life; that it was absorbed into rebirth to something greater.[111] When his disciple Marie-Louise von Franz wrote about the *Passion of Perpetua* – what is probably the most penetrating essay on this text – she showed a Perpetua whose death was not an ending, but the final ripeness completing a process of development in which the battle between elements in the unconscious culminates in the yielding of the 'I' to the greater self. This is what Jung himself called the *Passion des Ich*. I have no intention of using Freud or Jung, or both, to explain Perpetua and martyrdom; but their language, and their disagreement, can carry us along for a moment. Perpetua desires

---

[108] Lundberg 1942.

[109] Tertullian, *De baptismo* 16, pp. 290–1; and *Tradition* 19, p. 41: 'Si apprehenditur catechumenus propter nomen domini, ne faciet cor duplex propter testimonium. Si enim uiolentia ei infertur et occiditur, cum peccata sua nondum remissa sunt iustific-abitur. Accepit enim baptismum in sanguine suo.'

[110] Freud expounded this in his essay of 1920, *Beyond the Pleasure Principle* (Freud 1986, pp. 218–68).

[111] For Jung's view, see for example 'The Visions of Zosimos' in Jung 1967, pp. 57–108; and Jung is followed closely (although with more attention to the historical circumstances of 'archetypes' than he usually gave) by Franz in her essay on Perpetua: Franz 1951.

death in the full sense of an ending to life; but she also sees this death as a growth. In this she stands for that feeling for the fecundity of death which although it is not always acted out in martyrdom, is a feature of the early Middle Ages, visible in the conception of Christ's death as a nourishing of mankind,[112] in the saint's rejection of his family in the interests of the higher life *coram deo*[113] and – for example – in the architectural association between the *martyrium* and the baptistery.[114] The full force of the meaning of death in this time only dawns on us when we recognize how death as entry into an undisturbed quiet which is the negation of life – the quiet of Perpetua's garden – is also the growth and increase of rebirth. The martyr, in other words, takes up the death which negates life and brings it back to intensify death as fulness of life. It is only in death that he can stretch out to the object of his desire, which is, as it were, the other side of death; for death is the divide across which he must stretch *and* the possibility of stretching across it. Christianity rests perhaps more on this attitude to death as an ultimate ripeness than on any other premise; but it is only in some periods, in nervous times impatient for perfection and suffering from the strain of belief, that the need for immediate satisfaction in death makes martyrdom a common solution.

Perpetua lived in such times. The prologue to her diary explains how her martyrdom is a prophetic moment, in keeping with the 'abundance of grace in this final stage of time'.[115] It is not difficult to see how the simplicity of prophecy – the presence of Spirit in time, the commitment to the 'now' which brings to an end all the waiting of history – and the simplicity of death run close to one another; but perhaps most expressive of the search for simplicity,

---

[112] Cf. Bynum 1987, mainly on the period from the twelfth century.

[113] Theis 1976.

[114] Grabar 1946; for the extreme view that the entire iconography of the catacombs refers to baptism, Martimort 1949. Krautheimer 1942, p. 137, gives evidence for the existence of baptisteries in the catacombs of Priscilla and Pontianus.

[115] *Pass. Perp.* 1.3, p. 106. The three ages of Montanism are described by Tertullian in this same language of completion or ripeness: 'Tempus, inquit, omni rei [Eccles. 3:17]. Aspice ipsam creaturam paulatim ad fructum promoueri. Granum est primo, et de grano frutex oritur, et de frutice arbuscula enititur; deinde rami et frondes inualescunt et totum arboris nomen expanditur, inde germinis tumor et flos de germine soluitur, et de flore fructus aperitur. Is quoque, rudis aliquamdiu et informis, paulatim aetatem suam dirigens eruditur in mansuetudinem saporis. Sic et iustitia . . . primo fuit in rudimentis, natura Deum metuens; dehinc per legem et prophetas promouit in infantiam, dehinc per euangelium efferbuit in iuuentutem, nunc per paracletum componitur in maturitatem' (*De uirg. uel.* 1.5–7, p. 1210).

or finality, in times of confusion is Perpetua's exchange with her father on his first visit to the prison:

'Father, do you see this vase or water-pot, or whatever it is?'
'Yes'
'Well, could it be called by any other name than what it is?'
'No'
'Well, the same with me. I can't be called anything other than what I am, a Christian.'[116]

The sense of destiny, of a truth already present – of a simplicity in which all straining and desire is brought to rest, in which the sound of a word is bound intrinsically to the thing it means – recurs in the four dreams. Like the death for which they prepare, the visions stretch across to the other side, to the object of faith and desire, able to do this by the nature of dream and vision, which are projections from the material world into the world of the imagined. In Perpetua's own expression, they are a *fabulari cum domino*. The speech of prophecy and the seeing of dream or vision are in the end no different:

She speaks with angels [said Tertullian of a Montanist prophetess] and sometimes with the Lord; she sees and hears the hidden truths (*sacramenta*).[117]

Making immediate these *sacramenta*, vision does what death does; and in *Perpetua*, vision is thus more than a preparation, more than her effort to reconcile herself to what must come, to 'develop' herself by coming to terms with conflicting aspects of her unconscious mind; it is a *pre-enactment* of death. It is in this spirit that the prologue-writer – who understands the content of the diary better than has often been supposed – runs together prophecy, dreams and visions, and martyrdom. But if dream pre-enacts death in *Perpetua*, so too does sacrament. This is most obviously true of Perpetua's own baptism – 'the Spirit told me

---

[116] *Pass. Perp.* 3.1–2, p. 108: 'Pater, inquam, uides uerbi gratia uas hoc iacens, urceolum siue aliud? et dixit: Video. et ego dixi ei: Numquid alio nomine uocari potest quam quod est? et ait: Non. sic et ego aliud me dicere non possum nisi quod sum, Christiana.'
[117] *De anima* 9.4, p. 792: 'conuersatur cum angelis, aliquando etiam cum domino, et uidet et audit sacramenta' (cf. n. 87, above). For Tertullian in the *De anima*, dream is as it were the soul's direct perception. One might compare this confidence in dream and its interpretation – Perpetua knows without hesitation what her dreams mean – with the complexity of Aelius Aristides' dreaming, but also with the later misgivings of the church over dreams and their right understanding. See Aelius Aristides, *Sacred Tales I*; and for the attempt to keep dream within the limits of hagiography, Le Goff 1988, pp. 193–231.

that I should seek nothing from the water other than the suffering of the flesh' – which like dream is at once a preparation, a strengthening of resolve towards death and a pre-enactment in which death is already accomplished; but it is also true of the eucharist and baptism within the visions: the 'eucharist' of cheese in the first vision, set against the background of a contradiction between the confusion, difficulty, fear of the ladder and dragon, and the peace of the garden; then the 'baptism' of Dinocrates. We must try to appreciate the three rhythms as they play over one another: dream, sacrament, death, each making present to the senses what is on the other side:

I came to, still chewing something sweet, I don't know what. I told my brother straightaway, and we knew there would be a suffering (*passionem*); and we began to have no hope in the world (*in saeculo*).[118]

'I don't know what' (*nescio quid*): a detail conveying ingenuously that uncanny sensation of returning from dream to waking, a transition which for many at this time, including Aelius Aristides, would have held a deep fascination; but the feeling familiar to the dreamer of coming back from somewhere else is then infinitely deepened – again without a whisper of literary artifice – by the message the dreamer has brought back, that the prisoners are to give up hope in this world. The contrast between dreaming and waking turns out to be one between the next world and this one.

In the two visions of Dinocrates, the contradictions which dominate the first vision are replaced by an impression of frustration at separateness – a separateness perhaps reminiscent of Tertullian's intuition of the distance between God and creation.[119] Perpetua sees her young brother, who before death had already been shunned for the ugliness of his sores. Between Perpetua and Dinocrates is a great chasm,

so that each of us was unable to reach the other.[120]

The chasm separates the dreamer from the figure of the boy, but – the vision coming to Perpetua within her prayer – it seems also to be a gap between prayer and its answer. It is also the frustration of Dinocrates' thirst, his *labor* as he stretches upward to the rim of the

[118] *Pass. Perp.* 4.10, p. 112. [119] See above, pp. 53ff.
[120] *Pass. Perp.* 7.6, p. 114.

piscina he cannot reach.[121] This may be a thirst drawn from the scene of the entry of the Orphic 'thirsty ones' into Hades, but it is baptism too, and harks back to Perpetua's baptism after arrest.[122] The drinking from a *piscina* – a fish-pond or swimming-pool – is an anomaly not unlike the milking of cheese in the first vision, and just as the milking of cheese apparently conveys the eating and drinking which together make up the eucharist, so the drinking from a pool suggests baptism as both a drinking and an immersion. The drinking in baptism may at the same time be a reference to the unity of baptism and the eucharist.[123]

Vision, like the death it anticipates, stretches out across contradiction or separateness; and likewise the sacrament within vision. In the third vision the rim of the pool has lowered. Dinocrates, his wounds closed into scars, drinks 'endlessly' (*sine cessatione*) from a bowl attached to the side of the pool, which re-fills constantly. Once hot (*aestuans*), now he is cool (*refrigerans*); punished, he now plays. His pathetic desire to drink is slaked: he is *satiatus*. But there would have been no desire without the earlier frustration, without the chasm, just as in baptism there can be no resurrection – and no rebirth – without death. Symbol itself, or sacrament, like

---

[121] Ibid. 7.9, p. 114: 'et cognoui fratrem meum laborare'.

[122] Dronke argues that Perpetua, who is *liberaliter instituta* in the text (*Pass. Perp.* 2.1, p. 108), would have been dreaming not about baptism when she dreamt of Dinocrates, but about the 'thirsty ones' of Orphic myth. The *locus tenebrosus* from which Dinocrates emerges would therefore be Hades, not a prototype of purgatory (cf. Le Goff 1981, pp. 74–7). Many of Perpetua's vision-images – the dragon for example, and the *lanista* – are as much pagan as Christian in reference, but in the circumstances – Perpetua's recent baptism, the established association between baptism and martyrdom, and generally the carrying over of pagan imagery into Christian at this time of *crisis* – the case for a purely pagan Dinocrates is laborious. Perpetua had in mind both pagan and Christian imagery, an assumption made (sometimes with gay abandon) by Franz 1951.

[123] Cf. *Corpus Hermeticum IV*, pp. 150–1 (second/third century AD), describing a Gnostic baptism in the cup or chalice (κρᾱτήρ) filled with mind, thus a dipping in a cup rather than a drinking from a pool: 'He filled a great chalice with mind, and sent it down to earth; and he appointed a herald, and bade him make proclamation to the hearts of men: Hearken, each human heart; dip (βάπτισον) yourself in this chalice, if you can, recognizing for what purpose you have been made, and believing that you shall ascend to him who sent the chalice down. Now those who gave heed to the proclamation, and dipped themselves in the bath of the mind, these men got a share of *gnosis*; they received mind, and so became complete men.' (I have altered Scott's translation of κρᾱτήρ from 'basin' to 'chalice': see Lampe 1961, p. 776; Festugière 1938, who, referring to the same Hermetic text, suggests that the combination of drinking and dipping here and elsewhere might be an expression of the continuity between eucharist and baptism. He also suggests that the combination recalls another sense of *baptizein*, that of 'to get drunk' or 'be drunken', and this in turn suggests Dinocrates' playfulness after he has drunk. Since Perpetua, *liberaliter instituta*, would almost certainly have known some Greek, it is fair to assume that she had this sense somewhere in mind.)

death, is at once the divide which separates and the possibility of stretching across it.

But in *Perpetua*, this divide is also the divide between the suffering of one person and that of another, the distance crossed by compassion. Dinocrates cannot only be Perpetua's childish self, that part of her still attached to the world and hindering her development to death. He must also be taken literally as another person, whose suffering is necessarily remote because it is someone else's, but all the more remote – indeed utterly – because he has died:

And it astonished me that he had never come into my mind till that moment, and I grieved at the memory of his death.[124]

Dolui commemorata casus eius; and a little later, she grieves at the sight of him trying to drink: *dolebam quod et piscina illa aquam habebat.*[125] She had already used the same phrase of the episode of her father's beating: *et doluit mihi casus patris mei*. 'It was as if the rod had beaten my own back', she says, 'and so I grieved' (*dolui*) for his sorry old age.'[126] This compassion which bears no fruit, ending only in pity and in the contempt which is so close to pity, is the contrary of the compassion for Dinocrates, which reaches its mark.

And I had faith I could help him in his trouble.[127]

There is a harshness too in passing so abruptly from Perpetua's loss of anxiety about her own child –

As God willed, the child no longer hankered after the breast, and my breasts no longer gave me pain, so that I was troubled neither by care for the child nor soreness in my breasts[128]

– to her anxious prayer for Dinocrates. But the negative content in pity and in resignation to loss of the child is the condition of that other more potent compassion in which the suffering of another is successfully taken on. It is perhaps not surprising that

---

[124] *Pass. Perp.* 7.1, p. 114.   [125] Ibid. 7.8, p. 114.

[126] Ibid. 6.5, p. 114; and again at 9.3, p. 116, her father's last visit described with the dispassionate objectivity of a pity become resignation: 'ut autem proximauit dies muneris, intrat ad me pater meus consumptus taedio, et coepit barbam suam euellere et in terram mittere, et prosternere se in faciem, et inproperare annis suis, et dicere tanta uerba quae mouerent uniuersam creaturam, ego dolebam pro infelici senecta eius'.

[127] Ibid. 7.9, pp. 114–16: 'sed fidebam me profuturam labori eius'.

[128] Ibid. 6.7, p. 114. Perpetua had given her child to her father: above, p. 75.

compassion should follow the pattern of the negative and the positive found in sacrament, dream and death: the suffering in which compassion is based is after all a foreshadowing of death. The desire to make immediate what lies on the far side of sacrament or death, and thus to relieve the effort of belief, is also the desire to reach the suffering of another. Augustine will show how compassion for the suffering Christ, and therefore love, is integral to the understanding involved in sacrament;[129] and in monasticism we see the attempt, through asceticism, to repeat – to take on by a kind of compassion – the 'death' of poverty, and thus to lay hold of a final ripeness, of the *eschaton* within life; and in this vein we might interpret the winning of the golden apples in Perpetua's fourth vision.[130] In liturgy this contiguity of pain and satisfaction, the finally inexplicable fact that truth is within suffering, is echoed in the juxtaposition of penitence and relish,[131] and in the punishment, like that of the three boys in the fiery furnace, which is also a consolation.[132]

The martyr's desire was not always the same as Perpetua's. It might be gripped tight within the fortitude of Polycarp, resembling nothing so much as the *amor fati* of the Stoic,[133] the steadiness before death of the one 'possessed of truth' (*compos ueritatis*):

no one would want to be killed unless possessed of the truth[134]

as Tertullian put it. Or it might bubble up into a desire for death which is more or less openly a sublimation of the erotic, as in the story of Thecla – 'martyred' three times – in the *Acts of Paul* (*c.* 185–195). Thecla's propulsion towards death follows logically from her repudiation of sexuality, and from the moment when, a betrothed woman, she first heard Paul preaching, and was 'dominated by new desire and fearful passion'.[135]

The martyr has seized death as the object of desire; he has made real and tangible what to others remains the imagined content of faith. This accomplishment enables him to take the power of his

[129] See below, pp. 104ff.   [130] *Pass. Perp.* 10.8, p. 118.
[131] Thus Seamus Heaney, commenting on his *Sweeney Astray:* Heaney 1983, Introduction.
[132] *Gelasian*, no. 427, p. 69: 'Flammae lux quippe dicenda est ... quae tribus pueris in camino sentencia tyranni depositis uitam blandimentis mollioribus reseruauıt.' And on the same ambiguity in the 'baptism of fire', Edsman 1940.
[133] Cf. *Apologeticum* 1.12–13, p. 87.
[134] *Scorpiace* 8, pp. 1083–4.
[135] *Acts of Paul*, p. 355. On the date of the *Acts*, Hennecke–Schneemelcher 1965, p. 351.

persecutor into his own hands. When he is offered the alternative of making the pagan sacrifice or going to the beasts, it is he who chooses:

Hilarianus the governor said to me [Perpetua], 'Spare your father's white hair, spare your little son. Make the sacrifice for the salvation of the emperors.'
'I will not', I replied.
'Are you a Christian?', says Hilarianus to this.
And I reply, 'I am a Christian.'[136]

Tertullian, in character, noted the satisfying paradox of this refusal:

When your power against me is, unless I so will, no power at all, your power depends on my will, not on power in you.[137]

In *Perpetua*, baptism – and sacrament generally – is both a preparation for and a pre-enactment of death. There is nothing to be had 'from the water' but the 'suffering of the flesh'. In the liturgical performance of baptism, the power which comes of seizing on death in this way is the power of the word over the object. It is that phenomenon so inaccessible to the modern mind, the literal truth of symbol. Augustine goes some way towards an account of it.

---

[136] *Pass. Perp.* 6.3, p. 114. The interrogations of martyrs read something like parodies of the interrogation of the candidate before baptism (cf. *Tradition* 20, p. 42), sometimes including renunciation, repentance and confession of faith: thus *Martyrdom of Polycarp* 9.2–12.1, pp. 220–5.

[137] *Apologeticum* 49.5, p. 169; and *De fuga* 9.4, p. 1147 (on power arising out of the 'shame' of martyrdom): 'Publicaris, inquit, bonum tibi est; qui enim non publicatur in hominibus, publicatur in domino. Ne confundaris; iustitia te producit in medium. Quid confunderis laudem ferens? Potestas fit, cum conspiceris ab hominibus.'

Chapter 3

AUGUSTINE

The genius of Augustine was able to address the crucial question concerning baptismal conversion, the question which in Ambrose or Cyprian or Tertullian remained implicit: how does the moment of baptism stand in relation to the drawn-out living of the Christian life which follows it? How does the rite in its brevity bear on the longevity of *peregrinatio*, the pilgrim journey of the soul towards God?[1] This question, and the answer which Augustine gives, is psychological: it has to do with the individual soul. The question, however, leads Augustine to a theology of sacrament, and of baptism in particular, which is at least open to the political and social role taken on by sacrament in the period of the Merovingians and the Carolingians. In this as in much else, Augustine was the *Janus bifrons*, looking back into Late Antiquity and forward into the Middle Ages.

On the face of it, Augustine seems to have attributed to baptism primarily the role of exorcism: the negative function of removing original sin in the child, or in the case of the adult convert, both original and personal sins. Baptism, he said, is a momentary happening. It does away with the fever itself, but it does not heal the weakness which follows on fever. It pulls out the arrow of evil, but does not heal the wound. As a mere preparation in this sense, it is to be distinguished from the constructive process of renewal (*renouatio*), the day-to-day progress of the soul towards its maker, lived out in the tension of hope and faith.[2] For Augustine, the essential of the Christian life is in *peregrinatio*, the pilgrimage of the stranger in the Earthly City towards the City of

---

[1] *De trin.* 14.17, p. 454: 'Sane ista renouatio non momento uno fit ipsius conuersionis, sicut momento uno fit illa in baptismo renouatio remissione omnium peccatorum.'

[2] Ibid.: 'Sed quemadmodum aliud est carere febribus, aliud ab infirmitate, quae febribus facta est, reualescere; item aliud est infixum telum de corpore demere, aliud uulnus quod eo factum est secunda curatione sanare: ita prima curatio est causam remouere languoris, quod per omnium fit indulgentiam peccatorum; secunda ipsum sanare languorem, quod fit paulatim proficiendo in renouatione huius imaginis.'

God where he will find rest. Baptism, apparently, provides no more than the possibility of setting out.

Yet this view of baptism as an external operation disconnected from the subsequent history of the will – a momentary irruption of the divine – is only a part of what Augustine meant. The theology which makes infant baptism in the first place a remedy for the affliction of original sin turns out to be the same as Augustine's mature theology of the dependency of the human will on divine will. But this dependency is above all a co-operation, an encounter between man and God, a relation and in a sense a covenant. The essential thing about the soul is not that it has fallen from God, but that it is, or at least bears in itself, the image of God, and therefore carries the seed of a return to God. This is the theme of the great work *On the Trinity* completed in 419. If we dig further into Augustine's notion of baptism and infant baptism, we begin to see how it is linked to a broader conception of sacrament and of what he calls the *cultus Dei*, and how, by way of this idea of cult, it participates in the general motion of the will towards its divine origin. Sacrament is no longer a mere sign pointing to a reality outside itself, but is itself an act of the will. And the first, momentary, act of healing, the pulling out of the arrow, and the long convalescence which follows it, are continuous rather than cut off from one another. They are both a 'reform' – in the sense of a re-shaping to an original form – of the soul to identity with the incarnate Christ, so that now the 'moment' of healing appears as a brief intensity into which the extensive pilgrimage of the soul, its journey of penitence, is compressed, and from which the pilgrim sets out. The 'cult of God' and the 'day-to-day progress' (*quotidiani accessus*)[3] flow into one another. The sacramental and the ethical become one. It is by understanding this that we will understand Augustine's view of baptism.

In the time of attachment to Neoplatonism which preceded his conversion and even to some extent persisted after it, Augustine thought little about the sacramental side of religion.[4] His attention was turned away from the material and the bodily and the changeable, and inward to 'that which is'. Christianity was still the 'true philosophy'. Between the mind in its pure contemplation of

---

[3] Ibid.
[4] On Augustine's development, Adam 1932; Marrou 1938; on his ideas about sacrament, Van der Meer 1961, pp. 275ff.

truth, and the light of truth infusing it and which gave it the power to contemplate, there stood no material obstacle; and so Christ was the *exemplum uiuendi* who led the wise man in his search for wisdom.[5] There is no trace yet of the abject submission of man to his own worse nature, nor of justification as the taking on of a new nature by a gift of grace. Still holding these earlier views, it is to be expected that on the whole Augustine treated sacrament cursorily: he describes in the *Confessions* his surprise when a friend had recovered from a dangerous illness, and had changed his life in keeping with the baptism he had received while still unconscious on his sickbed.[6] But he did not dwell on the reasons for this, and when it came to describing his own baptism, he was quite summary. Similarly, when he talks of the interpretation of signs in his book *On Christian Education*, he seems still, at times, to be thinking about the discovery of meaning in signs principally as an intellectual exercise, despite his clear statement in the early part of the book that the Christian sign incorporates the love of God. In short, Augustine's conception of the whole complex of 'symbol', comprising not only sacrament but the half-hidden meanings in the Bible and even in the created world, is subject to the same kind of development as any other part of his thought. Indeed, it always lies very close to his thinking on the most eminent of all Christian symbols, the Incarnation: as Augustine grew older, as he passed first to Christianity, then to the priesthood and then became bishop, he abandoned the 'intellectual' Christ, Christ as *logos* of the Father and a being indistinguishable from the operation of the purified mind, and embraced the man-Christ who could only be approached in the anxiety of faith, hope and love. Sacrament makes possible the approach to, and ultimately the identity with, this Christ of the affections.[7]

REMEMBRANCE

The approach is in the first place an act of remembering: but as Augustine writes in his second letter to Januarius (letter 55), the

[5] *Confessions* 7.23, p. 107; and cf. Adam 1932, pp. 29ff.
[6] *Confessions* 4.7–8, pp. 43–4.
[7] Adam 1932, pp. 39ff. And see Auf der Maur and Waldram 1981, seeing in Origen's view of catechesis and baptism a meeting of word, belief and sacrament, of the ethical and the sacramental, which is not far from Augustine's thinking.

memory does not always work in the same way, and may have quite different implications. Why is it, Januarius has asked, that Easter falls on a different day each year, whereas Christmas is always on the same day?

First you should know [writes Augustine] that the birth of Our Lord is not celebrated as a sacrament, but is merely the occasion on which we call to mind (*in memoriam reuocari*) that he was born. To do this, we need only mark out the day on which this event took place, with a devotional feast, as it recurs each year. There is however sacrament in any celebration where commemoration is made of a past act, in such a way that something is signified or understood, and that this something is received in holiness. This is how we make the Passover (*Pascha agimus*): in it we call to mind not only what was done, in other words that Christ died and rose again, but other things witnessed in this connection too, and which have to do with its sacramental significance. For as the apostle says, 'he was handed over to death for our sins, and raised to life for our justification' (Rom. 4:25).[8]

The Hebrew *Pascha*, as Augustine rightly points out, is not the *paschein* of the Greeks and the *pati* of Latin. It does not refer to a time of suffering but to a time of 'crossing over'. It is a *transitus*: 'And so the transition from this mortal life into that immortal one, from death to life that is, is what is handed over (*commendatur*) in the Passion and resurrection of the Lord.'[9]

There is therefore a 'weak' and a 'strong' sense of remembering: an event may be recalled simply as an occurrence in the past; or it may be recalled for the meaning it had then and still has now. In this strong or absolute recollection, the past is 'handed over' and becomes as though not past at all. This commemoration, however, is not wholly passive: its sources and its energy are not only in the outward act of celebration but in an inward act of faith: 'This transition is done by us now through faith.' And since faith

---

8   *Ep.* 55.1, cols 204–5: 'Hic primum oportet noueris diem Natalem Domini non in sacramento celebrari, sed tantum in memoriam reuocari quod natus sit, ac per hoc nihil opus erat, nisi reuolutum anni diem, quo ipsa res acta est, festa deuotione signari. Sacramentum est autem in aliqua celebratione, cum rei gestae commemoratio ita fit, ut aliquid etiam significatur intelligatur, quod sancte accipiendum est. Eo itaque modo agimus Pascha, ut non solum in memoriam quod gestum est reuocemus, id est quod mortuus est Christus et resurrexit, sed etiam caetera quae circa ea attestantur, ad sacramenti significationem non omittamus. Quia enim, sicut dicit Apostolus, "Mortuus est propter delicta nostra, et resurrexit propter justificationem nostram" [Rom. 4:25].'

9   Ibid.; and on Augustine's correct interpretation of *Pascha*, Mohrmann 1958, pp. 205–22. For Christmas as *sacramentum*, however, in Rome of the mid-fifth century, see *Sacramentarium Veronense*, pp. 157ff, and especially no. 1241 on p. 158. Cf. Bourque 1948, p. 143; and Botte 1932.

'works through love' (Gal. 5:6), and since hope, like faith, requires the patience to hope for what is not yet seen (cf. Rom. 8:24), this crossing over, this burial with Christ in baptism – for the *transitus* of Easter is also the baptismal renewal – is an act of faith, hope and love. The 'strong' memory, it now appears more clearly, is not detached application of the mind; it requires all the force and decisiveness, all the ethical strength, which outside the confines of the celebration will be called on for the Christian existence. It is as if because of the commitment it demands, the brief passage of the rite contains *in nucleo* the entire pilgrim condition of man: it is pregnant with meanings which outlive it. With a *catena* of quotations from the Pauline epistles, Augustine reiterates this principle, that the narrative past of the Incarnation, death and resurrection, and with it the hoped-for future of an existence 'with Christ in God', are made present insofar as they are brought alive in faith:[10] 'the old man in us has been crucified with him; and we have risen with him' (cf. Rom. 6:6–11); 'you have undergone death, and your life is hidden away now with Christ in God' (Col. 3:3); we live in hope of the day of resurrection when 'this corruptible nature of ours will put on the incorruptible, this mortal nature immortality' (I Cor. 15:53). Everything in these passages strains to abolish tense by making tenses conflict: in faith the Christian 'crosses over' with Christ, and in his hope he already finds what is hoped for: 'in hope we are saved' (Rom. 8:24). In its mortal journey, the church waits to become what it has been: it hopes for the past. There are shades here of Augustine's reflections on the nature of time and eternity in book 11 of the *Confessions*, where he wrestles with the impenetrable paradox that time past and time to come appear to have no existence outside the present time of memory and expectation.[11] The more we think about past and future, the more we become aware that they are in our thinking and therefore in the present. Just as in the *Confessions* Augustine pictures the reflective mind naturally, almost inevitably, rising out of the duration of time to the eternal present, so here he evokes the evanescence of time under the pressure of a remembering which is at once a hoping.[12]

---

[10] *Ep.* 55.2, cols. 205–6.   [11] *Confessions* 11.17, pp. 202–3.

[12] *Ep.* 55.2, col. 206: 'Hoc igitur uniuersa ecclesia, quae in peregrinatione mortalitatis inuenta est, exspectat in fine saeculi quod in Domini nostri Jesu Christi corpore praemonstratum est, qui ex mortuis primogenitus, quia et corpus eius cui caput est ipse, non nisi ecclesia est.'

The remembering which goes on at Easter, quite distinct from the merely historical recollection of the Nativity, involves the whole motion of man towards the God in whose image he is made: it is the motion of faith, hope and love, or, to put it in the language which Augustine uses in book 14 of the *De trinitate*, the movement of wisdom towards its origin.[13] If we read this book, with its remarkable evocation of the natural return of the soul to its maker, and then turn to the *commemoratio* of the letter to Januarius, we can hardly fail to recognize the similarity in what is being described. It is of little importance that in the very same book Augustine makes his distinction between the 'one moment' of baptism and the extended effort of 'reform to God': we have only to read the account of his own conversion in the eighth book of the *Confessions* to know how charged the moment could be; or to think of what he says about the act of sacrifice in the *City of God* to gain an impression of the moment spilling over into, and filled with, the 'day-to-day progress'.[14]

In the *De trinitate*, Augustine offers an analysis of the soul, formed in the image of the Trinity, and therefore with an innate capacity to find rest in the fulness of the Trinity. Much as the mind reflecting deeply on the passing of time finds itself somehow lifted out of time, or the church in its hoping for the past (that is, for the culmination of history in death and resurrection) in some sense finds its hope fulfilled, so the soul in its capacity for God rises towards participation in him. This is the movement of the *cultus Dei*:

To put it briefly [the soul] worships the unmade God of whom it has been made capable by God, and in whom it is able to participate. And so it is written, 'The worship of God is wisdom' [Job 28:28]: [the soul then] will be wise not by its own light but by taking part in that higher light.[15]

As oil rises to the surface in water, Augustine says elsewhere, the soul makes its upward journey; and he expresses his delight in this phenomenon when he points out that it is as though a weight were to defy gravity, and move up instead of down.[16]

[13] *De trin.* 14.12, pp. 442–3; and *passim*.
[14] *Confessions* 8.25, p. 129; *De ciu. Dei* 10.6, pp. 278–80. On the idea of reform in the Fathers, Ladner 1959.
[15] *De trin.* 14.12, p. 443; on the Plotinian idea of the light from above, *De ciu. Dei* 10.2, p. 274.
[16] *Ep.* 55.10–11, cols. 213 (oil in water), 214 (weight rising).

This return to God, considered psychologically as it is in the *De trinitate*, is once more an act of memory. It is a commemoration.

As image of the Trinity, the soul is made up of three parts:[17] memory, understanding and love or the will. In its fallen state, the divine content of the memory is 'forgotten', and love is love of self. The soul, unaware of the story of its own creation and destiny except as a fragment of the past, turns in on itself and remains incapable of growth. And yet fallen man still 'walks in the image': the very vice of his self-love is the grounds of his metamorphosis to God-love, a truth which can be tested by the simple observation that a man will always hold fast to his soul, recognizing instinctively that all else in the world is inferior to it. He can never quite forget what he is. In these circumstances, redemption, the *regressus ad Deum*, amounts to an activation of what is in the memory by the will. This involves all three parts of the soul: the true content of the *memory* is brought to light by the *understanding* which has the power to see into memory, and which has been moved to action by the *will*. The process is analogous to speech, where language, stored passively in the mind's memory as words, is brought to the surface by thought acting in the service of will.[18] In the case of redemption, this Trinitarian activity is called by Augustine a 'being remembered':[19] very much like the individual or the church at Easter, the soul is brought round to memory; is made the subject of a remembering. It undergoes the same experience as the man who fails to recognize someone he has once met, and then has his memory jogged by a detail and suddenly recalls the face. Like the man in his embarrassment, the soul 'goes back into the memory' (*redit in memoriam*).[20] This whole account of reform or renewal is typically Augustinian in its refined sense of the involuntary nature of the exercise of the will. The man who suddenly recognizes a face is not entirely master of himself: he remembers, but is also part of a 'remembering'. Is his experience any different from that of the church at Easter, as it

---

[17] For what follows, *De trin.* 14.10ff, pp. 440ff.   [18] Ibid. 13.20, pp. 418–19.

[19] Ibid. 14.15, p. 450: 'Sed commemoratur, ut conuertatur ad Dominum, tanquam ad eam lucem qua etiam cum ab illo auerteretur quodam modo tangebatur.' Before his conversion, or *reformatio*, man has forgotten the history of God's presence, but not the presence itself, for this is imprinted on him, 'sicut imago ex anulo et in ceram transit, et anulum non relinquit' (ibid., p. 451). And see Plato, *Meno* 81c ff., pp. 302ff, for a classic example of the Platonic origins of this thinking about memory, and particularly for the connection between virtue and learning as recollection.

[20] *De trin.* 14.13, p. 444.

'goes back into its memory' and sees that it is the body of Christ? The *cultus Dei* as the soul's wisdom – *cultus Dei sapientia est* in Augustine's unusual translation of Job 28:28 – is also the *cultus Dei* of sacrament, an equation made still clearer by the treatment of the eucharist in the *City of God*. In sacrament and in the ethical life towards God, *cultus* is the motion of participation in God which is at the same time granted by God.

Wisdom, however, is the fruit of education: like the man unable to recall a face, the soul needs to be reminded of its own capacity. And the significance of the past is only known after the story of the past has been told:[21] the commemoration which occurs in sacrament is in this way dependent on the lesser, historical memory, and Easter is not quite so separate from Christmas as might at first appear. Significance, in other words, must be taught, and it is this teaching which occupies Augustine to some extent in the second letter to Januarius,[22] but more fully in two treatises, *On Christian Education*, (*De doctrina christiana*), and *On Catechizing* (*De catechizandis rudibus*). Indirectly, the content of these works – especially the brilliant psychological insights into the processes of teaching and understanding in the discussion of catechizing – point to the vital educational element in liturgy generally. At one level, ritual is an extended history lesson, conveying the Biblical past in its lections.[23] The alternative history offered to Clovis or even Charlemagne must have held them almost spellbound. But then out of the historical arose something more intense: we can see how in the twelfth century John Beleth or Hugh of St Victor drew the sacramental from the historical, drew an 'absolute remembering' from the weaker recollections of history, concentrating the past with such energy that it repeated itself. Repetitions of this kind are already inherent

[21] Ibid. 14.15, pp. 449–50, speaking of man unable to recall his own beatitude, but brought round to belief in it 'dignis litteris Dei sui, per eius prophetam conscriptis, narrantibus de felicitate paradisi, atque illud primum et bonum hominis et malum historica traditione indicantibus'.

[22] *Ep.* 55.3ff, and especially 9–13, cols. 211–15 and 15, cols. 217–18, this last on the number symbolism behind the forty days of Lent and the fifty days between Easter and Pentecost. Having said that this first stage of 'educational' significance serves a purpose as long as it is not used to excess, and as long as the ultimate significance of sacrament is always kept in mind, he is quite happy to indulge it at some length: he is evidently fascinated with number symbolism.

[23] Thus Augustine in *De cat. rud.* 3, p. 24, running together Rom. 15:4 and 1 Cor. 10:11, writes: 'Omnia quae ante scripta sunt, et figurae nostrae fuerunt; et in figura contingebant in eis; scripta sunt autem propter nos, in quos finis saeculorum obuenit.'

in Ambrose's notion of typology, and they go back much further, perhaps providing the basis of the Fourth Gospel and of Jewish ceremonial.[24] They are all annihilations of time which come about only through an awareness of being in time. And this double movement of historical and sacramental remembering, conveyed here by Augustine, reflects the duality of the Christian's own attitude to his past: for him, the promise made to the Jews has been fulfilled, and the Old Testament lies in the fulness of the New. As far as his own life is concerned, however, he cannot take this fulness for granted; he is condemned by his weakness to live historically, as though the Old had not yet been taken up into the New.[25] In this sense, he must live through the transition from Old to New, aspiring to the fulness of recollection but able to reach it only in a few privileged, sacramental, moments.

When he writes to advise the deacon Deogratias about catechizing, in a long letter of about 405 (*On Catechizing*), Augustine shows how catechism is precisely this work of harvesting 'the fulness of time' from the transience of history. In his learning of Biblical history, of the passage of the Old Testament into the New, the catechumen awaiting baptism accepts into himself the significance of the past, and history is robbed of its contingency. This can happen because he is taught that the sublime principle underlying all the events and stories of the Bible is *charitas*: love. The Incarnation is no more than the complete expression of this love:

If, therefore, Christ came chiefly that man might learn how much God loves him, and learning this might begin to be fired with love for him by whom he was loved in the first place, and so might love his neighbour at the bidding and after the example of the one who made himself man's neighbour at a time when man was not his neighbour but was wandering far away from him; if, moreover, all divine Scripture that was written before was written to foretell the coming of the Lord, and if whatever has since been committed to writing and established by divine authority tells of Christ and counsels love, then it is evident that on these two commandments of the love of God and the love of our neighbour depend not merely the whole law and the prophets, which at the time

[24] Cf. Cullmann 1966; Baumstark 1958, pp. 164–74, on Easter as 'a feast of idea'.
[25] So *ep.* 55.14, col. 217: 'Sed tamen quia ipsa spes ex promissione ueritatis certa nobis est, cum diceret, "Consepulti igitur sumus illi per baptismum in mortem", subiunxit et ait, "ut quomodo surrexit Christus ex mortuis per gloriam Patris, ita et nos in nouitate uitae ambulemus" [Rom. 6:4]. Ambulamus ergo in re laboris, sed in spe quietis: in carne uetustatis, sed in fide nouitatis.'

when the Lord uttered these precepts were as yet the only Holy Scripture, but also all the inspired books that have been written at a later period for our welfare and handed down to us.[26]

The main body of catechesis is in the Biblical narrative: the catechist must begin at the beginning with the Creation, go over what he feels to be the most instructive episodes of the Penta-teuch, the historical books and the prophets, go on to the New Testament, and finally say something about the history of the church up to the present day.[27] Thus the catechist recounts the story of the ages of man, including the sixth which begins from the entry of Christ into the world. But as he does so, he cannot avoid the patterns lying beneath his story, so that as the tale unfolds it seems at once to look backward and forward: the old prophesies the new, the new makes manifest, 'annunciates', the old. Augustine conveys this with a parable drawn from the Old Testament: as Jacob put out his hand first when being born, not his head, and with his hand held on to the foot of his brother born before him, so in the course of history, Christ-the-head followed in time the hand of the patriarchs and prophets who went before him. In time the hand outstripped the head, but in the order of things, the head comes first. Christ thus *precedes* the prophets who foretold his coming.[28]

At every turn, though, the attention required to see something more than history in history is rendered psychological, as though it is the very experience of the catechumen. The principle of all sacred history is the love which loves mankind despite its faithless wandering; and the succession from the Old Covenant to the New is the change in the believer from the religion of fear to that of love:

in the Old Testament the New is concealed, and in the New the Old is revealed. In keeping with the concealment, men of the flesh with their fleshly understanding were then and are now, the victims of the fear of punishment. But in keeping with revelation, men of the spirit with their spiritual understanding . . . are made free by the gift of love.[29]

In the God-man are brought together as if in a single moment the whole past of concealment and revelation, for although he is a manifestation, his true nature remains concealed: he is the

---

[26] *De cat. rud.* 4, p. 28. [27] Ibid. 3, p. 22.
[28] Ibid. 3, pp. 22–4. [29] Ibid. 4, p. 28; and see Christopher's note on p. 157.

exemplum humilitatis, who despises the good things of the earth and endures all earthly ills;

he refused to be made king by men, because he was showing the way of lowliness to those wretches whom their pride had separated from him; and yet the whole creation bears witness to his everlasting kingdom. He hungered who feeds all, he thirsted by whom all drink is created . . .; he was wearied with earthly journeying who has made himself the way to heaven for us; he became as it were one dumb and deaf in the presence of his revilers, through whom the dumb spoke and the deaf heard; he was bound who has freed men from the bonds of their infirmities; he was scourged who drove out from men's bodies the scourges of all pains.

And so on until the sudden relief of resurrection: 'But he also rose again, never more to die.'[30] But in this back and forth of hiddenness and openness – and this is what Augustine is saying throughout – mankind, or the particular catechumen, recognizes himself. Hearing these stories, he is thrown back on himself: finding himself loved by him whom he fears, his fear turns to love;[31] confronted with the sublime lowliness of the God-man, his conceit turns to humility.[32] In short, he comes to understand the significance of history, and this significance is his own capacity for the divine, whether this be called wisdom, faith, the *cultus Dei* or *charitas.* The story of the God-man, being a story of an act of love and of the humility which brings love by stooping to the loved one, elicits the *experience* of love and humility from the objective fact of love; elicits the eternity of emotion towards God from the history of this emotion. Thus, through story, Christ 'acquires [us] from time'.[33] Redemption is, in this

---

[30] Ibid. 22, pp. 96–8.

[31] Ibid. 5, p. 30: 'De ipsa enim seueritate Dei, qua corda mortalium saluberrimo terrore quatiuntur, caritas aedificanda est, ut ab eo quem timet, amari se gaudens, eum redamare audeat eiusque in se dilectioni, etiamsi impune posset, tamen displicere uereatur.'

[32] Ibid. 4, p. 30: 'Quia ergo caritati nihil aduersius quam inuidentia, mater autem inuidentiae superbia est: idem dominus Iesu Christus, deus homo, et diuinae in nos dilectionis indicium est et humanae apud nos humilitatis exemplum, ut magnus tumor noster maiore contraria medicina sanaretur. Magna est enim miseria, superbus homo, sed maior misericordia, humilis deus.'

[33] *Sermo* 363.3, col. 1638. Symbol, as we have seen from Ambrose, has this same power to make a bridge between the learnt fact and the felt experience, because like story it has its own integrity – it stands on its own – and yet invites the participation of the listener whom it touches by its familiarity. In contemplating the story or symbol, the soul becomes the sense of what it contemplates. Thus Augustine on the role of likeness (*similitudo*) in sacrament (*ep.* 55.11, col. 214): 'Ad ipsum autem ignem amoris nutriendum et flatandum quodammodo, quo tanquam pondere sursum uel introrsum

sense, a matter of learning a story intimately; and education, which begins with the recital of a story, leads ultimately to deification.

None of this could happen however – the soul could not be awakened to itself, the catechumen could not be taught to recognize himself in the mirror of the past – if man were not already in some way implicit in the story, so that as he learns he is also 'being remembered'. Karl Adam saw Augustine's own conversion as a struggle between his conscious opposition to Christianity and the memory of his mother's religion 'rooted in his subconsciousness'.[34] When he encourages Deogratias in the difficult task of catechizing, Augustine treats the Old and the New Testament and the passage from one to the other rather as though they were a subconscious memory to be raised to the surface of the mind. Freud held dreams to be a form of remembering, and he argued that the unhealthy mind can be healed if it lifts these dreams out of the unconscious and comes to terms with their meanings. Augustine's education of the Christian soul is a psychoanalysis in which the dream content is made up from the Bible; the catechumen is healed insofar as he understands himself as the product of the *sense* of the Biblical past. Like Freud's patient, his responsibility to himself is also his submission to something greater than himself, to the principle at work in his own formation; he must 'receive the significance in holiness', as Augustine put it to Januarius.

SACRAMENT AS LANGUAGE

This 'receiving of significance' only comes after the process of learning: the mind has to be built up in readiness. The treatise *On Catechizing* shows how this might be done by the catechist for the catechumen; and the second letter to Januarius, after speaking of the 'strong' memory of the Easter *commemoratio*, goes on to

referamur ad requiem, ista omnia pertinent quae nobis figurate insinuantur; plus enim mouent et accedunt amorem, quam si nuda sine ullis sacramentorum similitudinibus ponerentur. Cuius rei causam difficile est dicere. Sed tamen ita se habet, ut aliquid per allegoricam significationem intimatum plus moueat, plus delectet, plus honoretur, quam si uerbis propriis diceretur apertissime.' The whole question of symbol and story, vital to the understanding of the Middle Ages, has been made critical in the writings of Bultmann on the Bible as myth and on the need to 'demythologize': see Bultmann 1972.

[34] Adam 1932, pp. 14ff.

describe how this is based on the weaker recollections of 'congru-ence':[35] it is suitable, for example, that Easter, the season of 'newness of life' (*innouatio uitae nostrae*), should be celebrated in the first month of the year; or that the three great epochs of history, the time 'before the Law', the time 'under the Law' and the time of Grace, should correspond to the three days of the death, burial and resurrection of Christ, and thus to the three days of Easter. But a distinction is to be made between the mere 'usefulness' of such likenesses, with their ability to invigorate and uplift, and the austere simplicity of sacrament.[36] Likenesses of one kind or another, designed to draw the mind to a better under-standing, can be taken in great numbers from all sorts of natural phenomena: 'from the winds, the sea, the land, from birds, fish, sheep, trees or men'. Sacrament, on the other hand, can be made only from a few things: water, corn, oil and wine.[37] No harm will come of the multitude of likenesses, however, unless it is held to be a system and a method for divining the future. If this happens – and Augustine believed it had happened both among the Jews and in Greek and Roman paganism – the religious mind is duped, persuaded to fritter away its energies on fatalism. In its efforts to foresee the outcome of actions, and thus to find safe harbour in the storms of human life, it is 'dashed against the rocks of a wretched servitude, shipwrecked of its free will'.[38] These lesser likenesses are all very well, as long as they are seen to point to something beyond themselves; but as soon as they become a refuge to those who cannot bear the strain of faith and hope – the strain incurred by free will – they act only to frustrate the possibility of reform. The movements of the stars, the ebb and flow of the sea, the whole flux of nature, can be no more than the

---

[35] *Ep.* 55.8, col. 211: 'figurae congruentia'.   [36] Ibid. 3, cols. 206–7.

[37] Ibid. 7, col. 210.

[38] Ibid.; for a similar argument, directed particularly against Porphyry's inconsistency in taking up the pagan gods despite his philosophical monotheism, *De ciu. Dei* 10.26ff, pp. 300ff. In the letter to Januarius (*ep.* 55) the emphasis of the argument is on worship directed towards the one source of freedom, and is therefore in the first place (at this point anyway) about freedom of the will in sacrament; in the *City of God* the emphasis is on worship towards the single source of happiness or beatitude: if the angels and demons countenanced by Porphyry and other Neoplatonists are concerned for man's happiness, then they will understand and expect that man should address himself to the source of this happiness, and not to themselves. The demons and angels may be imitated, but not invoked. Augustine classes the various acts of pagan magic and divination as theurgy: for an interesting account of how Denis the Areopagite turns this term to his own purposes, associating it with a sacramental deification which has at least some points in common with Augustine's own notion of *cultus Dei*, see Louth 1986.

source of eloquence *about* the divine.[39] They are the means of 'insinuating' the truth, and not the truth itself: if the sun is in the so-called sign of Aries at the time of Easter, well and good, but the significance of Easter does not depend on this coincidence, nor on any other.[40] In all this, Augustine distances himself from the Stoic and the Manichee and from the tendency to fatalism and demonology in late Roman religion generally – it can be seen in the various documents of the *Corpus Hermeticum* as well as in the practices of the Mystery religions – but equally from those Christian authors, Firmicus Maternus and Tertullian among them, who, in their very opposition to paganism, absorbed at least some of its habit of finding God in nature.

The distinction between pagan and Christian cult is clear in Augustine's mind: the pagan mistakes God for his creation, and falls into fatalistic polytheism. The distinction within Christian symbol is less straightforward: the likeness of mere allegory, says Augustine, is to be subjugated to the fulness of sacrament; 'congruence' to true significance. But if we scrutinize some of the passages of the second letter to Januarius, we find soon enough that the education of the mind *towards* sacrament merges with surprising facility into sacrament itself. The cross, for example, carries a number of meanings:[41] the cross-bar, where the hands are fixed, conveys the joy (*hilaritas*) which comes of working for rest. This is explained by a pun: the hands mean work; and as narrowness is despair – here Augustine plays on the two senses of *angustia*: physical narrowness and moral distress – so the breadth of the transverse is the labourer's joy. The elevation of the head is the expectation of judgement. The upright of the cross occasions another pun: its length is the patience of the long-suffering (*longanimes*). The depth to which it is sunk into the ground is the *secretum sacramenti*. But what begins as word-play quickly turns to the earnestness of the *cultus Dei*, for the knowledge of the cross in its physical dimensions is suddenly more than it seemed: what at first was nothing more than an allegory pointing to the labourer's joy and expectation and patience becomes *by the very attention*

---

[39] *Ep.* 55.7, col. 211: 'Si quae autem figurae similitudinum non tantum de coelo et de sideribus, sed etiam de inferiori creatura ducuntur ad dispensationem sacramentorum, eloquentia quaedam est doctrina salutaris, mouendo affectui discentium accommodata, a uisibilibus ad inuisibilia, a corporalibus ad spiritualia, a temporalibus ad aeterna.'

[40] Ibid. 8, col. 211.

[41] Ibid. 14, cols. 215–16.

given to it, the joy itself and the expectation and the patience.[42] Standing before the picture of the crucifixion in his mind's eye, and remembering to himself not only this but the 'clarity' of the resurrection which follows it, the Christian or the catechumen finds that he understands the sense of this *triduum* of transition insofar as he has faith in the sense and is able to hope for it; in other words, insofar as he is moved towards it, and is able 'to be dissolved' into it (cf. Phil. 1:23).[43] Understanding is not finally cognitive or aesthetic: it is existential. How else, Augustine asks, are we to grasp Paul's notion of baptism as death and burial with Christ? The difficulty of taking in such an image is precisely the difficulty of the human predicament. It requires the same resources of the will to confront the meaning of baptism, the eucharist or Biblical history as to sustain the tension of a life lived between Two Cities.

The metaphor of the Two Cities is the epitome of Augustine's mature philosophy. Mankind in its ambivalence is caught between its own weakness, the result of being 'born in Adam', and its possible strength. Salvation is not in any resolution of this tension, but in a continuous movement between its two poles. Faith, hope and love are the 'virtues' which allow this movement, at least in its positive direction, to take place: together, these qualities are gathered under the name of wisdom. The movement

---

[42] Ibid., col. 216: this ethical interpretation of an image is accomplished by way of Ephes. 3:17–18: 'May Christ find a dwelling-place, through faith, in your hearts; may your lives be rooted in love, founded on love. May you and all the saints be enabled to measure, in all its breadth and length and height and depth, the love of Christ.'

[43] *Ep.* 55.14, col. 216: 'Ea uero quae nondum uidemus, et nondum tenemus, sed fide et spe gerimus, in alio biduo figurata sunt. Haec enim quae nunc agimus, tanquam clauis praeceptorum in Dei timore confixi ... Quod ergo inquit, "dissolui, et esse cum Christo" [Ephes. 3:17–18], inde incipit requies, quae non interrumpitur resurrectione, sed clarificatur; quae tamen nunc fide retinetur, "quia iustus ex fide uiuit" [Hab. 2.4]. "An ignoratis", inquit, "quoniam quicumque baptizati sumus in Christo Iesu, in morte ipsius baptizati sumus? Consepulti ergo illi sumus per baptismum in mortem" [Rom. 6:3–4]. Unde, nisi fide?' The whole passage is highly characteristic of Augustine's approach: it shows how he tends to begin from the intuition of revealed, Biblical symbol, in this case the *triduum* of crucifixion, burial, resurrection, goes on to expound it and then returns to it, reminding us how close exegesis is to liturgy – itself a reflection on Biblical imagery, but a reflection performed; it shows how this liturgical or exegetical reflection, by an act of interpretation, intensifies into a single moment the antithetical 'farness' and 'nearness' of the Biblical past; it shows the strength of emotion in the act of interpretation; and it shows how Augustine, far from putting all the emphasis on the first day of the *triduum*, with its sombre note, regards the events of all three days as a whole, death, burial and resurrection implicit in one another. On this, and on the figure of the cross in literature and art, Ladner 1983, pp. 197–208; Schiller 1972, pp. 88–164.

which occurs in sacrament is the same movement, and follows the same circular path: it begins in God and ends in him. We can see the circularity in Augustine's allegory of the cross: into the simplicity of sacrament – water, corn, oil and wine – flows all the diversity of lesser likenesses. At first these lesser likenesses seem arbitrary, perhaps a little ridiculous. But assumed into sacrament, they have a new complexion: it is as if they were 'meant' all along, like the apparently arbitrary asides in a play which fall into place at the dénouement. The circularity of sacrament, however, is more prominent than in theatre, and stronger. By themselves, the simple elements of bread, wine, water and oil *could* mean so many things that their bare presence sets the process of understanding in motion. There is something important here for the whole nature of worship, a problem closely related to the 'frankness' of Ambrose's sacrament.[44] The elemental, humble, quality of sacrament is like a myth: it suggests possibilities, invites interpretation. Able to stand on its own – in the sense that it is *res divina*[45] – it nonetheless demands involvement. This is again the difference which marks off Christian cult from pagan: the pagan in his worship is bound by the rules dictating human and divine action, by which he hopes to predict and with luck determine the future. As Augustine complains against him, he even tries to bind his own gods, thus belittling their power in the very act of worship. The Christian rejects this false science of theurgy, and regards everything in heaven and earth as meaningful only in its relation to the all-powerful God beyond them. His salvation is in right understanding.[46]

The circularity of likeness and sacrament, reminiscent of the circularity of memory, is expressed in the four books *On Christian Education* (the first two books of which were written in 396–7, the last two completed by 427)[47] as a philosophy of signs. And what is stated hesitantly in the second letter to Januarius is here developed more fully.

The purpose of the book is to show how education is a matter of learning to read the Scriptures in the right way. Addressing the

---

[44] See above, pp. 69ff; and for a fascinating treatment of the 'frank-speech' (*parrhesia*) of medieval saints, a phenomenon perhaps not unrelated to the frankness and simplicity of sacrament, see Murray 1978, pp. 393ff.

[45] *De ciu. Dei* 10.6, p. 278.

[46] Ibid. 10, *passim*.

[47] See the remarks on date in Joseph Martin's preface: *De doctrina christiana*, 'praefatio', pp. vii–xix.

Christian rather than the catechumen, it goes into problems of interpretation at greater length than the letter *On Catechizing*, but the principles are the same in both books. All instruction, says Augustine at the opening of his treatise on education, has to do with signs or things (*signa, res*).[48] Signs, although they are things in themselves, are also signs of things other than themselves: so wood is a thing, but the wood which Moses cast into the bitter waters is a sign. All signs are things, but not all things are signs. The only thing which is truly a thing in this full sense of not being a sign of anything else is God, who is unchanging and has reference only to himself. At the very outset, then, Augustine has described the convergence of the intellect, in its appraisal of all the things in the world, on the one true thing which is God: those who think of God in a sensual way, as dazzling light, for example, or even those who see many gods all equal to one another, are striving for the true apprehension of God, who is the being than whom no superior being exists.[49] The approach to God, however, is not just a matter of intellect, of seeing correctly the relation of sign to thing; it also involves the moral question of happiness. For some things are to be used (*uti*), some to be enjoyed (*frui*):[50] to use something is to use it in order to have something else which is worth having for itself; and to enjoy a thing 'is to rest with satisfaction in it for its own sake'.[51] The man who attempts to enjoy what should be used is acting toward the sign as though it were a thing: on the way to his father's home, he is distracted by the beauty of the scenery and forgets his destination.[52] God is the one proper object of enjoyment; and the path leading to the 'native land' of enjoyment, the attitude which makes it possible to use the things of the world in the interests of enjoyment, is purity of the soul.[53] The moral impact of this is clear enough when Augustine says that to follow only the letter of Scripture, to fail to raise one's eyes 'to drink in the eternal light', is to subject understanding to the flesh, and thus to bring death to the soul.[54]

---

[48] For what follows, *De doctrina christiana* 1.2ff, pp. 7ff.

[49] Ibid. 1.7, p. 10: 'Omnes tamen certatim pro excellentia dei dimicant nec quisquam inueniri potest, qui hoc deum credat esse, quo est aliquid melius.' An anticipation of Anselm's definition of God in the *Proslogion*.

[50] *De doctrina christiana* 1.3–5, pp. 8–9.

[51] Ibid. 1.4, p. 8.   [52] Ibid.   [53] Ibid. 1.10, p. 12.

[54] Ibid. 3.5, p. 83: 'Neque ulla mors animae congruentius appellatur, quam cum id etiam, quod in ea bestiis antecellit, intellegentia carni subicitur sequendo litteram.'

Reading is a moral act. To suppose, as the Jews did, that the temple was merely a sacred building and not a sign of the eucharist, or that Israel was a nation and not a presentiment of the universal church, was to fail God.[55]

The art of reading is a gift, however. To be able to 'raise the eyes upward' from sign to thing is to allow the soul to be taken up into the motion towards the enjoyment of God. This is the movement of love.[56] To be moved in this way is only made possible by the descent of Wisdom into the flesh of humanity, an event which causes 'a change in the affections' of man by his assimilation to it.[57] In the God-man, the movement of love has come to fruition, and the thing, instead of being separated from the sign, lives within it, is reconciled with it. To put this slightly differently: signs mean more than they say. Insofar as their meaning is understood, they become bound up with their meaning, associated with it, even indistinguishable from it. But understanding depends on love, and love is a gift. More exactly, it is the gift of Incarnation, the supreme *exemplum* of love.

Understanding, then, or reading, or the perception of sacrament, is a re-enactment of Incarnation. We can only speak of God because words are signs of things other than themselves, just as

---

[55] Ibid. 3.6, pp. 83–4. History thus becomes sign, and in becoming sign, is at once suppressed (made relative to an ultimate sense) and kept on (affirmed in its concreteness, in the specificity of event); in this vein, compare the use made by Augustine of Tychonius' fourth rule for the interpretation of Scripture, the distinction between *species* and *genus*: ibid. 3.34, pp. 106–10, where, with a tendentiousness which now seems astonishing, he explains how the recriminations against Israel in Ezech. 36:17–29 were said of the carnal, historical Israel, while the blessing of Israel in the same passage was a prophecy of the New Testament. This typological notion of a history which transcends itself is the basis of the liturgical *anamnesis* (see below, pp. 167–73). Typological exegesis is also one of Augustine's chief weapons against the Manichaeans, for it preserves the Old Testament – which since Marcion had been one of the main objects of attack of the Gnostic dualists – without succumbing to it.

[56] Ibid. 3.10, p. 87: 'Non autem praecipit scriptura nisi caritatem nec culpat nisi cupiditatem.' And: 'Caritatem uoco motum animi ad fruendum deo propter ipsum et se atque proximo propter deum; cupiditatem autem motum animi ad fruendum se et proximo et quolibet corpore non propter deum.' This movement is a movement towards the truth which begins in the truth, towards *res* which begins in *res* (ibid. 1.3ff, pp. 19ff); it is a movement founded on prayer, so that the Christian teacher must retire to drink in the word and only then will he be ready 'to belch out what he has drunk'; and thus a movement founded on inspiration (ibid. 4.15, pp. 138–9). Eloquence comes not from the study of the Ciceronian canon, although this may be of use, but follows naturally from wisdom (ibid. 4.6, pp. 121–3; cf. *De lib. arb.* 1.11.4.10, p. 213: 'Aderit enim deus et nos intelligere quod credidimus faciet', the same principle applied more widely; and Marrou 1938, pp. 505ff, on eloquence in Augustine).

[57] *De doctrina christiana* 1.11–17, pp. 12–15.

Christ as man is a 'sign' of God.[58] But in using language, the mind suffers constant frustration in its attempt to represent its conceptions by the signs of words. Speech makes the quick intuitions of the mind seem all of a sudden grey and dull. Deogratias writes to Augustine almost in despair. In his effort to express the truth of Christianity to the catechumens assembled before him, he finds himself not only unable to do it, but repelled from the whole exercise by a kind of *ennui*, a *taedium animi*. Rather than drain himself in 'vile and abject' words, he longs to take refuge in the silence of his own understanding. The terrible gap between the mere 'noise' of speech and the sense it is supposed to put across has thrown Deogratias into melancholy.[59] But in this gap, Augustine replies to him in his long letter *On Catechizing* (c. 399), is the secret of the truth: from across the gap, love urges us forward, to turn boredom into delight, noise into understanding. And to cross the gap is to be assimilated to Incarnation: 'For however much the articulations of the voice differ from the quickness of our understanding, the mortality of flesh will always differ far more from equality with God.'[60] Just as God abased himself in Christ, making himself weak to the weak, so as to gain the weak for himself, so the teacher must stoop to his pupils, feeding their feeble understanding and taking joy from their growth. As Christ-the-teacher was like a nurse (*nutrix*) cherishing her children, murmuring to them the broken words of love, so must the catechist be; and with Christ he must be the mother-hen, her wings drooping over her brood, defending and nourishing her chicks. For love, like the mother, only eats when it has given its children to eat: and so the teacher should not rest contented with his own knowledge.[61]

---

[58] See ibid. 1.6ff, pp. 9ff.

[59] *De cat. rud.* 10.14, pp. 44–6: 'Hoc autem scio, non tam rerum quae dicendae sunt, quibus te satis noui paratum et instructum, neque ipsius locutionis inopia, sed animi taedio fieri; uel illa causa quam dixi, quia magis nos delectat et tenet, quod in silentio mente cernimus, nec inde uolumus auocari ad uerborum longe disparem strepitum.' For the date of Augustine's reply, see Van der Lof 1962.

[60] Ibid. 10.15, p. 48: 'Si ... curam gerimus quemadmodum longis et perplexis amfractibus procedat ex ore carnis, quod celerrimo haustu mentis imbibitur, et quia multum dissimiliter exit, taedet loqui, et libet tacere, cogitemus quid nobis praerogatum sit ab illo qui demonstrauit nobis exemplum, ut sequamur uestigia eius. Quantumuis enim differat articulata uox nostra ab intelligentiae nostrae uiuacitate, longe differentior est mortalitas carnis ab aequalitate dei.'

[61] Ibid., pp. 48–50. For the notion of Christ as teacher, *De doctrina christiana* 3.6, pp. 83–4. The image of the mother-hen with her brood suggests the pelican of the *Physiologus*, who is consumed with love for her young; the young, however, peck at the parents'

When one person speaks to another, or when the teacher speaks to his pupil, he does not simply make a statement of what he holds to be true, to be acknowledged by his hearer and taken away. He has something in mind, expresses it, inadequately, in words, and thus *invites* his hearer to understand what he means. His speech will be effective not as a map of truth, but as an *address* to the particular listener. Language is *ad hominem*. It works by stirring his affections (*affectus animi*) to a discovery of the original meaning, to pass from sign to thing, from mere sound to sense.[62] Augustine is keenly aware of the immediacy of speech: discourse, he remarks to Deogratias, 'bears a facial expression'.[63] It discloses the mood of the speaker. It changes according to whether it is spoken to

a cultivated man or a dullard, a fellow-citizen or a stranger, a rich man or a poor man, a private citizen or a public figure, a man with some official authority, a person of this or that family, of this or that age or sex, from this or that school of philosophy, or from this or that popular error . . . In keeping with my own varying feelings my discourse opens, proceeds, comes to an end.[64]

Meaning in language therefore depends as much on its ability to join souls together in sympathy as on the content of what is said: 'For the capacity of the soul for sympathy is so great that when people are affected by us as we speak, and we by them as they learn, we live in one another; and thus both they, as it were, speak in us what they hear, while we, after a fashion, learn in them what we teach.'[65] Words achieve their end by virtue of the love which carries them: according to the brotherliness, fatherliness, motherliness with which they are said.

Language, then, involves much more than getting the right sign for the right thing. For it works by a *sympathy* between speaker and listener; this is what Augustine calls the *affectus animi compatientis*, 'the power of the compassionate soul'. And the sym-

---

faces, and the parents peck back, killing them; after three days' mourning, the mother makes a gash in her side (likened in the Christian commentary on the text to the wound in Christ's side) and the blood drips on to the dead chicks, reviving them: *Physiologus* 6, p. 17 (i.e. the Latin *Versio B* of the fourth century). The vital point made by Augustine, however, is that this assent is the assent of *charitas*, and therefore ethical in its implications: language for Augustine is above all a vehicle to Wisdom, and thus a performance of Wisdom, rather than an end in itself.

[62] *De cat. rud.* 2.3, p. 18.   [63] Ibid. 15.23, p. 66.
[64] Ibid., pp. 66–8.   [65] Ibid. 12.17, p. 54.

pathy which binds men is no different in kind – only in object – from the sympathy binding man with God. The ultimate language is therefore the language of Incarnation, by which God speaks to man; and the ultimate act of understanding is understanding that the self has its origin in the God-man. In the letter *On Catechizing* and in the book *On Christian Education*, we see the process by which speech between man and man *becomes* speech between man and God.[66] We see how the soul is educated to 'suffer with', and thus identify with, the death and resurrection of Christ. The moment of this identity, a moment of ritual deification from which proceeds the long duration of the ethical life, is the moment celebrated and repeated in sacrament. And in both these treatises of Augustine, we see how sympathy is awakened first by the telling of the story which has its epitome in Incarnation, and then – or rather at the same time – by the way the story is told: by the teacher's 'address' to his pupils. The 'absolute remembering' with which the soul lives the passage of Old Testament into New as though it were autobiography, goes hand in hand with the words of the story-teller.

In the *City of God*, Augustine states baldly the movement of sympathy in sacrament: the cult of God, he says, is the cult offered to the one true God who 'makes his worshippers into gods'.[67] The very imagery of *cultus*, with its connotations of tilling the earth, has about it the ambiguousness of sacrament.[68] The earth shapes the tiller, nourishes him, embraces him and makes him grow; and in the *poiēsis*, the 'making' of the liturgy, the worshipper is himself created anew, made into a god. This creative embrace, a making which is also a being made, is the essence of medieval liturgy, with its constant petition for the gift it is unworthy even to ask. It is the essence also of the great image-themes in liturgy: rebirth, death and resurrection, sacrifice. In all of them, the phenomena of life – natural birth, death, corruption and rejuvenation in Nature, adversity, pain, offering, self-sacrifice – are shown to mean more than themselves, to be given as well as taken. We can sense the same 'meeting of creativities' in the cult of the saints, where the character and powers of a particular saint are

[66] See also *Confessions* 10.2, p. 155.
[67] *De ciu. Dei* 10.1, p. 273: 'Hanc ei tantum Deo deberi dicimus, qui uerus est Deus facitque suos cultores deos.' On Augustine's notion of deification, through sacrament and otherwise, Bonner 1986.
[68] Cf. *De ciu. Dei* 10.1, p. 272.

fashioned by a community's needs, but then turn back to shape the community. In the liturgy, it is perhaps at its strongest in the great 'making' of the Roman baptismal *anamnesis*, which by telling the 'story' of water in the Bible, builds up the myth of a re-creating, re-forming substance, so that by the end of the recitation, the speaker finds himself succumbing to it, absorbed into it.

Liturgical language concentrates the 'compassion' awakened by normal speech. It is a quickening of ordinary language. As men 'live in one another' when they talk, each straining into the other's mind to catch the 'thrust of thought' (*ictus intelligentiae*)[69] behind his words, so in liturgy and prayer, they approach the divine through dialogue. In the dialogue, sign and thing echo back and forth with the effort of understanding:

> Ignis creator igneus
> Lumen donator luminis
> Vitaque uitae conditor
> Dator salutis et salus.[70]

This is the first stanza of a hymn for the nocturnal blessing of the candle copied into the late seventh-century *Antiphonary of Bangor*:

> Fire's fiery creator,
> Light-giving light,
> Life and source of life,
> Giver of salvation and salvation.

Not only the words, but the natural elements too, fire, light and later in the hymn the night-darkness and the wax of the candle, make up the language of this dialogue. In the solemnity of the hymn, the vague quotidian consciousness that in Nature might be a presentiment (rather than a dwelling-place) of the divine is given explicit and direct statement. The fire and the light are of a sudden overwhelmingly more than themselves. The night is the night of

[69] *De cat. rud.* 2.3, p. 18.
[70] *Antiphonary of Bangor*, p. 11. The manuscript is Irish but this hymn, with some others in the collection, is thought to have a continental origin: see Stevenson 1987, p. lxxxvi. The imagery of the bee and the wax in the sixth, seventh and eighth stanzas, and even some of the words used, are borrowed from the fourth *Georgic* of Virgil, but carry a Biblical-liturgical sense. The effect of the whole is an appearance of simplicity, but open to complex interpretation, as in sacrament itself.

the Israelites in their migration, lit by a column of fire, a night of rejoicing (*noctis gaudia*) despite its darkness, a migration from death to life.[71] Present here are Augustine's two themes of 'remembering' and of the *charitas* which works within language. The monks of Bangor (whether or not they composed this hymn) recall in their vigil the Israelites' crossing of the desert, and in doing so remember it as their own crossing; and through the words, the imagery, the fire and the light and dark, they are brought to the effort of understanding, to the love which resolves sign and thing.[72] This power of language, and especially of liturgical language, to 'make' those who speak it, to invigorate the natural motion of the soul, is more than a philosopher's idea. It is one of the fundamental reasons why sacrament *works*, throughout the Middle Ages and no doubt beyond them too.

GOOD AND EVIL: THE PROBLEM OF ORIGINAL SIN

Looking back at Augustine from the vantage-point of the Middle Ages, it is easy to suppose that he was more than anything a spinner of doctrines. He made clear statements about predestination, original sin, the power of evil, the Trinity, the status of heretical sacrament, which then passed into the medieval world view. It is important to understand, however, that this is only a part of the truth, perhaps even a small part. Augustine was not 'dogmatic'. His great talent lay not in the statement of Christian teaching, but in the expression of the grounds of this teaching, and the grounds of Christianity he drew from his own life. In his hands, the apparently dry husk of dogma is made into experience: or rather it is shown to be the fruit of experience. It is treated almost as a kind of shorthand used to describe concentratedly the breadth of existence. This does not make it any the less true: the Incarnation is not just a sign of the condition of man, but its sum. And Augustine always offers the opportunity of seeing the Incarnation not as something to be learnt but as something done. The bent of his mind, particularly in later years, was towards the

[71] *Antiphonary of Bangor*, p. 11 (2nd stanza):

> Ne noctis hujus gaudia
> Vigil lucerna deserat,
> Qui hominem non uis mori
> Da nostro lumen pectori.

[72] Ibid., 3rd stanza.

ethical, the psychological, the aesthetic, the confessional. In the *Confessions* themselves, especially in the eighth book, are some of his most earnest attempts to find those points of tension, 'fault-lines', where the divine and human wills meet. What else is the incident in the garden, when Augustine hears a child's voice saying the words 'Take up and read', but a meeting of this kind?[73]

Sacrament is also meeting: meeting between sign and thing, mother and child; sound and sense; it is God's reaching down into man and man's effort to fulfil his creation 'towards the image of God'.[74] We have seen how this meeting comes about through an act of faith, hope and love: how the virtues demanded by sacrament are not confined to sacrament but are the virtues of the ethical life. There is no real distinction, says Augustine in the tenth book of the *City of God*, between the 'cult of God' by sacraments, and the cult performed 'within ourselves'.[75] God – he goes on in the spirit of the letter to the Hebrews – 'does not want the sacrifice of butchered animals, but the sacrifice of a contrite heart'.[76] The ethical offering, which is at bottom a self-offering, is therefore indistinguishable from the offering made in cult: it cannot be said that what goes on in the rite is the sign of the moral life lived outside it; but rather, the rite is itself an authentic act. A symbol, for Augustine, as for Ambrose, is not there to be scrutinized for its meaning; it is there to be performed. And the rite is not a theatre of ideas, demanding the allegiance of the mind, as it sometimes tended to become under the pressure of the juridical temper of the twelfth century. It is not an ideology in this way, but a free exercise of the will, or better, a meeting of the will with its origin.[77] Augustine's notion of *cultus*, ritual performance, as moral action, is interesting not just as an idea of its time, but as an observation – and a brilliant defence – of one of the ways in which ritual works. In this sense, it is curiously reminiscent of the approach of some anthropologists. Above all, it recalls what

---

[73] *Confessions* 8.29, p. 131.

[74] On Augustine's notion of man created *ad imaginem dei*, and on the related concepts of *similitudo* and the *regio dissimilitudinis*, Ladner 1959; Markus 1964.

[75] Thus 'we are all the temple and each one of us is a temple', and the heart is an altar: *De ciu. Dei* 10.3, p. 275.

[76] Ibid. 10.5, p. 277.

[77] Ibid. 10.3, p. 275: 'Ipse fons nostrae beatitudinis, ipse omnis appetitionis est finis ... Bonum enim nostrum, de cuius fine inter philosophos magna contentio est, nullum est aliud quam illi cohaerere, cuius unius anima intellectualis incorporeo, si dici potest, amplexu ueris impletur fecundaturque uirtutibus.'

Clifford Geertz says about rituals – the cock-fight in Bali for example – as a heightened performance and display of social values, a potent mixture of tradition and interpretation.[78]

Already we have seen the moral implications of remembering and language. In the *City of God*, talking of sacrament in general and the sacrifice of the eucharist in particular, Augustine deals with this moral aspect on its own ground. Sacrifice, he explains, is identity with Christ, or 'coherence with him', as he puts it, by the offering of the moral self which is at the same time the condition of belonging to the body of which Christ is the head, the *societas Christiana*.[79] The centre of this complex of ideas is the sacrifice of self, called by Augustine 'compassion', *misericordia*, in order to distinguish it from the holocausts and the butchered offerings of the old law.[80] The sacrifice of compassion is directed inward, *in seipsum*, and outward to others, *in proximos*. It is an offering of the body 'as a living victim' (cf. Rom. 12:1ff), in other words 'temperance' in the use of the body; and a 'remaking' (*reformatio*) of the soul (cf. Rom. 12:2). Both inward and outward offerings, and the offering of both body and soul, are only true sacrifices when they 'refer' to God, and so the entire exercise can be resumed in the two commandments which are at once the hidden truth in the Old Testament and the revealed truth in the New: love God and love thy neighbour (cf. Matt. 22:37–40).[81]

[78] Geertz 1973, pp. 412–53.   [79] *De ciu. Dei* 10.6, p. 279.

[80] For this and what follows, ibid., pp. 278–9. The sacrifice of the Old Law is the 'sign' of the sacrifice of the New, and so it can be said that 'In that sacrifice which he said God does not want is signified the sacrifice which, he added, God does want.' The power of sacrament to make visible what is not visible is therefore a question of its ethical content: the tension between the seen and the unseen in water or bread or wine is the product of, as well as the cause of, the moral tension of the peregrination towards God. This is what lies behind his remark that 'Sacrificium ergo uisibile inuisibilis sacrificii sacramentum, id est sacrum signum est' (*De ciu. Dei* 10.5, p. 277). Augustine deals with miracle in similar terms, as a making manifest of what is hidden, and at the same time as an incitement of the soul towards its origin; but, as for Walt Whitman, there is nothing in the world which is not a miracle, all of it stemming from the one great miracle of creation. Again, though, God is not in the known quantities of Nature, but in its unknown origins: 'Deus, qui fecit uisibilia caelum et terram, non dedignatur facere uisibilia miracula in caelo uel terra, quibus ad se inuisibilem colendum excitet animam adhuc uisibilibus deditam' (*De ciu. Dei* 10.12, p. 287). The development in the Middle Ages of the idea of sacrament and miracle as forces independent of the soul's movements is a thing of great historical significance. It is important, for example, that Augustine was not concerned with the question of real presence, and although it makes an interesting exercise, it misses the point of his thinking to ask whether or not he believed in the real presence in sacrament: see Van der Lof 1964.

[81] *De ciu. Dei* 10.5, p. 278.

Christ is a joining together of God and man; sacrament is a performance of this joining, an 'absolute' memory of it enabling man to 'cross over' to God; and thus the symbol in sacrament bears out its original meaning of a 'throwing together', a *symbolon*. But the sacrifice of self by which the offerer is thrown together with God is also his membership of the Christian society: 'The true sacrifice is thus any work which acts to bind us with God in a holy society, done towards that final good from which we have the possibility of being truly blessed.'[82] However much it is *done* by men, it is *res diuina*, an act of God; in the end, it is even the sacrifice *of* man, for it is nothing other than man's consecration in the name of God, by which he dies to the world so as to live for God. Echoing the baptismal theme of death and burial in Christ in Romans 6:3ff, Augustine is here talking as much of baptism as of the eucharist: both are equally 'true sacrifices' of the self.

These threads of sacrifice are drawn together in the image of the body of Christ: the *misericordia*, or self-offering, the throwing together of man and God, the membership of the 'redeemed city', are all the act of a *single body*. In the act of sacrifice, the moral offering of self is *the same as* the offering made by the Christian society of itself, and both are *the same as* Christ's self-offering: for in offering himself, Christ is offering his body which is at once the assembly of Christian society and the self. At the Last Supper, Christ 'carried his own body'; he was both priest and sacrifice.[83] The individual in his *misericordia*, and the assembly in the rite, imitate this act, imitate the identity of priest and sacrifice, so as to become part of it. Becoming part of it they join themselves to Christ not only as victim, but as priest, and so, in worshipping God, 'they are made gods'. In this way, Augustine's notion of justification as an act of mediation is transferred, in all its efficacy, to the *cultus*. The man of faith, by the association of his humanity with the humanity of Christ, is taken up into Christ's divinity; or, in the language of the *cultus*, being made the sacrifice offered by

---

[82] Ibid. 10.6, p. 278.
[83] Ibid., p. 279: 'profecto efficitur, ut tota ipsa redempta ciuitas, hoc est congregatio societasque sanctorum, uniuersale sacrificium offeratur Deo per sacerdotem magnum, qui etiam se ipsum obtulit in passione pro nobis, ut tanti capitis corpus essemus, secundum formam serui. Hanc enim obtulit, in hac oblatus est, quia secundum hanc mediator est, in hac sacerdos, in hac sacrificium est.' For this idea of Christ 'carrying himself in his own hands', *Enarr. in ps. xxxiii, sermo* 1.10, pp. 280–1; and see Van der Lof 1964, pp. 295ff. It is a theme taken up in the early twelfth century by Gilbert Crispin in his *De altaris sacramento* 25, p. 128.

Christ, he becomes Christ-the-priest. Here is the last word, bringing to fruition all the education to remembrance and understanding which went before it. In this sacrament of personal and corporate deification, in this bringing together of bodily acts into one bodily act which is infinitely more than itself, the 'moment' of meeting, the *punctum temporis* of the *Confessions*, is taken out of the confessional and put into the ritual. In the unity of the moment, or of the body, or of the bread, wine, oil and water of sacrament, the human meets the divine as though in a vortex.

Yet this whole view of sacrament as meeting and dialogue, stated so vehemently in the *City of God* and examined so subtly in the letter *On Catechizing*, apparently fades to nothing before Augustine's teaching – developed from *c.* 406 onward – that mankind, and thus the child at birth, inherits the sin of Adam.[84] In this perspective, baptism is suddenly exorcism again: it has the exact and negative function of removing the adverse judgement incurred by 'birth in Adam'. The rite loses all its ethical colour: instead of something done by the candidate, it becomes something done to him. This is doubly true, moreover, because not only is the subject of the rite unable to free himself from a condition he did not make for himself, but he is often, in practice, an infant or child incapable of willing for himself, or of understanding the rite at all. For Augustine's espousal of original sin led him, and the church with him, to support what had in any case long been customary and common, the baptism of infants.[85] The combined effect of original sin and infant baptism thus appears to make the

---

[84] On the development of Augustine's view of original sin, see the clear and subtle account in TeSelle 1970, pp. 144ff, 258ff, 278ff. Also, Beatrice 1978. Both authors argue that the doctrine of original sin was not developed by Augustine solely as the result of his controversy with the Donatists and Pelagians: it was already inherent in the teachings of Cyprian and Ambrose, and, Beatrice believes, in certain Judaeo-Christian traditions, including that of the Encratics. Also, Gross 1960. And Büchler 1928, pp. 207–11, on the two-and-a-half-year debate between two rabbinic schools, the Shammaiites and the Hillelites, in *c.*AD 66, over the question whether it would have been better for man had God not created him. The Shammaiites, who took the pessimistic view, prevailed. Their discussion involved not only the view that birth led inevitably to suffering (cf. Ecclesiastes, Job), but also 'the premise that man was constitutionally liable to sin' (p. 208). On the background to the idea of original sin in Late Antique culture, Dodds 1965, pp. 23ff; Jeanmaire 1952.

[85] On the baptism of infants, Jeremias 1967, Cullmann 1948, Dujarier 1962, all arguing in favour of infant baptism in New Testament times; and Aland 1963, who believes that although infant baptism may have existed before 200 (when it is attested in Tertullian and Hippolytus), it would have been rare. For a thorough review of the problem, Hubert 1972. Also see Didier 1959, with a useful collection of texts.

candidate a vessel, an involuntary being, a theatre of good and evil. There is here at least the basis of a genuine conflict within Augustine's thinking: on the one hand he wants baptism (whether infant or adult) as part of the *cultus*, to be *transitus*, dialogue, meeting, a ritual expression of the soul's capacity for God; on the other hand, partly in response to the Pelagians, he presents it as a substitution of good for evil, with no reference to the personal will of the subject. Small wonder that Julian of Eclanum accused him of a relapse into Manichaeism.[86]

In a rather altered form, this conflict, above all a conflict about the will to good and evil, is the *leitmotiv* of medieval baptism. Baptism in the central Middle Ages is a ritual renewal of community; still associated with the Paschal season, it mimes both the rebirth of Nature and of the celebrating, offering people, and thus reflects to perfection the bond between largely agrarian societies and the earth they work. It is very much a *cultus*, a tilling, with all the complex sense of reciprocity and transformation and transfiguration that this has: the birth of the new is the death of the old, death is a rebirth, death is within life not outside it.[87] But – and in this the Middle Ages departs from Augustine – the work of tilling is the work less of the individual soul as it becomes part of the 'city redeemed' than of the community as a political and social organism, a thing of this world. The rite is in a sense prepared by Augustine but quite different from his meaning, political and social. Infant baptism is a concise, rich expression of the forces of consensus by which a community exists, and sits well in a society where the social and the celestial are not at odds as they are in Augustine's vision, but, at least potentially, overlap. Besides all this, however, the Middle Ages took up the other side of Augustine's thinking, his account of baptism as remedy, especially when they had in mind infant baptism. Baptism 'in a moment' removes the sinful condition to which man is born. This satisfies the deep conviction of the Middle Ages – not divorced from the predominance of the collective – that man is a *victim* with little to say in his own fate. At best he is tragic, at worst pathetic or just pitiable, like Lucretius' defenceless child, who

---

[86] See Brown 1969, p. 370.
[87] On these themes, Baumstark 1958, pp. 169ff; cf. in the early twelfth century, Rupert of Deutz in *De diu. off.* 4.19, p. 136: 'noua ecclesia "pulchra ut luna" ad plenitudinem proficit, ut crucifixo plena luna Christo commoriens et conresurgens illi in baptismo copuletur'.

like a mariner tossed on savage waves, lies on naked ground, helpless of all that gives life. Poured forth in pain from his mother's womb, thrown by Nature on to shores of light, he fills the air with his sad wailing. Hardly surprising when he has nothing left to do in life but weather its adversities. And yet the animals flourish. The ploughing-cattle and the wild-beast need no rattles to play with. They have no use for the soft broken words of the suckling nurse. They don't change their clothes for the weather, don't need weapons or high walls to keep possessions safe. Why should they when earth herself, and Nature in her copious artistry, bring forth all to all?[88]

Here is a melancholy and almost ageless impression. Without apprenticeship, said Montaigne as he quoted this passage, man can do nothing but weep.[89] Augustine too had a strong sense of the weakness of the child as the weakness of man; but for him, as for the Middle Ages, the weakness was also the sinfulness. It is because sin 'inhabits the limbs' of the infant that he protests with screams at his baptism.[90] Sin is the cause not only of the death that will come to him, but of the frailty to which he is born: it is an effect and a symptom of his condition. Yet for Augustine this image of man is ambiguous. If the child is a victim, he is also a victim of the possibility within him of becoming more than his old self. The infant in his weakness, he says in the *City of God*, is like the arrow whose 'impetus increases in proportion to the backward extension of the bow'.[91]

The Roman rite of baptism in the Middle Ages – the liturgy of the *Hadrianum* for example, which provided the basis of Carolingian liturgical reform – gives a performed expression of both these attitudes to good and evil, the static and the dynamic.[92] From an early date, families were 'rushed to the water' with their newly born, fearful of the judgement the children might receive if they died without baptism. Parents baptized their children not just because they were part of the same household, as the early

[88] *De rerum natura* 5.ll.222–34, pp. 213–14.
[89] *Apologie de Raymond Sebond* (*Essais* II.12, I, p. 501). Montaigne is arguing with this view: 'nostre police n'est pas si difforme et desreglée'.
[90] *De pecc. mer. et rem.* 1.26–7, pp. 67–8. Here Augustine echoes Lucretius in his depiction of the infant's weakness compared with the young of other animals; the infant has feet but cannot walk, hands but cannot grasp, and his intelligence is so slight that he cannot even find the breast that nourishes him.
[91] *Di ciu. Dei* 13.3, p. 387; cf. Ladner 1959, pp. 154ff, on the distinction between Augustine's *renouatio in melius*, and the *renouatio in pristinum*, in other words to the state of man before the Fall, in Origen and others.
[92] On these themes, see below, ch. 4.

church had done, but also – and more urgently – because they might otherwise be taken up rightfully by Satan. In the meantime, the form of the rite became more and more removed, bound up with exorcism, and tended to lose the subtle combination of decision and submission which characterized Hippolytus' 'crisis' and Ambrose's baptism of conversion. Yet for all this, the ethos of catechism, repentance, change of heart, in short the idea that baptism was not opposition but *transitus*, never fell away. It was lodged in the continuing association of baptism with Easter; in the idea, familiar to Alcuin, that penitence was baptism repeated. No doubt it persisted in the apprehension of death and rebirth as parts of an endless cycle in man and Nature; and it was kept up by the preaching of the missionaries, for whom baptism remained above all a 'crossing over' from paganism. Throughout the early Middle Ages, we must reckon with this ambiguity: the rite of baptism, and above all the baptism of infants which was generally the norm, was a 'passage from death to life' – in the words of the anthropologists a rite of passage – but this passage might be conceived as a once-for-all triumph of good over evil, a slaying of the dragon to which the baptized infant might or might not be loyal as he grew up; or, quite differently, as an image, and an intense enactment, of the continuously repeated ethical journey from sin to repentance and back, which far from being limited to the rite, overflows, as it were, from the rite into the pilgrimage of life.[93] This ambiguity is an inheritance, in a sense the misunderstood inheritance, of Augustine.

Augustine's view of good and evil changed perhaps more than any other part of his thinking. Only after 406 did he come to a fully fledged theology of original sin.[94] In his three books *On Free Will*, written between 388 and 395, he argues from Neoplatonic premises against Faustus the Manichaean, his one-time master. His object – and he is clearly still arguing partly with his old Manichaean self – is to show that evil is no more than contingent. Strictly, it has no being. For since the good is the perfection of form, and being is dependent on form, sin, which is a movement away from the good and therefore from form, is a departure from being. Evil, towards which sin moves, is not-being; it has no existence outside the acts or tendencies which cause it. And where

[93] For all this, see below, chs. 4 and 5.
[94] On the stages by which Augustine came to the full dogma of original sin, Sage 1967; and see above, n. 84.

good acts build up to fulness of being, to the perfect form, evil acts pass away in the doing. The will, meanwhile, is not divided into the two wills of good and evil, but is a single will, a *uis media*, whose relative content of good or evil is determined by what is willed.[95] Here is a firm answer to the Manichaean belief that man is prey to the two opposed forces of good and evil. On the other hand, in reducing evil to Nothing, and seeing sin as a mere tendency to Nothing, Augustine tends to diminish the hold which sin has over the will. This is typical of Augustine of this time: he is still thinking with Neoplatonic tools. Ethics is a matter of attachment to being and form, to the immutable principle.[96] Good and evil are simple objects of choice, and it is within man's capacity to make this choice for himself.[97] Certainly, he is born in Adam, and therefore receives into himself at birth the mortality of the flesh; but his imprisonment in the body is not in itself the cause of his destruction. It does not fix him in not-being. He is only guilty in this sense when he chooses to sin. This humanist optimism is close to the Pelagianism against which Augustine later made such a firm stand. Man, he still thought, is able not to sin; the soul is not irrevocably subject to the body, but able to control it.[98]

Infant baptism has no obvious place among these views. Baptism was a deliberate, knowing, statement of intention, and although the practice of baptizing children had long been familiar, baptism was commonly put off to an age when it was felt the danger of grievous sin had abated, and sometimes, as we have seen, until shortly before death. Augustine himself was 'seasoned with salt', i.e. received into the church as a catechumen in a rite in which salt was placed on the tongue, soon after birth; but he was only considered seriously for baptism (by his mother) when as a boy he fell ill with bad stomach pains. In the event, he recovered,

---

95 *De lib. arb.* 1.12, p. 227 (on the will determined by what is willed – and compare the later idea in the *City of God* that an emotion is an act of the will whose nature is determined by its relation to what is willed: *De ciu. Dei* 14.6, p. 421); *De lib. arb.* 2.20, p. 273: 'Si enim formae perfectio bonum est, nonnullum iam bonum est et formae inchoatio. Ita detracto bono ex deo, nulla ergo natura est quae non sit ex deo. Motus ergo ille auersionis, quod fatemur esse peccatum, quoniam defectiuus motus est, omnis autem defectus ex nihilo est, uide quo pertineat, et ad deum non pertinere ne dubites.'
96 Ibid. 2.13, p. 262.
97 Ibid. 3.22, p. 313.
98 For the Platonic background to these views, *Republic* 38, pp. 334–8.

and his baptism was put off again, until he was finally baptized after his conversion, aged thirty-two.[99] The story tells us much about the prevailing view of evil: on the one hand, it was felt that there was sin in the child which must be stilled, on the other that, if possible, each postulant to Catholicism should make his or her own, willed, profession through the medium of baptism.

In the past, Tertullian, Cyprian and Ambrose had all taught that both body and soul were affected by sin from birth, and all of them attributed this to association with Adam's disobedience. Man is 'infected by his own sin', said Tertullian, intimating that the *tradux peccati*, the passage of sin from one generation to the next, was to be found in sexuality.[100] Yet although they seem to have held that the soul incurred guilt as well as punishment for sin from this infection, none of them could bring himself to believe that the guilt was wholly beyond the reach of human will and effort; and none was able to state definitely that original sin made the baptism of infants *necessary*. Tertullian, for all his sense of the power of sacrament to bring about change, could not permit such an apparent denial of the individual's power to will change in himself.[101] Besides, he said, the baptism of infants was more or less an invitation to the sponsors to perjure themselves.[102] So, when he talks about infant baptism, Tertullian abandons the 'infectious seed' and describes the childish soul as 'alone', attached neither to God nor devil, a being morally neutral.[103] Cyprian and Ambrose, both of whom, unlike Tertullian, accept the established custom of baptizing infants, still tend to play down the effect of Adam's sin on the child, and leave the connection between original sin and baptism vague. Cyprian thought that a baby's squalling was a kind of prayer, and while agreeing that the child has taken on sin at

---

[99] *Confessions* 1.17–18, pp. 9–10; and for the similar case of Jerome, Kelly 1975, p. 7. For Augustine's earlier puzzlement over the virtue of infant baptism, *De quant. animae* (written 388) 36.80, col. 1080.

[100] *De testimonio animae* 3, p. 178: 'homo a primordio circumuentus, ut praeceptum dei excederet, et propterea in mortem datus exinde totum genus de suo semine infectum suae etiam damnationis traducem fecit'. For this clearly stated doctrine of traducianism, i.e. the passage of sin from man to man by generation, see also Tertullian, *De anima* 39.1, p. 843; *De res. mort.* 49.6, p. 991.

[101] He comes close however in *De baptismo* 1.1, p. 277: 'De sacramento aquae nostrae qua ablutis delictis pristinae caecitatis in uitam aeternam liberamur.'

[102] Ibid. 18.4, p. 293.

[103] *De anima* 11.6, p. 797.

birth, he puts all the stress on its coming to him from outside: it is alien to him, affecting him less because it is not his own.[104] And Ambrose, in his book *On Abraham*, while expressing a philosophical belief in the salvation of mankind as a *genus*, tells us that the individual can only sustain the salvation of his kind given the protection of a purged mind. This, says Ambrose, is the allegorical significance of God's command to circumcise. Such protection is needed in young and old alike: 'no time is empty of blame ... Every age is stained with sin, and thus ready for sacrament.' But just as circumcision guards against bad habits learnt from others, above all idolatry, so (it is implied) baptism cuts away 'bodily excesses' from the mind. There is no doubt of the necessity of the rite, at least at some stage in life: without it, the mind will be inveigled from innocence to sin. Despite this rudimentary notion of the inevitability of sin, however, Ambrose is wedded to belief in the native goodness of the *genus*.[105] Confronted with the question whether a child who dies unbaptized is worthy of the 'honour of heaven' he admits he does not know, evidently falling back on Tertullian's contention that the childish soul is neutral.[106] Like Augustine in the books *On Free Will*, Ambrose is inclined to think of evil as bodily and contingent; infant baptism, accordingly, he thinks of as a protective device, perhaps in the tradition of the Greek idea of the baptismal *sphragis* or seal, a mark on the soul to stand guard over it.[107]

In this hesitancy between incipient sin and innate good lie the

---

[104] *Ep. 64 (ad Fidum)*.
[105] *De Abraham* 2.81, col. 519: 'Nec senex ergo proselytus, nec infans uernaculus excipitur, quia omnis aetas sacramento idonea.' And ibid. 2.83, col. 521: 'Ergo haec ratio est quod omnis mens quae non fuerit circumcisa a superfluis corporalibus, et purgata solemni munere, ut exuat se passionibus et uitiis, interibit. Non caro, inquit, interibit, quia potuit salua fieri, si habuisset purgationem; nuda autem praesidii et incircumcisi cordis colluuione infirmior salutem generis sui non potuit seruare.' Here as always in Ambrose it is virtually impossible to extract straight doctrine from a discourse based in the figurative and the ambiguous: his thinking is affective.
[106] Ibid. 2.84, p. 521; cf. Augustine, *De lib. arb.* 3.23, for the notion that infants, baptized or not, share the same middle state.
[107] Cf. Ambrose, *Explanatio symboli*, p. 13. On the *sphragis* and its development as a Christian and baptismal idea, Dölger 1911; Ysebaert 1962, pp. 181–426; Lampe 1967. On the connection between 'sealing' and the seal of the Good Shepherd, Quasten 1939. Faced with the rites of sealing – the component rites of baptism all seem to have been thought of as acts of sealing (see Ysebaert and Lampe) – Augustine is always at pains to show how despite their apparent exteriority and involuntariness, they are signs of the interior responsibility demanded of the candidate: thus his *Sermo. ex. coll. Guelf.* 3.4, pp. 454–5.

fragments of an unmade idea, a half-spoken dogma.[108] To speak it outright would be to make of man the victim of good and evil, and baptism – apparently – the imposition, rather than the taking on, of a new nature. It would be to go against the whole conception of sacrament and symbol as an ineffable encounter between man and God, a meeting of wills; it would be to eclipse the human will, to remove the essential ambiguity in sacrament. It was Augustine who with an insight resembling prophecy took up the fragments and made them into a whole, and yet did so without losing his grasp of the freedom of the will.

In the books *On Free Will* Augustine depicted man standing before good and evil much as if he were standing before light and dark. He could choose to go towards good, or towards the absence of good which is evil; to walk into the light or the absence of light which is dark. Now, from *c*. 406, and then repeatedly and often more aggressively in the arguments he drew up against Pelagius and his disciples in the years from 411, he presented a very different picture, in which freedom, instead of being in *choice*, was in a relation of *obedience* between man and God. The Pelagians believed in the innocence of man. Sin, for them, was the incidental result of ignorance and bad habit, and baptism a straightforward refusal of the life of sin.[109] To combat what he regarded as a blithe reliance on human volition, Augustine, in effect, stood his old argument on its head. Already in *c*. 406, in his work *On the Literal Interpretation of Genesis*, he had come to the opinion that mankind, and each soul within it, was in no position to make a simple choice between good and evil, because it was itself a part of the history of good and evil: the race of man was a *massa damnata*, involved in a fatal movement towards evil. This

---

[108] The dogma was made explicit in Ambrosiaster's commentary on Romans (written sometime between 363 and 384); but Ambrosiaster (Erasmus' name for pseudo-Ambrose), who was perhaps a convert from Judaism, combined this unequivocal view of original sin with a humanistic and Jewish interpretation of the resistance to sin, founded on the argument that Christianity was a confirmation of the Old Law and in no sense an abrogation. The gravest sin therefore, is not the sin 'in Adam', but the personal sin done 'in the likeness of Adam's transgression' (cf. Rom. 5:14); and those who have sinned only through ignorance of the law (i.e. before Sinai) or through ignorance of Christ, are *reseruati sub spe* until the coming of Christ: *Comm. on Rom.* 5.12ff, pp. 165ff. Ambrosiaster does not mention the case of the infant's sin and punishment.

[109] Thus infant baptism, which they accepted as customary, was an embarrassment to the Pelagians: see *De pecc. mer. et rem.* 1.34–5, pp. 63–5, for Augustine's ridicule of the Pelagians, who had defended their position on infant baptism by claiming that it effaced the baby's own sins.

was true in the sense that any man or woman was born with a tendency to sin which he took from the sexual act by which he was put into the world. The tendency also took a mainly, though not wholly, sexual form, being most apparent in sexual desire (*concupiscentia*), a desire which, however firmly it might be resisted, could never be rooted out.[110] The tendency to sin was not itself sin, but at once the 'daughter of sin', i.e. the result of a sinful act, and the 'mother of sin', i.e. the cause of sinful acts.[111] However, not only did the tendency inevitably lead to the sin, but it was, in some sense, itself the source of a guilt sufficient for eternal deprivation.

Original sin is therefore this notion that 'through one man sin entered the world', so that 'by the trespass of one, many died' (Rom. 5:12). Sinfulness, then, the tendency to sin, is still a movement towards not-being, but it is a movement in which man is necessarily caught up: he is in it by his very existence. Far from being the object of choice, sin enslaves; and worse, because it is in him and he is in it – because it 'inhabits' him and yet is more than him – it is a self-enslavement, and from self-enslavement, as from sleep, the self cannot make itself free. Instead of being free to choose, the individual is unfree *if* he chooses, being incapable of choosing what would make him free; freedom is therefore in obedience to the good which gives him this possibility.[112] The falcon is free, in this theory, not in the wildness of his own flight, but in obedience to the falconer to whose will he has become attuned.

The rhythm by which the soul becomes free is the rhythm of sacrament. As the will must become more than itself by obedience, so the word or the water is made more than itself by the movement it brings about. Here again is Ambrose's Naaman, made to pass from the finitude of mere water to the infinity of what it means; and here too is Augustine's catechumen. Baptism is that 'tiny point', as the fourth-century inscription in the baptistery

---

[110] *De nupt. et concup.* 1.19, pp. 233–4, 1.24, pp. 239–40. For the subjection to the senses, even after rebirth, and not to sexual concupiscence alone, *Confessions* 10.41, pp. 176–7. For the idea that vestiges remain of man's power, before the Fall, to control all his organs by a will informed by reason, see *De ciu. Dei* 14.24, pp. 446–8, where he lists cases of those who can sweat at will, imitate birds, etc., swallow vast numbers of objects and then regurgitate them one by one at will, and so on.

[111] *De nupt. et concup.* 1.24, p. 240.

[112] Ibid. 1.23, pp. 238–9.

of Santa Thecla, Milan, calls it,[113] at which the soul crosses over from the slavery of choice to the freedom of obedience, from the necessity of sin to the possibility of not sinning. And the essence of the rite is not in the conflict between two wills, as might appear, but in the metamorphosis of the single will as it turns from willing one thing to willing another. It is this moment of metamorphosis, a mysterious time in which bad and good, 'falling and rising',[114] embrace one another in the soul, which fascinates Augustine in the *Confessions.* How is it, he asks, that the quiet is greater when it follows a storm, that a friend's recovery gives more relief than if he had never been unwell, that a thing lost and found is more precious than something never lost in the first place? The deeper the sorrow, the greater the joy which comes of it. This is true of the death and resurrection of Christ.[115] It is true too of the passage from slavery of self to 'falling on God',[116] the passage from necessity to possibility. It is here, *in* this crossing and in its inexplicable poignancy, that Augustine finds God; in the relation between the Two Cities, and not just in the City of God. This enigma is as much a characteristic of baptism as it is of the conversion which he is describing here in the eighth book of the *Confessions.* The new does not destroy the old; the old wood is cut back to make way for the new, which nonetheless grows from it (cf. Rom. 11:17ff).

In this implication within one another of the tendency to good and the tendency to evil – in this concealment of good in evil and evil in good which we have already seen played out historically in the Old and New Testament – is not only the ritual movement, but the movement of right action towards God: the movement of reform and renewal. Baptism is thus the source of repentance, or turning, as well as its outcome. But just as the Incarnation did not save man except through the faith and hope it initiated, so the baptism which 'repeats' it saves the catechumen only insofar as it arouses in him the same faith and hope. The rite, like the event of death and resurrection, occurs *once* in each person; but the act of crossing which it brings on, the *transitus*, precisely because its accomplishment is in the crossing itself and not in a state of rest,

---

[113] *DACL*, I, col. 1386 (attributed to Ambrose: see below, pp. 270–2).
[114] *Confessions* 8.8, p. 118; and cf. ibid. 10.4, p. 156: 'mutans animam meam fide et sacramento tuo'.
[115] Ibid. 8.6, p. 117.   [116] Ibid. 8.27, p. 130.

must – unless it is wholly rejected by the one who undergoes it – go on happening again and again.[117] In other words, as Augustine made clear against the Donatist heretics, a person can only be baptized once, but, 'for as long as he makes the journey', he will continue to fall and to reconcile himself through repentance. In baptism he is given the possibility of becoming more than his old self; falling short of this ideal, he must aspire to return to it. So, after passing across the Red Sea, he must wander in the desert in hope, eating the manna of his new condition, subject always to temptation.[118] Here is the *decursus et recursus* described in the twelfth century by Guibert de Nogent in his autobiography, the 'running back and forth' of the penitential remembrance of the baptismal vow; the idea – stated with enormous emotional force in Guibert's opening pages – that in baptism the child is *chosen*, and that like the Israelites, his justification is in his living up to his chosenness by a constant regression to God.[119]

Yet this 'running back and forth' from self to God, this 'falling and rising' which is the movement of baptism and of the repentance flowing out of it, can so easily seem a much simpler thing, a substitution of good for evil. It can so easily fall from ambiguity into the dualism of possession by good or evil. 'Oh', says Augustine after the Easter vigil, 'you who have been baptized, "you were once in darkness, but now you are light in the Lord" [Eph. 5:8.].'[120] Or in another sermon, 'he made sheep out of wolves. That is grace.'[121] Baptism, from this point of view, is one side of an antithesis:

whatever is born of this concupiscence of the flesh is as born to the world not to God. It is born to God, however, when it is reborn from water and the Holy Spirit. The guilt of this concupiscence, incurred by generation, is dismissed only by regeneration.[122]

And again:

All who are born are damned; none is free except by being reborn.[123]

---

[117] For the statement of this principle in a mystical rather than a sacramental context, see *Enarr. in ps. xli*; and Gregory of Nyssa, *In cant. canticorum, hom. xii, PG* xliv, col. 1025: 'Who desires to see God, sees him whom he desires by always following him, and the vision of his face is the ceaseless journey toward him.' On this, Ladner 1959, p. 103, n. 76.

[118] *Sermo* 363.3, col. 1637.

[119] *Monodiae*, p. 2.

[120] *Sermo* 225.4, col. 1098.

[121] *Sermo* 26.5, col. 173.

[122] *De nupt. et concup.* 1.19, pp. 233–4.

[123] *Sermo* 294.16, col. 134.

There is no meeting of wills here, or so it would seem; only the act of one divine will as it destroys the force of another in a passive receptacle. In his zeal to do justice to the compulsion of evil in the soul, to silence the optimism of Pelagius and Julian of Eclanum which in many ways was still a more familiar outlook in the world of Late Antiquity, Augustine was prone to express himself in the language of dualism. He fell back on the sentiments of his Manichaean youth, partly in response to controversy, but also because those sentiments were still there. In the formal sense, he was well able to defend himself against the charge of lingering Manichaeism; but the language of its metaphors remained, and we can only suppose that it was this which more than anything impressed a large part of his audience, at least that part of it more attuned to the imagery than the philosophy. To such people, as they listened to Augustine's sermons, there might well seem to be two wills rather than one will coloured by the value of the thing willed. 'We were not, and he made us: we had perished, and he found us', runs one of the sermons on baptism.[124] In the *theology* of this sermon, the soul is redeemed by its condition of fear, and like the Israelites before the Pharaoh's army passes from fear to faith. The torpid awareness of the inability not to sin rises up in faith. But in the *imagery*, the devil binds and baptism liberates, the 'enemy' drops deep into the sea like a dead-weight, or is devoured by the earth. The difference raises questions of interpretation: the liturgy, as we shall see in more detail, may be a theological interpretation of images, or it may be a submission to images.[125] There is little doubt that the great medieval scenes of the Last Judgement, the Harrowing of Hell, the slaying of the dragon by the saint, often represent a submission to images of good and evil, and thus to the outward fact of good and evil. In some degree, the strain of passivity in the moral outlook of the Middle Ages can be traced to the emphasis which Augustine placed on the necessity of sin, and more particularly to the imagery with which he gave force to this teaching.[126]

---

[124] *Sermo* 363.2, col. 1635.   [125] Below, ch. 4.

[126] This process can be seen in the interpretation of the 'ransom theory': the idea, taken from I Peter 1:18–19 and Col. 2:14–15 but which goes beyond both these texts, that the devil acquired a right over man after the Fall. This right God was compelled, or chose, to abrogate by buying it back with his own blood; or, in a more detailed variant, by allowing the devil to exercise his right of death on the one man not subject to it, and thus trapping him with his own zeal, as in 'a mousetrap'. Augustine, however, was careful to fit this into his notion of evil as a motion away from God and therefore from being, and

THE LETTER TO BONIFACE AND THE SOCIETY OF THE HOLY SPIRIT

There remains the stumbling-block of infant baptism: if the child is born to a *massa peccati*, he must be baptized urgently, and certainly before he dies, in order to avoid eternal banishment from the vision of God. Augustine made no bones about this;[127] and later, in most of the kingdoms of western Europe, it became the law of baptism *quamprimum*, 'as soon as possible': 'The mass-priest must preach to men the true faith and tell them homilies and visit the sick, and baptize children, as soon as they can most quickly be brought to baptism', wrote Ælfric to Wulfstan of York in about 1006.[128] With the practice of baptism *quamprimum*, the
baptized once more seems to be the object of a metamorphosis rather than the one who makes it happen.

The need to baptize early, the necessity of infant baptism rather than its possibility or desirability, is perhaps the most obvious legacy of Augustine to the Middle Ages. We shall see how deep it runs. And yet this is not Augustine's last word. In his reply to Bishop Boniface of Carthage, he suggests two approaches to the problem of will and faith in infant baptism which in their brevity and obscurity provide a fitting codicil to his conception of sacrament in general. It is clear from these answers, even from a certain impatience in Augustine's attitude, that the question of infant baptism will always be a question, will always elude a formal solution and will always in the end be a matter of the authenticity of the will, not of the logic of dogma.

How, Boniface asks Augustine, can the parent or sponsor of a child at baptism be sure that he is not lying when he answers for the belief of his charge – responding 'He believes' to the priest's question 'Does he believe?' – when he cannot know what the child will become, nor even what is in his mind at present? He might be a good-for-nothing in the making, a thief for example, suggests Boniface. Augustine's answer begins obliquely. 'The

---

so to avoid giving autonomy to the devil: the right, he seems to be saying, is not a right at all, but an illusion (*De nupt. et concup.* 1.23, pp. 238–9). In the image though – either in a painting or a sculpture or in the mind – captivity by the devil is likely to seem real enough. On the ransom in 1 Peter, Boismard 1956; and in the Fathers, Rivière 1928, 1930, 1933; and see the excellent and balanced account in TeSelle 1970.

[127] *De nupt. et concup.* 1.20, p. 235 and *passim*.
[128] *Ælfric's First Old English Letter for Wulfstan*, in *Councils and Synods* 1.i, p. 294.

sacrament of faith', he tells Boniface, 'is in a certain way faith itself.' Just as we might say, 'Tomorrow is the Lord's passion' or, 'Today the Lord has risen', knowing perfectly well that these things happened many years ago, so sacrament, because it is based in a likeness of the thing of which it is a sacrament – as Easter is the likeness of the passion – is, in a way, the thing of which it is a likeness. And so the sacrament of faith, i.e. baptism, is faith.[129] Here we recognize the familiar pattern: language, meaning more than it says, becomes what it means; the will, in its obedience to what is willed, becomes that which it wills; and the memory, in remembering, causes to happen again. To say of infant baptism, however, that it *is* the faith it signifies, and the will implied in this faith, is the most radical possible statement of this intuition: it means that the child believes and wills its own baptism.[130] This is true not just in the diluted sense that in baptism he is given a protection against temptation, a warrior's shield to fend off sin; nor because Augustine assumes he will undergo a successful Christian education; but because he only is at all insofar as he is, or becomes, what happens in his baptism: he only is insofar as he is now and will be the meeting between what is 'given' and what is 'taken', between the 'making' and the 'being made' which is at the centre of human willing. He is both symbol and reality of what it is to will.

The same reciprocity is at work in the 'social' aspect of baptism. One of Boniface's questions is whether the effect of infant baptism

---

[129] *Ep.* 98.9, cols. 363–4: 'Sicut ergo secundum quemdam modum sacramentum corporis Christi corpus Christi est, sacramentum sanguinis Christi sanguis Christi est, ita sacramentum fidei fides est.' In a champlevé enamel of *c.* 1156, an artist, possibly Godefroid de Claire, has depicted this idea on a retable: within a circular medallion, winged Faith carries a font, and round the inner edge there runs the legend, FIDES BAPTISMUS (Swarzenski 1974, pl. 167, fig. 366, and p. 68).

[130] Augustine leaves the role of the will imprecise, suggesting that it is there in a sacramental form as conversion; and in a potential form as protection ('tutelam aduersus contrarias potestates'), *ep.* 98.10, col. 364; and as incitement and aid to the reasoning will ('cum autem homo sapere coeperit, non illud sacramentum repetet, sed intelliget, eiusque ueritate consona etiam uoluntate coaptabitur', ibid.). This last is evidently the *gratia adiutoria* bestowed in baptism: see Garrigou-Lagrange 1954. Compare Augustine's remarks about the baptismal Creed as *speculum fidei*, a mirror of faith in which the self can see what it ought to be, and at the same time a *lorica contra aduersitatem*: Sermo 58.13, col. 399. Some of this sense of baptism as a mirror is taken up in the practice of 'dévotion au baptême' in seventeenth-century France: see Bremond 1967–8, 9, pp. 1–42. The distinction, however, is that in this pious practice the Christian remembers what he has become by baptism, while for Augustine it is more a matter of remembering what happens in the transition of baptism.

depends on the good faith of those who offer the child. If the parents believe baptism to have physical powers of healing, or if they have him baptized and then subject him to some kind of sorcery, is the effect of the rite negated?[131]

It was the Donatists of North Africa who, inspired by the memory of Cyprian of Carthage and others, had conceived sacrament as the operation of a pure, closed church, sealed against the outside world like a ship against the waters or like a walled garden.[132] Baptism administered outside this pure vessel was ineffectual — Cyprian had argued this himself against Pope Stephen — and so, the argument ran, a candidate who had been baptized by heretics and now wished to enter the true church, must be baptized again.[133] The efficacy of sacrament, Augustine had replied to them in the battering-ram of his polemic *On Baptism* (401), is not in an idealized assembly with its ideal ministers, nor in the purity of its ritual performance: it is an act of God, which passes through the church, but is in no way possessed by it. For the church is not, Augustine insisted, a perfect enclosure from evil, but is necessarily and constantly engaged with the world. Rather than a ship, it is a threshing-floor, an *area* in which the chaff is always being separated from the wheat in a continuous process.[134] There can be no question of re-baptism, since baptism is irreversible, and, in its divine origin, complete; it marks the candidate with a character, a sign of the divine presence, whether or not he is among heretics,[135] and the repentant heretic is not to be baptized again, but reconciled to the church.

In both his questions — the question about answering for the infant's belief, and the one about the blasphemous parents —

---

[131] *Ep.* 98.1–6, col. 359–62.

[132] On the Donatists, Monceaux 1912, 1920, 1922, 1923; Frend 1952; Brown 1969, pp. 212ff. For the image of the ship, i.e. the ark, and the garden with its (baptismal) fountain, Cyprian, *ep.* 69.2, 751: 'Si autem hortus conclusus est sponsa Christi quae est ecclesia, patere res clausa aliena et profanis non potest. Et si fons signatus est, neque bibere inde neque consignari potest cui foris posito accessus ad fontem non est. Puteus quoque aquae uiuae si unus est, idem qui intus est, uiuificari et sanctificari foris positus ex illa aqua non potest, ex qua solis eis qui intus sunt usus omnis et potus concessus est, quod et Petrus ostendens unam ecclesiam esse et solos eos qui in ecclesia sint baptizari posse posuit et dixit: "in arca Noe pauci id est octo animae hominum saluae factae sunt per aquam, quod et uos similiter saluos faciet baptisma" [1 Peter 3:20–1], probans et contestans unam arcam Noe typus fuisse unius ecclesiae.'

[133] Cyprian, *ep.* 74; cf. Augustine, *De baptismo.*

[134] Augustine, *ep.* 98.5, col. 362.   [135] Ibid.; and *De baptismo* 4.15, pp. 247–8.

Boniface is evidently worrying about the implications of a church which is not committed to absolute purity. What happens when the gates are opened in this way? How can we be sure that sacrament works at all if it is no longer the preserve of a caste, if it no longer springs from the fountain in the walled garden? We can be sure, Augustine replies, because it works by the will of the Spirit. If the parents practise sorcery on the child after baptizing him, or offer him for baptism with magical rather than properly religious intentions, although they are members of the church, they have no effect on the rite; and although they are homicides with regard to themselves, they are impotent with regard to the baptism, having put themselves outside the act of Spirit which makes sacrament work. There is here a reminiscence of the argument that evil has no being: for the purposes of the rite, the wayward parents might as well not be there. The evil soul cannot communicate itself, since it falls away from the very principle that binds souls together: it is still enslaved in the *massa damnata*. The unity of the church, the rallying-cry which the Donatists took from Cyprian, is thus a matter of what the church might be, not what it already is.[136]

This does not mean, however, that the ritual community gives nothing to sacrament. Far from it, for the sacrament is the product of the 'society of the Spirit'; in other words (Augustine seems to say), the church's making of sacrament is not a simple act by the church, but a part of its effort to be at one with the will of the Spirit. It reflects exactly his teaching of will as obedience to will, but this time in the 'universal society of faithful and saints' rather than in the individual soul.[137] Once again the rite is between the Two Cities. And the child, while his reason still 'sleeps',[138] is caught up in a social act of will which is also an act of God. He is beyond the reach of his parents' wrongdoing, because there now begins in him, even if he does not remain true to it in later life, the will to the good: 'The Spirit of rebirth is common to the adults who offer and the child they offer: and so, through this society of one and the same Spirit, the will of the offerers takes effect on the child offered.'[139] Now that the atavistic sin of his first birth has been loosed in him, he can do wrong only by his own will. It is in

---

[136] *Ep.* 98.1–6, cols. 359–62.   [137] Ibid. 5, col. 362.
[138] Ibid. 4, col. 361.
[139] Ibid. 2, col. 360; cf. *De baptismo* 4.25, p. 260, for the contrary case of the robber on the cross who wills his own *conversio cordis* without the outward form of baptism.

this moment of rebirth that he can be said to begin to have a will of his own, even though he wills by virtue of others who will in him.

In what follows we must try to see how this notion of a social will, at work within the individual from childhood onward, expressed by the ritual of infant baptism, becomes in the ages that succeed a social will in the more down-to-earth sense: a will not only of the 'society of the Spirit' but of the society of men and of this world; how baptism, and ritual generally, become in this way political. And we must try to follow the complex process by which the 'logic' of sacrament apparently taught by Augustine vies with the 'authenticity' of sacrament which is at the heart of his teaching. We must see how the tendency to formalism which he rejected, and the conception of the *cultus* as wisdom which binds the rite to the ethical life beyond it, both survive into the early Middle Ages in their different ways.

Chapter 4

FROM AUGUSTINE TO THE CAROLINGIANS

Augustine provided ways of thinking about what happened in sacrament, and addressed particular problems in baptism and the baptism of infants. From the fifth century, the tendency was to take the emphasis away from Augustine's ethical account of sacrament, with its reliance on the personal virtues of faith, hope and love, and put it more on a conception of sacrament as the collective performance of the 'society of the Holy Spirit', or of the assembly of believers in its capacity for God. Until the late eighth century, when the relation between conversion and baptism was raised again by Alcuin and Paulinus of Aquileia against the background of the mission to the Saxons and Avars, there were few theological treatments of liturgy. The literature about baptism in these years was occupied principally with the form of the rite, the exact manner in which it should be done, and this remained true for the most part even in what Alcuin said. There was a move away from the reflective sacrament of the Fathers, in other words, and towards the security, the certainty, given by the enactment of the forms themselves: by performance in this restricted sense. The concern with form – which as I will try to show was, in the long term, more apparent than real – takes on a special urgency in the case of infant baptism. Here, the child, unable to think or believe or answer for himself, is *answered for;*[1] and so for him the liturgy works, it seems, not from anything in him, but simply by his subjection to its form: to an order of words and actions spoken and done by others. By the look of it, then, all this makes infant baptism a perfect metaphor of the absorption of the individual into the collective, and into the formal idea of the collective expressed in the church. It simply says better what other sacraments would also say in this period, that the soul has no autonomy, but is good or bad according to its mute obedience to

[1] Caesarius of Arles, *Sermo* 229.6, p. 910.

130

fixed forms representing the eternal. In the first two parts of this chapter I will deal mainly with this aspect, with infant baptism as 'ritualistic', and with the apparent ritualism of the society which conceived it. In the third section I will argue that the forms of the rite are not evidence of a new theurgy – an abandonment to the rules of magic – but are more fully understood as a kind of setting of the stage, enhancing rather than blocking the soul's intuitions.

INNOCENCE, IGNORANCE AND INTENTION IN THE CHILD

Shortly after Augustine's teaching about original sin and the resulting necessity of infant baptism, there is some evidence of resistance to so hard a saying. From fifth-century southern Gaul there survives an epitaph, cut in stone, dedicated by stricken parents to their son Theudosius, who had died unbaptized. It now stands in the church of Brignoles, near the Mediterranean port of Toulon:

Worthy child, circled round by the rampart of the cross, innocent, undarkened by the filth of sin, little Theudosius, whose parents in purity of mind intended to bury him in the holy baptismal font, was snatched away by shameless death; yet the ruler of high Olympus will give rest to any member lying beneath the noble sign of the cross, and the child will be heir to Christ.[2]

There is a note of hesitation here about the place of ritual and symbol in the new religion. It would not have been easy for Theudosius' parents – who are obviously still thinking of the Christian God in a classical vein, as the 'ruler of Olympus'[3] – to come to terms with the idea that their son *had to be* baptized in order to be heir to Christ. They were more inclined to feel, and certainly they wished to feel, that despite his lack of understanding, he would be saved because he had done nothing wrong;

---

[2] *Corpus Inscriptionum Latinorum* XII.5750 (cited by Didier 1959, p. 125):

> Insignem genitum crucis munimine septum
> Insontem, nulla peccati sorde fucatum,
> Theodosium paruum, quem pura mente parentes
> Optabant sacro fonte baptismate tingui
> Improba mors rapuit: sed summi rector Olympi
> Praestabit requiem membris uti nobile signum
> Praefixum est crucis, Xpique uocabitur heres.

[3] On this kind of classical language in Christianity, Dölger 1950, pp. 70–7.

because he had been born into a Christian family who intended to baptize him, and because he had been buried with a Christian burial 'under the noble sign of the cross'. The inscription betrays the educated, still classical, Christian belief which goes back to the gentle spirit of Minucius Felix. Yet Theudosius' parents could not be as confident as Minucius Felix had been early in the third century. Their assertion that they had intended to baptize the child, and the emphasis on innocence and the power of the cross, make it clear that they knew about the doctrine of original sin. Their prayer is anxious: the desire it voices reminds us of the extreme recourse of those fourteenth- and fifteenth-century parents who rushed with their stillborn or dead child to a shrine, where the little corpse would breathe again for just long enough to be baptized, before flying off to heaven.[4]

Theodosius' parents are determined, however, that their son should not be the victim of a ritual shortcoming. More important for them is their affection for him, and the faith they wish to pass on to him. Perhaps they took solace from the local theology of Lérins, the two islands off Cannes, where the monks – among them Vincent of Lérins and Faustus of Riez – no doubt partly inspired by the writings of John Cassian, taught a concise, humane, even classicizing doctrine of co-operation between grace and the individual will. Since the Reformation this has been called Semi-Pelagianism because of the large part it gave to the personal will in salvation.[5] It may be, too, that in a general perspective, pessimism about the natural condition of man persisted side by side with this brighter view of things, and often in the same minds, through Late Antiquity and the early Middle Ages, neither of them able to oust the other. It is as though the Christianity of these centuries aspired to a sinlessness, to an original goodness in man, which was denied by its own doctrine of original sin. This ambiguity in the soul comes across most strongly perhaps in the ideal of the monastic life; in Gregory the Great, writing to the monk Secundinus in May of 599, it still leaves a question over the problem of the infant who dies before baptism:

Why is the child, who had done nothing, not clean in the sight of Almighty God? Why is the Psalmist, born of lawful marriage, 'conceived in iniquity' [Ps. 50:7]? Why is a man not clean unless he has been washed

4   Saintyves 1931, pp. 167ff.
5   See, for example, Vincent of Lérins, *Commonitorium*.

in the water of baptism? Why does every man die in Adam, if he is not held by the chain of original sin?[6]

Gregory gives Secundinus his answer in the end – man is indeed born to sin, being the branch of a rotten root – but he delivers it without much conviction. He cannot warm to this theme as Augustine had done.

Concern for the child's soul occurs again in a liturgical setting in the two Masses of the Innocents in the *Leonine* or *Verona Sacramentary*. In the prayers said at this feast, we can hear an echo not only of the innocence of Theudosius in the eyes of his parents, but also of their feeling that the destiny of the child and that of his parents, or of the community into which he has been born, are one and the same. The new-born are saved by natural affections to which the ritual forms give expression, and not by the forms themselves. These prayers, covering little more than a folio of the seventh-century manuscript (composed, however, probably in the mid-fifth century),[7] throw sudden light into the vexed question of the medieval view of childhood. They make nonsense of the idea put forward in modern historical writing that a 'category of childhood' had to wait for the bourgeois family of the seventeenth century with its at once down-to-earth and sentimental image of its own children. Until this time, it has been held, the child was either a Renaissance putto or nothing more than a scaled-down adult.[8] There can be no doubt, however, that earlier ages had their own, quite definite and often sentimental, versions of childhood. It is easy enough to find evidence of impatience with children or lack of interest in their world, or even hostility towards them, but the same could be said of modern times; and besides, a view which denies to the Middle Ages any sympathy for children ignores the whole genre of

6 *Registrum* IX.148, p. 703.
7 On the date of the MS, Mohlberg's introduction to *Sacramentarium Veronense*, pp. xxv–xxvi; on the date of the Mass of the Innocents, Bourque 1948, p. 143.
8 For a statement of these views, Ariès 1960; for modifications of it, Schmitt 1983; Le Goff 1973, both using the *exemplum* as the main source for attitudes to children. Also see Arnold 1980. For the ninth century, the book of advice sent by Dhuoda, a Frankish noblewoman, to her son, shows how deep could be a mother's sentiments. She is writing to a sixteen-year-old, but the book contains reminiscences (Dhuoda, *Manuale*, esp. ch. vi). Earlier, Gregory of Tours, *History of the Franks* 5.34, p. 296, speaks with much emotion of children wiped out in an epidemic. Against this, the remark of a Merovingian saint's life: 'Nascit puer, uagit in cunis, alitur in lacte, et quid amplius?' (*Passio Preiecti, MGH Pass. Vitaeque Sanct. aevi Merov.*, p. 227, cited Riché 1976, p. 230 n. 349).

Apocryphal literature which grew out of the story of the Christ-child.[9]

What we see in the words of the *Leonine* however – and this does seem peculiar to an earlier, pre-bourgeois society – is the ability of the adult community to see itself in the child, and conversely to see in itself the qualities of childhood. There is a 'category of childhood' in other words, but it allows the man to be seen more readily in the child and the child in the man:[10] 'Look down, Lord, on these gifts . . . , and permit, we ask, that we might be able to imitate the sincerity of [the Innocents] whose venerated childhood was given over to you.'[11] In this and other *libelli* – as the prayers of the *Leonine* are called – the virtues of the child, his innocence, purity, simplicity, even his ignorance, are taken up by the adult assembly. As ethical principles they are imitated; but they are imitated through the mediation of the offerings made in the Mass: 'Look down, Lord, on these gifts . . .'. And because these offerings are not just gifts made among men, but establish a relation with God, the moral virtues which are

9 Thus the *Protoeuangelium of James* and other texts in Hennecke–Schneemelcher 1963, pp. 374ff.

10 Cf. Curtius 1953, pp. 98–101, on the *topos* of the *puer senex*. The relation between child and adult in medieval liturgy – and society – is a rich subject. Ernst Kantorowicz's study of the iconography of Candlemas or Hypapante (2 Feb.), the feast celebrating the purification of the Virgin and the blessing of the Christ-child by the aged Symeon (cf. Luke 2:21–39), shows from the mosaic of this scene in the basilica of Sta Maria Maggiore, Rome, how it was used to depict not only the motif of the *puer-senex*, but also that of the historical renewal of Rome by Christianity, the passage from Old to New Testament and law to grace, and generally the notion of the withering of the old and the growth and potency of the young (Kantorowicz 1965, pp. 25–36: '*Puer exoriens*'). The feast of the Circumcision (1 Jan.), close to baptism both by its season – six days before Epiphany and its commemoration of Christ's baptism – and in its liturgical themes of *purificatio mentis*, *noua creatura*, etc., provides another occasion to dwell on the child–adult relation. The illumination which depicts this feast in the *Fulda Sacramentary* (fo. 17v), shows Mary and Joseph with the Christ-child outside the walls of Jerusalem, and opposite them (to the right in the frame), a group of five *parentes* (the word is written in gold lettering above the figures), apparently suggesting the association between the purification of Christ (or the child as Christ) and that of the community of his *parentes*, his kindred.

11 *Sacramentarium Veronense*, no. 1290, p. 165; and a benediction on the feast of the Innocents in the *Liber Sacramentorum Gellonensis* (eighth century, of the 'Eighth-Century Gelasian' type, from Guilhem-le-Désert), which associates the adult community both with its own children-to-be-baptized and with the Innocents. The Latin of the prayer is, however, so muddled that the exact sense remains hard to get at: 'Concede quesumus domine plebem tuam innocentum per gratiam qui tibi consecrasti primitias martyrum ab innocentiam paruulorum. – Seruetur hic populus purgatus baptismate qui tibi platita fecisti innocentiam per cruorem. – Ut illuc suo interuentu grex accedat per lauacrum ubi felices paruuli rore sanguinis gloriantur in perpetuo' (no. 2066, p. 288; I have omitted the additions and deletions to the Latin by Dom Dumas in his edition).

passed through them gain association with a divine origin. The notion that a child is virtuous already invokes the givenness of virtue, its origin beyond the personal will; now this is confirmed, played out in the act of sacrificial offering. If the offering, or rather the response made by God to offering, conveys this sense of virtue as gift – a sense which Augustine tried to clarify theologically – the offering itself is nonetheless an act of personal and social intention; and the child is caught up in intention, despite his own lack of it:

God, who bestows on the hearts of children yet without knowledge the benefits of your sacrament, permit, we ask you, that those lacking our awareness of faith should always receive the fulness of mercy.[12]

As Augustine knew, the *cultus dei* is dialogue with God: invocation and response, offering and response; but the dialogue is no mere spectacle: it mimes the inward condition of man, whose own power to invoke is itself a response; and whose possibility of being just, in Pauline language, is in justification. In the liturgy, moreover – the liturgy of the Innocents but that of infant baptism too – the child, passive yet involved in the collective will, stands as an abbreviated figure of the same dialogue. In another prayer of the *Leonine*, this gives rise to a meditation on the antithesis between the will-less Innocents and salvation by confession:

In the precious deaths of these little ones, murdered for the infancy of your Son Our Lord and Saviour by the deathly Herod, we know the great gift of your mercy. [In these Innocents] it is the power of grace alone that burns, not the will; they made an act of confession before they could speak; suffered passion before they were members of the Passion; were witnesses of Christ when they did not yet know him.

The final imprecation resolves the antithesis in an appeal to divine good will:

O [God] infinitely benign, who does not suffer that those slain in his name should die, even when they have no experience of the merit which brings glory, but fulfils in those shedding their own blood the saving rebirth, crediting to them the martyrs' crown.[13]

The Innocents are thus will-less martyrs, rather as Augustine conceived the baptized infant as a believer; and like the water of

12 Ibid., no. 1284, p. 164: 'Deus, qui bonis tuis infantum quoque tui nescia sacramenti corda praecedes: tribue, quaesumus, ut nostrae conscientiae fiduciam non habentes, indulgentia semper copiosa praeueniat.'
13 Ibid., no. 1286, p. 165; cf. *Missale Gothicum*, nos. 46ff, pp. 14ff, with emphasis on the irony of the children's, i.e. the Innocents', faith going before that of the adult community.

baptism, the blood of the Innocents, besides being real blood, is a reconciliation of weakness and power: through the blood the Innocents offer themselves, and God responds by 'fulfilling in them the saving rebirth'. What they lack in will, knowledge, understanding, is made good by the gift of will and knowledge and understanding; and this gift, which is the child's predicament but also that of mankind as he stands before God, is condensed in symbol: in water, blood, bread, oil and so on.

To know anything about the force of medieval ritual, its efficacy, we must take account not just of its outward forms, but of the struggle which goes on within it between form and content, between sacrament and confession; between the language and the emotion it expresses – the *sonus oris* and *ictus intelligentiae* of Augustine – between the structural and the existential. In what follows I will try to suggest some of the relation between the formal power of infant baptism, and its power to express the predicament of man before God.

EXORCISM AND THE STRESS ON FORMS

In the official teaching of the church on infant baptism, the notion of an effective, ritual sympathy between assembly and child was put aside. In the articles of the council of Orange, convened in 529, Augustine's doctrine of sin was resumed for posterity. The canons have a legislative brevity which pares down the living organism of original argument to the abruptness of dogma. Almost all the canons are either adaptations or excerpts from Augustine, with a few elaborations made by the anti-Pelagian apologist Prosper of Aquitaine.[14] A letter of Pope Felix IV, itself an amalgam of Prosper and Augustine, served as a preamble to the council, and a part of this then found its way into the canonical collection of Dionysius Exiguus.[15] Caesarius of Arles, the moving spirit behind the council, sent a record of its proceedings to Felix, who died before returning judgement; his successor in the see was a friend of Caesarius', Boniface, who duly gave the council papal approval.[16]

The meaning of the council of Orange for baptism is plain: the

[14] Hefele–Leclercq II.2, pp. 1085–110; and *PL* LI, cols. 723–30. Cf. Plinval 1958; Cappuyns 1934.
[15] Hefele–Leclercq II.2, p. 1188 n. 1.
[16] Only Boniface's reply survives: Mansi VIII, cols. 735–7.

soul as well as the body is corrupted by the sin contracted from Adam; in this inheritance there is sin, and not just punishment for sin, and therefore death to the soul and not to the body alone; since the Fall, justification is by faith alone, observance of the law is not enough; faith comes only with grace, and baptism is the vehicle of grace. Baptism, then, is not a participation of man in his own journey to freedom, but a liberation to which he is subject. The articles have taken up Augustine's logic of baptism, leaving behind the theology of will and symbol which underpins it:

Concerning the repair of free will [opens the thirteenth canon] the liberty of the will weakened in the first man cannot be repaired except by the grace of baptism; once lost, it cannot be given back except by the one who gave it, and about this, Truth itself has spoken: 'if the son has made you free, you will be free indeed' [John 8:36].[17]

Instead of a drama of *transitus*, baptism has become a play of symmetries over the child (or adult): grace against sin. It has shed the subtler part of Augustine's theology of sacrament, which saw in it a metaphor of the soul's return to its own divine origin, and has become once again, as Augustine himself put it, 'the pulling out of the arrow' rather than the healing of the wound: an operation on the child, rather than a meeting in him between will – either social or individual – and grace. Losing its intrinsic ethical content, it has become a formal exercise in power.

Over the centuries, the effect of this makes itself felt in the shape of the liturgy. The old rite of baptism, an expression of personal 'turning' made up of questions and answers which took up and echoed the give and take of catechesis rather than being cut off from it, must somehow express the entry of the new-born into the social group. One result of this disequilibrium is that the form of the rite, instead of inviting understanding, is severed from it; the form imposes its authority as though from outside: its importance comes to lie less in the questions it asks and the faith it awakens than in its own content or structure. We can see this effect in certain details: first, the season of baptism.

The proper seasons for baptism, at least in Rome, were Easter and Pentecost; celebrated at these times – and this is to leave aside the Gallican and Celtic association of baptism with Epiphany – baptism drew to itself the collective experience of the *pascha*, or of crossing-over (*transitus* in Augustine's translation), from death to

17 *PL* LI, col. 726.

life, sorrow to joy, humiliation to triumph, birth to rebirth.[18]
The Easter–Pentecost ruling remained in force until the twelfth
century and beyond, but certainly from the sixth century, we
begin to see signs in the legislative documents of the competing
desire to baptize children, and especially sickly babies, as early as
possible (*quamprimum*, in other words with no regard for season):
'and if, as is very common, the infants are weak' says the council
of Girone in Catalonia, in 517, 'with no appetite for their
mothers' milk, they are to be baptized even on the same day, once
they have been offered'.[19] Here in a few words is a quick but
exact impression of the infant mortality which it would be
impossible to express in figures in this period, and of just how
urgent infant baptism must have seemed to most communities.[20]
Later, against the background of mission and conversion in
Francia and England of the ninth century, king and church
legislated with one voice in favour of early, non-seasonal baptism,
moved not only by a theological anxiety about original sin, but by
the practical political desire to establish Christianity and weed out
the vestiges of paganism: 'And if an unbaptized child is brought
suddenly to the mass-priest, . . . he must baptize it immediately in
haste, so that it does not die heathen.'[21] In the Carolingian
councils and capitularies particularly, the correct way of adminis-
tering baptism, confession and communion – especially for the
sick – stands at the centre of the administrative effort to give
Christianity, and its political masters, firm roots in the countryside: to colonize the 'heath'.[22] With this went a certain emphasis

[18] See the letter of Pope Siricius to Bishop Himerius of Tarragona (late fourth century):
PL, XIII, col. 1135A. Siricius, recognizing the emergency baptism of children, or others –
those on the brink of shipwreck for example – about to die, nonetheless insists on the
proper seasons of Easter and Pentecost, and prohibits the celebration of baptism at
Christmas and Epiphany.

[19] C. 5, Mansi VIII, col. 549.

[20] Russell 1958, p. 35, table 38, maintains that infant mortality was considerably greater in
the Middle Ages than child mortality; but see the critical review by Amimann 1962; and
a reserved review by Van Werrecke 1960. Also on this Russell 1965, esp. pp. 86–7.

[21] *Ælfric's Pastoral Letter to Wulfsige III*, bishop of Sherborne (dated 993–5), c. 71, in
Councils and Synods I.i, p. 210; thus also *Ælfric's First Old English Letter* (c. 1006), ibid., p.
294; *Canons of Edgar* (1005–8) dictates baptism within seven days of birth: c. 15, ibid., p.
319; *Laws of Ine* (688–726), within thirty days: ibid., p. 319 n. 2; and cf. ibid., p. 453.

[22] Council of Paris (829), c. 48, *MGH Conc. aevi Karol.* I, pp. 642–3 (cf. cc. 6–10, pp. 614–
16); council of Aix (836), c. 16, ibid., p. 714, on the difficulty raised by the proliferation
of rural parishes in these times of pagan conversions: the councils call for a policy of one
priest to one parish. On the education of priests about baptism, *Admonitio Generalis*
(789), c. 70, *MGH Capit. reg. Franc.* I, p. 59; council of Turin (813), c. 18, *MGH Conc.
aevi Karol.* I, pp. 288–9.

on formal observance, on doing things the right way, a concern which emerges clearly from the exasperation of Boniface, the Anglo-Saxon missionary, at the bungling Bavarian priest who baptized 'In nomine patria et filia etc.' But the idea of correct observance was also, in the missions of Willibrord and Boniface, and then still more rigorously in the time of Alcuin, a question of the Roman observance, so that here, the efficacy of baptism is bound up more closely than ever with broader issues of church and politics.[23] The baptism of infants, it might be said, is now a political purification as much as a religious one.

If baptism was to be not only baptism of infants, but, often, baptism out of season too, and therefore detached from the Easter symbolism of *transitus* and conversion (or the Pentecost symbolism of illumination), it is not surprising that its form should also have been radically reduced:

And I believe [said Ælfric of Winchester in the first decade of the eleventh century] that if you see a child about to die and, taking up some water, you say, 'In the name of the Father and of the Son and of the Holy Spirit may this water be blessed for baptism', and, taking up the child, you say, 'I baptize you in the name of the Father and of the Son and of the Holy Spirit', and if the child comes up out of the water alive, he is saved.[24]

Such brevity was perhaps already common by Ælfric's time. On the other hand, there was a reluctance, perhaps an inherited incapacity, to abandon the wealth of ritual significance which made baptism an act of the collective will expressed in symbol. The tendency to formalism, to a rite which separated priestly power from the response of the liturgical crowd, was always balanced against the full-blown, participatory rite from which it derived. In this sacrament of adult initiation, addressed – for the

---

[23] Letter of Pope Zacharias to Boniface, *MGH Epist. Mer. et Kar. aevi* I, p. 336; and *PL* LXXXIX, col. 929. Cf. *Responsa Stephani papae II, PL* LXXXIX, cols. 1026–7 (Stephen's answers to queries put to him during his negotiations with Pepin, king of the Franks, at Quierzy over Easter of 754). Baptism administered *modo sic rustice*, 'In nomine Patris mergo, et filii mergo, et spiritus sancti mergo', is valid, but the priest who administers it, if he also does not know whether he was consecrated by a bishop, is to undergo lifelong penance in a monastery, and is to lose his priestly status. The priest who performs baptism in wine when in an emergency water cannot be found bears no blame; likewise the priest who pours the water over a sickly child, avoiding the risk of full immersion. In all these cases, it is emphasized that validity lies in the invocation of the Trinity. For the view that the efficacy of baptism is this period lay principally in the observance of correct forms, Angenendt 1987.

[24] Letter of Ælfric to Wulfstan, in *Councils and Synods*, I.i, p. 250.

most part – to infants, the tension between form and content was carefully maintained. The effort of maintaining it is evident in southern Gaul in the early sixth century when Caesarius of Arles pressed his congregation to offer their children for baptism at least a week before the ceremony itself, and preferably during Lent.[25] In ninth-century Fulda it comes across from a letter of Rabanus Maurus, advising priests in recently converted regions not to insist too much on the 'legitimate times' of Easter and Pentecost: parents had been forced to swear on oath that their baby was on the brink of death before being admitted to the font; unable to tell for sure whether he was ailing or healthy, they shrank from possible perjury, and, often, were faced with the sudden death of a child unbaptized. 'How absurd this is', comments the compiler of the collection of letters, 'is easy to see.'[26] The attachment to Easter which had in the early church been a natural expression of repentance and progression could now be something like an embarrassment.

Another sign of growing formalism is in the new wording of the Carolingian rite of baptism. The Roman rite known as the *Gelasian*, the Frankish versions of this known as *Eighth-Century Gelasians*, and the *Ambrosian* or *Milanese* rite, made baptism – even infant baptism – interrogatory by prefacing each immersion into the water with a question from the Apostolic Creed. In this way, the act of washing was also an inquiry into belief in the three persons of the Trinity:

Credis in deum patrem omnipotentem?
Respondet: Credo.
Credis in Iesum Christum filium eius unicum dominum nostrum natum et passum?
Respondet: Credo.
Credis et in spiritum sanctum, sancta aecclesia, remissionem peccatorum, carnis resurrectionem?
Respondet: Credo.[27]

[25] *Sermo* 225.6, p. 89; *sermo* 229.6, p. 904.
[26] *Epistolarum Fuldensium fragmenta*, in *MGH Epist. Karol. aevi* III, p. 522.
[27] *Gelasian*, no. 449, p. 74. This formula is still found in the twelfth-century liturgies of Milan and Aquileia: Paredi 1935 for Milan; and for Aquileia, the rite of Cividale, of c. 1300, ed. Quarino 1967, pp. 131–2. Cf. Ambrose, *De sac.* 2.7.20, p. 68. The form also remains in the twelfth-century liturgy of Catalonia–Narbonne: see Gros 1975, nos. 55–6, pp. 37–101, at p. 58. It persists elsewhere too, as in the mid-eleventh-century sacramentary of St Denis, MS Paris BN lat. 9436, fo. 50, where its appearance is evidence of the continuing use of the *Gelasian* after the draughting of the *Gregorian*.

The *Hadrianum*, a version of the *Gregorian Sacramentary* sent by Pope Hadrian to Charlemagne in the 780s as part of the re-organization of the Frankish liturgy on Roman lines (the original is lost but mainly recoverable from copies), and the *Supplement* which was then added to this book, probably by Benedict of Aniane, turn this question-and-answer form into a simple indicative:

Et ego te baptizo in nomine patris [first immersion]. Et filii [second immersion]. Et spiritus sancti [third immersion].[28]

It may be that the *Hadrianum* – which has added the indicative form to the original *Gregorian* – and its *Supplement* are trying to make things easier for the unschooled priests of Francia who seem to have found even the shorter baptism hard to master.[29] If this were so – and it is suggested not only by Boniface's letter to Zacharias but by the appearance of the short form in Gallican books earlier than the *Hadrianum*[30] – it should not distract us from looking at the new rite as a dramatic whole. In the *Supplement* to the *Hadrianum*, a clear effort has been made – evidently by Benedict of Aniane – to introduce a break between the 'adult' and 'infant' rites.[31] After the threefold renunciation of Satan, the priest proceeds to the font and blesses the waters before addressing to the godparents, who are holding the children, the three Credal questions; he then baptizes the children in the indicative form: 'Et ego te baptizo . . . .'. The implications of this go

[28] *Hadrianum Supplement*, paras. 1084–5, p. 378.   [29] For this argument, Gy 1982.
[30] For details of this Gallican usage, Andrieu's introduction to *Ordo XV*, pp. 85–90, where he argues that the indicative form has a Visigothic, and ultimately oriental, origin; and that an important reason for taking it up was that it expressed at once Trinity (in triple immersion) and unity (in single formula). The *Sacramentary of Angoulême* combines the pouring of water with immersion, and an interrogatory with an indicative form, suggesting strongly the difficulty of articulating an adult rite with the practice of infant baptism: 'Et antequam perfundas eum aqua interrogas ei uerba symboli et dicis. Credis in deum patrem omnipotentem. Respondet credo. Credis in ihm xpm filium eius unicum Deum nostrum natum et passum. Respondet credo. Credis et in spiritum sanctum, sanctam ecclesiam catholicam . . . Respondet credo. Et cum interrogas per singulas uices, mergis eum tertio in aqua his uerbis. Baptizo illum in nomine patris et filii et spiritus sancti, ut habeas uitam aeternam' (no. 2004, p. 138). That the text has infant baptism in mind is clear from the next rubric: 'Postea cum ascenderit ad fonte infans . . .'. A similar confusion appears in the *Missale Gothicum*: 'Dum baptizas interrogas ei et dicis: Baptizo te . . .' (no. 260, p. 67). It may be that the indicative form first enters the Roman rite in the baptism of the sick: it occurs in the order for baptism of the sick in the *Hadrianum Supplement* (probably a seventh-century rite), paras. 981–4, pp. 335–6; and cf. Gy 1982, p. 68.
[31] On the authorship of the *Supplement*, see Deshusses' introduction, pp. 63ff.

deep: whereas in the *Gelasian* practice the parent or godparent answered for the child while he was being dipped, so that adult understanding was inseparable – dramatically speaking – from infant passivity, here in the *Supplement* the questions and answers were cut off from baptism itself. Baptism is thus an action on the child, an application of forces to him. It is as though one takes stock of the understanding assumed by the questions in the moment between the questions and the baptism, and then delivers it to the child who is an object of the questions. Abandoning the confusion of roles which bound adult and child together, the *Supplement* does away with the fiction that the child can answer for himself; he is now will-less, in keeping with his inherited loss of will in Adam. The richer imaginings of the *Leonine* feast of the Innocents have faded away; and the priest meanwhile, instead of being in dialogue with the assembly even at the heightened moment of the immersion itself, is now much more firmly represented as the broker of ritual power. This shift in priestly function, which is visible in the same period in the new rite of anointing the hands at ordination,[32] marks an aloofness of priest from people which will become important in the ecclesiological development of sacrament from the ninth to the twelfth centuries.

One further example of these changes can hardly be ignored: the purpose of the scrutinies up to the sixth century is described by John the Deacon, a Roman writing to Senarius, a high official of the court at Ravenna, in about 500. They are called scrutinies, John says, because in them

We examine (*perscrutamur*) the hearts [of the *electi*] about the faith, as to whether the holy words have lodged in their minds after the renunciation of the devil, whether they have understood the grace which is to be from the Redeemer, whether they confess belief in God the Father Almighty.[33]

The three scrutinies of the Roman rite are thus a growth from the custom mentioned by Hippolytus of examining the *electi*, those in the final stage of the catechumenate, on their progress towards the crucial moment. Even John, who was writing when infant

---

[32] Père Gy (Gy 1978) argues that this emphasis on the sacredness of the priest's hands – a natural expression of the sacredness of the priest himself – lies behind the new practice, enjoined by the *Libri de synodalibus causis* of Regino of Prüm (*c.* 906), of communion taken in the mouth (and not in the hands first) by adults. For Regino's text see ibid., p. 118.

[33] *Epistola ad Senarium* 4, p. 173.

baptism was already the norm, may, however, be giving a learned rather than a realistic description of the sense;[34] a century or so later, in the Roman *Ordo XI*, the number of these meetings increased from three to seven, and for entirely artificial reasons: it is fitting, says the compiler of the *Ordo*, that just as the seven gifts of the Spirit are bestowed after baptism, so the candidate should be prepared by seven scrutinies falling between the third week in Lent and Holy Saturday.[35] Again, the idea of the rite as a meeting of human and divine will – Augustine's idea of an ethical sacrament – has withered away; the overall effect of *Ordo XI* is to turn scrutiny from instruction and examination into exorcism: into an objective purification from evil. To make the number up to seven, *Ordo XI* has ignored the three old Roman scrutinies of the third, fourth and fifth Sundays in Lent, and attached the label 'scrutiny' to the rite of entry into the catechumenate (*ordo ad caticuminum faciendum*), to that of the 'opening of the ears' (*apertio aurium*), and to that of *effeta* on Holy Saturday which includes a recitation of the Creed, originally by the *electus*, now by a godparent. None of these had been scrutinies in the *Gelasian* from which they are borrowed. The compiler has then added four further week-day scrutinies simply by repeating the *ordo ad caticuminum faciendum* four times.

With this more than ever the rite has shifted from expression to form: since the *ordo ad caticuminum faciendum*, now repeated five times in Lent, is a sequence of exorcisms, the dominant key is that of exorcism or purification. More radical still, the *effeta*, which intertwines objective exorcism and subjective reununciation – as well as the recital of the Creed – and the *Apertio aurium*, which is a homiletic, and highly allusive, commentary on the first words of each Gospel, on the Creed (of Nicaea-Constantinople) and the Lord's Prayer, are both made to serve this dominant key of exorcism. Throughout, the balance which the Fathers had seen in sacrament between the voluntary and the involuntary, between the individual 'turning' towards Truth, and the Truth to which the soul turned, had been upset by the spectacle of a child, perhaps no more than a few weeks old, offered up to what was still essentially an adult rite. The great themes of enlightenment – 'annunciation', 'showing', 'opening', of *reformatio* and *illuminatio* –

[34] Andrieu, introduction to *Ordo XI*, pp. 383–4.
[35] *Ordo XI*, no. 81, p. 442. And for this and what follows, Andrieu's introductory discussion, pp. 380–408.

the images which suggest an active change in the soul towards
ueram conuersationem, are rendered passive.[36] And catechesis, the
process of learning how to distinguish good from evil, becomes an
external operation of the removal of evil: exorcism. If the
candidate desires baptism, or thirsts for it as the deer of Psalm 41
thirsts for water, he does so only insofar as the congregation thirsts
through him; the compelling image – and the reality, because this
is what is done in baptism – is now that of purification. The
child's powerlessness in baptism was thus an exact symbol of his
parents' sense of passive weakness – and of fear – before the
prospect of Judgement.

We can gain no idea of the force of infant baptism, its
continuing power to compel, unless we see that the parents – and
with them the whole liturgical crowd assembled at the Paschal
baptism – imagined themselves in the child.[37] They as much as

[36] *Ordo XI*, nos. 42ff, pp. 427ff; and *Gelasian*, nos. 310ff, pp. 48ff. Thus in *Ordo XI*, the
Praefatio symboli, introducing the *Traditio symboli* (no. 61, p. 433, the text changed only
slightly from the *Gelasian*): 'Dilectissimi nobis, accepturi sacramenta baptismatis et in
nouam creaturam sancti spiritus procreandi, fidem, quam credentes iustificandi estis,
toto corde concipite et animis uestris bonam [Gelasian: ueram] conuersationem mutate
ad Deum, qui mentium uestrarum est inluminator; accedite, suscipientes euangelici
symbolum, sacramenti a Deo inspiratum, ab apostolis institutum, cuius pauca quidem
uerba sunt sed magna mysteria.' In the reply made by Maxentius of Aquileia to
Charlemagne's letter on baptism, he turns scrutiny as test and examination of faith – as it
had been for the older tradition, including John the Deacon – into scrutiny as exorcism:
'Scrutinium namque est inquisitio et inuestigatio, quia opera diaboli et eius pompae,
quae primum hominem in paradiso per prauam suggestionem mandato dei separauer-
ant, et uas illud ex limo terrae formatum et animatum ueneno suae malitiae infecerant,
per ora sacerdotum et manus impositionem scrutiniatum atque purgatum, et eiectum
exinde spiritum immundum' (*Ep. ad Carolum* 2, PL CVI, col. 52) Theodulph of Orléans,
in his reply, seems to think the scrutinies unnecessary to infants, *Lib. de ord. bapt.*, col.
228B: 'Qui uero illius iam aetatis ut rationem credulitatis suae reddere possint, diligenti
examine scrutandi sunt'; and he takes the historical view that the child becomes a
catechumen not in order to learn, but in order that *antiquus mos* be maintained: ibid.,
col. 224B–C. Neither the *Hadrianum* nor its *Supplement* mention the scrutinies, but the
Hadrianum refers to the *Apertio aurium* with the words *Post pisteugis* (*sic*), i.e. 'after the
Creed' (no. 359, p. 182). In view of what Theodulph says, this may mean that scrutinies
had been abandoned; more likely though, they were to be supplied from *Ordo XI* or a
similar source.

[37] An unusually precise example of this occurs in the *Sacramentary of Marmoutier*, a version
of the *Hadrianum* copied *c.* 845 – and the basis of the edition of the *Supplement* by
Deshusses – where in the *ordo ad caticumenum faciendum* the regeneration of the child
turns into that of the adult community in the course of a single prayer: 'Preces nostras
quaesumus domine clementer exaudi, et hunc electum tuum crucis dominicae cuius
inpraessione cum signamus uirtute custodi, ut magnitudinis gloriae rudimenta seruans,
per custodiam mandatorum tuorum ad regenerationis peruenire gloriam mereamur'
(*Hadrianum Supplement*, no. 1066, pp. 371–2; for the *mereantur* of other MSS, see
apparatus on p. 372).

their children were adrift on stormy seas, in desperate need of a 'helmsman': such is the metaphor of the Lenten liturgy which is taken up by the Anglo-Saxon poem *Andreas*.[38] These were times when the smallness of the soul in the face of good and evil was represented most accurately in exorcism. Exorcism in the *Gelasian* or *Ordo XI* is a more subtle process than it might at first seem to be. Awakening desire and disgust, it does after all involve the self, the personal will. But the immediate impression left by exorcism is of a magical-medicinal cure; or of a purification which ignores the willing subject. And it is this first sense which is borne out by much of the context of medieval notions of good and evil.

The body, in the exorcisms of the *Gelasian* or *Ordo XI*, is in the first place a passive object, stricken with disease and blindness and bound with chains: and because what happens to the body is a way of saying what happens to the soul, the soul too is passive: 'Expel from these [your servants (*famulos*)] their blindness of heart, break apart Satan's stranglehold which binds them down.'[39] Humankind has been founded; it must now be refounded, become a race renewed. As in Paul's theology of the old Adam and the new Adam, the will in its individual capacity tends to be swallowed up by Adam and Christ as types of the old condition of man and the new. And the body undergoing these rites of cleansing – which, we should recall yet again, is usually in the early Middle Ages the body of a child – is little distinguished from the dumb ritual matter of salt and water and oil: 'I exorcize you, creature of salt . . .'.[40] The body, like the elements, is worked on by a medicinal magic which separates the dirt and darkness of the diabolic from the *seruus dei*: 'You will have no share with the servants of God . . . Give honour to the Holy Spirit in his coming.'[41] And so the devil is forced to recognize his own fraudulence and give up his pretensions. In this battle between gods, he must go into retreat before superior powers; acknowledge the separation which since the fall of angels has been his lot. Exorcism, in other words, works on the principle of dualism which Augustine had found it so hard to resist, especially in the rhetorical warmth of his sermons. Salvation, in this view of things, seems to happen more in an external physical process than in the soul.

---

[38] *Andreas*, esp. lines 235–468. [39] *Gelasian*, no. 285, p. 43.
[40] Ibid., no. 288, p. 43; *Hadrianum Supplement*, no. 1068, p. 372.
[41] *Gelasian*, no. 294, p. 45; *Hadrianum Supplement*, no. 1075, p. 375.

Evil, in such portrayals, is not an absence or a mere failure of being, as Augustine described it to his Pelagian opponents; it is a positive presence, a concrete condition. It is not not-being, but bad being. This is hardly in doubt if we consider the early medieval picture of hell: hell is a place of physical pain and moral suffering. Although it represents a Fall, it is not a falling away from being but another kind of being, symmetrically opposed to heaven. The symmetry, and thus the positive quality of evil, is brought home resoundingly in the Anglo-Saxon account of hell as 'the deep surge down under the headlands in the low abyss', an image which had all the precision and immediacy that an island people, with its poetry of seafaring, would naturally give it.[42] This impression of evil as another kind of being, and one which had little to do with a discerning, willing intention, had ancient roots: it was partly a legacy of the Gnostic element in Christianity, itself – as we have seen – intertwined with the old Jewish teaching of the Two Ways; and it was preserved by the common motif of the seven deadly sins, a Babylonian idea, and then later again a Gnostic one, which associated sin with the dangerous journey of the soul through the seven heavens, and thus tended to make of it a metaphysical and astrological disorder more than a moral choice.[43] But within Christianity, the perception of evil as positive in this way was bound to become more forceful as it was solidified in certain images, which in time grew into common-places, so that evil tended to be conceived more and more as exterior and immovable. This is true of the two great myths of the 'ransom theory' and the 'harrowing of hell', both of which dramatize the opposition between good and evil by showing mankind as the object of conflict between Christ and Satan: man is enslaved by the devil after Adam has played into his hands, and only Christ, who is not subject to the devil nor to the death which he inflicts, can release him. This is the 'ransom theory'.[44] The 'harrowing of hell' tells the story of Christ's descent into Satan's gloomy empire to vanquish his hold over mankind, and lead the ancient just up to their 'homeland', into the 'renowned citadel'.[45]

[42] *Christ and Satan*, p. 126; and cf. the late eighth-/early ninth-century ivory plaque representing the Last Judgement (the first known example of this theme in the West) with Hades swallowing the damned: Beckwith 1972, no. 4.

[43] Bloomfield 1952, pp. 1–104.   [44] On the doctrine of ransom, Rivière 1934.

[45] These images are from *Christ and Satan*, pp. 131–2. For the early history of the *descensus ad inferos*, and particularly on the association between water and the lower world in Judaism and early Christianity, Lundberg 1942, pp. 64–72.

It should be said that in a poem such as *Christ and Satan*, an Anglo-Saxon treatment of this story, the opposition between high and low, Christ and Satan, is cast as an invitation to moral reflection: it is an opposition between pride and righteous humility, and thus an appeal to conscience. At the same time, though, it is hard not to feel that the repeated association of Satan with lowness, darkness and perhaps most of all with the false word, and of Christ with 'the habitation above', light and true words (including the promises of prophecy which he now fulfils), must have hardened the episode into a story of embattlement over man's soul, rather than within it. In the case of the ransom theory, which hinges on the disputed possession of rights over man, such hardening is clearer still. Like many peasants, the soul was unfree. A similar idea of redemption makes an earthy appearance in the story of a slave-woman in tenth-century Winchester. Fettered and chained by her lord, whom she had aggrieved in some small way, she was condemned to be heavily beaten the following day. Passing the night in abject prayer for the intervention of St Swithun, the chains fell from her feet as dawn broke. Rushing to Swithun's tomb, her hands were freed too. Her angry lord, 'not on his own will but forced by God', let her go away unharmed.[46] As in the 'ransom theory', the woman gained her freedom by the prevailing of one lord over another.

How much has this to do with baptism and its exorcisms? The view of man as little more than the object of rights, unable to gain his freedom except by being made 'serf of God' (*seruus dei, famulus dei*), is already written into the liturgy of exorcism:

God of Abraham, God of Isaac, God of Jacob, God who counselled the tribes of Israel and freed Susannah from false accusation, we beg and implore you, Lord, to give their freedom to these your servants also (*ut liberes et has famulas tuas*).[47]

The will is servile. We have already seen it being treated like a patient under the priest's medicine. It is also – obviously enough in baptism – a contaminated substance which needs washing clean: 'that the heart purged in the divine font ... become a temple made holy to God';[48] or, in the inscription of the baptistery of

---

[46] *Miraculi S. Swithuni*, cols. 67D–68A.
[47] *Gelasian*, no. 295, p. 45; cf. *Hadrianum Supplement*, no. 1076, p. 375.
[48] *Gelasian*, no. 294, p. 45; *Hadrianum Supplement*, no. 1075, p. 375.

Mainz, 'Here the flock is dipped in the pure waves, so that the sheep does not carry its dirty fleece too long.'[49] All this connected imagery encourages the soul to see itself not as freely choosing between right and wrong, but as the object of right and wrong. The tenor of exorcism, the whole notion of a bodily purification which is also a purification of the soul, introduces a strong element of determinacy into the conception of good and evil. The priest comes to resemble at once a doctor and a herald of battle to be done by God and Satan; in this role, he conducts the operation by which the devil is forced to 'step back from this servant of God',[50] to 'acknowledge [his] sentence and give honour to the living God'.[51] The candidate is a vessel to be emptied and filled; or a stained cloth to be scrubbed clean.

As well as purification from what is thought of as the physical stain of sin, exorcism – and baptism generally – brings a sudden clarity; a shaft of light which transforms chaos into order. It re-enacts the first and greatest of exorcisms: the Creation; and it is by virtue of God-the-Creator that exorcism works: 'I exorcize you creature of water, by God the Creator of all that is sweet who with his word separated you in the beginning from the earth.'[52] In baptism, the child was re-created, and so removed from the anarchy of his first birth.[53] He was made clear in the way that God made matter clear, separating water from land and naming the animals. Nor should we suppose that an early medieval congregation pressed too hard the theology of Creation from Nothing: this was an age with a gift for seeing the physical shape of evil, in leprosy, plague, poor harvests, bad kings, Vikings on the rampage, heretics and 'fallen' women. In other words, Creation was creation from bad matter, from chaos, not from Nothing. We see a reflection of this in some of the perceptions of the child

---

49 Quasten 1939, pp. 223–4.
50 *Gelasian*, no. 296, p. 45; *Hadrianum Supplement*, no. 1077, p. 376.
51 *Gelasian*, no. 292, p. 44; *Hadrianum Supplement*, no. 1072, p. 374.
52 *Sacramentary of Angoulême*, no. 2000, p. 138.
53 A number of words are used in the liturgies to express the broad idea of 'reform': *refectio* (*Gelasian*, no. 382, p. 61); *renovatio* (ibid., nos. 337, 377, pp. 54, 60); and most frequently, *regeneratio*, as in ibid., nos. 450, 451, p. 74, etc. The rite for reconciling penitents in the *Gelasian* also uses *reformatio* (ibid., no. 359, p. 57). The sense of clarity at Creation, and repeated in the ritual present, is especially striking in the opening of the benediction of the Easter candle on the vigil of Holy Saturday: 'Deus, mundi conditor, auctor luminis, siderum fabricator, deus qui iacentem mundum in tenebris luce perspicua retexisti, deus, per quem ineffabili potentia omnia claritas sumpsit exordium . . .'.

who was to be re-created. For the child at this time represented the uncertainty of the future: in an age of high infant mortality he was full of possibilities both good and bad. He might live and perpetuate a lineage or renew a community, or he might fade within hours. He was an object of anxiety and hope. Like other marginal figures, he was peculiarly susceptible to other-worldly influences: from Augustine we know of the belief that a demonic child might spit out the host in sacrilege;[54] and Burchard of Worms, near the year 1000, lays down a two-year penance for any woman who has driven a stake through the body of an unbaptized child, intending to prevent it from returning to do harm to the living.[55] On the other hand, the child was an instrument of prophecy, after the example of John the Baptist, the greatest of child-prophets,

who when yet a child in his mother's womb leapt with prophetic joy at the imminent salvation of man; who at his conception wiped away the blot of his mother's barrenness, loosed his father's tongue at his birth, and alone among the prophets pointed his finger at the redeemer of the world whom he had foretold.[56]

Not every child, it is true, was a John the Baptist or a child-Christ as he appeared in the infancy Gospels; on the other hand, these figures acted as archetypes for those that came after them, the 'normal children' of history; and in the ritual context of baptism itself, the child was assimilated to Christ, and thus, presumably, in a sense, to the Christ-child.[57] The ordinary child also held promise of a humbler kind: the promise of a young boy which the

[54] *Ep.* 98.4, col. 361.   [55] Burchard, *Decretum* 20, *PL* CXL, col. 947.
[56] *Sacramentarium Veronense*, no. 254, p. 33; cf. Luke 1:5–66. In the woman of the Middle Ages, barrenness was an affront, and yet her virginity was an object of respect; and her fruitfulness, however desirable, could never be dissociated from the uncleanness of her body, particularly from menstruation and childbirth itself. For a ritual of 'churching', or purification of the mother after childbirth, Franz 1909, pp. 224–5. On the particular ways in which menstruation and childbirth were associated in the Middle Ages, Wood 1981. And on all these ambiguities, see the very rich study in Bynum 1987.
[57] In a tenth- or early eleventh-century walrus ivory carving of the Baptism of Christ, related in style to the Benedictional of St Æthelwold from Winchester or Ely, the figure of Christ is that of a child, who cowers slightly before the Baptist (Beckwith 1972, no. 14); for two earlier examples, Dalton 1909, no. 9: ivory panel showing on the right Christ among the doctors, on the left the Baptism of Christ (fifth century, Dalton argues for western provenance, p. 8), where the baptized Christ is a small child standing in the Jordan; and no. 10: a Baptism of Christ in ivory, where the Christ is 'of juvenile aspect' beardless against the bearded Baptist (sixth century, Egypt or Syria).

tenth-century *Romano-Germanic Pontifical* celebrates in its ritual for the first hair-cutting;[58] and the connection made between the child and fate is borne out by the frequent employment of children to draw lots in Late Antiquity and the Middle Ages.[59] Like the forest, the child was untilled, a place of spirits both good and bad; and like the forest, the child could be reclaimed.[60]

Seen like this, original sin was no more than a learned statement of a less conscious disquiet about new-born babies and even children. A child upset the balance, introduced something shapeless into the social fabric. A *Life of St Odo of Cluny* breathes a sigh of relief when Odo's little nephew is baptized by the saint and almost immediately vanishes heavenward, after an adventure during which the boy and his nurse had been captured by Normans, and escaped by night across the river Seine.[61] The text is a model translation of liturgy into story, showing one of the ways in which liturgy entered into the minds of its congregations: for Normans read Satan and his pomps; for the river read the water of baptism, as well as the Jordan; the journey of the boy and his nurse is clearly a 'passage' or *transitus*, and the night suggests the vigil of Easter Saturday, the 'legitimate time' of baptism. The role of the nurse is less obvious, but she is presumably the church, nurturing and protecting through the journey, until the child is brought back to her. Showing through this story is the medieval ideal – actually performed in baptism – of reducing the 'passage' of life, the treacherous time of waiting, so radically that birth is as nearly as possible reduced to death. Odo's baby nephew (young enough to have a *nutrix* with him) remains just long enough for

---

[58] 1, pp. 3–4.   [59] Courcelle 1953.

[60] Le Goff 1988, pp. 47–59, stresses the medieval conception of the forest as an empty space, at once promising and dangerous. The sense of expectancy vested in the child is conveyed by a Roman prayer for Candlemas (on this feast, see above, n. 10): 'Perfice in nobis quaesumus domine gratiam tuam, qui iusti Symeonis expectationem implesti, ut sicut ille mortem non uidit, prius quam Christum dominum uidere mereretur ita et nos uitam optineamus aeternam. Per dominum' (*Hadrianum* no. 127, p. 124). The possibility which is in the child as he is offered to Simeon's blessing, and the answering expectancy of Simeon reflect the more general principle that the story of the life, death and resurrection of Christ contains in its brevity the long story of all that has gone before (the history of Israel) and all that is to come (the *consolatio* of Israel) (Luke 2:25). The transaction is between the *puer* looking forward and the *senex* looking back. Does the theme of the *puer–senex* recur, for example, in the Winchester (or perhaps Ely) ivory of the Baptism of Christ (see above, n. 57). On the *puer–senex*, Curtius 1953, pp. 98–101.

[61] *Life of St Odo of Cluny* 16, cols. 69–70 (I am grateful to Dr Patricia Morison for this reference).

this brief but victorious encounter with Satan's army, and then, in body as well as ritual metaphor, returns whence he came.

Baptism reclaims the child. The salt of wisdom, writes Theodulph of Orléans – responding to Charlemagne's encyclical letter on baptism (812) – will cure those who receive it from any 'flux or flow which might be in them'. He is talking about the practice of placing salt on the candidates' tongues in the third week of Lent in the *Gelasian* and *Ordo XI*. Like Lot's wife, who was turned into a pillar of salt when she looked back on the road from Sodom (cf. Luke 17:32), the catechumens are forbidden to turn back to the place of their imprisonment.[62] In a similar vein, Alcuin – taking up the ancient symbolism of 'sealing' – stresses how the anointing of chest and shoulders just before immersion is a closing-off of the whole body to the devil: 'defences are laid all around'.[63] Alcuin has a liking for the orderly, systematic element in ritual, partly for political reasons. But the desire in this letter to Oduin (and elsewhere) to make baptism an act of definition is a tendency he would have found in the liturgies themselves. The *Gelasian* for example (and then *Ordo XI* and the *Hadrianum Supplement*) divides the little catechumens into male and female in the ceremonies of exorcism, and addresses each group separately: 'This to be said over the females', 'This over the males' and so on.[64] But in an order of scrutinies from a north Italian city – probably Grado or Brescia or Pavia – dated by its editor to the eighth century, the sensitivity to forms, and to their precise expression in gesture, is in a class of its own. Behind the text we can picture the involvement of a whole city and its hinterland in a long ritual of assemblies and separations. On thirteen occasions, the families of the children to be baptized bring the children and

---

[62] *Lib. de ord. bapt.*, col. 226: 'debent accipere salem sapientiae, ut quidquid in eis fluxum et fluidum est, uerbi dei sale curetur, et . . . memores sint uxoris Lot'. Theodulph is taking up a theme used by John the Deacon in his letter to Senarius (*Epistola ad Senarium* 3, p. 172), and again by the commentary which accompanies this text in the *florilegium* on baptism (attributed to Alcuin by Wilmart): Wilmart 1933, pp. 158–9. This idea of ridding the child of flux recalls a twelfth-century story, in the *Life of St Otto of Bamberg*, telling how Otto, during his mission to the Pomeranians, finds some children playing in the street. He asks them which of them are baptized, and tells those who identify themselves that if they wish to 'keep the faith of their baptism', they must shun their unbaptized playmates. Eventually the pagan children, 'quasi de infidelitate confusi et exterriti', succumb to Otto's persuasions, and are baptized themselves (*MGH Script.* xii, p. 813).

[63] *Ep.* 134, p. 202; *ep.* 137, p. 214: 'ut undique muniatur'.

[64] *Gelasian*, nos. 293–7, pp. 44–5; *Ordo XI*, nos. 18–25, pp. 422–4; *Hadrianum Supplement*, nos. 1073–9, pp. 374–6.

their older brothers and sisters to the cathedral. At each session, the catechumens are shut out from the assembly, carried presumably by their sponsors. As Lent draws on, more families arrive from outlying villages, and offer their children to the 'scrutinies', so that progressively the rite reflects a meeting, a concentration of the city and its hinterland within the city walls: a centralizing and a tightening of kin-relations.[65] The prayers, appropriately, dwell on both 'family' and 'people', suggesting a process of integration between the two. Throughout, the rite is occupied with formal rhythm, with what amounts to a ritual choreography, so that the gathering of Israel 'from the scattered peoples' of Ezechiel 28:35 – the reading for the fourth Saturday in Lent here – resembles a Dance of the Blessed. The deacon turns to the south to pray; he bends; he rises; he bends towards the priest and the priest turns to the assembly. The catechumens stand with their families in the choir. They stand 'with grace and reverence'; in a circle; or they bend towards the priest as the priest bends towards them.[66] From the cathedral they process to the church of Santa Maria on Holy Saturday; after the Gospel, the catechumens leave and stand outside the doors; when two antiphons have been sung, the doors are opened by two deacons carrying olive branches, one of whom leads the female candidates back within, the other the male. And after all the opening and closing of Lent, the distinction between holy and profane is reiterated with chanting:

> The catechumen, let him leave.
> The heretic, let him leave.
> The Arian, let him leave.
> The Manichaean, let him leave.
> The Bonosian, let him leave.
> The pagan, let him leave.
> The Jew, let him leave.
> The incurable, let him leave.[67]

The Christian is the one who has learnt, even carried by his sponsor, to take part in this solemn, exclusive, dance.[68]

[65] *North Italian Services*, pp. 7–31.   [66] Ibid., pp. 10ff.
[67] Ibid., p. 24. For Bonosian, follower of Bonosus (d. *c.* 400), who denied the perpetual virginity of Mary, see references in *ODCC*, p. 189.
[68] An example of what has been called a Dance of the Blessed is in Bamberg cod. bibl. 22, fo. 4r, which illustrates the text of the Song of Songs glossed by an abbreviated version of Bede's commentary on the Song of Songs (see following paragraphs). The illumination interprets Solomon's stately procession in the Song of Songs (the *ascensus purpureus* of the commentary) as a mannered dance, upward past the figures of *ecclesia*, the Virgin,

The dance is the antithesis of the chaos represented by Jews, pagans, and Bonosians. It is a mannered performance of an ideal world, a world from which all the 'impurities' have been sloughed away, a Utopia of forms. In it, the determinist vision of ethics which attaches naturally to exorcism has developed into an aesthetic vision of perfection. It is a perfection recognizable in Bede's vision of the church as the bride of the Song of Songs – a vision perhaps conceived in Bede's youth – of a church without spot or wrinkle, whose essential characteristic is her beauty.[69] In one passage of his *Commentary on the Song of Songs*, Bede makes clear the practical connection between baptism and the attainment of this beauty. The church, he explains, is without spot or wrinkle

not because any of the saints can be innocent of all blame or perfect in virtue in this life . . . but because the church is holy insofar as she is the church of Christ, true in faith and pure in deed; and insofar as any impurity or wickedness which cleaves to her, being no part of her, may be forcibly purged away the quicker for its foreignness. John has something similar to this: If a man is born from God, he does no sin, for God's seed stays in him, and born from God, he cannot sin [cf. 1 John 3:9]. Insofar as the seed of God's grace, by which we are reborn, stays in

who holds out the chalice, and thus to the crucified Christ, from whose side issues the nurturing blood of the eucharist. The movement of the dance is that of a helix: it moves round, but it also progresses upward, through baptism and the eucharist. It is as though the purely cyclical is broken by a linear progression from sin to beatitude (cf. Hanning 1979 on the circular dance in fourteenth-century England as an image of futility). The artist has also expressed the progress of the dancers as a transformation worked by baptism: those who have not yet reached the font are of various race, colour and sex; those after it have become a nation of priests, kings and prophets (cf. 1 Peter 2:9). On the facing folio is a *maiestas* of unusual power, suggesting – in contrast to the earthbound agitation of the dancers on the left – the uncanny weightlessness of the angelic liturgy, where all movement has been turned to harmony. The formal perfection of the *maiestas* is conceived, through colder colours, as distant, whereas the figures of the left-hand page have a certain familiar warmth. On this double page, see Fischer 1926, pp. 4–6; and Mayr-Harting (1991), II, ch. 1. On dance as a theological image in the Middle Ages, Meyer-Baer 1970.

69 Thus Bede, *In Cant.* 3.4.9, p. 257: 'Tota quidem forma tui corporis, quo per mundum longe lateque dilataris, o ecclesia catholica, pulchra mihi et immaculata appares.' For a highly stimulating account of this and other themes in Bede's commentary, Riedlinger 1958, pp. 72–88. Riedlinger suggests that Bede may have composed this commentary in his youth, on the grounds of its energetic and optimistic mysticism. Hurst in his edition (*CCSL* CXIXB, *praefatio*) mentions the lack of evidence for dating, and concludes, 'Cum ratio certa absit, illa circa A. D. 720–730 scripta iudicari possunt', in other words in Bede's later life: he was born in 672/3 and died in 735. On the work within the Song of Songs tradition, see also Ohly 1958; and on the relation of earthly to heavenly church, Congar 1968, pp. 104–27.

the just man, he cannot sin. Insofar as he does sin, the grace of rebirth works in him again, freeing him as time requires.[70]

In this lies all the subtlety of medieval idealism, troubled over the sin which cuts man off from God, the church on earth from the heavenly church, and yet always – with more or less confidence – questioning or even ignoring this estrangement. But Bede, perhaps inspired not just by his own youth but by the youth of his people,[71] does more than question: he offers a way of seeing which makes the heavenly church, in a real sense, indistinguishable from the earthly. He has gone beyond the vague Platonism which had informed the views of Origen and Augustine on the church; he has avoided the moral optimism of Julian of Eclanum who put the heavenly church simply in good action in the world.[72] He has said instead that the heavenly church is present in potentiality, in the possibility of not sinning, which even if in each individual it is only a possibility, is present insofar as he does not sin. It is present in the seed sown in him at baptism. For Bede, the image of this possibility is the beauty of the bride; and equally, we might say of baptism that the clarity which it brings out from chaos, the beauty of its forms, is the image of the heavenly in man. Liturgical forms, then, which at first appear to be nothing more than the counterpart of man's prostration before God – especially in the case of infant baptism – are also a playing out, as it were, of the presence of a mystical church in the midst of the earthly. Or, more exactly, liturgy is a representation through forms of the world insofar as it is heavenly: in its capacity for eternity.

Elsewhere, there are other symptoms of an idealistic turn of mind expressed in liturgy, although lacking the elegance of Bede's conception. The bishops who replied to Charlemagne's questions about baptism – despatched in 812 – stressed in their letters the mystical and eschatological dimension of baptism, while some of them, much like Bede again, balanced this carefully against its moral aspects. Theodulph of Orléans, for example, saw the closing rites of baptism – the putting on of white robes, anointing with chrism, laying-on of a 'mystic veil', laying-on of hands by the bishop and eucharist – as various ways of representing the access to the heavenly made possible by baptism. The donning of

---

[70] *In Cant.* 3.4.7, p. 254 (cited Riedlinger 1958, pp. 84–5).
[71] Cf. Riedlinger 1958, p. 84.   [72] Ibid., pp. 72ff.

white robes is thus not only a reminder of cleanness, and of the 'newness' of baptism, but presents a spectacle of 'the angel's glorious beauty';[73] and both the anointing with chrism and the placing of a 'mystic veil' over the head are for him signs that baptism is entry to an eternal kingship and priesthood, to a 'chosen race, a royal priesthood, a consecrated nation, a people God means to have for himself', in the words of 1 Peter 2:9.[74] And this in turn leads one to reflect on the complex of ideas studied by Ernst Kantorowicz, by which the king is made Christ-like at his anointing.[75] At least in his liturgical persona, the Carolingian or Ottonian king was Christ-like even to the point of being at once God and man. To this it is reasonable to respond that if the king was Christ-like by anointing, so were all his subjects by their baptism; and that in the body of the child in baptism, as much as in the body of the king by his consecration, the ideal and the real were joined.[76]

WILL TO FORM

Forms, however, only represent – as we have found out from Bede – what the soul might become. Their beauty, and the clarity of form which is sculpted out of chaos in exorcism, is not simply the beauty of the soul, but the possibility in the soul. Forms represent not what the soul is, but the soul's striving, the effort with which it reaches above itself. There is no form – because nothing to represent – without this striving. If this is true of infant baptism in particular, it is because the whole complex of forms and ideas and experience brought into play at Easter or Pentecost still applies when children are baptized. We have seen how legislation and pastoral theology from Caesarius onward tried to

---

73 *Lib. de ord. bapt.* 14, col. 233: 'et nos albis post baptismum induimur uestibus, ut munditiam teneamus in opere quam accepimus in regeneratione, seruantes et nostram innouationem, et angelici splendoris decorem'. And consider the ethical idealism inherent in the notion of the seven gifts of the Holy Spirit, stressed by Theodulph as a part of confirmation, ibid.

74 Ibid. 16, col. 235.

75 Kantorowicz 1957; and Kantorowicz 1952 for the Patristic origins of the doctrine that sacramental grace involved a *Christomimesis*.

76 Thus baptism is assimilation to Christ's death, burial and resurrection, after Rom. 6:3ff.: the *florilegium* on baptism attributed to Alcuin by Wilmart takes up this Pauline idea and relates it to the symbolism of immersion and emergence from the font (Wilmart 1933, p. 161); the Carolingian authors follow the *florilegium*, here as often. For this sense of identity with Christ, also see below, pp. 159–67. And on the associations between baptism and the anointing of the king in art, Hoffmann 1968.

keep a balance between the urgency of saving infants from original sin – a purely functional baptism – and the association between baptism and the 'feasts of idea' of Easter and Pentecost;[77] now in the letters of the Carolingian bishops to Charlemagne, answering his queries on baptism, there is plenty of evidence that the balancing act has lost none of its importance.[78] It goes on at least into the twelfth century. In view of it, it is reasonable to suppose that even emergency, non-seasonal baptisms were deeply coloured with ideas carried over from Easter and Pentecost. We can still assume, in other words, that baptism was a performance, and not just an abbreviated, unexplained visitation made by God to the soul. It was a performance in the broad sense of a theatre expressing the striving of the soul from the earthly to the heavenly.

For liturgy begins with the earthly, with the privileged elements of water, fire, oil, bread, wine. This was Tertullian's problem[79] – the 'stupidity' of water – and it remains Theodulph's:

Since the element of water is the most appropriate among all the elements of this world to the grace of purging, vivifying, re-making, it is reasonable that the grace of baptism should be conferred on it. After all, when the spirit of God was borne over it at the beginning of the world, it conceived the power (*efficaciam*) of regenerating men; and the dignity of purging them it took to itself when it flowed from Christ's side. So, through this visible element the invisible thing is signified, and as the water cleans the body outside, so the soul, in some hidden way, is purified by the water's mystery.[80]

What has Theodulph done here? He has wound into a single thread the physical, ordinary functions of water – it washes and it nurtures life – with the presence of spirit in water, by way of its Biblical sense; and in doing this he has fused together the sensation of water as a familiar, everyday thing, having certain uses and

---

[77] See above, pp. 137ff.
[78] See, for example, Leidrad's paragraph on the infant in baptism as penitent, by virtue of his godparents' responses: *Lib. de sac. bapt.* 10, col. 868.
[79] See above, ch. 2.
[80] *Lib. de ord. bapt.* 13, col. 232: 'Quia ergo elementum aquae in hoc mundo omnibus elementis purgandi, uiuificandi, recreandi gratia aptius est, non immerito ei baptismi dignitas confertur, quia et regenerandorum hominum efficaciam, cum spiritus dei in mundi primordio super id ferebatur, concipiebat, et purgandorum, cum ex latere Christi proflueret, dignitatem capiebat. Per hoc etenim uisibile elementum res illa inuisibilis signatur, ut sicut aqua purgatur exterius corpus, ita latenter eius mysterio per spiritum sanctum purificetur et animus.' Cf. Jesse of Amiens, *Ep. de bapt.*, col. 790.

properties, with the conception of the spirit. The arc of meaning which moves from sensation to idea, from the cleaning of the body to the purging of the soul, is therefore attributed to the object which gave rise to it.[81] The simple water which fills the bath turns out to be the water impregnated by spirit at Creation. The Biblical – and with it the 'absolute' authority of the Bible – invades the ordinary. And it will never be clear – to the 'liturgical' mind – whether this metamorphosis occurs in the object or in the eye of the mind, the subject. Outward and inward have become indistinguishable. Is baptism the descent of the Spirit, or the aspiration of the soul to the Spirit? It is both at once. In this confusion of subject with object, made possible (as we shall see) by the origin of both in the act of Creation, is the life-blood of sacramental efficacy. It must be stressed, because it was precisely this which Berengar of Tours, writing in the mid-eleventh century about baptism and the eucharist, tended to obscure: for him, two things happened in sacrament, one in the elements, and another, inspired by it but not the same, in the mind.[82] The controversy over the sacraments – mainly the eucharist – in the eleventh and twelfth centuries was in this way the result of a misunderstanding of the part-hidden theological content of liturgy.

Liturgy, the theatre which surrounds sacrament, does not ask the mind or the soul to think, without more ado, of bread somehow being body, or water being spirit. There is no change of substance or essence, as there would be for those who defended what they saw as the integrity of the eucharist against Berengar. Liturgy consists rather in ordinary actions which come to be seen *sub specie aeternitatis*, as actions of the spirit;[83] or, equally, of

---

[81] In reflecting on the phenomenology of medieval liturgy, I have learnt a great deal from Paul Ricoeur's conception of myth and symbols as enactments of implicit philosophies of will, which philosophy in the formal sense can identify, understand, 'repeat' and make coherent (Ricoeur 1960).

[82] *Rescriptum contra Lanfrannum*; and see below, pp. 221–3; 243–54.

[83] Compare Alcuin's remarkable and lucid paragraph on this: 'Tria sunt in baptismatis sacramento uisibilia, et tria inuisibilia. Visibilia sunt sacerdos corpus et aqua. Inuisibilia uero spiritus anima et fides. Illa tria uisibilia nihil proficiunt foris, si haec tria inuisibilia non intus operantur. Sacerdos corpus aqua abluit, spiritus sanctus animam fide iustificat. Et hoc est, quod apostolus ait: "Cooperatores enim dei sumus" [3 John 1:8]. Cooperatur homo spiritui sancto in salute hominis; sed et ipse homo, qui baptizandus est, cooperari ambobus debet in salute sua, id est spiritui sancto et sacerdoti humiliter corpus praestare ad sacri mysterium lauacri et animam uoluntarie ad catolicae fidei susceptionem' (*Ep.* 113, p. 165).

ordinary language, in its everyday, functional usage, refracted in the light of benediction, or language as God's word. In the blessing of the waters on Holy Saturday, the raising up of ordinary language and of ordinary action are run together:

Be present and merciful, Almighty God, to us who keep these your commands, breathe on us your goodness, speak in your mouth the benediction of these simple waters, that they might have strength (*sint efficaces*) not only for the washing of bodies which they do by nature but equally for the purification of minds.[84]

The washing of the body is the washing of the soul. The immersion in water is the baptism of Christ in the Jordan, and therefore the descent of the Trinity, and it is the death, burial and resurrection of Christ.[85] There is no equation between object and meaning, but a 'bringing out' of one action from another; or the 'opening' of a banal, finite action, limited by its purpose or its physicality, to the infinite freedom of God's action. This power, or efficacy, in liturgy is thrown very wide. In the institution of godparenthood and coparenthood, social relations and ordinary blood kinship are made open to a kinship in the spirit;[86] in ordeal, it seems, judgement by a community of one of its members according to *fama* or reputation is transformed into, and made to originate in, the absolute judgement of God.[87] And in this bringing out or opening is the creativity of liturgy: for liturgy is the medium in which the ordinary – war, peace, punishment, physical desire, kinship, pacts – is made transparent to its divine origins.[88] Liturgy, then, is the theatre in which the soul strives beyond the ordinary; and the forms to which it gives so much emphasis, by putting before the soul an illusion of bodily perfection – rhythms of perfect equilibrium like Boethius' music of the spheres or the fluttering of a seraph's wings – represent the beauty of which the soul is capable. But they only represent the beauty, and this we should bear in mind.

---

[84] *Gelasian*, no. 447, p. 73: 'Haec nobis praecepta seruantibus tu, deus omnipotens, clemens adesto, tu benignus aspira, tu has simplices aquas tuo ore benedicito, ut praeter naturalem emundationem, quam lauandis possunt adhiberi corporibus, sint etiam purificandis mentibus efficaces.'

[85] Theodulph, *Lib. de ord. bapt.* 13, col. 232. [86] Lynch 1986.

[87] Cf. Hyams 1981; Bartlett 1986. [88] On this, see below, pp. 159ff.

SEEING INTO THINGS

If we listen to Leidrad of Lyon, writing to Charlemagne in his *Book on the Sacrament of Baptism* (812), we catch at once an impression of the soul's striving:

> The baptized are clothed with white garments, so that the attire of the outward man should show the cleansing and the renewal of the inward. For whoever is brought across from the domain of shadow into the dominion of light and clarity, thereafter uses white clothing after the example less of Jesus son of Joseph than of Jesus son of God.[89]

Here Leidrad benefits from the Vulgate's failure to distinguish the names Joshua and Jesus, Joshua being in the first place the high-priest who rebuilt the temple in Jerusalem during the time of restoration in the sixth century BC (cf. Zach. 3); and from the failure to tell apart Josedech father of Joshua and Joseph father of Jesus. The confusion brings home the theology of fulfilment which Leidrad goes on to outline:

> For what was fore-shadowed in Jesus son of Joseph was fulfilled in Jesus son of God. So it was that the prophet Zachariah said: 'Jesus stood before the angel very vilely clad, and the angel gave it out to his attendants they should take away these vile rags from him. Guilt of thine, said he, I have set by; thou shalt have new garments to wear instead. A clean mitre they should place on his head. And about him they put new garments' [Zach. 3:3–5].[90]

There follows Leidrad's exegesis, itself made up of a skein of Biblical references, and – as in Ambrose but also much of the more emotive homily-writing of the ninth and tenth centuries – weaving imagery and ideas into one cloth:

> Done in part by the Lord Jesus Christ, this is fulfilled all the more in his members, and daily. It might be said that the Lord put on vile clothing when 'knowing no sin He was made sin for us' [2 Cor. 5:21], 'took our infirmities upon himself and bore our sicknesses' [Matt. 8:17]. Yet since there was in him no guilt to carry away, but 'he was wounded because of our guilt' [Isa. 53:5], the vile garments were taken from him with the wiping-away of our sin, so that rising in him, we hear, after our baptism: 'Behold thou shalt have new garments to wear.' And so the Song of Songs asks: 'Who is this who makes her way up' all in white [S. of S. 3:6; 8:5]? Then we receive anointing on the head as though in fulfilment of

---

[89] Leidrad, *Lib. de sac. bapt.* 8, col. 865.   [90] Ibid.

the words: 'A clean mitre they should place on his head. And they put new garments on him.' And again, 'once you were the darkness, now you are light in the Lord' [Eph. 5:8]. Whoever has escaped the darkness of Egypt through baptism, and is made the body of Christ, is deservedly clothed in white garments. The flesh of Christ was buried wrapped around with a clean shroud. Whoever rises from the dead with Christ by passing through the holy font is deservedly clothed in white. The holy angels who witnessed Christ's resurrection came in white garments.[91]

This passage is rich in theatre. Its subject is the identity with Christ brought about by baptism; but it puts across this idea with a series of quickly juxtaposed scenes, and these in turn are dramatic developments of a number of symbols – shadow and light, filth and whiteness, sickness, wounding. There is thus a progression beneath the surface of Leidrad's words, from 'symbol', in the sense of bodily action or sensation which gives rise to meaning, to drama, and thus to idea. The progression is a 'bringing out' of meaning. Leidrad is demonstrating what it is to attend to liturgy: an idea which taken on its own would be prohibitively rarefied, that of being made one with the man-God, is made a sensation in the flesh, because it is shown to have originated in sensation. So it is that the idea of good-against-evil which is (apparently) applied to the child in baptismal exorcism has its roots not only in the thoroughly material belief in the devil and his minions, but also in the difference evoked in the prayers between bad and good smells, between ugliness and beauty, between bad and good medicine.[92] Exorcism, which seems more than any other part of the rite to treat both body and soul as objects, is thus nevertheless – and at the same time – a stimulus to disgust and pleasure in the subject. If the devil smells bad, he demands a subjective reaction; he cannot remain only an idea, or a part of the form of the liturgy.

The theatrical content of Leidrad's 'pictures' raises questions about the relation of liturgy to theatre. There is a picture of Christ

---

[91] Ibid., cols. 865–6.

[92] For smell, *Orationes super electos ad caticumenum faciendum* in *Gelasian*, no. 285, p. 43: 'et signum sapienciae tuae inbuti omnium cupiditatum fedoribus careant, et suaui odore praeceptorum tuorum laeti tibi in aecclesia deseruiant'. Cf. *Hadrianum Supplement*, no. 1065, p. 371. And Leidrad's remarks on the sense of smell becoming a sense of Christ (on the touching of nostrils and ears on Holy Saturday): 'Ille enim tactus ad odoratum fideles prouocat spiritalem, ut non corporis sed mentis sensibus Christum inaestimabili suauitate sentire possint, et dicere ei, "Post te in odorem unguentorum tuorum curremus" [S. of S. 1:3]' (*Lib. de sac. bapt.* 2, col. 858). For the medicinal metaphor, *Gelasian*, no. 288, p. 43; *Hadrianum*, no. 1068, p. 372.

exchanging clean for vile clothing, then other, subsidiary pictures, of Christ wounded on the cross, the bride of the Song of Songs, the crossing of the Red Sea, the burial of Christ, his resurrection, the angelic chorus. But the drama of these scenes is not their fundamental element. It is there to help across from bodily sensation to meaning, and from ritual present to Biblical past, by enlisting the emotions. Rather than the identity with Christ which is the end-product, it arouses sympathy.[93] In this way, it is a middle-stage. Here in Leidrad, the chief emotion is brought on by the story implicit in each scene of pathos turned to the whiteness of glory. The emotion aroused by passion become triumph is already not uncommon in Carolingian times, and is the main ingredient of the ninth-century *Dream of the Rood*, the Anglo-Saxon poem whose theme is Christ as suffering king. The insistence of Leidrad's address, the inclusion of the urgent inter-rogatory voice of the Song of Songs: 'Who is this who makes her way up?', the effect of repetitions which nonetheless build on one another, and the tumbling succession of images and ideas, all suggest the style of Biblical commentary which Beryl Smalley called exclamatory.[94] Such a style, like the theatrical episodes themselves, encourages the soul in its desire for meaning.

The 'bringing out' of meaning from the brute matter of the world makes up a great current in the medieval way of thinking. We can see throughout the liturgy the effort to look behind the appearance of things and history and the cycle of the year, to the truth which sustains them. Everything that meets the eye is a 'covering', obscuring yet suggesting the truth beneath. William of Conches and others in the twelfth century, who, following Plato's *Timaeus*, were concerned with this interior meaning in the cosmos, developed systematic theories to explain how man can 'interpret' the physical stuff of Creation.[95] William attributes the power to interpret to those faculties planted in man – sense, imagination, reason and intellect – which give him a natural sympathy with created things, making it possible for him to see through the surface of the world – the things in it – as an image of the archetype present in the mind of God-the-maker when he created it from nothing. Seeing through the world as it appeared

[93] For something resembling this sympathy, compare the idea of *compunctio* mentioned in *Regularis Concordia* 37.4, pp. 36–7.
[94] Smalley 1964, p. 45.
[95] On this theme in the thought of the twelfth century, Dronke 1974; and Gregory 1955.

161

to his senses, man was able to penetrate to its 'causes', with much the same movement of mind by which he saw through the surface, or covering (*integumentum*), of a text – in this case Plato's *Timaeus*. Investigating the 'causes' of the world, man found that the world had its origin in 'creation from nothing'; its cause, that is, was entirely other than the world itself. It lay outside. Nor was it a cause in the modern, scientific sense, for although it might be called objective, independent of man's understanding (*intellectus*), it was bound up in the moment of creation and, in its very origin and purpose, with the capacity of man to investigate or perceive it, to uncover it.[96] A sixth-century prayer in the so-called *Old Mozarabic Missal*, a blessing of the palm (or olive or willow) on Palm Sunday, is not saying anything very different when it speaks of the 'intuiting' of God's work:

Holy Lord, Eternal Father, Almighty God, who through your Son and our Lord Jesus Christ created all things from nothing, and by the power of the Holy Spirit provided the world's engine with its motley armoury of creatures, that man, created by you and lit with your unending light, looking upon (*intuens*) the effects of your awesome work, might unloose a surge of praise for all things to the Creator of all that is . . .

The two sides of Creation – man and matter – lean towards one another, mindful of their shared origin. Nature is a showing forth of God, a theophany, while man, as he looks on it, understands this showing for what it is. The prayer can therefore go on to speak of 'viridity', the rising sap, of the palm-tree, as the desire for innocence and victory in the perceiving soul:

Humbly we bow down and beseech you, that you might look down on these growths from the palm-tree or willow or olive in their greenness,

[96] *Glosae super Platonem* 32–4, pp. 98–102. The progression from sense to intellect in man, from perception of *rei presentis* (*sensus*), to perception of *rei absentis* (*imaginatio*), to the power to discern the properties of bodies and the differences between them (*ratio*), to *intellectus*, 'the force by which man perceives the incorporeal' allows in the first place an introspective cognition of the Creator as other than his Creation, for man, seeing in himself (by reason) the conflict between the weight of the body and its movement, knows that movement comes 'of another'; inquiring further, he sees in himself 'a certain spirit' which does this moving; and since spirit is in conflict with gravity, he knows again that it must have been put in him by the wisdom 'of another'. It is not the wisdom of another creature, so it is clearly that of the Creator. At the same time, the capacity of man to understand, what William calls his *ingenium*, permits an understanding of the world outside him, and in the end of the anatomy of 'creation from nothing' – and therefore again of the otherness of God in the *diuisio bimembris* of the world as efficient, formal and final cause (i.e. God's essence, his wisdom, the archetype in his mind at creation), and as material cause (the world as generated and in time).

and bless them and sanctify them with your strength, so that by the example of those who met you with palms as you hurried into Jerusalem, thus fulfilling what had been foreseen and singing glory in harmony with the prophet's praise, we too, taking up their innocence in our minds, might be made acceptable to offer you the sacrifice of our praises; that when you come to make judgement of the world, striving for the forgiveness of all sin, we, just as now we stand holding these leafy sprays, might then be worthy to take hold of the palms of victory.[97]

This is a complex prayer, with its reflection on the fulfilment of history in Christ, in ritual act and then in Last Judgement; but its central motif is the sympathy binding created man with created palm, enabling the one to 'see into' the other. The worshipping subject and the symbolic object have found themselves to be effects of the same cause.

The history of this insight into matter-as-manifestation – a seeing through to what is absolute in matter – would make up a large part of the history of the European imagination. Its theologians are pre-eminently pseudo-Denis, John Scot Eriugena and the cosmologists of northern France in the twelfth century, above all William of Conches and Bernardus Silvestris.[98] Thirty odd years ago, Von Simson suggested, with great aplomb, that the first Gothic – principally Suger's St-Denis and the cathedral of Chartres – owe their new form precisely to pseudo-Denis' theology of light as physical and symbolic disclosure of the eternal. If this makes Suger too much the intellectual (he was an earthy enough type, as his language betrays), and – as Christopher Brooke has written – ignores the stone-mason architects with whom he worked, there is still something in it. The Gothic

---

[97] *Liber ordinum*, cols. 179–80: 'Oremus. Domine sancte, Pater eterne, omnipotens deus, qui per Ihesum Christum filium tuum dominum nostrum cuncta ex nicilo procreasti, et uirtute sancti spiritus uariis ac multimodis creaturis mundi machinam perarmasti, ut homo a te conditus ac tue eternitatis lumine inlustratus, tuorum intuens opera mirabilium tibi laudes pro cunctis persolueret conditori omnium rerum: te supplices inploramus ac petimus, ut uiriditatis arbuscule ramos palmarum, salicum uel oliuarum tua uirtute benedicere ac sanctificare digneris, ut eorum exemplo qui tibi Iherosolimam properanti occurrentes cum ramis palmorum, conplentes uaticinia ac prophetarum laudibus gloriam concinuerunt, nos quoque mente eorum innocentiam possidentes, acceptabiles tibi nostrarum mereamur offerre sacrificium laudum: ut quum [ad] iudicandum ueneris mundum, adipiscentes cunctorum ueniam delictorum, sicut nunc coram te horum tenuerimus ramuscula frondium, ita mereamur percipere palmas uictoriarum. Amen.'

[98] Cf. Gregory 1955, esp. pp. 41–121.

building is still, in part anyway, a making-manifest of the principles hidden in matter, and 'brought out' by geometric design.[99] Liturgy too is an understanding of what is being made manifest, although it is true that in liturgy the 'understanding' is weighted more towards sense and emotion than intellect. It has more in it of desire, fear, sadness, joy, than of investigation; it is carried on the back of Leidrad's dramatizations and the Mozarabic 'unloosing of praise', rather than by the liberal arts which gave the twelfth-century cosmologists their vantage-point. On the other hand, there is among the rites of baptism at least the vestige of an appeal to the mind, in ceremonies like that of the 'Opening of the Ears' (*Apertio aurium*), reminiscent of Ambrose's notion of the 'eyes of faith' as against the 'eyes of the body'. In the 'Opening of the Ears', the Biblical text is approached as a veil which the perceptive faculties, properly attuned, are peculiarly able to penetrate, because the text which 'announces and shows', and the mind which attends to it, have the same author.[100]

Leidrad, in the passage quoted, gives a forceful example of how fully sensation and intellect embrace one another over the transforming interval of liturgy. He concentrates on two symbols to convey identification with Christ: whiteness and the body of Christ. Whiteness is perhaps odd as symbol, in that it suggests that angelic or super-angelic state where symbol is no longer needed. It suggests the untouchable pallor of death, and accordingly there is already something non-sensual about it. It lacks the fulness of an elemental symbol which makes us want to grasp it in the hand or touch it or smell it (oil, chrism), and thus somehow possess it. With body though – the body of Christ which is no less body than any other body – Leidrad is able to make us feel how 'things', or bodies generally, are at once palpable, tangible, present, available and satisfying, and yet impenetrable, inexplicable, distant and unsatisfying. This double experience of matter is not only sensation or perception, but theology: the body of Christ in which the little neophyte now participates – and which he thus possesses and possesses him – is more pitifully distant than any body. This is confirmed in two pictures of Christ as Jesus-cum-Joshua, and

---

[99] Von Simson 1956, esp. pp. 3–58; and Brooke 1969, esp. p. 128, on the limitations of Von Simsom's intellectualized Suger.

[100] *Gelasian*, no. 300, p. 46; *Ordo XI*, no. 45, p. 428 (for 'adnuntiet et ostendat'); and *Gelasian*, no. 310, p. 48 (*praefatio symboli ad electos*); *Ordo XI*, no. 61, p. 433 (see n. 36 above for quotation).

Christ buried in a shroud, his aloofness confirmed by whiteness in both scenes. Here is the moment of *Noli me tangere* over again.[101] And as the dramatic issues into theology, the same distance re-emerges as the theory of the scapegoat. Christ is not sin but has taken on sin 'for us'. Yet the distance is finally resolved in an act of penetration; difference collapses into sameness, because 'done in part by the Lord Jesus Christ, this is fulfilled all the more in his members'. The ritual act of covering the child's body in white clothes is exquisitely poised between the respectful distance of imitation, and the uninhibited fulness of identity.

In a blessing of the waters in the *Leonine Sacramentary*, the circle of understanding what is being made manifest, instead of working through drama or the Mozarabic 'intuition', is thrown before the imagination with the abruptness of a challenge, in the demand that God's hand be in the water: 'may your hand be hidden in this water'.[102] But the suddenness of this demand raises another possibility. Liturgy, it seems, and its symbol, as well as involving the movement with which the mind and the object come together and make meaning, may sometimes place the accent on presence. Instead of carrying the mind towards an idea, the physical element may be seen to hold the idea within itself. The imagination, instead of seeing through the object, instead of seeing what is behind it or what it points to outside itself, cleaves to it, finding fulness within it. It is as though the object soaks up meanings; it has density, or what has been called the 'condensation' of symbol.

---

[101] Thus the homily appearing in five MSS from the eighth to the twelfth centuries, attributed by Saxer to Optatus of Milevum (d. 392), which dwells on the tension in this instant when the gardener is recognized as Christ, but cannot be touched: 'Et illa [Maria Magdalene] dixit: Domine, quare non mihi permittis, ut te tangam uel fimbriam uestimentorum tuorum? Ego non debeo tangere, quem tangebant aegroti et sanabantur? Tu in ligno pependisti, et in sepulchro iacuisti, tu paradisum reserasti: admitte me ad hortum deliciarum tuarum. Sanasti Euam, iocunda Mariam. Ostendisti mihi uitem tuam, laetifica me de uindemia tua. Et dominus: Vade, inquit, ad palmites meos apostolos et ad Petrum.' Here too, as Saxer's notes show in intricate detail, the moment of identification with Christ which is also distance from him, is the moment of baptism. The baptized enter the homily as those who benefit from the fecundity of Christ's death: they are the *lilia renatorum* pushing up in the garden where Mary meets the gardener-Christ; the *renouata uindemia*. So the growth which grows from suffering, a kind of consummation, is juxtaposed with the aloofness of Christ, the impossibility of consummation or its postponement. See Saxer 1970 for text and commentary. On the theme of desire and fulfilment in sacrament, above, ch. 2.

[102] *Sacramentarium Veronense*, no. 1331, p. 170.

It is like a vortex into which everything falls.[103] In this way, with miraculous naivety, the physical becomes an end in itself. There is no going beyond it, because no need to go beyond it. As Gothic enacts the true principles underlying matter, so Romanesque expresses this complementary effect of real presence in matter. The Romanesque facade is a living being, defying the apparent lifelessness of its materials. Its zoomorphic figures – as Meyer Schapiro has shown[104] – far from being subject to the architectural forms which enclose them, make use of the forms as a frame to leap about in.

The extreme sensuality of this perspective, in which meaning is held fast by the object – and of which the effect is no doubt to be sought in the capacity of the unconscious mind to project its own contents on to external objects – is surely the great accomplishment in the twentieth century of Henri Gaudia–Brzeska and Henry Moore. Both these sculptors, and others like Brancusi, have resurrected, out of the upheaval of Modernism, the 'primitive' innocence of an affinity with matter. In Merovingian and Carolingian times, this is the innocence of Christ's body in the bread and wine of the eucharist – an innocence already being questioned in the mid-ninth century by Ratramnus in his separation of the historical body from the 'figurative' body and blood of the altar.[105] Body, to this ingenuous power of imagining, is the apex of matter, and in the cult of relics we get a glimpse of how even a fragment of body is enough to hold an endless breadth of senses. Finally, though, the two ways of seeing are continuous. Insight and the feeling for presence fold into one another. To see the sap of Creation rising in the tree is to see the absolute presence within it in the perspective of its own origin, and therefore as a potency of growth rather than a stasis sufficient unto itself. Insight or *intuitio* sees the object as 'expression of'; the sense of presence sees it as a fulness in its own right. One brings out idea from thing,

[103] Compare Victor Turner's notion of the 'condensed' symbol in Turner 1967, pp. 19–47; and Ricoeur 1960, pp. 158ff, on the relation between the totality of possible meaning in the world and the contingency of symbol: 'Cette totalité, tellement signifiée et si peu vécue, ne devient disponible qu'en se condensant dans des êtres et dans des objets sacrés qui deviennent les signes privilégiés de ce signifiant total.'

[104] Schapiro 1977, pp. 265–84.

[105] Thus Ratramnus, *De corp. et sang. dom.* 97, col. 169A: 'euidentissime monstratum est quod panis qui corpus Christi et calix qui sanguis Christi appellatur figura sit, quia mysterium, et quod non parua differentia sit inter corpus quod per mysterium existit et corpus quod passum est'.

the other rests in the thing. But there is no more between them than a shift of emphasis.

HISTORY AND REPETITION

The power to bring out from sense to idea, as well as the more immediate awareness of presence, is enhanced by the setting of liturgy within the seasons, the metaphoric use it makes of the cycle of the year and its variations: the time of sowing, the time of reaping, of little and plenty. All liturgy – the sanctoral as well as the temporal – depends on this immediate sense of time as experience; it is, in this way, a performance of time. But as with the physical matter of the world, it does not leave time to its immediacy, but makes from it an idea of time. For liturgy enacts the Christian view of a time which loses itself in eternity.[106] It brings out eternity from time. In another part of his letter, Leidrad refashions this liturgical performance of time as a poetic one. This is how he represents the baptismal *anamnesis*, the prayer which recalls the 'history' of baptism from the beginning of time:

So, the unruly universe, without its ruddy sun and its sallow moon and its winking stars, pressed down on ungathered and invisible matter with the hugeness of its abysses, with its formless shadows. Only 'the Spirit of God was borne over the waters', like a charioteer, and in a figure of baptism, brought about the birth of the world. Between heaven and earth looms the vault, and according to the etymology of the Hebrew tongue, the sky, or 'Samaim', comes from the word for water, and the 'waters which are over the sky' are set apart for the praise of the Lord. Then in Ezechiel the crystal is extended over the cherubim, and crystal is water but more compact and dense. Firstly living creatures come out of the water, and he lifts the winged faithful from the earth to the sky. Man is fashioned, and the sacraments of water are poured between the fingers of God. Paradise is planted in Eden, and one font is divided into four springs, and it is these that Ezechiel sees afterwards in his vision as they gush from the temple and, flowing against the rising sun, give life to the bitter dead waters. The world sins, and cannot be purged without the water's flood; the moment the foulness is well and truly despatched, the dove of the Holy Spirit flies down to Noah just as it flies down to Christ in the Jordan, and announces peace with the branch of healing and light. Pharaoh with his army, not wanting the people of God to make their way out of Egypt, is suffocated in a type of baptism; and in the Psalms it is written of his death: 'You have strengthened the sea in its virtue, in the waters you have smashed the dragons' heads.' And so serpents and scorpions and all withered things are cut to pieces.

These are the great events in the history of the sacrament. From them Leidrad passes to a mosaic of lesser water-incidents:

Abraham and Isaac dig wells; foreigners chase them away, the city of Beersheba is the city of the oath, and so the kingdom of Solomon takes its name from the springs. Rebecca is found at the well, Rachel is greeted with a kiss from her suitor beside the waters, Moses saves the daughters of Midian's priest from a rebuff at the open water-hole.

The rhythm picks up as the flood of history pours itself out. It quickens to the climax of Christ-in-water. But the more urgent and breathless the succession of events, the more apparent it becomes that they are all one event repeated. The difference between happenings vanishes into the oneness of the 'voice of the Lord over the many waters', and the flood of history flows into the vessel which contains it:

'The voice of the Lord is over the face of the waters. The Lord is over the many waters. The Lord fills the flood with his presence.' [And now stepping unexpectedly from water itself to the water of fecundity and cleanness, Leidrad brings on the bride of the Song of Songs, and thus, by allusion, the church:] 'Her teeth are like a flock of shorn sheep which have come up from the washing-place, all of them bearing twins, none barren among them.' Micah prophesies about the grace of baptism: 'He will have mercy on us, he will drown our iniquities and thrust all our sins to the deepness of the sea.' Ezechiel says: 'Yes, I shall single you out among the peoples, I shall gather you from every land, I shall pour clean water over you, and you will be cleansed from your wickedness.'

The culmination of these images of a timeless water is Christ in the Jordan, and from this absolute moment Leidrad makes time a slow, deliberate descent to the ritual present:

The Saviour himself, after baptism and the blessed waters of his bath in the Jordan, makes of water the first sign; and this man who had begun with water, ended with water. His side is split with a spear and the sacraments of baptism and martyrdom are laid down together. After his resurrection, he sends his disciples through the entire world, saying to them: 'Go, teach all the nations, baptizing them in the name of the Father, the Son and the Holy Spirit.' And then: 'The man who believes and has been baptized will be saved.' From that time the apostles began to teach and baptize; and for their part, people believed and were baptized. So, anyone who is to be baptized is first taught so he may

From Augustine to the Carolingians

believe; he is instructed in the faith. This is being a catechumen, which means one who is taught.[107]

[107] *Lib. de sac. bapt.* 1, col. 855: 'Igitur rudis mundus, necdum sole rutilante, nec pallente luna, nec astris micantibus, incompositam et inuisibilem materiam abyssorum magnitudine, et deformibus tenebris opprimebat. Solus "spiritus dei" in aurigae modum "super aquas ferebatur" [Gen. 1:2] et nascentem mundum in figura baptismi parturiebat. Inter coelum et terram medium exstruitur firmamentum, et juxta Hebraici sermoni etymologiam, coelum, id est "Samaim", ex aquis sortitur uocabulum, et "aquae quae super coelos sunt" [Gen. 1:7] in laudes Domini separantur. Unde et in Ezechiel crystallum super cherubim uidetur extensum [cf. Ezech. 1:16, 10:10], id est compactae et densiores aquae. Primum de aquis quod uiuat egreditur, et pennatos fideles de terra ad coelum leuat [cf. Gen. 1:20–2]. Fabricatur homo [cf. Gen. 1:26–7], et inter manus dei aquarum sacramenta uersantur. Plantatur paradisus in Eden, et unus fons in quattuor principia diuiditur [cf. Gen. 2:10–14], qui postea secundum uisionem Ezechielis prophetae egrediens de templo, et contra solis ortum uadens, amaras aquas mortuasque uiuificat [cf. Ezech. 47:1–12]. Peccat mundus, et sine aquarum diluuio non purgatur: statimque columba spiritus sancti expulso alite teterrimo, ita ad Noe, quasi ad Christum in Jordanem deuolat, et ramo refectionis ac luminis pacem orbis annuntiat [cf. Gen. 6:5ff, 8:6–12]. Pharao cum exercitu nolens populum Domini exire de Aegypto, in typo baptismatis suffocatur; et in psalmis de interfectione illius scribitur: "Tu confirmasti in uirtute tua mare, contriuisti capita draconum in aquis" [Ps. 73:13]. Unde et reguli et scorpiones arentia quaeque sectantur: in ara mutatur sacramentum crucis, et LXX palmae apostolorum dulcoratis legis gurgitibus irrigantur [cf. Ezech. 15:27]. Abraham et Isaac puteos fodeunt [Gen. 26:23–5]; repugnant allophyli, et Beersabeae ciuitas juramenti, regnumque Salomonis nomen sumit a fontibus [cf. Gen. 21:22–32]. Rebecca inuenitur ad puteum [cf. Gen. 24:10–21], Rachel propter aquas supplantatoris osculo salutatur [cf. Gen. 29:1–9], Moyses filias sacerdotis Madian aperto puteo ab injuria uindicat [cf. Exod. 2:11–17]. "Vox Domini super aquas" [Ps. 29:3]. "Dominus super aquas multas." "Dominus diluuium inhabitare facit" [Ps. 29:10]. "Dentes ejus sicut grex detonsarum ouium, quae ascenderunt de lauacro, omnes gemellos habentes, et sterilis non est in eis" [cf. Cant. 4:2, 6:6]. Micheas de gratia baptismi uaticinatur: "Miserebitur nostri, demerget iniquitates nostras, et projiciet in profundum maris omnia peccata nostra" [Mic. 7:19]. Ezechiel ait: "Tollam uos quippe de gentibus, et congregabo uos de uniuersis terris, et effundam super uos aquam mundam, et mundabimini ab omnibus iniquitatibus uestris" [Ezech. 6:24–5]. Ipse saluator post baptisma et sanctificantes suo lauacro aquas Jordanis, primum signum ex aquis facit; et qui ab aquis coeperat finiuit in aquis. Latus percutitur lancea, et baptismi pariter atque martyrii sacramenta funduntur. Post resurrectionem suam mittit discipulos in mundum uniuersum, et dicit eis: "Ite, docete omnes gentes, baptizantes eos in nomine Patris, et Filii, et Spiritus sancti" [Matt. 28:19]. Et iterum: "Qui crediderit et baptizatus fuerit, saluus erit" [Mark 16:16]. Ex illo ergo tempore coeperunt apostoli docere et baptizare; gentes autem credere et baptizari. Ergo qui baptizandus est, prius docetur ut credat, id est instruatur fide: hoc est enim catechumenum esse id est instructum.' The reference to Beersheba and the kingdom of Solomon is obscure: the 'kingdom of Solomon', or Israel, was referred to as the country 'from Dan to Beersheba' in Judges 20:1, and, through a misunderstanding of the Hebrew, Beersheba was thought to mean 'well of the oath'. The whole nation, Leidrad is thus saying, takes its name from the water of a well. On the four rivers of Paradise as a type of baptism in Carolingian art and literature, Underwood 1950. It is temping to see in Leidrad's *anamnesis* an echo not only of the liturgy but of Tertullian, especially in view of the famous 'Agobardinus' MS – a copy of a number of Tertullian's works containing the autograph of Agobard of Lyon (MS Paris, BN lat. 1622); but this volume neither includes Tertullian's *De baptismo*, nor mentions it in the list of contents on fo. 1v (the MS has lost a number of folios: see Tafel 1925, p. 48).

169

There is much here that goes back to Augustine's ideas about a 'strong' remembering by which the soul recognizes its source and returns to it. But in Leidrad – and in the liturgy he is expounding – theory becomes praxis. We are aware in Leidrad of a sense overridden in Augustine by theological idea, of time as the fabric of history. Time is no mere image of eternity, a shadow on the wall of Plato's cave dimly reporting a truth which lies elsewhere; it is the substance in which eternity happens. Events recalled are not just things in the mind, but things in the world. In the idiom of medieval exegesis, they belong to the literal sense before they can belong to the allegorical or mystical. So, the ineffable paradox of Christian time as a linear time which is also a time of returns to the beginning, to man as image of God which is what he was at Creation, is not intellectualized but brought to life in the quick–slow rhythms of the *anamnesis* (or Leidrad's rendering of it) as they play over the fundamental, unchanging principle beneath them. Linear, historical time, we are made to feel, is also – equally – a series of repetitions or returns.

The partly unconscious process into which *anamnesis* (or 'not-forgetting')[108] draws the mind goes something like this: confronted by the original water of Creation, the memory, at first over-whelmed by the distance between itself and what was, is made to feel by a 'genealogy' of water (comparable with the Tree of Jesse or the genealogy of Christ in the opening verses of Matthew) that the ancient, Biblical water is after all immediate, present here and now. So, the remote past – infinitely significant because bearing in it the *manus absconsa*, the hidden hand of God-the-maker – issues on to the familiarity of the ritual present; and conversely, the everyday water comes to bear an infinite significance since it is now shown to reach back into the beginning of time. But as it follows this progression, a different kind of awareness dawns on the mind. The suggestion of continuity, made all the more irresistible by the element of difference in each water-episode (difference throwing sameness into relief), is built up to such a pitch, and the verbal parataxis so insistent, that the episodes come

108 On 'remembrance' or *anamnesis* in liturgy, Casel 1926; and on the related notion of the 'feast of idea', distinguishing mere commemoration from the great feasts (like Easter, Pentecost, Epiphany) which carry into the liturgical present 'ideas' at work in salvific events, Baumstark 1958, pp. 154–74. For references on the controversy raised by Casel's 'mystery theology of liturgy' – of which *anamnesis* is the lynchpin – see Jones Wainwright and Yarnold 1978, pp. 15ff and 24ff. And see also Dix 1945, pp. 243–7.

to seem repetitions of an idea. This is not quite time taken up into an eternal present of reflection, as in Augustine's *Confessions*. The event is still conceived of in time; it remains external and independent of the mind. But in the perspective of repetition, the time itself in which the event stands loses its essential quality of time-passing, with all that this means by way of change, progression, decline, difference. The connections which link one event with another through history, conveyed in this passage by the image of the four rivers flowing down from Eden, serve in the end to emphasize the single principle of connection from which all history, in all its diversity, is generated. And this one connection, perhaps fleetingly glimpsed in the four springs of Ezechiel's vision 'flowing against the rising sun', has its reflection in repetition. *Forma fluit, manet esse rei*: 'Form passes away, the essence stands', said Bernardus Silvestris.[109] The process becomes clearer by analogy: it is like looking at an album of snap-shots of a person one knows well. She is shown from childhood to her present middle-age. At first it is the change over time which is striking; but leafing through the pages, the recognition grows that what is now, and familiar, though different from what was, is merely a development of more basic characteristics which have always been there. The past in this way, is a making-manifest of what has always been there; and to read it over, or listen to it, is to see into this absolute continuum – and thus to see repetition where once there was change.

This capacity to pierce history and lay it bare is a transference of, and an intensification of, the perception of matter as a 'covering' of Creation. The same insight is at work in both cases. The individuality and concreteness of things (or happenings) is not weakened by the knowledge that beneath the dance of forms is a single, undivided stress of being, but enhanced by it. It is true of the sacramental vision generally that the more sensible a thing, the more urgent its physical presence, the more possibility it has to be made more-than-physical; and the more firmly situated in time an event, the more it stimulates to a conception of repetition, and even of the absence of time reflected in repetition. It is the two sides of this relation which are carried, undivided, in the idea that

---

[109] The whole passage is very apt: 'Si tamen inspirat uerum mens conscia ueri, / Rem priuat forma, non rapit esse rei. / Res eadem subiecta manet, sed forma uagatur / atque rei nomen dat noua forma nouum. / Forma fluit, manet esse rei, mortisque potestas / Nil perimit, sed res dissociat socias.' (*Cosmographia* pt ii: *Microcosmos*, 8.11.41ff, p. 138.)

Christ, or the present ritual action, is the fulfilment of time-past and time-to-come. In him, as in the present moment of liturgy, all time is resumed, rather as in the depiction of his baptism in the Middle Ages, the water is so often shown heaped up round his body as though the heap of water is the fulfilment of the Jordan's flow through time.[110] Past time (or Biblical history representing past time) is thus conceived as being annihilated by Christ's repetition of it once-for-all; and yet because he repeats it more perfectly – or rather makes its sense more manifest – he also confirms it, and opens the way to the possibilities of progress (towards him) and decline (from him). And the same double-vision is beautifully expressed in the liturgical topos of *renouatio in melius*, 'renewal for the better':[111] change for the better exists against the backdrop of sin, change for the worse. It is therefore a progression. Equally, however, it is a repetition of what has been, of what is visible in the original act of Creation.[112] And so, the cleansing away of the 'old squalors' – in a *Gelasian* prayer – is the

[110] Bede expresses this notion of fulfilment as a reversal of time in the moment of Christ's death-and-resurrection: 'Quaerendum autem cur noctem dominicae resurrectionis euangelista describens ait, "Vespere autem sabbati quae lucescit in primam sabbati" [Matt. 28:1], cum consuetus ordo temporum habeat uesperam magis tenebrescere in noctem quam in diem lucescere. Sed mystice loquens euangelista quantum dignitatis haec sacratissima nox de gloria deuictae mortis acceperit insinuare studuit dum eius exordium quo deuotae Christo feminae in obsequium illius uigilare coeperunt insequentem iam diem lucescere perhibuit. Nam dominus auctor et ordinator temporum qui in ultima noctis huius parte surrexit totam eam nimirum eiusdem resurrectionis luce festiuam reddidit et coruscam. Siquidem ab exordio mundanae creationis usque adhuc ita temporum cursus distinguebatur ut dies noctem praecederet iuxta ordinem uidelicet primae conditionis. Hac nocte per mysterium resurrectionis domini temporum ordo mutatus est. Nam quia nocte surrexit a mortuis die uero sequenti eiusdem resurrectionis effectum discipulis ostendit ac participato cum eis conuiuio ueritatem uirtutis eis mirantibus simul et gaudentibus astruxit rectissime nox illa sequentis diei coniuncta est luci ac sic temporum ordo statutus ut dies noctem sequatur' (*Hom.* 2.7, *In uigilia paschae*, pp. 226–7).
[111] On this theme, Ladner 1959, esp. pp. 153–212: the return in Augustine and the subsequent liturgical tradition is a return to Creation rather than to Paradise. To some extent, this nuance distinguishes Augustine and the West from the Greeks (but see following note).
[112] Cf. Boas 1948, on 'primitivism' in the Middle Ages, and ideas of redemption as return to origins. On the theme of baptism as both a return to Paradise and on anticipation of Judgement, *Liber Sacramentorum Gellonensis*, no. 2009, p. 271: 'BND [benedictio] IN VIGIL PASCHE . . . Et quos ueteribus maculis baptismatis emundauit unda sacrata per lauacrum, tue protectionis auxilium purgati, tales ante te represententur in iudicium quales nunc processerunt ex baptismo. – Et qui te miserante reuocati sunt in paradisum, non patiaris exules fieri renascente conmisso.' And cf. Le Goff 1977, pp. 46–65, for an essay on different views of time in the Middle Ages, but mainly distinguishing cyclical from linear time.

rediscovery of a 'new childhood in all its innocency'.[113] Rebirth, which with death-and-resurrection is the central image in baptism, is these two irreconcilable things at once: a washing clean from the stain of first birth, and a return to the innocence of birth. With this conjunction we have come back to the theme of the *Leonine* mass for the Innocents, salvation through the unknowing child, whose innocence is his faith, and inspiration to the faith of his parents.

BETWIXT AND BETWEEN

The insight into things and the insight into history come together in the *Gelasian* benediction of the baptismal chrism, where the thrust of growth in the 'fruit-bearing wood' of the olive-tree, with its origin in Creation, is juxtaposed with an *anamnesis*, or Biblical history of oil: the anointings of David and Aaron, the olive-branch brought to the ark by the dove of peace, Christ anointed in the Jordan.[114] But there is another kind of insight too, another mode of participation by the worshipping subject in the liturgical object. Baptism, like the rites of burial, or marriage, or the eucharist itself, or penitence, is a 'rite of passage'. It involves a crossing-over, a *transitus* or *pascha*, from one state to another. Insofar as transition is an accomplished fact brought to bear, in the abstract, by the adult community on its unwitting children, it remains an observance of forms. But if we remember that the community saw itself in its children, attributing to them its own experience, we can see that the passage undergone is genuinely a passing-across, a change in being, with all the changes of a hazardous sea-crossing, and even the fears and hopes of Jonah in his whale.

Passage is insecurity, the vagrancy of *peregrinatio*. It is the suspense of being cut off equally from what has been and what will be; the condition – that of the penitent – of having been thrown out of the wedding-feast.[115] But it is in this time of estrangement that the soul understands most acutely what it is

---

[113] *Gelasian*, no. 448, pp. 73–4: 'Discendat in hanc plenitudinem fontis uirtus spiritus tui et totam huius aquae substantiam regenerandis fecundet effectu ... Hic natura ad imaginem tuam condita et ad honorem sui reformata principiis cunctis uetustatis squaloribus emundetur, ut omnis homo hoc sacramentum regenerationis ingressus in uera innocentia noua infantia renascatur.'

[114] Ibid., no. 386, p. 62.   [115] Ibid., no. 365, p. 58.

estranged from. The Middle Ages is full of examples of truth found through hardship, from the perseverance of the epic hero in the face of failure (Beowulf's pessimism comes to mind, or Ruodlieb's honourable exile), to the melancholy lyric of the seafarer in the Anglo-Saxon poem, who for all his 'mere-weariness', cannot refuse the call of the whale-path, reasoning with himself that in this

> ... dead life
> On loan and on land, I believe not
> That any earth-weal eternal standeth
> Save there be somewhat calamitous
> That, ere a man's tide go, turn it to twain.[116]

The so-called *Prayer of St Brendan* depicts the saint between shore and shore, above and below, left and right, addressing his God as he crosses the seven seas. 'This prayer was given him', says the preface, 'after seven years of Easter spent seeking the promised island, and he celebrated Easter on the sea for seven years running.'[117] The whole journey in other words was an Easter, a *pascha* or crossing-over. The preface is probably an addition made in the eleventh century to the main body of an eighth-century prayer, but the text as a whole is an echo of baptismal exorcism, both in its phraseology and in the general notion of a liberation by transition through water. The one essential difference is that here the soul cries out before God for its own delivery:

Deliver me, Lord God Almighty, from all dangers of earth, sea and water, from the apparitions of beasts, the beast that walks on four legs, the fowl that flies, the serpent that crawls. Defend me, God, from fire, from lightning, from thunder, from hail and snow, from the rains and the winds, from the dangers of the earth, from the whirlwind and the earthquake, from every evil, from the hunter and the hater, from the evil eye, from words, from the dangers of men in the world and of the dark, from the arrow that flies by day and the sinister commerce of the night. Protect me from every anger that does down good.[118]

In this appeal for safety from everything that is shifty, everything that is uncertain or of unseen origin, the form of exorcism has

[116] Translated Ezra Pound, in Pound 1975, pp. 35–8, at p. 37.
[117] *Oratio s. Brandani* 1, p. 1.
[118] Ibid. 10, pp. 18–20. The baptismal background to the prayer is confirmed by its use of the form *Epheta, quod est adaperire* (3, p. 2), from Mark 7:32 and in the *Gelasian* rite of baptism: no. 420, p. 68.

given way to the desire for exorcism, expressed in the soul which is still passing-between. It is still what anthropologists have called 'liminal'.

Anthropologists – Van Gennep who first isolated the concept of the 'rite of passage', and more recently Victor Turner[119] – have also asked why these crossings-over should exercise such extraordinary power over belief and emotion. A part of the answer is suggested by Brendan's prayer: the acute uncertainty of *pascha* brings a confessional response, first by way of *lorica*, the litany of protectors who being invoked become integral to the person invoking –

These and all the saints with the perfect Trinity, are the protectors (*loricae*) of my soul and spirit and body, with all their members within and without, from the sole of my foot to the crown of my head[120]

– then in explicit confession –

Before you, my Creator, I make confession of all my vices . . .[121]

The precariousness of being 'betwixt-and-between' causes the soul to cry out, to throw itself upon the God within. To do otherwise, as Guibert de Nogent told himself in the 1120s, would be to fall foul of despair:

Surely it is a better thing to strive for you for a time, even for a moment to breathe you in, than outright to forget all remedy and despair of grace? And what is despair other than a wanton wallowing in the mire of shame? For where the spirit gives up its struggle with flesh, the substance of the unhappy soul is beaten down as pleasure spends its forces. It is then that a man is submerged in the water's swell, taken down into the deep; his strength forced down from the well's mouth to the mound of falsehood.[122]

Guibert, a 'sick soul' if ever there was one, is a long way from Brendan's heroic, incantatory, defiance of the monstrousness of evil; but both – Brendan on his surging sea, Guibert with his mortal fear of the heaped up water and the well's depth – express what it is like to be 'inside' the exorcism of baptism.

But there is another inflexion in the liturgy – and the religious psychology – of passage. In the Roman prayers (both *Gelasian* and

[119] Van Gennep 1960; Turner 1967, pp. 93–111.
[120] *Oratio s. Brandani* 10, p. 18. On the *loricae*, Gougaud 1911, 1912.
[121] Ibid. 11, p. 20.   [122] *De uita sua* 1, p. 6.

Gregorian) for the benediction of the Easter candle on the vigil of Holy Saturday, the transition is from dark to light, as well as, by implication, from death to resurrection, servitude to freedom, pain and punishment to relief, and so on.[123] But in the brief space of these images of turning, all the long turning of the forty days of Lent, and even the shorter 'rite of passage' of the three days (*triduum*) of Thursday, Friday and Saturday, are concentrated. In this concentratedness, rather than one thing being true after another – light after darkness, joy when pain has gone – two contradictory things are seen to be true at the same time. This is the paradox of the simultaneity of day and night, of night as inexplicable illumination. It might invite an effort to understand better, a deeper reflection prompted by the bewildering confusion of opposites. Victor Turner, pointing out that the subject in the liminal stage of a rite of passage sees the things he has seen before but in a quite different order (the female put with the male, the good with the bad and so on), says that for this reason 'liminality' might be called 'the realm of primitive hypothesis, where there is a certain freedom to juggle with the factors of existence'.[124] But here in the rites for the Easter vigil, the contradictions seem to go beyond any reflection. They bemuse. They stop the mind in its attempt to interpret, and invite reverence not reflective participation. For

This is the night of which it is written, And the night will be lit up as day, and the night will be my illumination in the garden of love.[125]

This is the impenetrable event, no longer intelligible or open to 'intuition', of the lighting of the Paschal candle at night; of Christ dead *and* resurrected; Christ as the Lucifer or light-bringer, 'who did not know the Fall'. Before the 'great mystery and awesome sacrament of this night', this 'miracle of the resurrection of the Lord', when 'the age-old shadows sense day brought over them, and death once damned to eternal night stands stupefied at its own imprisonment', it is only possible to 'heap up praises'.[126] Confu-

---

[123] *Gelasian*, nos. 426–8, pp. 68–9.
[124] Turner 1967, p. 105; and on p. 106: 'Liminality may be partly described as a stage of reflection. In it those ideas, sentiments and facts that had been hitherto for the neophytes bound up in configurations and accepted unthinkingly are, as it were, resolved into their constituents.'
[125] *Hadrianum Supplement*, no. 1022, p. 361: 'Haec nox est, de qua scriptum est, et nox ut dies inluminabitur, et nox inluminatio mea in deliciis meis.'
[126] *Gelasian*, nos. 426–7, p. 69.

sion at being neither one thing nor the other has given way to wonderment at being both at once. In the emotions and in theology, 'our necessary sin of Adam'[127] makes a coincidence of opposites with the death of Christ which destroys it. It is true too that in the emotions, and in the moral life which is embryonic in liturgy, this 'happy blame' (*felix culpa*)[128] – the knowledge that sin is beneficial because of the redeemer it demanded – is a fact of experience. Despair and joy do coincide; melancholia is the necessary condition of mania; and repentance depends on remembrance of past sin and the certainty that it cannot be avoided. But the predominant key of the blessing of the candle – the prayer which most fully characterizes the Holy Saturday time of betwixt-and-between – in both *Hadrianum Supplement* and *Gelasian* is one of respect before an operation of infinite delicacy, which exceeds all understanding. It is the operation of the Christ-like bee, for (in the words of the *Gelasian*)

When we wonder at the origin of this substance [the wax of the candle], we find ourselves praising the bees and their beginning. Bees are frugal in harvest, chaste in giving birth. They build cells out of waxen liquid, of a kind that human art, for all its mastery, cannot equal. They pluck flowers with their feet, and afterwards the flowers are not so much as bruised. They give birth not in labour, but gather up the already conceived foetuses in the mouth and let forth a swarm. It was in this way too that Christ issued, miracle-like, from the Father's mouth. In the bee is a fruitful virginity innocent of labour, taken up by the Lord when for love of virginity he took to himself a mother in flesh.[129]

There is no question here of 'participation'. This image of frail, incomprehensible beauty, far from exciting the mind to penetrate with understanding, demands of it an attitude of respect. The bee

[127] *Hadrianum Supplement*, no. 1022, p. 361: 'O certe necessarium Adae peccatum nostrum, quod Christi morte deletum est.'

[128] Ibid.: 'O felix culpa, quae talem ac tantum meruit habere redemptorem. O beata nox, quae sola meruit scire tempus et horam in qua Christus ab inferis resurrexit.'

[129] *Gelasian*, no. 428, p. 69: 'cum igitur huius substanciae miramur exordium, apium necesse est laudemus originem. Apes uero sunt frugalis in sumptibus, in procreatione castissimae. Aedificant cellulas caereo liquore fundatus, quarum humanae peritiae ars magistra non quoequat. Legunt pedibus flores ut nullum damnum in floribus inuenitur. Partus non aedunt, sed ore legentes concepti faetus reddunt examina, sicut exemplo mirabili Christus ore paterno processit. Fecunda est in his sine partu uirginitas, quam utique dominus sequi dignatus, carnalem se matrem habere uirginitatis amore constituit.' This form of the *Exultet*, the 'Romano-Gallican', also occurs in the *Hadrianum Supplement*, no. 1021, p. 360. For other versions, and a bibliography to these prefaces, *Corpus Praefationum*, pp. cff.

– after the bee of Virgil's *Georgics* from which this eulogy borrows – plucks without bruising the tender skin of the flower; it brings forth its young with no sexual contact and by a painless gathering motion. Sensibility in this benediction – and above all in this song of the bee – is the impossibility of possessing with the senses; and from it arises an attitude of bowing down before rather than a movement of seeing into. And this sensibility must have been translated into the lambent ritual gesture which the historian can only guess at from miniatures and frescoes; the fluent but endlessly careful gesture, for example, of Joseph of Arimathea and Nicodemus as they lift Christ from the cross and lay him in his place of burial, in the Egbert Codex (Trier, Stadtbibliothek, cod. 24, fo. 85v, of about 977–93).[130] Or again, it is perhaps visible in the essential strangeness of the child-catechumen: 'Behold', Jesse of Amiens writes to the priests of his diocese, probably in 812, 'those who have professed belief in him, and yet Jesus did not give himself to them in belief: such are the catechumens.'[131] In these aspects of liturgy, there is a resistance to resolution, a remoteness which can only be looked on from afar, and which – curiously – brings us back to the formal, Utopian, dance where we began. And yet the beauty of the bee is not form as possibility, or availability of the heavenly; it puts before the worshipper precisely the unavailability of form, the awesome *distance* of the *Maiestas*.

All this is to say that infant baptism was many things at once. It was, as yet, no hindrance, but rather a stimulus, to the religious imagination that a child should be led through the forms of an adult experience. The child, along with the water, palm-branches, salt and oil, was himself a symbol – perhaps the principal symbol – in which the action of sacrament took place. He was the focus of the rite. But it remains to say something about this ability of the adult community to see itself in its children, and to explore some of the reasons why it became so difficult to do so. From the characterization of early medieval baptism, we must pass to the story of its decline.

[130] See facsimile edition by Schiel 1960.
[131] *Ep. de bapt.*, col. 785; and cf. Augustine, *De diu. quaest. ad Simplic.* 1.2.2, p. 25.

Chapter 5

THE DIMINISHING OF BAPTISM

BAPTISM AND CONFIRMATION

In fifth-century southern Gaul, and then, independently, in eighth-century Germany and elsewhere, the rite of confirmation, which had been integral to baptism, was sheared off from it. It was performed later, and by the bishop.[1] In both southern Gaul and in Germany, the change was a change in practice, to meet a particular difficulty: bishops could not get out into the countryside to baptize all those who needed to be baptized, and so they agreed that they could fulfil their function as bishops by simply 'confirming', or finishing off, the baptism given by a deacon or a priest.[2] In Carolingian times, confirmation was often deferred for some years after baptism, either because the bishop could not get out to visit all the villages of a large diocese, or because, confirmation now being associated with a new degree of commitment, it was refused until later in life.[3]

If this began as no more than a need to meet the circumstances, it almost immediately – in the fifth century and the ninth – came to represent a rupture in the liturgy. It broke apart the two elements held in tension by liturgy: the tension between the symbol as a gift of being and as the recognition, the working through, of this gift in the conscious mind; between the child as potential and the child making good – or failing to make good – this potential; between perception and understanding. The *Gelasian* expresses some of this in a strangely intense prayer:

God, in whose foresight are present all times gone by, and who does not wait for what will be, give lasting effect of solemnity to the action we

---

[1] Buchem 1967, for the change in southern Gaul; Fisher 1965 for the later change, and its effect of disintegrating the unity of the rite of baptism; and Mitchell 1966.

[2] Buchem 1967, pp. 87ff; Jerome (d. 420) mentions the difficult journeys made by bishops to perform the laying on of hands after baptism in remote villages (*Contra Luciferanos* 9, *PL* xxxiii, cols. 172ff); and see Gregory the Great, *Registrum* 11.3, p. 831.

[3] Thus Jonas of Orléans, *De inst. laicali* 1.7, col. 133.

once did and now remember, that what we pass through in our memory we may hold to in the things we do.[4]

In this way the *Gelasian* recalls, with that 'strong' remembering which makes time stick to eternity like iron filings to a magnet, the baptism celebrated a week and a day before, on the vigil of Holy Saturday.[5] In this philosophical prayer, all time is reduced to the ritual instant, so that the moral aftermath of baptism is a sequence of re-possessions of the original moment. Everything I do is a matter of the power of my memory to recover this first moment. Penitence is a remembering of the same kind. It goes back in time, 're-forming' what was once formed, and so reversing the course of sin.[6] But the beginning which is remembered and repeated in what follows – especially when this beginning is *infant* baptism, or the oblation of children to monasticism which is cognate with it – is a submission of the will as much as an exercise of the will. The premise of all liturgical offering, of prayer itself, is that God is infinitely more than man. This 'infinitely more' is expressed in absence. In making an offering, I ask for this absence to become a presence; or, put another way – and this is how Anselm of Bec put it in his *Cur deus homo*, which takes up the rhythm of liturgy in this respect – I ask for infinitely more than my due. I have strayed from God; being only man I cannot by my own lights get back to him; he gives me the capacity to return.[7] In Anselm it is by becoming the God-man that God

---

4   *Gelasian*, no. 504, p. 81 (*Orationes et praeces de pascha annotina*): 'Deus, per cuius prouidentiam nec praeteritorum momenta deficiunt nec ulla superest expectacio futurorum, tribue permanentem peractae quae recolimus solemnitatis effectum, ut quod recordatione percurrimus, semper in opere teneamus.'

5   For this remembering, see above, pp. 89–98.

6   *Gelasian*, nos. 358–9, p. 57 (*Ordo agentibus publicam paenitenciam*): 'Deus humani generis benignissime conditor et misericordissime formator, qui hominem inuidia diabuli ab aeternitate deiectum unici tui filii sanguine redemisti: uiuifica itaque tibi nullatenus mori desideras, et qui non derelinquis deuium, adsume corruptum ... Nesciat quod territ in tenebris, quod stridit in flammis, atque ab erroris uia ad iter reuersus iusticiae nequaquam ultra nouis uulneribus saucietur, sed integrum sit ei atque perpetuum et quod gratia tua contulit et quod misericordia reformauit ...'.

7   Anselm, *Cur deus homo*; and see the essay on sacrifice by Hubert and Mauss: after a study of Hebrew and Vedic sacrifice, they conclude that sacrifice is not in the first place expiatory (in other words by an act of cleansing re-establishing the external order of purity which has been infringed), but rather establishes a *rapport* between presence and absence: 'Pour que le sacrifice soit bien fondé, deux conditions sont nécessaires. Il faut d'abord qu'il y ait en dehors du sacrifiant des choses qui le fassent sortir de lui-même et auxquelles il doive ce qu'il sacrifie. Il faut ensuite que ces choses soient près de lui pour qu'il puisse entrer en rapport avec elles, y trouver la force et l'assurance dont il a besoin et retirer de leur contact le bénéfice qu'il attend de ses rites. Or, ce caractère de pénétration intime et de transcendance est, au plus haut degré, distinctif des choses

confers this capacity; by this means, because God is both man and God in Christ, the freedom of the will is not eclipsed by the gift. In liturgy, this circularity by which the will does not merely succumb but becomes more than itself is enacted in offering, a giving in which infinitely more is received than is given; or, in what would come to be thought of as the metamorphosis of the elements: the bread and the wine, becoming the body and blood of Christ, become infinitely more than themselves without ceasing to be themselves.

What I began by calling 'the tension within liturgy' is therefore two tensions closely bound up: the implication of all time in a beginning; and the growth of the will to something more than itself. The separation of confirmation from baptism – in itself apparently a small matter – introduces a quite new way of thought, or at least it is a symptom of a new thinking.

For confirmation now serves as an extension of the first moment of baptism into the aftermath of baptism. It is a hinge articulating baptism with what comes later, so that baptism now comes to seem 'that which is given', and the moral life a continuous effort to sustain what has been given, with confirmation the middle term between them.[8] This is put with a simple metaphor. Confirmation 'strengthens'. When it was first detached from baptism in southern Gaul in the fifth century, confirmation meant only a 'finishing off' of what had been begun; a 'sealing', as the Fathers had called it.[9] But now it is made, by Faustus of Riez in the 450s – who was perhaps partly inspired by the suggestion in the liturgy of Pentecost with which confirmation was traditionally associated, that this feast was at once a 'finishing off' of the period which had begun at Easter, and a 'going out' from it –

---

sociales. Elles aussi existent à la fois, selon le point de vue auquel on se place, dans et hors l'individu' (Hubert and Mauss 1899, p. 306). The sacrificial rhythm of liturgy, or the rhythm of Anselm's theology, is not quite in line with the one found by Hubert and Mauss, however: the 'more' of liturgy is not the quantitatively more of the society over the individual (the quantitatively more of Durkheim's 'collective representations'), but the qualitatively 'more' of the infinite over the finite. This qualitative difference, which prevailed in the thinking of the Middle Ages, is the reason why an anthropology of the Middle Ages – in the sense given to anthropology since the eighteenth century, the study of man as man – is not enough on its own. See Dupront 1987, pp. 466–77, for some remarkable pages on this. On the oblation of children to the monastic life, Leclercq 1968.

8   Thus baptism and confirmation are two sacraments to Rabanus Maurus: *De inst. clericorum*, col. 316B; and see Leidrad, *Lib. de sac. bapt.*, col. 865: 'Ergo in baptismo fit remissio peccatorum, in impositione manuum conferuntur dona uirtutum.'

9   Buchem 1967, pp. 129–30 and pp. 141–2; and on sealing in baptism, Lampe 1967.

confirmation was made by Faustus to look forward to the difficulty of holding fast to the new being taken on in baptism. In a child, it is not the innate faculty of mind, but the education;[10] in the apostles, it is not knowledge of Christ – this was not enough: Peter denied Christ – but the power of the Spirit given at Pentecost to the apostles; the power with which they then set off into the world.[11] In Faustus, baptism and confirmation are held in delicate balance – a Semi-Pelagian balance. The essence of the moral power in man is the strength to hold the wisdom of the world in contempt (what he calls 'the contempt of salvation'); it is the monastic power to refuse the world. Its source was both the new-born and the in-born. Baptism makes this power into something new; confirmation strengthens what was already there, the *munus naturae* ('gift of nature').[12] Faustus has his penny and his cake: baptism causes a radical change in being, but confirmation stresses continuity from the natural capacity of man. He calls the capacity, both the new and the innate, *sensus rationabilis*. It is the power to 'discern good from evil', and act accordingly.[13] But in balancing the two sides of man, what had been given him which he could not possess himself, and what he was born with, Faustus tended to isolate them from one another.

For the Carolingians, who do not seem to have paid much attention to Faustus until he was included, in the middle of the ninth century, in the important collection of canons known as the False Decretals, confirmation was less an anticipation of the moral life after baptism than the link between the authority of the rite (as *opus operatum*, as form, as totality, a thing wholly finished and sufficient to itself, a ritual act which took its effect from the outward form, the words and actions done *rite*, correctly) and the moral life (which is never finished). It was the moment, like the moment of Pentecost which it still resembles, of going out from innocence into the world. It states once and for all the integrity of baptism; it 'finishes off'. But it goes out from baptism:

[10] *Homilia in Pentecosten*, p. 41: 'Numquid prodest si quisquam parentum magnam paruulo conferat facultatem nisi prouidere studeat et tutorem?'

[11] Ibid., pp. 41–2: 'Vides quia cum spiritus sanctus infunditur, cor fidele ad prudentiam et constantiam dilatatur. Itaque ante descensionem spiritus sancti usque ad negationem apostoli deterrentur, post uisitationem uero eius usque ad martyrium contemptu salutis armantur.'

[12] Ibid., p. 42: 'De spiritu sancto accipimus uitae amore et gloriae ardore succensi ut erigere a terrenis ad superna et diuina ualeamus. Ad hoc enim sensum rationabilem et naturae munere et secundae natiuitatis reparatione suscepimus.'

[13] Ibid.

The shoot went out from the root of Jesse, and the flower from the root; it went upward, and the spirit of the Lord came to rest on it, the spirit of wisdom and of understanding, the spirit of counsel and of fortitude, the spirit of knowledge and of piety, and it was full with the spirit of the fear of the Lord.[14] (Isa. 11:1)

Taking this as their text, the Carolingian writers tend to oppose two movements: the downward movement from the norm, from wisdom to fear; and the upward, ethical movement, from fear to wisdom.[15] A little later, in the early 830s, Jonas of Orléans provided an image to reconcile the two. He wished to characterize the moral predicament of the Christian layman and the Christian king.[16] The layman, he said, and the king as the layman most obviously involved with the world, was one who looked into a mirror – a perfectly clear, undistorting mirror – to see whether he was still wearing the right clothes, or, even more worrying, whether he had lost his clothes altogether.[17] He looked back from the world at the innocence he had once, at the beginning, momentarily received, and he was ashamed. His shame, in keeping with the shift away from public penitence to an inward contrition of tears, was a private shame; for he was only looking at himself.

The mirror is various things. It is the moral norm: the principles which must be translated into practice in order to live well. This in turn is the norm as represented – for this is an age which succumbed to the illusion that truth could be established in the *ordo* of politics – in the bishop, or in the priesthood generally, and above all in the law, promulgated by bishop and priest.[18] It is, by implication, the confirmation which, it was now emphasized,

---

[14] See Theodulph of Orléans, *Lib. de ord. bapt.* 17, cols. 236–7, for the use of this passage; and Jonas of Orléans, *De inst. laicali* 1.5, col. 131.

[15] Theodulph, *Lib. de ord. bapt.*, col. 259. He associates this movement upward and downward with the relation between the 'plenitude', 'perfection' and 'universality' suggested by the number seven in the seven gifts of the Spirit, and the 'going forth' of the 'stock of David' (*stirps Dauid*) from the root – which is also the apostolic succession: ibid., cols. 236–8.

[16] Jonas of Orléans, *De inst. regia*, cols. 279–306; *De inst. laicali*, cols. 121–278.

[17] *De inst. laicali*, col. 127: 'Proinde scire debet unusquisque fidelis quia hoc nouo homine, Domino uidelicet Christo Jesu, indutus fuerit, licet in praesenti purpura et bysso, auro et gemmis ornatus incedat, miserabiliter tamen atque flebiliter in oculis maiestatis nudus existit: et si in hac nuditate diem clauserit extremum, non solum a rege Christo in futuro corripietur, sed etiam a nuptiali, aeternoque conuiuio excludetur.'

[18] Leidrad, *Lib. de sac. bapt.* 11, col. 869: 'Dicunt ecclesiastici doctores, speculum animae esse mandata diuina, ut unaquaeque fidelissima in eo intuens, deprehendat in semetipsa uel foeditatem uitiorum, uel pulchritudinem uirtutum.'

could only be conferred by the bishop. Again by implication, it was baptism: it was at baptism that the 'new man' had 'put on Christ' (Gal. 3:27), in other words, the new clothes of the virtues.[19] Liturgy had allowed the soul to catch the absence and the presence of God in that rare moment when they were in the same place. The saint, the man through whom acts of God were done, was made up of the same absence and presence. But now man was defined not just by the saint, but by the king. 'The king is so called by right ruling', explained Jonas (after Isidore of Seville): *rex a recte regendo uocatur.*[20] What he really is is in his very name. If he fails to be what his name says he is, he can no longer be this thing, but must be something else, a tyrant no doubt. His rule is therefore his moral responsibility to the name to which he must continually look back, the name given him by the priest.

The answerability of the individual soul to the image in the mirror, or to the image which he knows ought to be there but which is not, depends on the separation of two elements which in liturgy had been only one: the clarity of seeing, and the clarity of the idea of what should be seen. The self-knowledge which becomes now so much the centre of moral teaching is a knowledge of self against the objective standard of the law; the inwardness which marks the period from the ninth to the twelfth centuries is a function of a certain talent for perceiving the lineaments of outwardness. The sensitivity to character, to the experience of the hero in the romances, the attention to sentiment, the notion that penitence was above all personal grief over the loss of Christ,[21] in other words everything which began from a sharpened awareness of change in time was made possible by the focusing of the image of what did not change: the law in its purity. We should look at the origins of the clarity which allowed the image in the mirror to be focused.

---

[19] Jonas, *De inst. laicali* 1.2, cols. 125–8.

[20] Jonas, *De inst. regia*, 3, col. 287; Isidore of Seville, *Etym.* 1.29.3; 9.3.4. Cf. Pseudo-Cyprian, *De xii abusiuis saeculi*, p. 51.

[21] Alcuin exploits the tears of public penitence (see, for example, *Gelasian*, no. 358, p. 57: 'Moueat pietatem tuam, quaesumus, domine, huius famuli tui lacrimosa suspiria') in order to stress the private tears of contrition. This enabled him to call penitence a 'second baptism' in the traditional way, without losing the emotional force he wished to put into it, and which comes through in his poetry: 'Cur tu dulcis amor fletus generabis amaros, / Et de melle pio pocula amara fluunt?' (*Carmina* 204, *PL* CI, col. 795, cited by Driscoll 1986, p. 316; and see his comments, p. 291).

The diminishing of baptism

RITUAL TO RHETORIC: LITURGY AND CONVERSION

Attempts to convert those peoples occupying lands beyond the frontiers of Frankish Gaul and Germany, the Frisians and Saxons, remained sporadic until the arrival of the Northumbrian Willibrord in Friesland in 690.[22] Willibrord was followed by another Anglo-Saxon, Wynfrid, from Devon, who on his consecration as bishop by Pope Gregory II in 722 took the name of the Roman martyr Boniface. His missionary labours in Friesland, where he was killed by pagans on 5 June 754, and in the central German lands of Hesse and Thuringia where Christianity had not yet taken firm root, together with his establishment of the groundwork of diocesan organization in Germany, earned him the title 'Apostle of the Germans'. It was their combination of missionary thrust and administrative efficiency – bringing together the old Irish tradition of the missionary in exile and the still more ancient principle of centralization on Rome – which made the work of Willibrord and Boniface so lasting in effect. In the next great episode of mission, when Charlemagne brought down his hand on the still pagan Saxons of north-west Germany and on the Avars across his eastern borders, the same mixture of vigour and organization appears in the documents and handbooks of conversion, which by now have become more numerous.[23] Here in these books, made to teach priests and to teach priests how to catechize, we can see the systematic quality of mission in the way the material is put together; but more than anything we are made aware of the missionary's zeal to *persuade*. And his persuasion, it is clear, drew its themes, its images, its teaching, from baptism itself. It was as if the rite had been opened out into rhetoric; as if the stuff of liturgical symbol had been turned into argument.

In the capitulary he issued in 785, Charlemagne had forced Christianity on the recalcitrant Saxons by legislation.[24] No doubt he was determined to take full advantage of the baptism of their leader, Widukind. Failure to keep the fast of Lent was to be punished with death; any Saxon hiding from baptism would also be put to death; any who failed to give their child for baptism

---

[22] For this and what follows, Levison 1946, pp. 45ff.

[23] For the background to this, and the links between conversion and education, McKitterick 1977; on the various documents which set out to explain the rite of baptism in the context of conversion, Bouhot 1978; Bouhot 1980; Bullough 1983; and the list of manuscripts containing such documents compiled by Keefe 1984.

[24] *MGH Capit. reg. Franc.* I, pp. 68–70; cf. commentary in Halphen 1921, pp. 145–218.

within a year of birth without the permission of a priest would be liable to a fine double that imposed for refusal to do military service. Missionaries, particularly Irish missionaries, had been happy to smash pagan idols in order to bring home their point, but Charlemagne's sustained military aggression was something new. It was not long before the bishops began to react against it. After some preliminary murmurings they came together in the summer of 796 somewhere on the Danube to discuss the baptism of the Avars. Could this illiterate, 'brutish and unreasoning people' be expected to grasp the meaning of the new religion, they asked themselves, with the same readiness as, say, the eunuch baptized so abruptly by the apostle Philip (Acts 8:30–8)?[25] The eunuch, like St Paul at his baptism (Acts 9:9–18), knew what he was doing, and needed no preparation. But this people was 'rough in faith'.[26] It was obvious that they needed some grounding. The military campaign, Paulinus of Aquileia had written to Charlemagne, must not be confused with the war of the spirit: to defeat in battle was not the same as to convert.[27] Alcuin, more tactfully, praised the king for 'softening the hardness of the unfortunate Saxons', and depicted him leading the converted peoples before the throne of God;[28] but he went on to make the case for preaching. He quoted Jerome: 'It is not possible for the body to receive the sacrament of baptism unless the soul has accepted the truth of faith.'[29] These 'new peoples' were like children. Fed on solid food they would vomit. They must be given milk, or more literally they must not be forced too promptly to pay tithes and other exactions;[30] and above all they must learn 'a knowledge of the Catholic faith',[31] for 'A confession of the tongue makes for salvation only when it is held firmly as a belief in the heart.'[32] In

---

[25] *MGH Conc. aevi Karol.* I, p. 174.

[26] Cf. Alcuin, *ep.* 111, p. 160, lines 31ff; *ep.* 113, p. 165, lines 14–15.

[27] *MGH Conc. aevi Karol.* I, pp. 141–2 (in the proceedings of the council of Frankfurt, 794).

[28] *Ep.* 110, p. 157. On the development of the idea of holy war, and the crusade, out of the war of conversion of the heathen conducted by the Christian king whose duty it was to give increase to the Christian people, and on the liturgical expression of these ideas, Erdmann 1977.

[29] *Ep.* 110, p. 158, quoting *Comm. in Matt.* 4.28, *PL* XXVI, col. 218C.

[30] *Ep.* 110, p. 158.

[31] Ibid., p. 158: 'Illud quoque maxima considerandum est diligentia, ut ordinate fiat praedicationis officium et baptismi sacramentum, ne nihil prosit sacri ablutio baptismi in corpore, si in anima ratione utenti catholicae fidei agnitio non praecesserit.'

[32] Ibid.: 'Illa tantum oris confessio proficit ad salutem, quae firmiter cordis credulitate tenetur.'

this turn away from brute-force to benign persuasion, there is already a hint of liturgical image made into argument.

With time, this grows. Alcuin's first concern, admittedly, was that the order of baptism, what he called the 'rational order of holy baptism',[33] should be observed correctly. For this he drew on a document, usually referred to as the *Primo paganus* from its opening words, which seems to have originated in the seventh century, and was itself related to a *florilegium* on baptism which accompanies John the Deacon's letter to Senarius in the surviving manuscripts.[34] The *Primo paganus* was a matter-of-fact statement of the sequence of rites in baptism, and a brief explanation of their meanings: 'First the pagan is made a catechumen; as he comes near to baptism, he is to renounce the evil spirit and all his damnable pomps.'[35] And so on. This document – which anticipates the scholastic reduction of liturgical forms – had its roots beyond the *florilegium* on baptism, in the sixth-century letter of John the Deacon, and was copied down to the twelfth century.[36] Alcuin himself sent it to his pupil the priest Oduin, and to the monks of Septimania, the province of south-eastern Gaul, where the right conduct of baptism was made especially urgent by the custom of Adoptianist heretics in those parts of baptizing with only one immersion.[37] It provided the framework for the questionnaire on

---

[33] *Ep.* 134, p. 202: writing to his pupil Oduin, he wishes him to know the 'rationabilem sacri baptismatis ordinem'.

[34] John's letter and the *florilegium* are published in Wilmart 1933, pp. 153–79; *Primo paganus* is quoted *en bloc* in Alcuin's letters nos. 134 (to Oduin) and 137 (to the monks of Septimania): pp. 202–3, pp. 214–15. Bouhot 1978, pp. 280ff, argues that neither the *Primo paganus* nor the *florilegium* were the work of Alcuin, as Wilmart thought, but that the first is a pre-Carolingian document, probably from Rome, and that the second, which has three exact forms, originates in a seventh-century composition. For Bullough's belief that the *florilegium* may have been Alcuin's, Bullough 1983, pp. 42ff.

[35] Alcuin, *ep.* 134, p. 202; *ep.* 137, p. 214.   [36] Bullough 1983, p. 44 and n. 103.

[37] Alcuin, *ep.* 137, pp. 210–16. On the attempt to counteract Adoptianism by the liturgies, see Andrieu's introduction to *Ordo XV*, pp. 85–90 (and above p. 141 n. 30). For the letter of Gregory the Great which Alcuin says he cannot find in the book of letters sent him from Rome (*ep.* 137, p. 215), Gregory, *Registrum* 1.41 (to Leander of Seville), pp. 47–9 (at p. 48). Gregory defends the *consuetudo diuersa* of the one faith, and in doing so shows how important gesture was thought to be in the conveying of ideas and symbolic meanings: 'Nos autem quod tertio mergimus, triduanae sepulturae sacramenta signamus, ut, dum tertio ab aquis infans educitur, resurrectio triduani temporis exprimatur. Quod si quis forte etiam pro summae trinitatis ueneratione aestimet fieri, neque ad hoc aliquid obsistit, baptizandum semel in aquis mergere quia, dum in tribus subsistentiis una substantia est, reprehensibile esse nullatenus potest, infantem in baptismate uel ter uel semel mergere, quando et in tribus mersionibus personarum trinitas, et in una potest diuinitatis singularitas designari. Sed si nunc usque ab hereticis infans in baptismate tertio mergebatur, fiendum apud uos esse non censeo, ne, dum mersiones numerant,

baptism sent by Charlemagne to his metropolitan bishops in 812, and was the basis of many of the bishops' replies; and it was incorporated into the various versions of the handbook on catechizing which seems to have been initiated by Alcuin, and undertaken or directed by Arno of Salzburg.[38]

The question which lies behind this literature is, what is baptism? It was a question asked partly in response to the problem of intention raised by infant baptism, and partly by the circumstances of mission and the renewed importance of the baptism of adults.[39] The establishment of order in the liturgy, of which the most prominent example was the work of Benedict of Aniane on the *Gregorian Sacramentary*, was as vital – probably more – to the religious and political stability of Carolingian Europe, as any of the later debates on the eucharist or predestination.[40] But as the literature of baptism developed – and I am assuming that the various documents should be seen as articulated, at least loosely[41] – a second question, how to persuade the pagan to baptism, is added to the first and often pushes it into the background. As this happens, it is as though the curt sentences of the *florilegium* and the *Primo paganus* are opened outwards, leavened, and transformed into addresses or sermons. Alcuin writes in the new rhetorical vein to Arno of Salzburg in 796, playing on Arno's name which in its German form means 'eagle'.[42] Arno is the eagle, recalling the

---

diuinitatem diuidant, dumque quod faciebant faciunt, morem uestrum se uicisse glorientur.' Alcuin thus required three immersions as an expression of the unity of the Trinity against the Adoptianists; Gregory allowed the virtue both of single and triple immersion, but advised single immersion in Spain where triple immersion was associated with the Arian division of Son from Father in the Trinity.

[38] See Bouhot 1978, pp. 285ff. On Arno's handbook, below, pp. 189–95; on the incorporation into it of *Primo paganus*, Bouhot 1980, pp. 221ff (apparatus to text).

[39] Thus the Carolingian literature on baptism generally addresses itself to baptism as conversion, and Leidrad particularly stresses the connection between baptism and the preaching which must come after it – and thus the responsibility of priests to a sacrament which is, however, not affected by their lack of faith (*Lib. de sac. bapt.* 11, cols. 868–72); but the same literature shows awareness, already a little awkward, of the problem of intention in infant baptism (especially Leidrad, ibid. 10, col. 868: *De infantibus uel his qui pro se respondere non possunt*).

[40] Angenendt 1973.

[41] On this, Bullough 1983, pp. 42ff; Bouhot 1978.

[42] *Ep.* 113, pp. 163–6: 'Praesagum tibi nomen inposuere parentes; licet dispensationis dei ignari, apud quem omnia futura iam facta sunt. Qui te summa pietate caelestia ordinauit mysteria populis ministrare, et de alto supernae gratiae intuitu acutissimis spiritalium oculorum obtutibus fluctiuagos de huius saeculi salo pisces ad uiuificandum non ad mortificandum eruere, et sacro uitrei fontis lauacro abluere, et igne sancti spiritus ad epulas aeterni regis assare; ut uerus apostolicae uocationis auditor efficiaris.' For 'eagle' in Old High German (*aro, arin*), see Grimm and Grimm 1854 (1984), s.v. *AAR*.

eagle of the *Physiologus*[43] – a collection of animal fables and allegories originating in Egypt in classical times – the eagle looking down with narrow eye on the storm-tossed waves, swooping to catch fishes from them as though from 'the salt of the world'. He bears them away – in Alcuin's conceit – to life not death; he washes them in a glass font – an arresting image which suggests the association of water, light and fire in the liturgy of Pentecost[44] – and then 'roasts them in the fire of the spirit for the feast of the eternal king'.[45] He is thus the 'fisher of men', who 'casts the net of Apostolic preaching over the ocean of deepest paganism', at the bidding of Christ the helmsman – a metaphor which reminds one of the scene in the Old English poem *Andreas* where Christ steers the apostle Andrew and his thegns across swelling seas to Mermedonia.[46] Alcuin, apparently, is trying out on his fellow bishop the method of address *ad hominem* which Augustine had put forward in his book *On Catechizing* (*De catechizandis rudibus*). In a letter on the principles of teaching the pagan, he cannot help showing the kind of thing which might be done in such teaching.

But Alcuin shows less knowledge of the content of Augustine's book than Arno in his handbook.

Arno, bishop of Salzburg from 785 to 821, responsible for the mission to the Avars and later the Slavs, appears in the sources as Charlemagne's trusted adviser on the problems in religion and politics (and war) raised by the eastern frontier. The chief document of his activities is the book whose title he borrowed from Augustine's treatise: he called it the *Ordo de catecizandis rudibus uel quid sint singula quae geruntur in sacramento baptismatis*.[47]

---

[43] *Physiologus B*, p. 19: 'Cum senuerit, grauantur alae eius, et obducuntur oculi eius caligine; tunc quaerit fontem aquae, et contra eum fontem euolat in altum usque ad aerem solis, et ibi incendit alas suas, et caliginem oculorum comburit de radio solis; tunc demum descendens ad fontem trina uice se mergit, et statim renouatur tota, ita ut alarum uigore et oculorum splendore multum melius renouetur.'

[44] This triple association is clearer in the *Gelasian* (prayers for the octave of Pentecost (nos. 646–51, p. 101); but it remains in the *Hadrianum*, nos. 515ff, pp. 222ff (*passim*); and see the preface for the fourth day of Pentecost in the *Supplement*, no. 1617, p. 533, where *infusio* is an action of both water and fire:' ... cuius infusio, petimus ut in nobis peccatorum sordes exurat, et tui amoris ignem nutriat, et nos ad amorem fraternitatis accendat'. Water and light is suggested in the *infusio* of: 'sancti spiritus domine corda nostra mundet infusio et sui roris intima aspersione fecundet'.

[45] *Ep.* 113, p. 163.

[46] Alcuin refers to the 'two brothers', Simon Peter and Andrew, who labour to pull the nets in during the storm: *ep.* 113, p. 163. For the baptismal resonances in *Andreas*, below, pp. 201–3.

[47] On Arno's life, Ferluga, Hellman and Ludat 1977, pp. 131–3. On the text, see the acute remarks of Bouhot 1980, pp. 191–4 and 230–8.

This, a compilation of sources, was evidently put together by Arno – or under his direction – in response to the growing discussion of missionary methods, and in particular to Alcuin's call for preaching over war as the means of proselytising. The *Ordo de catecizandis rudibus*, which may in an earlier form have been sent in answer to Charlemagne's queries about baptism, incorporates *Primo paganus*, but goes far beyond the order of baptism contained in that brief text, providing to its user a catalogue of arguments towards conversion. The arguments themselves – drawn not only from Augustine's *On Catechizing* but from the *Instructio ad competentes* of Nicetas of Remesiana (bishop of Dacia from 395 to 415) and other sources – are often highly developed, assuming an earnest intelligence in their audience; and their arrangement, orderly but open-ended, would have allowed elaboration of some themes and suppression of others, and generally the adaptation to the demands of the audience which Augustine had valued so highly in his own advice on education towards baptism.

The depth of Arno's approach to persuasion comes across best from a comparison with Alcuin.[48] In Alcuin's mind, converting the pagan means putting before him first the doctrine of the immortality of the soul; and then drawing from this its consequences for retribution – eternity of bliss for the good man and eternity of pain for the wicked. When these notions have taken their effect, the Creed can be recited in good faith, and this makes baptism possible. He has more or less ignored the central, Christological sense of Augustine, which turns on the coincidence between the love of God for man enacted in Incarnation, and the love between man and man arising out of speech; between Incarnation and rhetoric. In the very act of addressing his listeners with love – by his attention to who they are – the preacher awakens the love required in them for an understanding, and so bears out the principle of Incarnation.[49] To this Arno's compilation does fair justice. Using Alcuin's letter to Charlemagne,[50] and Rufinus' translation of the *Recognitiones* of Pseudo-Clement,[51] he sets the flow of Augustine's teaching in a ritual frame, without losing sight of Augustine's psychology of fear become love through Incarnation:

[48] Ibid. [49] See above, pp. 98–109. [50] *Ep.* 110, pp. 158–9.
[51] *Ordo de catecizandis*, nos. 4–10, pp. 206–7 (Augustine); nos. 12–13, p. 108 (Ps.-Clement).

What is the principal cause of the advent of the Lord? [here Arno quotes and then expands from the fourth book of Augustine's treatise] The Lord came so that God might show his love for us, 'setting it before us' to great effect, 'because while we were still enemies to him, he died for us' [Rom. 5:8], and because 'the end of the law and its fulness is love' [1 Tim. 1:5; Rom. 13:10], 'that we should love one another' [John 13:34], 'and so that we should lay down our souls for our brothers as he laid down his soul for us' [1 John 5:16], and if we were slow to love him, the true God, 'who loved us first' [1 John 4:19] and who 'did not spare his only son but gave him over for our sins' [Rom. 8:32], we should not be slow in returning his love. There is no greater invitation to God than his pure and true love.[52]

The thicket of quotations from the Epistles, not found in Augustine, would provide to the preacher using the handbook a means of referring his speech back to Scripture. Arno goes on to copy what Augustine says about the effect of God's love expressed in humility on the soul swollen with pride, and then of the growth in the soul from the initial fear which is the occasion of conversion to the love in which it finds completion. Such passages could hardly be more relevant to Arno's task among the Avars, and to the background of conversion in war, with all that war must have meant for pride, humiliation and fear. By judicious selection, he has moved well beyond Alcuin's much more straightforward call for a persuasion based in the prospect of retribution. However orderly Arno's *Ordo de catecizandis*, it is the urgent work of a man with pagans on his doorstep.

Augustine had shown in the treatise *On Catechizing* how the words of the catechist have their fulfilment in the *cultus* of baptism. Ritual is rhetoric at its most intense, awakening the same effort of faith, hope and love, but crowding this effort into the single 'moment' of an act of belief. Now the movement goes the other way. The intensity of the moment is unfolded, so that stress moves back from the *cultus dei* itself to the time of preparation before it, when the soul is nourished with the arguments on which belief is built. In Arno's compilation there is a fine example of such an unfolding of liturgy. It is the speech of an unknown author to those who cannot believe in the resurrection of the flesh:

[52] Ibid., no. 7, pp. 206–7.

There are perhaps some in the church who wonder how the flesh can rise up again from dust. Why do they not wonder how God made everything from nothing? It is less to restore what was than to make from nothing what was not. The very elements of the world preach to us the image of resurrection. Every day the sun dies from our eyes. Every day it rises. The stars fade in the early hours and return in the evening. In the summer we see bushes heavy with leaves, flowers and fruit, and in the winter we see the same bushes stripped of leaf, flower and fruit, naked and dry. Then with spring come round again, when the wetness rises from the root, they are clothed with their beauty once more. Why worry about men when you can see this happen in wood?

But if they think about the dust of rotting flesh, these people say, How can bones and marrow and flesh and hair be restored in resurrection? If they ask these things, they should look at the tiny seeds of giant trees. If they can, they should look at them and say, Where are the massive strength, the stretching branches, the multitude and greenness of leaves, the varieties of flower, the richness, the taste and the smell of fruits? Do the seeds of trees have in them the smell or the taste which the fruit gives when the tree has grown? No. And if things which are not seen in the seed can be produced from it, why worry about the dust of human flesh and whether the form which is not visible in it can be restored from it?

Often though they make this silly objection [the preacher goes on, wearily now] the wolf eats a man's flesh, the lion eats the wolf, and the lion dies and returns to dust. If dust is raised up, how can the man's flesh be separated from the wolf's and the lion's? What can you say to this, except that they should ponder first how they came into the world, and then they will find how they will rise up?[53]

Bede, in his writings on time, associated the waning and waxing of the moon, and thus Eastertide, with the decline and restoration of the soul;[54] and now in this passage, the anonymous author (basing himself on Gregory the Great's *Homily on Ezechiel*) brings the familiarity of the seasons and natural growth into the same focus as the wholly unfamiliar, and apparently impossible, proposition

---

[53] Ibid., no. 36, p. 215. The text attributes this to Gregory's *Homily on Ezechiel*, but Bouhot identifies it as part of an anonymous *Sermo de resurrectione*, PL Suppl. 4, 1585–6, which uses Gregory's homily.

[54] *De temp. rat.* 54: 'Et ut uegetati diuersarum uarietate uirtutum, earumque foliis ueluti amoenae arboris adumbrationem uelati, tamquam laetae atque fructiferae segetes pullulemus in plenilunio, ut perfectum splendorem fidei et sensus gerentes a peccati tenebris segregemur; in reuersa eadem luce lunari ad caelos, quod a quinta decima luna fieri incipit, ut, quanto magni sumus, humiliemur in omnibus, dicentes cum apostolo singuli: "gratia autem Dei sum id quod sum" [1 Cor. 15:10].'

of the resurrection of the flesh.[55] The liturgical imagery of death-and-resurrection, rebirth and of 'viridity', the use of the potency of nature as a metaphor for the capacity of the soul, is now the material by which the missionary argues – and not without irony – from the possible to the impossible; by which he goes beyond the paganism of his audience.

To the sterility of paganism (as he sees it) he opposes the infinite fertility of Christianity. Akin to this is the missionary's argument against idols, 'the gods of the nations' of whom the Psalmist said, 'Eyes have they but they see not; they have ears but they hear not; noses have they but they smell not; they have hands but they handle not; feet have they but they walk not; and those who put their trust in them therefore become like them' (Ps. 113:5–8). Pope Boniface V quotes the Psalmist's words in his letter to King Edwin of Northumbria, and goes on to contrast the lifelessness of idols with the cross's power to redeem.[56] Idols are made from corruptible material; they are insensible; they are like stones fixed in one place; they do not have in them the breath of life. All this means that they can be broken up without any ill effects. When Bede tells the story of King Edwin's high-priest Coifi, rushing away from the council meeting which had finally accepted the Christian religion, and heaving a spear against the idol of his own faith, we catch with sudden clarity the intoxication of this destruction.[57] It is a destruction which renews, coursing with the adrenalin of new-found power.

To the author of Arno's passage on resurrection, the origin of the flesh and its destiny are almost equally unknowable. God's power to make from nothing, and his power to revivify dust, are intimations of boundlessness. The pagan Germanic world, it seems, already had a keen appreciation of the uncharted openness which lay before birth and after life. Among the early scenes of Beowulf, we hear of Scyld, chief of the Danes, who arrives in their land as a child, alone on a ship laden with treasure, and departs from them at his death once again 'into the power of the

[55] Cf. Tertullian, *De resurrectione mortuorum*, 12.4, p. 935: 'Reuoluuntur hiemes et aestates, et uerna et autumna cum suis uiribus moribus fructibus. Quippe etiam de caelo disciplina est: arbores uestire post spolia, flores denuo colorare, herbas rursus inponere, exhibere eadem quae absumpta sunt semina nec prius exhibere quam absumpta.' And then (12.6): 'Nihil non iterum est; omnia in statum redeunt cum abscesserint, omnia incipiunt cum desierint, ideo finiuntur, ut fiant; nihil deperit nisi in salutem.'
[56] Bede, *Hist. Eccles.* 2.10, pp. 168–71.
[57] Ibid., 2.13, pp. 184 and 185.

flood'.[58] Of unknown origin, this warrior returns to the unknown. He is like Bede's famous sparrow, whose flight convinces the members of Edwin's court of the value of Paulinus' Christian preaching:

This is how the present life of man on earth [says one of the King's chief men] appears to me in comparison with that time which is unknown to us. You are sitting with your ealdormen and thegns in winter time; the fire is burning on the hearth in the middle of the hall and all inside is warm, while outside the wintry storms of rain and snow are raging; and a sparrow flies swiftly through the hall. It enters in at one door and quickly flies out through the other. For the few moments it is inside, the storm and wintry tempest cannot touch it, but after the briefest moment of calm, it flits from your sight, out of the wintry storm and into it again. So this life of man appears but for a moment; what follows or indeed what went before, we know not at all. If this new doctrine brings us more certain information, it seems right that we should accept it.[59]

Here, it is true, Christianity is presented as the religion of 'more certain information', and it is the old religion which is associated with unknowingness. But this perhaps underlines something of extreme importance in the rhetoric of conversion: the power which Christianity offers the Germanic peoples – and particularly their kings – was that of the *familiarity* of the unknown. The cycle of growth and decay in the tree, or the familiar rise and fall of the seasons, are suddenly linked with the spectacle of eternity from which things come and into which they pass. The resurrection of the flesh, thus brought close to the births and deaths of nature, gives concreteness to eternity; as do the doctrines of the immortality of the soul and the future life, with which Augustine's catechist, and Arno's after him, are to begin their discourse. Paradise does not yet have the geography it will have by the time of Dante, but it is accessible enough to the senses and the mind, if only as the place where 'there will be no more death, or mourning, or cries of distress, no more sorrow' (Rev. 21:4–5).[60] It is familiar, in other words, as the antithesis of what is most immediately known. When Edwin's counsellor spoke about the sparrow, he was not just explaining what he would have to reject,

[58] *Beowulf*, pt I, lines 1–52 (quoted here in the translation of J. R. Clark Hall: Clark Hall 1911, pp. 20–2).

[59] *Hist. Eccles.* 2.13, pp. 182–5.

[60] *Ordo de catecizandis*, no. 18, p. 210. On the development of a geography of the afterlife, Le Goff 1981.

but was already opening his mind to the Christian conception of the unknown which lay before and after this life.

If the liturgy *celebrates* the familiarity of the unknown and infinite, the rhetoric of the missionary *argues* it, demonstrates it, persuades to it. We have seen how the liturgical image of a growth with infinite roots and infinite implications – the *uiriditas* of the Mozarabic blessing of the palm and of the Roman blessing of oil[61] – becomes an argument for the resurrection of the flesh. In another passage in Arno's missionary handbook, taken direct from chapters 36 and 37 of Augustine's *On Catechizing*, time is shown to have in it a principle of growth from and towards God.[62] This is the principle of prophecy, which in liturgy (as I have suggested) becomes *anamnesis*;[63] and it too can become the substance of persuasion. We can see how this is done in a slightly later document, but one which is almost as firmly linked up with the history of mission: the *Fulda Sacramentary* of about 975, designed, like many liturgical manuscripts emanating from this abbey, to further the cause of the Ottonian mission to the Slavs and Danes.[64] *The Order of Scrutiny* (*Ordo scrutinii*) in the *Fulda Sacramentary*, although apparently it envisages child-catechumens as well as adults, returns to the older idea of scrutiny as teaching.[65] It takes place on the Monday of the third week of Lent, the day of the first scrutiny, and it urges its hearers to understand how the history of man operates within them, individually:

Man, whom God created with good will in his image and likeness, hear this: tutored, a hearer, you are to be a catechumen. Lend your ear. Come

---

[61] See above, pp. 162–3.   [62] *Ordo de catecizandis*, no. 34, p. 214.
[63] See above, p. 172.
[64] See the introduction to their edition of the *Fulda Sacramentary* by G. Richter and A. Schönfelder.
[65] *Fulda Sacramentary*, no. 471, pp. 330–2. The rubrics specify that the candidates are children; the words address them as if they are adults, putting before them a history of their own decline in that of Adam and the fallen angels, as well as the *agnitio ueritatis* which will reform them; apparently remembering the age of its audience, it then begins to talk *about* the candidates to the adult assembly. Meanwhile the miniature accompanying this folio of the MS (the miniature is on fo. 214r: Tafel 42 in the edition) shows both children and adults at the scrutiny, some of the adults standing without children on their arms and therefore presumably undergoing baptism. This is borne out by the baptism scene on fo. 87r, where children and adults await immersion by Boniface (whose martyrdom is shown in the other half of this miniature: see Tafel 27, and below, p. 204). Clearly the text of the scrutiny has in mind children and adults to be baptized, and others present. (I am grateful to Henry Mayr-Harting for discussion of the miniatures, and for help with the whole question of conversion.)

to the knowledge of God. Give your name in this rite of registration,[66] and have it written in the book of life. Desire the grace of God and walk into life. For you are the one whom the one God has made and created holy, full of the quickness of reason, to serve him in a servitude of perennial glory. You are man, made and made ready to rebuild the ruin of angels. Your substance is from nothing, your body from slime. What you are and how you are, all is from nothing. And so you are the image of the maker, that standing firm under the gaze of the creator, you might be holy; a successor in heaven to the wicked fallen angels; unending in a world without end in your praises of the maker.[67]

From here the sermon goes on to the deception of man by the devil, and Christ's intervention to 'repair' (*ut qui cuncta fecerat ex nihilo te repararet ex aliquo*) the ill-effects of this in his capacity as mediator between God and man.[68] The possibility of repair thus presented is the possibility of life itself:

Today then, hear God speaking in me, who once spoke through Moses. Wholly aroused, be wakened: hear and feel the force of God, just as you were wakened when the author of life blew breath onto your face and you were made man with living soul.[69]

Vige ('be wakened' or 'take strength') suggests also the blooming of a plant. It is as though history is the thrust of growth as it is seen in man himself. But the metaphor of vegetal or temporal increase, of invigoration, turns attention from the *metamorphosis* of conversion (metamorphosis involving discontinuity), to its continuity. The missionary represents the resurrection of the flesh, and the taking on of Christianity by the pagan, not as terms of contradiction, but as a development – even if this is the *aporia*, the riddle, of the growth of an acorn into an oak, or, as in the parable, of the mustard seed (tiniest of seeds) into a mustard 'tree' (Mark 4:30–2; Matt. 13:31ff; Luke 13:18ff).[70] The tree may reach above the clouds, like Jack's bean-stalk, but it must still grow out of the

---

66 Referring to the writing down of the names of the candidates for baptism at the first scrutiny on Monday of the third week of Lent (*Fulda Sacramentary*, no. 471, p. 330).
67 Ibid.   68 Ibid.
69 Ibid., p. 331: 'Audi itaque hodie in me loquentem deum, qui olim locutus est per Moysen; totus sic excitatus uige, ut audias et sentias uim dei, sicut uiguisti cum insufflauit in faciem tuam idem auctor uitae et factus es homo in animam uiuentem.'
70 See Jeremias 1972, pp. 146ff, for the parable of the mustard seed, and the parable of the leaven which has the same sense. In both cases the Synoptics stress the contrast between the smallness of the seed (or quantity of leaven) and the great size of the tree (or great number of loaves), whereas the rhetorical context here expresses the continuity despite the contrast.

earth. How this must have appealed to the pagan king, whose power – it is tempting to think after Frazer's *Golden Bough* – was tied up with the fertility of the land and of lineage: *fecunditas terrae*, an influential Irish book on kingship calls him.[71]

In the *Gelasian* prayer quoted above, the 'times gone by' and the 'waiting for what will be' (*momenta praeteritorum-expectacio futurorum*) find their point of rest in God's 'foresight' (*prouidentia*), or of the baptism which is now being recalled.[72] Time has been absorbed into an absolute memory and anticipation. But before this stage has been reached, there must be a less intense view of things in which time still offers resistance; where it is still a process of unfolding. There must be a *narratio*, as in Augustine's catechesis. This *narratio* is far from alien to the liturgy: it is written into the whole idea of the New Testament as the fulfilment of the Old; the idea that the *figurae* of the Old Testament, which are – as this word with its origins in the Greek *schema* suggests – 'sketchy', shadowy, incomplete, not quite enough (but stretching forward to become enough), are completed in the *ueritas*, the truth, of the New; and that this process of completion is accomplished again and again in liturgy.[73] The persuasion of the missionary, and the use he makes of history in order to persuade, follow exactly the conception of a truth gradually unfolding to its full clarity. Bede's *Ecclesiastical History* is a tale in this vein. It opens with a description of the islands of Britain, among them Ireland, where snakes have been banished and deer abound, and altogether a land of plenty echoing the paradise of Eden.[74] Caesar and his Romans, whose coming is announced by two storms, strip this land bare. Then comes Augustine of Canterbury and the beginning of the long story of restoration, or completion, of what was promised in the opening scenes.

Bede (sanguine spirit) is so intent on the success of this story that he tends to ignore the real stuff of paganism.[75] He writes as though he has forgotten it. He wishes to lay before us the *process* of

[71] Pseudo-Cyprian, *De xii abusiuis saeculi*, pp. 51ff: the king is here the embodiment of people and land – 'pax populorum, tutamen patriae ... cura languorum ... temperies aeris, serenitas maris, terrae fecunditas' – but he is all this in the sense that his moral failure (his failure to be the *cor-rector* of his people) will result in material ills. Also see the interesting remarks of Sot 1988, on the *celeritas* and *grauitas* of the Merovingian kings, against their Indo-European background.
[72] Above, pp. 179–80.   [73] On *figura*, Auerbach 1959.
[74] Bede, *Hist. Eccles.* I.1, pp. 14–20. See comments in Kendall 1979.
[75] Mayr-Harting 1972, pp. 40ff.

conversion, but he is not so interested as he might be in the two stages of a metamorphosis – the before and after of Remigius' words to Clovis at his baptism, 'Worship what you have burnt, burn what you have been wont to worship' – the abruptness of which can be guessed at from the candid juxtaposition, in the ivory carvings of the Franks Casket, of the brutal tale of Wayland the Smith and the scene of the Adoration of the Magi. He is not even interested in the much less abrupt passage from the gloomy heroism of Beowulf – whose battles with Grendel and his mother are at least reminiscent of exorcism – to the combat of the saint with evil.[76] Rather, he tells the story of the progressive clarification of a landscape, a paradise, at first dimly perceived; of a sketchy picture filled in over time, until it takes on the sharp lines of *ueritas*.

Is this not the effect of Bede's handling of the conversion of King Edwin of Northumbria? To convey the development in Edwin's mind of a clearer perception – of a recognition of what is already there at hand – Bede tells three stories, each of them probably representing a different tradition.[77] This is not because he is muddled, or cannot choose between three accounts, but because he wishes to show the erratic path taken by an idea in the mind of this troubled man, 'who often sat alone in long periods of silence, speaking with himself in his inmost heart, thinking about what he should do, and which religion he should adhere to'.[78] The first story tells how Edwin married Ethelberga, the Christian daughter of King Ethelbert of Kent, who brought with her Bishop Paulinus. Paulinus is bent on the conversion of the Northumbrians. Shortly after their arrival, on an Easter Sunday, Edwin narrowly escapes assassination at the hands of the West Saxons, and that same night rejoices in the birth of a daughter. He promises Paulinus that if he should be victorious in battle against the West Saxons, he will throw down his idols and serve Christ. As a pledge of good faith (*pignus promissionis inplendae*), he hands over his daughter to be baptized, at Pentecost, by Paulinus. In the second story, Edwin, still deliberating on what he should do – unable, as yet, to fulfil his promise to Paulinus – is approached by Paulinus, who lays his right hand on the king's head. Suddenly,

---

[76] Colgrave 1958; Mayr-Harting 1972, pp. 220ff. On Beowulf's ambiguity, Wormald 1978. And Gregory of Tours, *History of the Franks* 2.31, for Clovis.

[77] See the editors' comments to this effect, in the edition by Colgrave and Mynors.

[78] *Hist. Eccles.* 2.9, p. 166. For the three stories, ibid. 2.9; 2.12; 2.13, pp. 162ff.

Edwin recognizes Paulinus as the 'stranger' (*ignotum*) who had once, when he was threatened with betrayal and death while exiled in the court of King Redwald of the East Angles, come to him with the same gesture, reassuring him that he would be spared, that he would overcome his enemies and surpass his own fathers in power. Before vanishing mysteriously, Paulinus hints at the full magnitude of what he has in mind, something which the king could hardly have understood until later:

But if he who foretells so much good as is to befall you, can also give you better and more useful counsel for your salvation and your life than any of your fathers or kindred ever heard of, do you consent to submit to him, and to follow his wholesome counsel?[79]

Edwin makes the promise to the stranger – for he has no idea of Paulinus' identity at this stage. When Paulinus lays his hand for the second time on the king's head, it is obvious that when he had spoken of 'salvation' (*salus*) and 'wholesome counsel' (*monita salutaria*) he had meant more than escape from physical death, or good advice about government – although he had meant these things too.[80] Edwin has therefore given two promises, one knowingly, the other with only half an understanding of its content. The third tradition now recounts the speeches of Edwin's counsellors in the *witenagemot*, first Coifi who takes the material-ist view that he has not had enough out of his assiduous attention to the gods, and then the counsellor who likens life to the flight of the sparrow through the hall at night, and the time before and after life to the uncertainty of the bird in the storm outside. The new religion is the religion of 'more certainty'.

Bede has emphasized not the contradiction between the idol and Christ, but the unfolding of one into the other; the slow growth of the seed. He has used the story – with its power to show each development implicit in the last – to imitate the course of time moving towards completion. So it is with time that the failure to recognize a strange figure or to understand what he says, gives way to recognition. The translations of large sections of the Bible into the vernacular (Saxon and Anglo-Saxon) constitute a recognition too. What was dimly seen – if at all – is brought close to hand in the new language. The fallen angels in the Anglo-Saxon translation of Genesis (which is a re-interpretation and not a

---

[79] Ibid. 2.12, p. 178.   [80] Ibid. 2.12, pp. 180–2, makes this quite clear.

translation in a straightforward, literal sense) defy God with a pride akin to Beowulf's resolution in the face of destiny. Caedmon chews over the cud of the Latin Vulgate and brings forth a song in his own tongue.[81] Translation, in other words, involves a conversion, a rumination in which what had been unclear is made familiar. But the translation of books of the Bible into the native tongue is also, in a sense, a translation of liturgy into story: it is part of that desire to persuade by unfolding the intensity of liturgical imagery, and to present it as a series of steps – a beginning, a middle, and an end – rather than a cluster of ideas and associations all in the same place. It is a translation from Christianity performed into Christianity explained, into Christianity as the fruit of experience, time, history; Christianity as a progression.

The association of these elements – translation into the vernacular, story-telling, and conversion – is evident in the collection of Old English poems contained in the Bodleian Manuscript Junius 11. The manuscript was put together at the turn of the eleventh and twelfth centuries; it is made up of verse translations (translations which liberally develop their themes, sometimes with the help of the Apocrypha) of extracts of Genesis, Exodus and the Book of Daniel, and closes with a verse account of the Harrowing of Hell and the Temptation of Christ in the desert (*Christ and Satan*). The episodes chosen from the Old Testament books are closely related to the readings for Holy Saturday in the *Gelasian*: Creation, the Flood, the sacrifice of Abraham, the crossing of the Red Sea and the journey through the desert, the three youths in the fiery furnace in Daniel.[82] On stylistic grounds, it is clear that the poems are by different authors (the *Genesis*-poem itself being a conflation of the work of at least two poets); but together – as their compiler obviously knew – they tell a single story, of the fall of man and his return, over the course of history, to wholeness. The events picked out are not juxtaposed, as though unconnected in time, as they are in the liturgical readings in which they seem to originate – or whose general pattern at least they follow; they are not event-ideas in this way, but are strung together in a different coherence, a temporal and linear coherence, a dramatic sequence in which each episode flows out of the previous one and into the

---

[81] Ibid. 4.24, p. 418. And see Delbono 1967 on the relations between translation into the vernacular and conversion.

[82] *Gelasian*, nos. 431ff, pp. 70–2.

next, giving an impression, overall, of development rather than repetition in different perspectives.

With great compassion for the condition of fallen man, the poems weave the complex tales of revenge, betrayal, seduction, the terror of the Israelites trapped between the sea and the advancing army of the Pharaoh, Daniel's unwillingness to tell Nebuchadnezzar the true and awful meaning of his dream, around the always present figure of the righteous man, who runs like a thread of gold through rough cloth – Adam himself, Noah, Moses, Abraham, finally Christ.[83] Like all good story-tellers, these poets wish to move their listeners by appealing to their moral experience: and so we are made afraid by the suspense as the embittered fallen angel, jealous of God's love for man, flies over the land towards the unprepared and doomed couple in Eden; and relieved when the people of Moses have all made their precarious journey across the floor of the sea, between the towering walls of water which threaten to break over them at any moment. We fall in willingly with the poet's conviction (he had after all to sing of heroes) that the man who stepped first into the opening in the water needed as much courage to do this as he would have needed to turn his face to the enemy behind. This series of stories, which may have been intended by the compiler as a form of catechesis, makes of Christianity a drama.[84] This is their power to persuade. They invoke in the listener, not the theoretical faculty, our ability to see through the veil of matter to the author of matter, but the moral faculty, our ability to discern evil from good within time – or, rather, the ability to suffer our inadequacy to make this discernment.

There are other Old English texts which give translations – in this sense of expansions in the native tongue – of liturgy. The epic poem *Andreas*, with its lingering attention to the sea and the crossing of the sea, its climactic episode of a wicked land purified by a flood that rises from a pillar in its midst, described by the poet as a drinking bout gone sour, alludes clearly enough to baptism.[85] Fittingly, towards the end of the story, the 'bitter beer-drinking' is sweetened – like the bitter waters of Mara,

---

[83] For this theme, see the excellent introductions in S. A. J. Bradley's collection of Anglo-Saxon poetry (Bradley 1982).

[84] Hall 1976, argues that the MS is compiled with catechesis in mind, perhaps along the lines of Augustine's *narratio* in the *De catechizandis rudibus*.

[85] Walsh 1977, makes a detailed study of the baptismal references.

sweetened when Moses threw a length of wood into them, this being a type of baptism – and the Mermedonians, other than the irretrievably wicked, are brought back to life from the flood waters and baptized. *Andreas* is in the first place a re-telling, in Old English, of the adventures of the apostle in the apocryphal *Acts of Andrew*. But while translating the Latin of the source into the language and idiom of his people, the poet has also, by laying stress on certain episodes – principally the 'water-episodes' – turned the rite of baptism into a narrative. *Andreas* is baptism put into a vernacular story, and so made accessible both in language and form. By being recast as a narrative full of local reference and therefore thoroughly familiar to its audience (for whom the epic story was one of the chief means of communication), the liturgy – which must have seemed at first a remote and perhaps merely magical spectacle to the Germanic peoples – was made into something compelling, close at hand.

A full perception of this process would require proper consideration of the relation between the story-form and the form of ritual. Here it can only be suggested that a story – not all stories it is true, but surely an epic like *Andreas* just as a novel – has force because it re-presents the situation of consciousness in time, the experience we all have of being pulled back towards the past by memory and its overtones of regret, forgiveness, nostalgia, jealousy, grief, and pulled forward into the future by desire, anticipation, fear, hope. In this way, the story 'happens to' its listeners. The anxiety of suspense brought on by the *Genesis*-poet in his account of the seduction of Eve is an implication of the listener's anxiety-in-time into the anxiety Adam and Eve *would* suffer if they knew what the listener can guess. We implore Eve not to eat the apple, but we know (even if we have forgotten the story) that she will. The listener's time and the story's time pass over and under one another. In the whole sequence of Junius 11, from fall to Christ, or in the sequence of *Andreas*, culminating in the flood in Mermedonia, the attention of the listener is carried along like this, his consciousness of the temporal sharpened again and again by suspense, by recapitulation and by the irony which stimulates both his memory and his anticipation. So, the story, moving forward from its beginning to its end, is the form not of the beginning and the end, but of the uncertain, and therefore anxious, elapse of time between them. Is it not significant, in this respect, that the Junius manuscript ends with the temptation of

Christ in the wilderness, as if to say that this state of anxiety-in-time is the condition of the moral life? The story, as it were, has no proper end.

In the context of conversion, story has been abstracted from liturgy, where it was only a part of the scheme of things. For in liturgy, story – temporality, sequence, the anxiety of being in time, the sense of loss over time – is held within the discipline of repetition, which brings back all time to beginning and end. In the intense, sacramental, moments of liturgy, the 'expectation' of completion yet to come, and the remembering of the completion that once was, are realized. Baptism *is* the Flood, the crossing of the Red Sea, the *triduum* of death-and-resurrection. This is what *anamnesis* means: the past is 'not forgotten'. It is repeated. But there can be no pure repetition.[86] In an absolute remembering, memory would be indistinguishable from event, and so there would be no awareness that one was the *same* as the other. If one thing is to be seen to be the same as another, it must be different from it. Remembering, if it is to be remembering and not a mystical identity between mind and object, will always have in it both the sense of loss in time (difference) *and* that of recollection (sameness); both time and not-time. Liturgy is centred in this joining of time and not-time. It joins story and the contrary of story. From this the missionary, wishing to speak to the world, detaches story.

If the poet-translator opened ritual out into story, hoping thus to convince his audience (whether pagan or already Christian) by an address to moral experience, the missionary-martyr, living out the association between baptism and death, offered something closer to proof. He demonstrated, bodily, the force of his arguments, and therefore the efficacy of his baptizing. When the lives of Boniface and other missionaries to the continent were set down, no special emphasis was laid on the connection between the work of baptizing and its culmination in martyrdom; but more than once, when an artist wished to reduce these life-stories to their essential elements, he chose to depict the two scenes of baptizing the heathen and martyrdom. In a late tenth-century manuscript of the *Life* of Kilian (a seventh-century Irish mission-ary to Germany), copied and illuminated at Fulda, the saint's baptizing and martyrdom (by beheading) make up only two

---

[86] For this analysis of repetition, Kierkegaard 1985, pp. 171–2; and see above, pp. 167–73.

scenes in a sequence of eleven miniatures.[87] But in three liturgical manuscripts of the same period, all from Fulda – that metropolis of Ottonian mission – and one of them the *Fulda Sacramentary*, the two episodes of the saint baptizing and the saint martyred stand alone to represent – in this case – the life of Boniface, accompanying the text for his feast on 5 June.[88] In the miniature on fo. 27r of the *Fulda Sacramentary*, Boniface baptizes in the left-hand scene, and suffers martyrdom on the right. The two events are divided by a Corinthian column. Baptizing, Boniface stretches his hand forward from the left in a gesture of blessing over the adult who is immersed to the shoulders in a font; to the right of the font, a priest lays his hand on the head of the immersed man, while behind him to the right of the picture, a group of five godparents, men and women, stand, one of them holding a child ready for baptism. On the far left, behind Boniface, a corresponding group of six deacons wait, one of them holding the white garment which will clothe the neophyte when he emerges. On the other side of the antique column this peaceful scene is mirrored with aggression. Instead of godparents and deacons in the wing, two bands of soldiers – their helmets mockingly taking up the tonsures of their counterparts – press forward towards Boniface in the middle. In the *Life*, Boniface forbids his *comitatus* of priests and followers to defend themselves,[89] and so in the picture, with an attitude of what seems to be deprecation, he bows his body and lowers his head before the soldiers, only holding up to them his Bible, against which a sword falls. At his back, from the viewer's right, he is stabbed in the shoulder with a spear. On the ground in both scenes, flowers push up, reminding the eye of the acanthus leaves of the Corinthian column above, and expressing no doubt the fecundity of both occasions.

There is a sense here of martyrdom not as baptism of blood – as it had been for Tertullian[90] – but as an affirmation of *baptizing*. Fulda, we have seen, was one of the centres of ritual persuasion –

---

[87] MS Hannover, Niedersächsische Landesbibliothek 189 (*Passio Kiliani*, fos. 1r–11r); on the text, see Kilian 1989, p. 217 (no. 202), and pp. 222–3, pls. 1–11 for reproductions of the miniatures.

[88] MS Udine, Biblioteca capitolare, cod. 75. v (fo. 43v); Bamberg, Staatliche Bibliothek, Cod. A II. 52 (fo. 126v). The scene from the *Fulda Sacramentary* (fo. 87r) is reproduced in Richter and Schönfelder's edition, pl. 27; the scenes from the Udine and Bamberg MSS on pl. 28.

[89] *Life of Boniface*, p. 56.

[90] See above, p. 79. For Fulda, see above, p. 195.

where the ritual of baptism was developed into a discourse of explanation and persuasion. In these pictures, it seems to present martyrdom as the ultimate eloquence of the preacher, the demonstration once and for all in action of what had been said in words: a kind of catechesis through blood. We might, as a coda to the discussion of liturgy and rhetoric, go further and ask what was the content of this eloquence in death. Boniface belonged with the Roman style of mission, its accent on administration, the politics of the church, the establishment of a diocesan structure – a tradition which still had its roots in Roman colonialism.[91] But his fervour, and the Fulda miniatures with their portrayal of humiliation, point to another strain. At one level, the meekness of Boniface before his persecutors echoes – from the other side of the pillar – the submission of the neophyte, naked, exposed, head lowered in baptism:

Here comes the Hun [Theodulph of Orléans had said] long hair bound; he was fierce once, but faith has brought him down.[92]

It seems the symmetry of the miniatures was not an idle one. The complex juncture of humility and power, in both king and priest, is a *motif* in Bede and Gregory the Great. So Bede's tale of King Oswin, first angry at Aidan because he had given away to a poor man the gelding Oswin had given him, and then humbling himself before the man of God when he reflects on what Oswin had done:

Is that brood of the mare dearer in your sight than that son of God the poor man?[93]

---

[91] Levison 1946, pp. 78–93; but see Markus 1970, for the argument that Gregory the Great abandoned the colonial model of mission, seeing from his correspondence with Augustine of Canterbury that the tactics of persuasion were called for.

[92] *MGH Poet. lat. aevi Carol.*, p. 484: 'Pone uenit textis ad Christum crinibus Hunnus / Estque humilis fidei qui fuit ante ferox.' Cf. Gregory of Tours, *History of the Franks* 2.31, p. 144 (baptism of Clovis).

[93] Bede, *Hist. Eccles.* 3.14, pp. 258–61 (this transl. is Thomas Stapleton's, in the sixteenth century); and see comments in Mayr-Harting 1972, pp. 95–6. For Gregory the Great, the effectiveness of the signs worked by the holy man is tied firmly to his self-knowledge and humbleness. He writes to Augustine of Canterbury after the conversion of King Æthelbert of Kent: 'Restat itaque, frater carissime, ut inter ea quae operante deo exterius facis semper te interius subtiliter iudices ac subtiliter intellegas et temetipsum, quis sis et quanta sit in eadem gente gratia, pro cuius conuersione etiam faciendorum signorum dona percepisti, et, si quando te creatori nostro seu per linguam siue per opera reminiscaris delinquisse semper haec ad memoriam reuoces, ut surgentem cordis gloriam memoria reatus premat.' (*Registrum* 11.36, pp. 926–7.) On the story of the Danish ruler who freed St Willibrord because he was so impressed with his courage (told by Alcuin, *Life of Willibrord*, transl. in Talbot 1954, p. 9), see Hill 1976.

asks Oswin. Was humility, we might ask, in priest or king, not a part of the power of priest and king because it was an aspect of their distinctiveness, their refusal to take part in the reciprocity of feud? But humility also awakens conscience, as Bede's story shows. The martyrs of the early church knew, and Tertullian made much of it, that the persecuted drew the power of his persecutor on to himself by refusing to parry it. Surely what was true then was true now, if in very different times. In an act of aggression against one who does not defend himself, the aggressor accuses himself. The lack of resistance sows at least a doubt in his mind. The deliberate humility of non-resistance – especially in a society dominated by feud and by a law based in the principle of compensation – breaks the pact of violence. It is one of those places where the give-and-take of the ethical and social, the system of balances, is opened out to something more than itself.

Did persuasion not begin like this, in the turning back of violence on itself? Did the humiliation of the baptizing martyr not make possible the humbling of the pagan in baptism?

SYMBOL TO ALLEGORY

The rhetoric arising out of the missions was an 'unfolding' of the intensity of liturgical signs, of Augustine's liturgical moment. It reaffirmed the importance of liturgy generally, and sacrament in particular – witness the new wealth of literature on the sacraments in the Carolingian age, and the attention given by homilists to liturgical subjects from Bede onwards. But with its tendency to address the individual, in what later writers would call his conscience,[94] to stress the moral as a separate issue from the sacramental, to stress what Hildefonsus of Toledo had called the 'journey made in the wilderness after baptism' with its labyrinthine, circuitous paths, the paths of error, effort, indecision which would become those of the quest for the grail in the twelfth century:[95] with all this, the momentary effulgence of baptism was pushed out on to the periphery. It was a mirror bearing the fixed image of the face that looked into it, the face as it had been in

---

[94] But note the use of conscience in the sense of moral conscience already in the *Gelasian* rite for the reconciliation of public penitents: (*Gelasian*, no. 360, p. 57): 'ut non plus ei noceat conscientiae reatus ad paenam quam indulgentia tuae pietatis ad ueniam'.

[95] See Hildefonsus' treatise, *Liber de itinere deserti quo pergitur post baptismum*, cols. 171–92; on the quest for the grail as a labyrinth, Doob 1990.

that first moment, and which therefore served to remind anyone looking into it of his failure to keep the image intact; of its tarnishing in time. There is something of this alertness to the ethical in Asser's *Life of Alfred* (*c.* 893): Asser presents a new hero, not the king-saint familiar from Bede, or the pagan hero of *Beowulf*, who is subject to the inevitability of providence or destiny, but the one who must learn, who will at times fail, who needs guidance in a struggle to get to something which always seems to be just out of reach. The picture is obscured perhaps by the ultimate success, by the re-assimilation of the king to a monastic stability in the end, but it is nonetheless there. Not for nothing is Alfred hounded into the marshes of Athelney. It is there too in the interest in character – the product of this learning in time – and in the formation of character. Einhard, writing his *Life of Charlemagne*, makes his hero almost a patchwork of the character traits of Suetonius' Roman emperors – but this does not mean that he was not interested in Charlemagne's character. He merely lacked the tools to describe it.[96]

In an atmosphere still recalling the problems posed by mission, but one almost visibly lit up by the monastic ideal, Bede lets us see into the beginnings of this changing relation between sacrament and ethical consciousness. His skill in shaping traditions to his own thinking without losing their integrity enables him at the same time to pass light-footedly between the different levels of Biblical exegesis, from literal-historical to allegorical, to moral, to mystical senses. His attention, however – and this is the greatness of his exegetical art – is turned in the end to the relation between the moral and the mystical. Evoking the beauty of an image, turning it in his hand so that it corresponds to a clarity of vision, he puts it before his audience as a moral exhortation; and whether he does this with a Biblical or a liturgical image – they are usually the same – the clarity itself of his interpretation has the effect of separating image from mind. He has made of Bible or liturgy something like an object of moral contemplation.

So, in a homily on John 11:55–12:11, the pericope for Monday before Easter, the two sisters, Martha and Mary, appear in this

---

[96] Thus Asser compares Alfred's search for wisdom, and for the learned men who will help him, to the flight of the bee, who 'per incerta aeris itinera cursum ueloci uolatu dirigens, super multiplices ac diuersos herbarum, holerum, fruticum flosculos descendit, probatque quid maxime placuerit atque domum reportat' (*Vita Alfredi*, p. 61). For Einhard's borrowings from Suetonius, see the comments made by Halphen in his edition.

contemplative half-distance. It is the occasion of the Paschal meal in the house of Lazarus in Bethany, when Mary anoints Jesus' feet with spikenard:

At the feast Martha serves, like the faithful soul bearing her devotion before the Lord. Lazarus is among the guests reclining with the Lord, since those raised from sin's death to justice are joined with others who rejoice in a justice of their own. This is the justice of the truth already present. Their penitence places them among the innocents. They eat the gifts of heavenly grace. It is good, too, that the meal should be celebrated in Bethany, the city on the side of the Mount of Olives, whose name means 'House of Obedience'. For the 'House of Obedience' is the church, loyally obeying the Lord's command. It is the city set on the Mount of Mercy which can never be lost from view; the city built from the side of its redeemer, or rather steeped in the water of washing and the blood of benediction flowing from the side of the one who died for it. Meanwhile Mary, Lazarus' second sister, with a gesture of great love, . . . took a pound of precious spikenard ointment and anointed the feet of Jesus and wiped them with her hair. Here she gave a sign not just of her own devotion but of the gentle bending of all faithful souls to the Lord. We know from Matthew and Mark however – and this is important – that Mary poured the oil over the Lord's head as well as his feet [Matt. 27:7; Mark 14:3]. And there is no doubt that this is the same woman who Luke tells us was a sinner, and came to the Lord carrying a pot of ointment, 'and standing near behind him, she began to wash his feet with her tears, and she wiped them with the hair of her head, and kissed his feet and poured ointment on them' [Luke 7: 37–8]. This is the same woman, but while on this occasion she bent down and anointed only his feet, weeping her tears of penitence, on the other occasion, taking joy from a good act, she showed no hesitation in rising up and anointing the head as well as the feet. One action suggests the first effort of the penitent, the other the justice of the perfect soul.[97]

---

97 *Hom.* 2.4, pp. 209–10: 'In qua caena Martha ministrat cum anima quaeque fidelis operam domino suae deuotionis inpendit; Lazarus unus fit ex discumbentibus cum domino cum etiam hi qui post peccatorum mortem resuscitati ad iustitiam sunt una cum eis qui in sua permansere iustitia de praesentia ueritatis exultant paenitentes simul cum innocentibus caelestis gratiae muneribus aluntur. Et bene eadem caena in Bethania celebratur quae est ciuitas in latere montis Oliueti et interpretatur domus oboedientiae. Domus namque oboedientiae ecclesia est quae fideliter domini iussis obtemperat et ipsa est ciuitas quae super montem misericordiae constituta numquam potest abscondi ipsa quae de sui latere constructa redemptoris, id est aqua ablutionis et sanguine sanctificationis quae de ipsius latere pro se morientis exiere inbuta est. Ubi etiam altera soror Lazari Maria in magnae indicium dilectionis sicut sequentia monstrant euangelicae lectionis accepit libram unguenti nardi pistici pretiosi et unxit pedes Iesu et extersit capillis suis pedes eius; quo non solum suae dat indicium deuotionis sed et aliarum fidelium deo animarum signat pietatis obsequium. Sed prius notandum quod sicut narrantibus

The homily is liturgical: the oil Bede has in mind is the chrism which will be blessed, after the public ceremony of penitence on Maundy Thursday, to be used for anointing after baptism. But what Bede does with liturgy is of great interest. In the notion of the 'truth already present' we recognize the theme of Bede's commentary on the Song of Songs. The possibility of not sinning, he had said there, contains at least something of the actuality of not sinning. In this Easter homily, Bede shows us this 'presence of truth' in the light – that least sensual of things sensed – in which we see the two scenes (Martha and Mary at the table, and the landscape, Bethany on the mountainside). The light is the light after exorcism, which has emptied matter of its physicality, and leaves behind only perfect clearness of vision: 'the city set on the Mount of Mercy which can never be lost from view'. The clearness is sustained in Bede's dramatic precision and his precision in defining meaning: Martha and Mary balanced against each other; the equilibrium of their respective devotions – Martha's labour and Mary's penitence; the Mary of Mark and Matthew linked with the Mary of Luke by the progression from effort (wiping the feet) to accomplishment (pouring oil on the head); and the line of meaning which runs from the obedience of Martha to that of Bethany, the 'House of Obedience', to the church-obedient, to the obedience of water and blood to the wound. The light which lights these scenes is never oblique, always even; it does not pose the question of origin. It does not *come from* anywhere, from over a horizon, or through a window. It is the perfect medium in which this lucid drama moves; a medium on the plane between sense and non-sense, or of sense purified, emptied, which is the adequate place for the meeting of Lazarus who was once dead, and his guests who are already as if dead; the point at which we see the possibility of truth turn into the actuality. The evenness of the light thus illumines a *fable:* a world where the sensual is emptied of sensuality – Lazarus and his guests sit down not to food but to 'the gifts of heavenly grace'.

Matheo et Marco didicimus non solum pedes domini Maria sed et nardo caput perfudit. Nec dubitandum est quin ipsa sit mulier quae sicut euangelista Lucas refert quondam peccatrix ad dominum cum alabastro uenit unguenti "et stans retro secus pedes eius lacrimis coepit rigare pedes eius et capillis sui tergebat et osculabatur pedes eius et unguento unguebat" [Luke 7:37–8]. Eadem ergo est mulier sed ibi pedes solum domini prona unguebat et hoc inter paenitentiae lacrimas hic autem inter gaudia iustae operationis et pedes unguere et ad caput quoque unguendum non dubitauit erigi. Ibi quippe rudimenta paenitentium hic iustitiam perfectarum designat animarum.'

Martha appears bent with labour, Mary bent with anguish, but what we see is the beauty of the lines, not effort or sorrow.

In another homily, for Holy Saturday, we get a better idea of how this concern to reduce the suppleness of imagery to the clarity of line, of an object seen, colours ethical discourse.[98] What Bede offers is the clear picture in the mirror – that unusual mirror which shows anyone who looks into it what he *should* look like (and what he *once*, for a brief moment, did look like). The text of this second homily is the healing of the deaf-mute (Mark 7:31–7). Jesus heals the deaf-mute by putting his fingers in his ears and touching his tongue with spittle, a gesture borrowed by the liturgy, where the priest touches the nostrils and ears of the candidate about to be baptized, with saliva, saying over him, as did Jesus over the deaf-mute, *Effeta, quod est adaperire*. Of this, Bede makes a moral allegory – so that baptism too becomes an allegory of the moral aftermath of baptism. It is not the moral life itself – but the moment to which it refers back. Tongue, nostrils and ears are the allegorical figures: tongue is honest speech (or slander), nostril the breath of God in the man who sticks to the truth, ear the hearing in which faith must be grounded. The cleanness of baptism is the moral cleanness of prudence and wisdom, and what matters most is that we should keep the effect of the rite as far as possible intact.

Bede's lucidity, the veil of light that he spreads over sacrament, is wrought out of a mastery of meanings; the tying up of all the loose ends, the tidying of troubling juxtapositions and awkward joinings and a resolution of the problem of meaning. The *aporia* – the uncertain element always present in the attempt to find meaning and to make meaning – has come to rest in the authority, the calm, of Bede's definiteness. This definiteness is founded in allegory – not the *allegoria* of medieval exegesis which can be many things – but the allegory which makes use of one thing, concrete and familiar, to mean another which is more abstract, in such a way that the importance of the first thing, the sign, fades away – mainly or entirely – once the second has been understood. Allegory is a kind of ladder climbed by the mind, from material sign to concept, which can be kicked over when it has served its purpose – the scales of justice, death the hag with her scythe, the ill omen of the crow, the shadows thrown on the walls of Plato's

---

[98] *Hom.* 2.6, p. 220–4.

cave by the sun.[99] In practice, it is an exaggeration to put it quite like this. The ladder is often needed again; a ghost of the physical, tangible sign lingers in the concept. We cannot dissociate justice from a particular statue, or victory from the Arc de Triomphe. But I will use 'allegory' to help to a better perception of 'symbol' which is so different, for this relation of meaning, where the clarity and sufficiency of the concept tends to empty the concrete thing (from which it started) of its concreteness. It replaces the palpable, the tangible, the desire to seize hold of, the plasticity, the sense of presence, with the disinterestedness of light.

Symbol is something else. In symbol, thing and idea affirm one another; and because it is never clear how the idea is in the thing or the thing in the idea, because meaning can never be distinguished from sign, the possibilities of meaning are *inexhaustible*. The benediction of the oil on Maundy Thursday – the oil to be used for the first of the two post-baptismal anointings in the *Gelasian* rite, and the oil of Bede's homily of Martha and Mary – will give an impression of this inexhaustibility. The prayer comes from one of the earlier, Roman, layers of the *Gelasian*, probably from the second half of the sixth century:

It is truly good, just, and right, and brings salvation, that we give thanks to you always, here and in every place, Lord, Holy Father, Almighty and Eternal God. In the beginning, with other gifts of goodness and piety, you told the earth to put forth the fruiting wood. Among the trees was born the olive, minister of this thick-running liquid, whose fruit now serves for holy chrism. For David, in prophetic spirit, knowing before their time the sacraments of your grace, sang a song about these faces of ours which would one day beam bright with oil. In another time, when the world's sins were expiated by a poured-out flood, the dove, acting out the likeness of a gift not yet come, announced with his olive-branch the return of quiet to the land. Then, in these recent days, the same thing was spoken out, with effects for all to see, when every sin was tossed into the washing destroying waters of baptism, and this anointing with oil makes our faces joyful and serene. Thus too you gave your servant Moses the command to make a priest of his brother Aaron, bathing him first in water and then pouring on to him this unguent. Afterwards there came a wider honouring, when your Son, our Lord Jesus Christ, had demanded to be washed by John in the waves of Jordan, and the Holy Ghost was sent down in the likeness of the dove, over your only-begotten, in whom, you showed in the testimony of the voice that followed, you were well pleased; and that this was he you

99 Cf. Ricoeur 1960, p. 23.

gave the plainest proof, because the prophet David had already sung that one would be singled out and anointed with the oil of rejoicing. We ask you, therefore, Lord, Holy Father, Almighty and Eternal God, through Jesus Christ your Son our Lord, bend down to sanctify with benediction the sap of this creaturely thing, and mix in with it the force of the Holy Ghost through the power of Christ your anointed, from whose holy name the chrism takes its own name, the chrism from which you have anointed your priests and kings, prophets and martyrs, that it may be to those who will have been reborn from water and the Holy Ghost the chrism of salvation, and that you give them a part in the life which has no end, a share in the glory of heaven. Through the same, our Lord Jesus Christ your Son.[100]

Every phrase, sometimes every word, is a little explosion of possible senses. The prayer is a 'horn of plenty'. No commentary on it would exhaust it, but any comment on it is an intrusion – for it cannot be known what it *did* mean, at a certain time, in a given place. Some senses, though, would have been hard to resist.

Everything is in the oil, the inner principle of the vital, which when smeared on the body – the chrism, a mixture of oil and balsam, would be smeared on the forehead of the baptized by the priest on the vigil of Easter, after the bath of baptism – makes manifest this inner principle, brings it to the surface, 'for all to see'. For oil is the fatty substance of life itself, the unctuous flow with

[100] *Gelasian*, no. 386, p. 62: 'Uere dignum et iustum est, aequum et salutare nos tibi semper hic et ubique gratias agere, domine, sanctae pater, omnipotens aeternae deus. Qui in principio inter cetera bonitatis et pietatis tuae munera terram producere fructifera ligna iussisti, inter quae huius pinguissimi liquoris ministrae oleae nascerentur, quarum fructus sacro chrismati deseruiret. Nam Dauid prophetico spiritu gratiae tuae sacramenta praenoscens uultos nostros in oleo exhilarandos esse cantauit. Et cum mundi crimina diluuio quondam expiarentur effuso, in similitudinem futuri muneris columba demonstrans per oliuae ramum pacem terris redditam nunciauit. Quod in nouissimis temporibus manifestis est effectibus declaratum cum baptismatis aquis omnium criminum commissa delentibus, haec olei unctio uultos nostros iocundos efficiat ac serenos. Inde eciam Moysen famulo tuo mandata dedisti, ut Aaron fratrem suum prius aqua lotum per infusione huius unguenti constituerit sacerdotem. Accessit ad hoc amplior honor, cum filius tuus, dominus noster Iesus Christus, lauare a Iohanne undis Iordanicis exigisset, et spiritu sancto in columbae similitudine desuper misso unigenitum tuum, in quo tibi optime conplacuisse testimonio subsequentis uocis ostenderis, hoc illud esse manifestissime conprobaris, quod eum oleo laeticiae prae consortibus suis ungendum Dauid propheta caecinisset. Te igitur depraecamur, domine, sanctae pater, omnipotens aeternae deus, per Iesum Christum filium tuum dominum nostrum, ut huius creaturae pinguidinem sanctificare tua benedictione digneris et in sancti spiritus inmiscere uirtutem per potenciam Christi tui, a cuius sancto nomine chrisma nomen accepit, unde uncxisti sacerdotes reges prophetas et martyres tuos, ut sit his qui renati fuerint ex aqua et spiritu sancto chrisma salutis, eosque aeternae uitae participes et caelestis gloriae facias esse consortes: per eundem dominum nostrum Iesum Christum filium tuum.' On the dating of this, Chavasse 1958, pp. 135–9 and pp. 164ff.

which life persists, the viscosity of its slow growth, the syrup hidden at its core, its secret exuberance – elevated now to the *ubertas benedictionis* (in the expression of another *Gelasian* prayer): the 'exuberance of benediction'.[101] The anthropologist sees it appear across a huge variety of societies, with a multiplicity which has its own exuberance:

Fat is the most primitive unguent, and is regarded in early thought as a very important seat of life. Ideas of sacredness are perhaps implicit in its ordinary use, inasmuch as it is animal substance. To take illustrations: the Arabs of East Africa anoint themselves with lions' fat, in order to acquire courage. The Andamanese pour melted pigs' fat over children to render them strong. The Namaquas wear amulets of fat. The Damaras collect the fat of certain animals, which they believe to possess great virtue. It is kept in special receptacles; 'a small portion dissolved in water is given to persons who return home after a lengthened absence . . . The chief makes use of it as an unguent for his body.' The fat of the human body possesses a proportionately higher sanctity and potency. It is especially the fat of the *omentum* (the caul) that is regarded as possessing this vital force . . . The Australian savage will kill a man merely to obtain his kidney-fat with which to anoint himself. It is believed that the virtues of the dead man are transfused into the person by anointing. It is regular practice throughout Australia to use for this purpose the fat of slain enemies. These natives also employ it to make their weapons strong; sick persons are rubbed with it in order to obtain health and strength. In India a prevalent superstition relates to the supernatural virtues of *momiai*, an unguent prepared from the fat of boys murdered for the purpose. Grease made from the fat of a corpse is a potent charm among the Aleuts . . . A piece of human kidney-fat, worn round the neck, was believed by the Tasmanians to render a man proof against magic influence. The virtues of human fat as a curative and magical ointment are well-known throughout the world. By its use love may be charmed, warriors rendered invulnerable, and witches enabled to fly through the air. Transformation into animals, as related by folklore, is effected by magical ointments, originally the fat of the animal in question.[102]

In the *Gelasian* blessing, the oil flows out from Creation, into the trees and their seeds and fruit. It is the *essence*, the fatty substance within history, determining the course of history from seed to maturity, promise to fulfilment. In its thickness (*pinguissimi liquoris; huius creaturae pinguidinem*) it suggests permanence, the abiding property of prophecy, its inevitability. It suggests the sap

---

[101] *Gelasian*, no. 1570, p. 228: 'Ita ueniat, quaesumus, sperate benedictionis ubertas, ut repleti frugibus tuis de tua semper misericordia gloriemur.'
[102] Hastings I, p. 550.

of the tree of Jesse, and of all the themes of descendancy in Old and New Testament. Oil soothes after a bath; it welcomes the returning hero and honours him; it softens and feeds nerve and skin. In the prayer, water and oil are always close. Aaron is washed in water and then anointed; the olive-branch brings an end to the destructive water of the Flood. Baptism is water *and* oil; oleaginous water, the water of life, nurturing and benign. It is as if oil is the essence of this nourishing water, the seawater seen by Michelet in *La Mer:*

Seawater, even the purest, sampled in mid-ocean, far from any admixture, is whitish and rather viscous. Pressed between the fingers, it forms *threads*, and slowly drips away. Chemical analyses do not account for this characteristic. There is an organic substance here which such analyses attain only by destroying, depriving it of its particularity, and brutally restoring it to the general elements.

The plants and creatures of the sea are dressed in this substance, whose mucosity, consolidated around them, has a gelatinous effect, sometimes fixed and sometimes tremulous: they gleam through a diaphanous garment. And nothing adds more to the fantastic illusions which the world of the seas affords us. Their reflections are singular, often strangely iridescent – on the scales of fish for instance, or on the molluscs which seem to derive from it the entire splendour of their nacreous shells.

This is what most attracts the child who sees a fish for the first time. I was very young when this happened to me, but I perfectly recall the intense impression. This brilliant, flashing creature, clad in its silver scales, cast me into amazement, inexpressible delight. I tried to capture it, but found it as difficult to catch hold of as the water that ran through my tiny fingers. It seemed to me identical with the element in which it swam. I had the vague notion that it was nothing but water, animal or animate water, organized water.

, Much later, having grown up, I was scarcely less amazed when I examined, on a beach, one of the Radiata. Through its transparent body, I could make out the individual grains of sand. Colourless as glass, barely substantial, shivering when touched, it looked to me as it did to the Ancients and even to Réaumur, who simply called such creatures *gelatinized water.*

How much more powerful such an impression becomes when one finds in their initial formation the yellowish-white ribbons wherein the sea produces a soft sketch of its solid fucus, the laminaria which, turning brown, attain to the solidity of leather hides. But still quite young, in the viscous state, in their elasticity, they have something of the consistency of a solidified wave, all the stronger for being softer.[103]

[103] Michelet, *La Mer* (quoted in Barthes 1987, pp. 41–2).

But oil is also the contradiction of water. Water destroys in order to wash: it is *aqua delens*. Water troubles, oil solaces, just as after the Flood, the raven flies off into the watery expanse, bringing back no news, and the dove carries back the olive-branch. In the Anglo-Saxon *Genesis*-poem, the raven settles ominously on a floating corpse. The special office of oil is not only to convey all that is vital, but to *show* it on the skin; to make it outward and evident 'for all to see' (*hoc illud esse manifestissime conprobaris*). In it, when it is smeared, the hidden seed is 'made plain'. 'Of the majority of early peoples', in condescending words written in the early years of this century, 'it may be said that grease and ochre constitute their wardrobe.'[104] Oil is mixed with paint and perfumes to attract. In the *Gelasian*, oil shows the exhilarated faces sung of by David (*uultos nostros in oleo exhilarandos esse cantauit*): the face of Christ-the-anointed at his baptism, when he was 'pleasing to God' (Matt. 3:17 etc.); the faces of the baptized; the faces of the saints: the 'priests, kings, prophets and martyrs'. The 'being' of the 'man of God' is expressed in his bodily beauty, the beauty of his face, his bodily form, his voice, his eyes. It was said of St Padarn the *gratia uultus*, the 'beauty of the face' – *gratia* with the double sense of physical beauty and supernatural grace – was enough on its own to reconcile two warring kings in sixth-century Wales.[105] This seems to be the proper sense of 'glory': it is when mere appearance, seeming, is transparent to truth.

The manifold associations of the oil go on. They are, after all, inexhaustible – inexhaustible because there can be no end to the *attempt* to reach back to the primacy, the innocence, of perception; to what cannot be fully said. Symbol, then, is that of which enough can never be said, and more can always be said.[106] It is both fertile and barren; it comprises both doubt and certainty, comprehension and frustration, presence and absence. The multiplicity of associations is the expression and the failure to express the integrity of the object in itself. Leo the Great (d. 461) talks about the same phenomenon in a sermon spoken on Easter Sunday. However difficult it is to go on speaking about the feast of Easter, it is not open to the priest to withhold speech about it,

[104] Hastings I, p. 549.
[105] Bieler 1936, p. 56; and see Bieler's remark on p. 53: 'Doch die körperliche Schönheit ist nur das Kleid, durch das der Adel der Seele schimmert, der das Wesen des *theios aner* ausmacht.'
[106] Cf. Ricoeur 1960, pp. 17ff.

since this subject-matter, being unspeakable, gives the power to speak. And what he says will not fall short, because he is talking about something of which enough can never be said. Human weakness succumbs to the glory of God, and, unfolding the works of God's mercy, will always find itself unequal to the task. We strain our senses, we put to it all our wits, we fail in speech. It is good – *and* too little – that we feel anything apt to God's magnitude. In the prophet's words, 'Seek the Lord and you will be strengthened; seek his face for ever' [Ps. 104:4]. No one is to presume to find all that he seeks. To fail to get somewhere is not to stop getting nearer. Of all the works of God in which the effort of man's admiration tires itself, what delights and overwhelms the mind's contemplation as does the Saviour's Passion? However often we think about his omnipotence – which is in him with the Father as one and equal essence – it is the humility in God which seems more striking than the power. It is more difficult to comprehend the emptying of divine majesty, than the raising up of humble form. But it helps us understand if we think that although the Creator is one thing, the creature another, one thing the inviolable godhead, another the flesh which suffers, the quality of both substances runs together in one person, so that whether weak or strong, the insults and the glory are together in this person.[107]

Prayer – and this is an account of prayer – is therefore two things. It is the exuberance of language, its associativeness *ad infinitum:* Leo talks about the *exsultationes spiritualium gaudiorum* (the 'floods of spiritual joy') which do not suffer us to remain silent. But it is also the restraint of language, the ability to say 'enough said', and so to re-affirm that 'enough can never be said'. The exuberant

[107] Leo, *Sermo* 62, cols. 349–50: 'Desiderata nobis dilectissimi, et uniuerso optabilis mundo adest festiuitas dominicae passionis, quae nos inter exsultationes gaudiorum silere non patitur: quia etsi difficile est de eadem re saepius digne apteque disserere, non est tamen liberum sacerdoti, in tanto diuinae misericordiae sacramento fidelis populi auribus subtrahere sermonis officium, cum ipsa materia, ex eo quod ineffabilis, fandi tribuat facultatem; nec possit deficere quod dicatur, de qua numquam potest satis esse quod dicitur. Succumbat ergo humana infirmitas gloriae dei, et in explicandis operibus misericordiae eius, imparem se semper inueniat. Laboremus sensu, haereamus ingenio, deficiamus eloquio: bonum est ut nobis parum si quod etiam recte de domini maiestate sentimus. Dicente enim propheta: "Quaerite dominum et confirmamini, quaerite faciem eius semper" [Ps. 104:4], nemini praesumendum est quod totum quod quaerit inuenerit, ne desinat propinquare qui cessarit accedere. Quid autem inter omnia opera dei, in quibus humanae admirationis fatigatur intentio, ita contemplationem mentis nostrae et oblectat et superat, sicut passio saluatoris? De cuius omnipotentia, quae ei cum patre unius et aequalis essentiae est, quoties, ut possumus, cogitamus, mirabilior nobis fit in deo humilitas quam potestas; et difficilius capitur exinanitio, quam seruilis formae in summa prouectio. Sed multum nos ad intellectum iuuat, quod licet aliud creator, aliud creatura, aliud deitas inuiolabilis, aliud caro passibilis; in unam tamen personam concurrat proprietas utriusque substantiae, ut siue in infirmitatibus, siue in uirtutibus, eiusdem sit contumelia, cuius et gloria.'

word reaches its object. It names a thing not to classify it, but to bring back the direct perception of it. For this to happen, there must already be a primal kinship between word and thing, a confidence that the word *is* the thing; a kind of naivety about language. The early Middle Ages possessed this confidence. Eric Auerbach attributed it partly to Augustine's use of *sermo humilis*, the common, unpolished speech of the people which was better able to carry the weight of teaching, precisely because it was 'nearer the ground' (*humilis*); and he saw the effect of this in the 'realism' of Gregory of Tours, who always allowed blood and spirit to sit side by side.[108] In more urgent circumstances, it shows through in the alliance, in the saints' lives, between word and miracle; the direct, unvexed, *efficacy* of the word in matter;[109] and it shows in this *Gelasian* blessing of the oil, with its numerous 'pictures' or scenes, juxtaposed around the running theme of the 'fatty liquid', whose slow, persistent vigour is irresistible. But in liturgy at least, there is no shortage of restraint. There is the restraint of fasting, and of exorcism – which elucidates and empties matter; and the restraint of the priestly language itself – a language which is solemn, *sollemnis*, in the double sense of the Latin word, both repetitious and heightened.

Bede has done away with the unease caused by this situation – the situation of abundance and restraint – by making a work of art: instead of concentrating on what cannot be said, he shows us what it would be like *if* enough could be said. He offers us an illusion.

The educational programme of the Carolingians, set out in the *Admonitio Generalis* of 789 – and pervading so many of the writings and institutions of the period, including the reform and Romanization of the liturgy – was a mission within the already existing body of Christendom.[110] It aimed to teach those who were Christian in name but little else, and to enforce practice by episcopal visitations throughout dioceses. It too was an exercise – enormous and sustained – in elucidation, and more than this, in *explanation*. Under the direction of monastic centres, Lorsch, Reichenau, Fulda, a special literature of liturgical explanation

---

[108] Auerbach 1965.
[109] Thus for example, *Life of St Martin*, 16, pp. 287–8: 'Deinde, aegram intuens, dari sibi oleum postulat. Quod cum benedixisset, in os puellae uim sancti liquoris infundit, statimque uox reddita est. Tum paulatim singula contactu eius coeperunt membra uiuescere, donec firmatis gressibus populo teste surrexit.'
[110] McKitterick 1977.

grew up in the mid-ninth century, in the form of handbooks which could be used by parish priests going about their work. There were *expositiones missae*, and *expositiones baptismi*[111] – these last looking back to, and sometimes borrowing from, the corpus of Carolingian letters on baptism, written to Charlemagne in 812. Rather as, between the late tenth and the twelfth centuries, the development of handbooks of canon law organized by subject-matter (and not chronologically, as they generally had been until now), and the development of clear principles for the use of these books, tended to make teaching into a method of judging, so the *expositiones* tended to make the sacraments of baptism and the eucharist into a kind of method for the implementation of the holy. The same thing can be seen at work in a more 'intellectual' handbook about the sacraments and other matters, with slightly more difficult content, like the book of Walafrid the Squinter *On the Origins and Growth of Certain Ecclesiastical Customs* (841) – although here the intent is also to explain the historical genesis of the rites, another interest already evident in some of the correspondents of 812. By establishing the principle that every liturgical action had a specific meaning, which connected it with other actions and their senses, the handbooks took the stress away from the finding and making of meaning by the assembly, or perhaps the individual, which was demanded by the very looseness of liturgical performance, and by this element of 'inexhaustible' possible meanings, and laid it instead on the *practice* of liturgical action.

A significant effect of this was that words also became actions, in a way which, I think, they had not been before. The liturgy is always a 'speech-act': a prayer, for example, is not just a statement for information, but a promise, a request, an act of praise, a lament. But in liturgy, words are not habitual actions. Even if they have a habitual, regular, unthinking aspect, they are never only this – this is no more than the formal aspect of liturgy, the aspect of restraint. Besides this, there is the rhythm of prayer as it passes from the sensual to the abstract (and back), in which, even if it does not understand, word for word, what it hears, a congregation recognizes its own standing in the world – its own standing between the 'enough said' and the 'always more to say'.

---

[111] On the *expositiones missae*, see the excellent article by Wilmart in *DACL* v, pp. 1014–27, which gives an account of the background and the different classes of *expositio*; for a list of the baptismal expositions, Keefe 1984.

With the systematic, and simplistic, explanation of meanings undertaken by the handbooks, this recognition, or participation – the impulse to make new meanings each time – is reduced to something more like the performance of habit.

But it is a bit more than habit. It is a practice, in the sense that it is done to achieve a known effect. Liturgy is liable to become, in these handbooks, a kind of machinery of salvation.

If the prayers of the *Gelasian* (and similar examples could be found in the other main liturgical books) talk of the hunger of the Roman people waiting for the wheat to be harvested, or the alarm caused by a thunderstorm, they do so in order to throw open these natural phenomena, and the emotions they arouse, to the 'unsayable' which Pope Leo had in mind.[112] The 'awe' induced by the thunder is both integral to the prayer *and* transcended by it. But the allegorical certainties of the ninth- and tenth-century priests' handbooks causes a short-circuit – the books identify a category of the holy, rather like the Polynesian *mana*, an unpersonified force lying somewhere between the natural and the supernatural, and they put it to use, by means of the artifice of liturgy and its sacrament. It becomes a reserve of potency. Sacrament, in other words, turns into magic: the mechanical, methodical use of the sacred to definite ends – a reversal, in fact, of the order of prayer, because it shuts in to the world instead of opening out from it. There is little surprise, in view of this, that the same handbooks which contain the *expositiones* often contain magical formulae for the improvement of health, or the deflection of disaster.[113] The intention is now not so much to do what the old prayers did, to turn the threat of a thunderstorm into an occasion of praise – 'may the threatening of power be made into the substance of praise'[114] but more to stop the storm happening again.

A prayer like this – and it is very representative – does not simply accept destiny, or succumb to threat. It *responds* to destiny

---

[112] *Gelasian*, no. 1604, p. 233: 'Oramus pietatem tuam, omnipotens deus, ut has primitias creaturae tuae, quas aeris et pluuiae temperamento nutrire dignatus es, benedictionis tuae imbre perfundas, et fructus terrae tuae usque ad maturitatem perducas, tribuas que populo tuo de tuis muneribus tibi semper gratias agere, ut a fertilitate terrae esurientium animas bonis affluentibus repleas, et egenus et pauper laudent nomen gloriae tuae. Per.'(Cf. Chavasse 1958, pp. 464–9, for the setting of this blessing at Pentecost.) For the thunder, nos. 1566–7, p. 227.

[113] Thus, for example, MS Vat. Pal. lat. 485.

[114] *Gelasian*, nos. 1566–1567: '. . . ut post noxios ignes nubium et turbines procellarum, in materiam transeat laudis comminatio potestatis'.

and threat. Do we not see a similar impulse in Roland, who responds to the destiny of defeat with the battle-cry, *Munjoie?* He is never resigned to his fate, but embraces it with glee – and so he refuses to blow the olifant and bring back the emperor's army until it is too late. Roland's fighting is a kind of praise. The tendency for sacrament to become magic came from the wish to use sacrament as a means of control, to make sacrament the *cause* of certain *effects* – ultimately the effect of salvation. It was this that made the Saxon monk Gottschalk (who died *c.* 869) so angry – the anger comes through unmistakably in his polemical prose. His anger brought him to the extreme view that each soul was predestined either to eternal fire or eternal bliss, irrespective of any action it might accomplish. The words of liturgy – like other words – could only be said with meaning by those destined to be *apud deum*, with God. Said by the others, they were vain. By no means, protested Gottschalk again and again, could a soul pre-destined to evil be freed by baptism.[115] Gottschalk threw away the artifice of sacrament (as he saw it) altogether, and thought of liturgy as no more nor less than the medium of expression of the blessed.[116] He anticipates, in this, those in the twelfth century, Abelard most obviously, who wished to make liturgy and sacra-ment the means of expression not of the predestined soul, but of moral intention.

[115] *De praedestinatione*, 3, p. 182: 'Nam si reprobi baptizati per sanguinem crucis Christi sunt redempti, ergo sunt etiam per ipsum saluati et liberati. Non autem per ipsum saluati et liberati quippe qui sunt ab ipso Christo rite satis morti sempiternae praeiudicati praedamnati praedestinati et ut ita dictum sit in illam iam iure praecipitati.'

[116] Ibid, pp. 181–2: 'Illa quam de sancta cruce antiphona debita ueneratione cantatis: "O crux admirabilis euacuatio uulneris restitutio sanitatis" clarius luce subuertit et pellit errorem qui confingitur quasi de redemptis in ea reprobis baptizatis. Namque cum constet quod nullatenus ipsa crux fuerit uel sit ullius illorum "euacuatio uulneris" uel "restitutio sanitatis", patet profecto quod eorum nullius ibi sit facta redemptio sed electorum solummodo ... "Nemo enim potest dicere dominus Iesus nisi in spiritu sancto" [1 Cor. 12:3] id est sicut a sancto exponitur Augustino: "Corde ore opere animo dicto facto, Nemo potest dicere dominum Iesum nisi in spiritu sancto." ' (The antiphon is from the rite for the exaltation of the cross, *PL* LXXVIII, col. 803D; Augustine's passage from his *In Ioh. euang. tr.* 74.1, p. 513.)

Chapter 6

THE TWELFTH CENTURY, OR
FALLING SHORT

The art of liturgical symbol is to accomplish what even in the so-called age of faith was that most difficult of acts, the touching of God by man and man by God as though it were something obvious. The Psalm says it without mincing:

As for me, I am poor and needy; but the Lord careth for me. (Psalm 40:20)

In the Vulgate, this is Psalm 39:18, and more abrupt still:

ego autem mendicus sum et pauper / Dominus sollicitus est mei.

Faced with Easter, Leo the Great sets side by side the obviousness with which words reach out in meaning, their exuberance, and the difficulty they have in doing so. From one point of view, there is always more to be said; from the other, enough has never been said.[1]

There was in the twelfth century a sense of loss. The interest shown in history is part of a preoccupation with what has been lost. Liturgy had always been, precisely, a denial of loss. The eucharist, in particular, had always denied the loss of the body of the God-man. It was a re-finding, again and again, of this lost, disappeared, body. But the controversy over the eucharist which began with the bitter quarrel of Berengar of Tours and Lanfranc of Bec in the 1050s shows how far a *worry* had developed over this daily re-discovery of a thing of the past. Was this body, after all, not lost? In what sense could it be said to be *here now*? If the body was here now, in these *species* of bread and wine, what could be said about the relation of the bread and wine to the body and blood? The terms in which the 'realist' Lanfranc – realist in his claim that the historical body, 'born of the Virgin', was the *essence* after consecration of the (deceptive, less real) *species* of bread and wine – affirmed the presence of this bygone body,

---

[1] See above, pp. 215–17.

amount, often, to a resignation to 'real absence'. Presence is an object of belief; but the object of belief has become an *incomprehensibile*, and belief itself, accordingly, a refusal to seek understanding: 'Do not seek what is higher than you', Lanfranc warns Berengar.[2] Sacrament, against this background, is a failure to accomplish; it affirms an inadequacy in the human perception of truth.

What I wish to describe is how this 'loss of body' apparent in attitudes to the eucharist runs parallel with a hesitancy over the capacity of the will to reach *its* object, which is apparent in the discussion of baptism, and, above all, of infant baptism. The 'theology of failure' which is built, by Abelard especially, on these inadequacies, and which is so much a part of the 'Renaissance of the Twelfth Century', finds itself very well expressed by what was coming to seem the oddity of infant baptism: the oddity that the sacrament of the will should be applied, willy-nilly, to a child.

'I' OR SELF?

Against Berengar's argumentative, obsessive 'I', Lanfranc puts the 'judgement of the crowd': *sententiam uulgi*.[3] Against Berengar's 'I think', the blunted thinking of instinct, opinion, faith. We take this antithesis of the 'I' and the crowd (heard already in the isolation of *Ego Berengarius*, the opening words of the oath of orthodoxy he swore under duress in 1059 in Rome)[4] at first as a thing of little importance – a commonplace of polemic in which one side feels it has with it the weight of general opinion, and the other clings all the tighter to his own because no one else shares it; the polemic of the complacent and the bloody-minded.

Lanfranc: You're on your own.
Berengar: You parrot the mob.

So we pass over the traded insults, waiting for the real stuff of argument. But as we search about in the argument for its nub, we begin to see how Berengar's jealously guarded 'I' (and equally

---

[2] Lanfranc, *De corpore*, p. 175; and p. 187: 'innotescit, quod uera Christi caro, uerusque eius sanguis in mensa dominica immoletur, comedatur, bibatur, corporaliter, spiritualiter, incomprehensibiliter'.

[3] For *sententia uulgi*, Lanfranc, *De corpore*, p. 156.

[4] Lanfranc, *De corpore*, pp. 151–2. On the circumstances of this oath, de Montclos 1971, pp. 163–79.

Lanfranc's crowd) are inseparable from the way they see the thing.

Why should the common opinion be more probable? asks Berengar. Is it not more likely to be the more foolish? The church is not the mob. It is the 'bride without spot or wrinkle'. It is common enough, for example, for people to suppose that man is made in the image of God in a literal sense, so that the lines of the body somehow follow the lines of God's body, or that God has cut himself into three parts. Are we to believe this kind of thing because the crowd says it?[5]

Berengar scorns. He is brittle and haughty, his prose repetitive and unplanned. The *Rescriptum contra Lanfrannum*, the one extended piece of writing that remains from him, leaves the abiding impression of a mind seeking meaning, and only able to begin by bringing down the assertions made by others. He despises Lanfranc, but needs him in order to say anything at all. The irritation of this predicament shows through in the *ad hominem* style of argument, in the frequent recourse to insult; but also in the awkwardness with which he states his case, the stuttering prose. The obsessive quality, the spleen characteristic of the victim of an injustice – this is how he thinks of himself – makes us less and less inclined to hear him out. He abuses the bishop of Vercelli, accusing him of rank depravity; he calls Cardinal Humbert of Silva-Candida, author of the 'realist' oath Berengar had to swear in 1059, a member of Antichrist;[6] and pulls Lanfranc's argument to bits – or tries to – with a mock patience which barely conceals his frustration. He is cut off, solitary and utterly contemptuous of a world so crass it could claim that the body of Christ *on the altar* was the body of Christ *born of the Virgin*, and thus that the body of Christ was corruptible, could be 'crushed by the teeth', as Humbert had put it in the oath.[7] His retirement to the island of Saint-Côme in the Loire, near Tours where he had been a canon and a master in the school, and his death on the island in 1088, is the fitting image of his isolation.

Down the Middle Ages there runs the great tradition of what

---

[5] Berengar, *Rescriptum contra Lanfrannum*, pp. 41–2.

[6] Ibid., pp. 48, 38. On Berengar 'in the grip of an obsession' as he wrote the *Rescriptum*, Gibson 1990, p. 16.

[7] De Montclos 1971, pp. 171–2: 'panem et uinum quae in altari ponuntur, post consecrationem non solum sacramentum, sed etiam uerum corpus et sanguinem domini nostri Jesu Christi esse, et sensualiter non solum sacramento, sed in ueritate manibus sacerdotum tractari, frangi, et fidelium dentibus atteri'.

Gilson called *le Socratisme chrétien*.[8] The imperative, Know Thyself, which Socrates borrowed from the Oracle at Delphi, is in Patristic times attached to the anthropology of Gen. 1:26–7:

And God said, Let us make man, in our own image and likeness; let us put him in command of the fishes of the sea, and all that flies through the air, and the cattle, and the whole earth, and all the creeping things that move on the earth. So God made man in his own image, made him in the image of God.

The Biblical concept of man made in the image of God makes of self-knowledge a consciousness not only of self, but of man; and not only of man, but of the *place* of man in the order of things. 'Know Thyself' has become a command to know what man is, in the sense of knowing where he is. He is not an angel, and not a beast, but he shares in the natures of both angel and beast. His soul (Dante would say later) was like the horizon, where the two hemispheres of pure spirit and irrational animal meet on one line.[9] The metaphor of the soul a horizon grows naturally from the Platonic tradition of man as a 'little world', a microcosm. In him is contained the material world of the senses, *and* the world of ideas.

Knowledge of self is therefore much more than the introspection of each into his own. Ultimately, it is a knowledge of things and of God, and of the right relation between them. It is first an understanding of, then a conforming to, the equilibrium of the triadic order of Creation: God–Man–Nature. God created Man over Nature. Biding by this equilibrium – being man – means making no claim to be more than man; and avoiding falling to something less than the condition of man. Morally, it means avoiding the counterfeit of both presumption and despair, the lures of *grandeur* and *misère*. It means keeping the soul level with the horizon, in a perpetual dawn-or-dusk: a *Dämmerung*.[10]

Man is the being who holds steady between angel and beast. This is what he finds when he looks within himself, a preordained

---

[8] Gilson 1944, pp. 214–33, for this and what follows.

[9] *De Monarchia* 3.16.3: Dante likens man to the horizon, alluding to the *Liber de Causis*, a collection of Platonic sentences chiefly from Proclus. But the *Liber de Causis* had likened the *world-soul* to the horizon. See Nardi 1930, pp. 100ff.

[10] 'The higher the ape goes, the more he shows his tail', goes the old proverb: see notes in the Arden edition of *Measure for Measure*, by J. W. Lever, p. 46; and the text on this page (which was quoted to me by John Ashton): 'But man, proud man / . . . Most ignorant of what he's most assur'd- / His glassy essence' (Act 2, sc. 2, lines 118–21).

equilibrium. Already in this there is something reminiscent of the 'symbol', and the prayer which articulates it. Symbol, rather than being suspended on the horizon between the angels and the beasts, or God and creation, is more inclined to *juxtapose* the two. It begins by exposing the distance which lies between them – this is perhaps one of the functions of exorcism – and then establishes the dialectic by which they are eventually fused. This is apparent in Leo's double characterization of a language of prayer which is empty with an emptiness calling to be filled; or in the distance between, and then reconciliation of, the solemn architecture of prayer and the specific, punctilious immediacy of the 'things' of liturgy: water, salt, bread, wine and so on.[11] But if liturgy begins like this, from a dialectic, it settles in the end for its own equilibrium in which the two extremes are resolved on a single line of horizon: the 'enough said' of Leo's Easter sermon, which includes in itself both the 'always more to be said' and the 'never enough said'. And so, in both its dialectic and its equilibrium, prayer, or symbol, follows – it enacts in a kind of theatre of consciousness – the condition of man as it is recounted by *le Socratisme chrétien*. In prayer, man acts out, demonstratively, the inward act of knowing self with which he perceives his position in the order of things: 'ni ange ni bête, mais dans l'entre-deux'.[12] The same staidness[13] is also at the heart of the monastic rule – the rule which perhaps finds its ultimate (because most conscious) expression in Bernard of Clairvaux: 'Know Thyself. There are two things that make us ignorant of ourselves ... Thinking ourselves more, or less, than what we are; and two things make us think like this: presumption and pusillanimity.'[14] Pascal, in the

[11] The litany is perhaps the extreme version of this sense of distance in the liturgy between the concrete and the ideal. Although litany, with its repetitiveness and list-making, may bring on a trance-like state of pure supplication – may, in other words, empty the mind of the concrete – it may equally cause the mind to react by springing back into the fulness of the concrete. This may happen rather as the rigours of a poem's form can draw attention all the more to the physical pressure of particular words in it. On 'pure praise', and the 'vacuousness' of the litany of the Jewish Hekhaloth hymns, Scholem 1955, pp. 57ff.

[12] Gilson 1944, p. 222.

[13] In Henry Vaughan's poem, *Man*, it is the animals that keep this 'staidness' or 'stedfast-ness and state', while 'Man is the shuttle, to whose winding quest / And passage through these looms / God order'd motion, but ordain'd no rest' (Vaughan 1914, II, p. 477).

[14] *Breuis comm. in Cant. Cant.* 22, col. 425 (quoted by Gilson 1944, p. 221 n. 2). In his studies on the text of Bernard's writings, Leclercq concludes tentatively that the *Breuis commentatio* is not among Bernard's works, but may have been delivered by the young Bernard as a sermon, and taken down by a scribe: Leclercq 1953, pp. 105–24.

seventeenth century, struck once more the balance between *grandeur* and *misère*, presumption and pusillanimity. Later again, Kierkegaard's most powerful writings are wrestlings with that impossibility of resolving the abyss between the two capacities in man, the sensual and the intellectual, an impossibility which he finds in himself – this is his knowledge of self – and which he calls doubt.[15]

The tragedy of Kierkegaard's doubt is not absent from prayer, or from man's introspective knowledge. The equilibrium of Bernard, or, a little earlier, of St Anselm's *Meditations*, is never complacent; it does not solve, put an end to, the problem posed by the dialectic of Creation from nothing. Man is in the middle of this dialectic: he belongs both to the God who has neither beginning nor end and to created nature with its plodding round of births and deaths. If the monk (Anselm or Bernard) makes of man's middle place a harmony, liturgy – for all its attention to form, especially in the Roman rite – tends more to promote the fluctuations on which this harmony depends. If the 'terror of my life' (*Terret me uita mea*) and the 'Jesus himself' (*Iam ipse est, iam ipse est Iesus*) of Anselm's first Meditation are held in a deliberate, artistic and literary balance which has the effect of pulling them up out of the primacy of the original emotions of despair and hope,[16] the equivalent alternatives of liturgy – death-resurrection, and the contradiction within exorcism: Satan and Christ, or sin and purity from sin – leave a more restless impression of back-and-forth. There is a unity of death-and-resurrection in the *triduum* of Easter, and a sense of fulfilment of the obvious in the spiralling movement from beginning to end of a Roman prayer, but the juxtaposition of death and resurrection, or of beginning and end, request and response, is never forgotten. It could never be forgotten, because liturgy is so much occupied with the dramatic movement towards and away from repose or equilibrium or satisfaction.

In this deep vein of man's reflection on man – a reflection on man and not on each man – knowing self, being knowledge of man as product of God, is also ignorance.[17] The act of self-knowing is always a response by man to the creation of man by God, but always an inadequate response. Seeking to know

15 Kierkegaard 1985, pp. 118ff.
16 Anselm, *Med.* i, in *Opera*, iii, pp. 76–9. For this interpretation, Pranger 1984.
17 Gilson 1944, pp. 224ff.

himself, man finds he does not know what he is, because he does not know what made him. Again, in prayer or self-knowing (which as we have said come to much the same thing), knowing and ignorance are in balance. This is a balance hard to maintain when the reflection on man becomes the self-scrutiny of *each man*; when confession turns to autobiography. Knowing self, as Gilson puts it, is not just the condition of resemblance between image and model, man and maker, but the individual consciousness which responds to this condition.[18] So, in the *Confessions*, Augustine, as it were, watches his own prayer. In the end, though, whatever disjointedness there was between prayer and consciousness of prayer, between the fact of resemblance and awareness of it, is mended. A worry remains. The two movements, God to man and man to God, do not always make a perfectly harmonious dance. Yet it is implicit in Augustine's account of conversion that they respond to one another ultimately; and this meeting, in one place, of what man is, and each man's response, between question and answer, is the essence of conversion. In the harmony of question and answer is the absorption of autobiography into confession, of the 'I' into the self, the individual into the man.

Yet the worry that consciousness will be estranged from resemblance cannot be put away. It lurks. The prayer of liturgy, partly no doubt because it is collective prayer – the speech of the *corpus quod est ecclesia* – does not succumb to it. But with the disruptiveness (the demographic growth, rapid economic change, technological development, break up of communities) which is so much a part of the turn of the eleventh and twelfth centuries, the anxious 'I' makes its re-appearance.

Something like this – the anxious isolation of 'I' from self – has occurred, for example, in Abelard, who is concerned, in the *Ethics* as much as in the *Historia Calamitatum* – where he tells the story of his own 'troubles' – with the singularity of experience. In the *Ethics*, whose sub-title, not for nothing, is *Scito te ipsum* (*Know Thyself*), what comes across first is the privacy of moral judgement. The privacy is borne out in the particularity of the examples, *exempla*, which form the subject-matter of the argument. Abelard's notorious (and perhaps misunderstood) argument that there can be no sin without intention to sin, so that sin, 'properly speaking', has nothing to do with action outside the

<hr>

[18] Ibid., p. 218.

mind, has the effect of making sin – and the whole apparatus which surrounds it of intention, consent, contrition – a matter of atomized, personal experience.[19] *Scito te ipsum*: knowing self is knowing myself, not the self. Abelard in the end goes further than this, but the delight he took in this part of what he was saying, his evident pleasure in the idea that sin was pure intention, gave it a high profile – and was one of the things that got him condemned at Sens in 1140.[20] As for the *Historia Calamitatum*, it can be represented as the story told by Abelard of how he discovers, and then learns to resign himself to, his own, singular *fortuna*: the *fortuna* of his own *ingenium* (a word so often used in the context of the schools of the early twelfth century, in this sense of individual keenness of wit, facility, and in Abelard associated with the quickness of the jousting knight);[21] the *fortuna* of his deserved castration (so he sees it) and his undeserved humiliation at the council of Soissons in 1121, when his book on the Trinity was burnt (*fortuna* is close to chance – it does not keep step with an order of justice, or not one that can be discerned);[22] the *fortuna* which makes him, almost desperate, a second Cain, *vagus et profugus*, the vagabond in flight before his persecutors, weighing seriously whether it might not be better for him to live among the

---

[19] For general introductions to the *Ethics*, see David Luscombe's edition, pp. xiii–xxvii; and Blomme 1958.

[20] *Capitula heresum Petri Abaelardi*, x and xi, pp. 50–1.

[21] *Hist. Cal.*, p. 63: 'Ego igitur, ... sicut natura terre mee uel generis animo leuis, ita et ingenio extiti et ad litteratoriam disciplinam facilis.' It is Abelard's *ingenium* which allows him to 'win' against William of Champeaux: p. 67, lines 145–52; and see p. 69, line 209. In the opinion of Walter of Honnecourt (fl. 1100), a monk who abandoned his position as *scholasticus* for a life of prayer in the monastery of Vézelay – and who, when asked by the brethren of Honnecourt to return to them, replied, 'Quaerite uobis alium uerborum uenditorem' (*Letter*, p. 170) – *ingenium* was likely to have mischievous effects on its owner, if it was not kept in check. He wrote to Roscelin of Compiègne, one of Abelard's teachers, and an early example of the 'wandering scholar': 'Laudabili uiges ingenio, quod similis eloquentia sequitur, immo ut prompta pedissequa dominum comitatur. Quibus duobus si tertium se coniungat, sobrius intellectus, idoneus diuinae philosophiae formaris discipulus' (*Letter*, p. 173). On the scourge, as St Anselm and others saw it, of the wandering scholar, seeking about the country to show off his talent, Southern 1990, pp. 175ff. The young Abelard is a prime example of such a wanderer: *Hist. Cal.*, p. 64, lines 28–30; the pleasure he takes in intellectual jousting is very much reminiscent of the jousting of those bands of *iuuenes* – the noble younger sons, unmarried and without land of their own – which were so common in the twelfth century: Duby 1964.

[22] *Hist. Cal.*, p. 89, lines 922–7: 'Paruam illam ducebam proditionem in comparatione huius iniurie, et longe amplius fame quam corporis detrimentum plangebam, cum ad illam ex aliqua culpa deuenerim, ad hanc me tam uiolentiam intentio amorque fidei nostre induxisset, que me ad scribendum compulerat.'

followers of Mohammed.[23] What seems to be an arbitrariness in the dealings of *fortuna* – its content of chance – lingers like a pallid image of that old teaching of the arbitrary: the teaching of predestination to good or evil, firmly associated with Augustine. Chance, like predestination, singles out *each man*, producing a threatened, sometimes bewildered 'I', the 'I' crying out in incomprehension, like Abelard in his exile as abbot of Saint-Gildas in Brittany, where the land reached its end: 'From the ends of the earth have I called upon thee, my heart heavy within' (Ps. 60:3).[24] But *fortuna*, or Abelard's version of it at any rate, and that of Boethius on which it was based, was also the contrary of predestination, for it was only, in the end, an apparent arbitrariness. Chance was a play of shadows, and behind it, somewhere, was the logic of *providence*.[25] Much of the skill of William of Malmesbury, as an historian, lies in his ability to relate the unruly course of chance events – the contingent – and then to suggest their true coherence and orderliness, their *prouidentia*, by the discipline of a literary form. The remarkable thing in Abelard's *Historia* is that he has refused to do this: he has allowed the relation between *fortuna* and *prouidentia* to remain a question. The happier message of the *Ethics*, that sin can only be by intention, is Abelard's attempt to rescue the true destiny which is providence, from the seeming destiny of chance occurrence. But here again, the attempt is made by turning attention to the *singular* in each moral experience: conscience in Abelard's *Ethics*, the faculty by which intentions are judged, is the power of each to review his own moral history.

Abelard's inability to find the logic of his particular fate is an aspect of his being alone. It is the singularity of his 'calamities' which afflicts him. One of the themes running through the *Historia Calamitatum* is the rupture between solitude – the much desired aloneness of the philosopher, or the monk: *monachos*, 'the one who is alone' before God – and what Abelard calls *fama*: *conscientia tibi, fama proximo tuo* ('conscience is for you, reputation for your neighbour'), he repeats after Augustine.[26] It has been said

[23] Ibid., p. 97, lines 1221ff.
[24] Ibid., p. 98, lines 1250–4: 'ibique ad horrisoni undas Occeani, cum fugam mihi ulterius terre postremitas non preberet, sepe in orationibus meis illud reuoluebam: "A finibus terre ad te clamaui, dum anxiaretur cor meum."'
[25] Ibid., p. 108, lines 1589–97. Abelard calls it *diuina dispositio* here.
[26] Ibid., p. 103, line 1399. Cf. Bynum 1982, p. 49 (on this passage from Augustine, and its aptness to the designs of the canons regular).

of the twelfth century that it is less a time of the 'rise of the individual' than a time of the individual in relation to others. Again and again, and most often among the canons regular, we catch the refrain of *docere uerbo et exemplo* – 'teaching by word and example'.[27] *Fama* suggests this relation between one and another, and its reconciliation of the inward of *conscientia* and the outward of *exemplum*. But in Abelard *fama* is often dogged by another word: *inuidia* (envy, dislike, grudge, unpopularity).[28] *Fama* is reputation and rumour, not necessarily bad; it is 'fame' in a modern sense, the regard for a great teacher, and, in Abelard's case, a witty performer in public. But it is equally, or more – in Abelard's mouth – the scorn of the public at the theologian who is forced to throw his own book on the fire;[29] or at the notorious lover unmanned in the night.[30] Abelard feared scorn as much as he delighted in dealing it out.[31] *Fama* is the critical separation of one solitude from another – and much of Abelard's literary production, and some of his verse as well as his theology, explores the predicament of those who are somehow severed from others. Samson, for example, in the *Planctus* which Abelard devotes to him, is

> Clausus carcere,
> oculorumque lumine
> iam priuatus,
> quasi geminis

[27] Bynum 1982, on teaching by word and example; and her essay on the limits of individualism in the twelfth century, Bynum 1980. Two important essays by anthropologists on the notions of 'person' and 'individual', broaden the whole subject immensely: Mauss 1966; and Dumont 1983, pp. 33–67. Dumont's essay argues that the individual is a category which develops in the West out of the peculiar ambiguity of Western monasticism, which requires of its monks that they be at once 'this-worldly' and 'other-worldly'; both separate from others, and among others. But it might be argued that this double-life (which is conspicuously absent from Indian monasticism) is a feature not of each monk with regard to other monks, but of the whole community with regard to the world. Something more is required to make an individual.

[28] In the immediate context of *fama*, *Hist. Cal.*, p. 103, line 1400. Again, p. 69, line 223 (the ill-will of Anselm of Laon), p. 86, line 824 (the *inuidia* of Lotulf of Novara and Alberic of Reims and others pressing for Abelard's condemnation at the council of Soissons in 1121; Alberic and Lotulf are Abelard's *emuli*, those who envy him: p. 83, line 708, p. 84, line 749, etc.) There is a whole vocabulary of ill-sentiment in Abelard, a lasting bitterness as well as a great effort to overcome it.

[29] Ibid., pp. 87–8.

[30] Ibid., p. 80.

[31] Clanchy 1990 suggests that Abelard scorns not only his teachers William of Champeaux and Anselm of Laon, but, in the *Theologia Christiana*, Anselm of Bec. Luscombe (forthcoming) believes that at least in this case, Abelard's face was straight.

ad molam sudans tenebris
est oppressus.

Incarcerated, the light of his eyes now plucked away, as if with double
darkness toiling at the mill, he is weighed down.[32]

The preoccupation with solitude gives to Abelard's teaching an
odd caste. The *Historia Calamitatum* is an *exemplum* addressed to
others in favour of the solitude – however hard to attain – of the
ideal philosopher. There is a friction in Abelard between the city
(Paris, but also, in the *Theologia Christiana*, the ancient city) and
exile from the city (the convent of the Paraclete which he
founded in the 'desert' near Troyes, and, equally, Diogenes the
Cynic and the other solitaries of ancient times).[33] Through the
exemplum the philosopher-monk communicated his solitude to
others. In the *Historia*, there is also a suggestion that Abelard is
allowing himself to be compared with the suffering Christ.[34] But
just as *fama* is a mark of separation between one and another, so
the imitation of the *exemplum* – and with it the *imitatio Christi*,
that twelfth-century motif which inspired so many to the life of
poverty and eremiticism – is a distancing of self from historical
Christ: something quite different from the liturgical or symbolic
power to remember absolutely, to 'make happen again' by
anamnesis.

The estrangement of the 'I', creating in Abelard's acute intelligence a tension not altogether negative, but echoing the resigned-
ness of the Stoics – the sense in Abelard that self-knowledge is a
bell cracked by doubt – develops in Guibert de Nogent into a self-
obsessiveness which brings us back to sacrament. Guibert's case
will help to show how this exorbitant 'I' is at odds with the whole
quality of sacrament. For Guibert's troubles, described in the
three books of *Monodiae* in which he speaks of his life and its
setting among contemporary events around the city of Laon, all
begin from his inability to get over a kind of dread of himself; and
this dread is first a dread of his own baptism. The story of
Guibert's birth and baptism takes up the giddy antitheses of

---

[32] See the study of this *Planctus* in Dronke 1986, pp. 114–49. I have used Dronke's edition
and translation.
[33] *Theol. Christ.* 2.67ff, pp. 159ff.
[34] The imitation is a gentle sub-text. Abelard, for example, protesting that his motives for
returning to the Paraclete (now Heloise's convent) were not the selfish and even sexual
ones of which he was accused, implies a comparison between himself and Christ
followed by women (*Hist. Cal.*, p. 103).

liturgical symbol, but without giving the solace, at the end, of ritual form. The child Guibert refused to be born.[35] Father, friends and family stood hopelessly round the bed, and began to fear for both mother and child. Guibert's mother had suffered abnormal pain through the whole of Lent, and now the birth was about to take place not on this day or that, but on the vigil of Easter, the Saturday which marks time between the two poles of death and resurrection. He was to be born at the intersection of despair and hope – on that day when the equilibrium which is man, the equilibrium of 'ni ange ni bête mais dans l'entre-deux', was at its most finely balanced:

O Lord God and Father, who gave me (who am bad – you know how and in what way bad) birth from this woman (who is really, not by some pretence, good), you have given me hope too, through her merit, something I would never presume to have had had I not, for a moment, out of fear of my sin, breathed again under your grace. You brought on this hope – is it hope, or does it just feel like hope? – by providing to me that I should be born, and reborn, on the most holy and highest day, the day most wished for by all Christians.[36]

The danger to mother and child became so great that the whole party rushed to the altar of the Virgin, and made a vow to offer the child, if he or she lived, to the religious life. Guibert is an offering, an oblate to the monastic life, before he is born. His birth, because it happens on the Easter vigil, and again now because it is bound up with the offering of the child – the birth is a sacrifice, echoing the sacrifice of the God-man – is already a rebirth. It is charged, and in the self-regarding, ornamented language of Guibert – a style ever in search of a choice turn, a style, like the man, ambitious to impress but imprisoned by itself, essentially cut off – it is melodramatic. What Guibert never recovers from is the terrible contradiction between the solemnity of his birth-baptism, which he interprets as an arbitrary gift of embarrassing magnitude, and the feebleness of the *oblatio* which was brought forth. After this beginning, so auspicious yet so unpromising, he will never find equilibrium:

Just then [at the moment of offering to the Virgin] a sickly little tyke spilled out, more abortion than child. He appeared on the day, yes, but

---

[35] For this and the following, Guibert, *Monodiae* 1.3, pp. 16ff. For Guibert, see Benton 1970.
[36] *Monodiae* 1.3, p. 16.

so wretched that any joy there was went on the mother who lived through it. So miserable was this weakling of a thing that for a second after his birth everyone thought they were looking at a still-birth. The frail shoots of rushes which come up in this country in mid-April could have been held up to my fingers, and it would have been the rushes that were fatter not the fingers. On the same day, as I was being carried to the saving font, a woman – I was told this story often when I was a boy and as I grew up: it was one of those old jokes – turned me round and round from one hand to the other, saying, Will he live, do you think? Nature nearly forgot herself, making this little thing with hardly a limb on it – it's come out more like a rough drawing than a body.[37]

The ornamentation in Guibert's expression is partly deceptive. It is not merely literary, for all its self-consciousness. Beneath it is a lively realism, as though the events and even the vernacular language is trying to break through. But it is also under strain from strong personal emotion (at least in this first book of the *Monodiae*), and some of the apparent trickiness of the style amounts to a kind of instability of both language and emotion: an instability which careers from one extreme to another, from despair to hope and back, without being able to settle for a measure between them. In one sentence, the infant Guibert is an *oblatio*, brought into potent proximity with the Christ-*oblatio* of baptism and the Mass; in the next an *abortio* (or *quiddam instar abortionis*, almost an abortion).[38] And when he puns on the near-death of child and mother together, he seems to be making an effort to snatch, for a moment, one of the things that matters most to Guibert throughout, the entanglement in one another of mother and son:

Now deathly grief for both of them cast down father, friends and kin, for while the child hastened the death of the mother, so the fate (*exitium*) of the child, as long as he found no way out (*exitus*) was a source of compassion to all.[39]

It is the condition of finding no 'exit' that afflicts Guibert through his autobiography: he will always be caught in the morbid antithesis laid down at his birth – *oblatio/abortio*. The misery of

[37] Ibid., pp. 18–20. The turning from hand to hand recalls the practices mentioned by Jean-Claude Schmitt in his book on Guinefort, the holy greyhound: new-born children who were sickly were thrown back-and-forth across a river, evidently in order to restore the child to itself after it had been occupied by a demon-child (i.e. had become a changeling); or they might be shaken up and down to frighten off any demons who were thinking about entering a child. Schmitt 1983, pp. 71ff.
[38] *Monodiae* 1.3, p. 18. [39] Ibid.; and see Labande's note 1, p. 18.

birth – its squalor, pain, the weakness of the infant – and the grandeur of the season of birth, will never be lived down. The contradiction will repeat itself, unforgivingly, in subsequent *decursus* and *recursus*,[40] the unrelieved alternation between lapses into the pit of culpability and escapes from the pit with the help of an arbitrary, not to be hoped for, hand.[41] In the saint of an earlier time, the coincidence of physical birth and baptism-birth was more or less taken for granted. Is this not why the baptism of a saint is rarely mentioned in the *Lives*? It goes without saying. The coincidence is an instance of that natural sympathy of which the saint is an avatar, which brings together the ground underfoot and the sky overhead.[42] Again, it re-affirms the equilibrium of man: not angel, not beast, but between them and both of them. But the saint's *measure* is what Guibert lacks. Liturgy (as I have suggested) risks the shock of juxtapositions: the smallness of the sign, its fragmentedness and the huge integrity expected of it. The difficulty suffered by Guibert makes a parody of such juxtaposition, withdrawing it from the staid rise and fall of the natural seasons – the reliable elapse of a time going round and round – into the frailty, the thinness, of the 'I'. Guibert seeks measure in his mother's beauty. He looks upon his mother as a work of art, as *the* work of art. She is an ideal of classical beauty: the beauty which is rescued from mere sensuality by proportion – *forma conueniens, apta diductio membrorum*.[43] For Guibert, as for the classical tradition to which he looks, proportion, the harmony of parts in the whole, is as much an ethical as an aesthetic quantity. It is the product of restraint, so that it is without difficulty that he passes from the classical to the monastic, from proportion in things to refusal of them: to the *certae castitatis frons seuerissima* (the hard features of certain chastity).[44] But these early years of the twelfth

---

[40] Ibid., 1.1, p. 2: 'Confiteor amplitudini tuae, Deus, infinitorum errorum meorum decursus, et creberrimos ad te miserationis internae, quos tamen inspirasti, recursus.'

[41] Ibid., p. 6.

[42] The *Life of St Rumwold* is his baptism: he lives for three days, during which time he instructs his parents as to the proprieties of his baptism, is baptized and preaches to the pagans of southern England where he is born. He is the *tyro Christi: Vita Rumwoldi confessoris*, Nov. III, pp. 685–90. The baptism of the saint seems more likely to be mentioned from the late tenth century on: thus the *Life* of Æthelwold by Wulfstan of Winchester (not before 998), pp. 8–9. I am grateful to Dr Katie Cubitt for these references.

[43] *Monodiae* 1.2, pp. 11–12. On the proportion of the humours, which Guibert also mentions in connection with his mother (p. 12), see Klibansky, Panofsky and Saxl 1964.

[44] *Monodiae* 1.2, p. 10.

century turned back to the classical without quite being sure of themselves. The classical, with its sense of equilibrium in proportion, especially human proportion – its *bonheur rapide*[45] – was not natural to this period as it was to the sculptors of Chartres at the end of the century. This is a time not of classicism, but of the imitation of classicism. Guibert, it has been said, was a man unable to confess his sin to others.[46] At the beginning of the second book of the *Monodiae* is his attempt, when elected abbot of Nogent, to make confession to his fellow-monks, but by way of a sermon. He remains, in the end, cut off from others, and with fewer moral resources than Abelard. Isolated in this way, the disproportion he finds in himself, the lack of measure between *oblatio* and *abortio*, leaves him sore. What to do? Guibert, incapable of confessing, projects his desire for proportion on to the work of art which is his mother. But behind the projection is always the worry that she is no more than an idol – a *mere* harmony of limbs – just as there would always be, in these early days of 'Renaissance', the fear that recourse to the ancient world was nothing better than a banquet for the senses.

The 'I', disoriented and experimental, shrank from the robust joining of physical and metaphysical in sacrament. A similar distaste made the heretic (the 'chooser': after the Greek, αἱρεῖσθαι, 'to take for oneself') draw back from sacrament. Early in the eleventh century there began to appear, in northern France and north Italy, groups of heretics who were identified in the first place because they preached against infant baptism, the eucharist, marriage and penance.[47] In the mature expression of heresy, given it by the Cathars of Languedoc in the late twelfth/early thirteenth centuries, there developed an 'alternative baptism', whose name in Provençal, *le babtisme espirital* (in Latin it was *consolamentum*) indicates how far it was thought of as a counter-rite to the 'material baptism' of Catholicism.[48] In this rite, there are no symbols any more – no physical objects laden with metaphysical cargo. The few material things which are there – a Bible, a table

[45] Focillon 1964, pp. 17ff, distinguishing classicism from the 'experimental' phase before it, but also from the academic which imitates it.
[46] According to Moore 1985, Guibert intends to confess through writing the *Monodiae*, but fails because he is unable to confess to his fellow-monks. The *Monodiae* are a failed 'Confessions'.
[47] Taviani 1979.
[48] *Rituel cathare*, pp. xv–xxvi for the *consolamentum*. On the background to the rite, Guiraud 1904; Thouzellier 1969.

covered by a cloth, the words of the sermon spoken by the ministering 'perfect', the act of laying on hands – all amount to a refusal of symbol, much as Christ's baptism (taken by the Cathars to have been a laying on of hands and not a water-baptism) is a refusal of the water-baptism of John the Baptist.[49] The material objects in this ritual are not used for their richness; they are not, as it were, ontologically a part of the rite. They have been put there to clear a space for the operation of individual choice – the moral choice to 'contemn the world' and everything in it.[50] The heretics are refusing what has now come to seem the fiction of sacrament. We can understand how they came to think of sacrament as a fiction (especially infant baptism which left no room for choice) if we see their protest as part of a wide initiative to place stress on the ethical side of religion: the relation between man and man.[51] Certainly, in raising questions about the ethical content of sacrament, they put their finger on a tender spot.

SACRAMENT AND MAKING

David Jones, a poet and a painter and a calligrapher, was concerned with what would happen to the business of making (from the making of a birthday cake to the making of a painting by Rembrandt) after the 'civilizational turn' which he felt was under way had had its full effect of giving pride of place to technology and the made-by-machine, over art and making-by-man. This was in the 1920s and later decades. The 'civilizational turn' of the twelfth century was not the same as the one David Jones had in mind (and which is still with us) – although the two turns share some ground. But the urgent sense of man as essentially a maker, whose own making which is free and playful, and even gratuitous, is a response to the original making which was the gratuitous act of Creation – this sense of man as *poeta* or maker, is inalienable from the working of sacrament. And the concern, in David Jones, that there has been a loss of the power to make, a withering in the maker's hand, helps us see what went on in the eleventh and twelfth centuries when sacrament was with-

---

[49] Ibid., p. xvi.   [50] Ibid., p. xix.
[51] Borst 1953, takes this view of the Cathar religion in general, and believes that the dualism of the Cathars was no more than a peg on which to hang their concern with the moral. Cf. Morghen 1968, to similar effect.

drawn from *poiēsis* into the intangible *mysterium* of metamorphosis — into a secret mechanics no less mechanical for being secret. Anyway, this is how David Jones put it in what he calls a fragment, written in *c.* 1938 and 1966:

A,a,a, DOMINE DEUS

I said, Ah! what shall I write?
I enquired up and down.
                    (He's tricked me before
with his manifold lurking-places.)
I looked for his symbol at the door.
I have looked for a long while
                    at the textures and contours.
I have run a hand over the trivial intersections.
I have journeyed among the dead forms
causation projects from pillar to pylon.
I have tired the eyes of the mind
                    regarding the colours and the lights.
I have felt for His Wounds
                    in nozzles and containers.
I have wondered for the automatic devices.
I have tested the inane patterns
                    without prejudice.
I have been on my guard
                    not to condemn the unfamiliar.
For it is easy to miss Him
                    at the turn of a civilization.

I have watched the wheels go round in case I might see the living creatures like the appearance of lamps, in case I might see the Living God projected from the Machine. I have said to the perfected steel, be my sister and for the glassy towers I thought I felt some beginnings of His creature, but *A,a,a, Domine Deus*, my hands found the glazed work unrefined and the terrible crystal a stage-paste ....*Eia, Domine Deus.*[52]

But what does sacrament have to do with making? And what do we mean when we say that man is essentially a maker, so that (combining the two ideas) sacrament is somehow essential to man — a process he cannot do without; cannot help, being what he is, entering into? These are the questions asked by David Jones in his essay on 'Art and Sacrament'.[53]

Sacrament, we have already found, is a re-presenting: a making

[52] Jones 1974, p. 9.   [53] Jones 1959, pp. 143–79.

again rather than a copy. Re-presenting (which under its temporal cloak is repeating) is a making again under a new form. Sacrament and art are thus allied in the most intimate way: they involve the same process. The artist, like the 'sacramental man', is the trunk of the tree through whom the things of the world, which he perceives in his senses – by his taking part in the world – become forms; by which the sap rises from root to crown. This is the image which gave Paul Klee the backbone to his lecture *On Modern Art*. Between root and crown a transformation has occurred: they *look* quite different from one another. Yet the crown is none other than the root under another form: it re-presents it. 'This is not a representation of a mountain, it *is* "mountain" under the form of paint', says David Jones' painter: 'Indeed', Jones adds, 'unless he says this unconsciously or consciously he will not be a painter worth a candle.'[54] The painter, then, or any artist – *poeta* – is a maker in this particular sense, that he makes signs which *are* what they are signs of. This identity between sign and thing, which is so recognizably the identity acted out in the Mass of the offering of bread and wine and the self-offering of Christ, is what distinguishes art from imitation – from what the psychologists call the *eidetic* facility: the power to copy, to represent rather than re-present, the *eidos* (the thing seen).[55]

How, though, in sacrament or art, can it come about that the sign (the painting, the Mass, the birthday cake) *is* the thing (the mountain, the self-offering, the day of birth)? This question worried Augustine when he tried to explain to Januarius why Easter was somehow more than just a recalling of something that happened 'in history', something apparently – and by the usual standards of common sense – lost to the past; gone with it.[56] The liturgy, and that long stretch of historical time – the early Middle Ages – which made the liturgy its natural expression, worried over this much less. In that *durée* more than in others, the identity of sign and thing seemed to go more or less without saying – and in this is the historian's headache. But the throbbing begins to calm once he dwells seriously on the proximity of sacrament and art. For what happens when the painter puts a scene on his canvas or *homo religiosus* gazes on the elements of the world offered to him as symbols – water, wine, bread, stone, fire – is that he carries across

---

[54] Ibid., p. 170.   [55] Read 1943, pp. 136ff.   [56] See above, pp. 89ff.

not what he sees, but the *idea* of what he sees – idea in the widest sense, including not only the intellectual but also the emotional reaction. What he paints, or sees in the liturgical elements, is not what he *beholds*, but what the scene or the element *is to him*. The painting thus re-presents not because it puts before the mind something which reminds it of the scene; it does not provide information of a kind that would enable a passer-by who had seen the picture, and now happened on the scene, to say, 'Ah! This is the stretch of the Thames painted by Dufy.' Or, if it does provide information, this is not what matters most about it; this is not what the painting was painted for. What matters about the painting is that it re-produces, 'under another form' as Jones puts it,[57] what the scene was to the painter; what he sees in it and not just what he sees. It is in this way that the painting – or the liturgical celebration – is a sign; and it is in this way that the sign *is* the thing it re-presents. What is repeated in the sign-cum-painting is the relation of artist to material; of *poeta* to *materia poetica*. And this relation is not any old relation, but the relation of making, or *poiēsis*. It is the same making which goes on in liturgy and its sign, so that, for example, the dunking of a child in water re-creates the death of Christ and his descent to break the gates of hell.

One is reminded by this power of re-presentation, of what Lucien Lévy-Bruhl, the French philosopher who wrote at the turn of this century, called the 'primitive mind'.[58] E. B. Tylor, and with him others of the 'école anglaise', had explained the apparent peculiarity of many 'primitive' customs by attributing them to a fundamental error in thinking. The 'savage' had got into the habit of assuming the figures who appeared in his dreams to be objective persons, with lives of their own, who visited him in his sleep. This assumption he had then applied to the phenomena surrounding his waking senses, seeking to explain to himself everything from thunderstorms to motorbikes (if he had seen a motorbike by now) by attributing to things he saw about him their own souls and their own independent lives. In his mind, not only animals, but clouds and rivers and rocks became 'persons', with their own wills and desires and dislikes and likes, and able to inter-react with one another. It was their inter-reaction that brought about storms and floods, as well as the functioning or dysfunction of the human body. The 'école anglaise' thus thought

[57] Jones 1959, pp. 173–4.   [58] Lévy-Bruhl 1951, for this and what follows.

that the mental processes of the 'savage' were no different from 'ours'. The 'savage' had simply made a wrong hypothesis at an early stage, and it had remained for religion (imperfectly) and then experimental science (fully) – this according to Frazer[59] – to put him right. It was all a matter of progress. The hypothesis of the animist who thought the world was full of inter-reacting souls was no different in kind from that of the scientist: exactly like modern science, the primitive mind posited a model of causation founded on the interplay of objective forces.[60] The difference between animism and science was that of two stages along a continuum. Against this, Lévy-Bruhl held that the primitive mind is not the child who fathered the grown man of experimental science, but does its thinking in a quite distinct way. The neuro-physiology is the same. The 'savage' sees a cloud or a motorbike in the same way. But having seen it, he conceives of it neither as an independent soul or will, nor (in the case of the cloud) as a formation of droplets out of vapour at a certain level of humidity and a certain temperature. Instead, he looks on phenomena as signs in whose significance he takes part. In this way of seeing the principal relation is not, in the first place, between things, but between seer and thing seen; Lévy-Bruhl calls it *participation mystique*.[61] It is this *participation mystique* which allows (again) the sign *to be* the thing it is a sign of. Of this, Lévy-Bruhl gives a gallery of fine examples, from the papers of ethnologists and sundry travellers, including George Catlin's report of the Mandan Indians of North America who reacted not without rancour when he made paintings of their bison: 'I know, one of them said, that this man put many bison in his book, because I was there when he did it, and since then we have had no bison to eat.'[62] And – in a story very suggestive for the study of the medieval representation of saints – when the Huron Indians of Newfoundland saw the images of St Francis Xavier and St Ignatius on the altar of the Jesuit missionaries, they

looked at them with awe, believing them to be living persons. They asked if they were *Ondaqui*. The word *Oqui*, and its plural *Ondaqui*,

[59] Frazer 1922, pp. 63ff.
[60] Lévy-Bruhl 1951, pp. 7ff. Lévy-Bruhl's first interest is to do no more than explore the virtues of a new hypothesis, namely that different institutions mean different minds.
[61] Ibid., pp. 68ff.
[62] Ibid., p. 42, quoting from an edition of Catlin's account of travels among the North American Indians published in Edinburgh in 1903, which, however, I am unable to trace.

signifies among them some divinity; in a word, what they recognize as above human nature. They asked also if the tabernacle was their house, and if those *Ondaqui* dressed themselves in the ornaments which they saw around the Altar.[63]

Whether or not this way of seeing should be called 'primitive' is a question all its own. Perhaps we should say, mimicking Lévi-Strauss, that 'savage thought' – *la pensée sauvage* as he calls it with some irony – is the thought of the artist or musician, or rather of anyone who puts things together to make something, whether old bits of cardboard box turned into a doll's house or the fragments of the *materia poetica* which go together to make up a poem (old bits of history, myth, legend, other poems, text-books on geology, closing time in a pub, Marxism, an argument over a hedge, whatever comes to hand).[64] Lévy-Bruhl, in his account, does not think of his primitive as a handy-man (the *bricoleur* of Lévi-Strauss), and this is because he thinks that *participation mystique* has its own logic, a logic which gives short shrift to the loose, chancy, business of things happening to come to hand. Lévy-Bruhl wanted to dispel any idea that the primitive was the romantic or intuitive or poetic. The associations made through *participation mystique* are not free; according to Lévy-Bruhl, the primitive, in following the direction of the sign, in catching hold of its meaning and thus 'taking part' in its motion, is not in any way making it for himself. It is not his meaning, but the meaning pre-determined by the society in which he lives. So the individual is subservient to a well-defined set of ideas which exist in the collective mind – Lévy-Bruhl calls them 'collective representations' after Durkheim – and which dictate the direction his own thinking must take.[65] These patterns of ideas, like the institutions of the society which forms them, have a clear structure: a logic of their own (and not the logic of 'making') to which the individual mind is subject.

Lévy-Bruhl, then, turns out to be not quite what was wanted. *Participation mystique* is all very well, but 'collective represen-

---

[63] Thwaites 1897, p. 256, quoted by Lévy-Bruhl 1951, p. 42. (I have given the English translation, from French, in Thwaites' edition of the *Relations*.)

[64] Lévi-Strauss 1962, pp. 26ff.

[65] Evans-Pritchard 1965 is a very fair critical essay on Lévy-Bruhl, presenting him not as erroneous in his theory of *participation mystique*, but as going too far, and not seeing what Evans-Pritchard himself stressed, that explanations of phenomena by the principles of witchcraft and by those of natural causation are not exclusive of one another. They co-exist happily in the mind. Evans-Pritchard gives a particularly clear summary of Lévy-Bruhl's use of 'collective representations'.

241

tations' are not. But on the way, we passed the handy-man, and it is surely he who gives us our answer. He again comes close to what liturgy or sacrament, and all *poiēsis*, does. For no one would want to make man-the-maker *wholly* free. He can only work with what comes to hand, and what comes to hand is not just the material – the cardboard boxes, the lump of clay, and so on – but the way the material has been used before: *tradition*, or what has been handed down. Tradition limits what can be done. In liturgy, which is itself a tradition, it limits the things that can be done with symbol. Some things and not others can be thought of a symbol, can be made from it; and since liturgy is a social tradition, it seems to make use of something like 'collective representations'. Liturgy then would be not a *poiēsis*, but something ready-made, a map whose legend tells us exactly how it should be read. And yet tradition is in practice always less than logical. It lacks consistency, contradicting itself or offering multiple possible interpretations of the same gesture or sign, often in a most confusing way: is baptism the Baptism of Christ or the death/resurrection? Are the three immersions in baptism the three persons of the Trinity or the three days of burial? How does the Purification of the Virgin and the meeting of the infant Christ with Symeon at Candlemas stand to infant baptism (the connection is suggested by a miniature in the *Fulda Sacramentary*)? Is the Mass an offering of self in parallel with Christ's offering of self, or an offering of Christ to God by man? Many possibilities arise, some no doubt more common, more natural or idiomatic than others at certain times or in certain places. Liturgy is a job-lot. It is a structure only in a loose sense. Some bits of it might be ignored at some times, stressed at others. Sometimes it is barely a structure at all: it is just bits and pieces that come to hand, that happen to be there, and which can be put together in many ways. It does not bind to a ready-made pattern of thought, but calls up the virtuosity of the maker. It is *bricolage* – the effect of past *bricolage*, and an invitation to further *bricolage*.

Sacrament does not come off the peg. It invokes the freedom of the handy-man to do what he wants with the débris that lies about. What does his freedom consist in? It is the freedom of origination:[66] to make what has not been made before – it is what David Jones calls the 'Gratuity Ness' of making[67] – which then issues in the virtuosity, the pure pleasure (or pain, some would

---

[66] Read 1943, p. 137: 'origination' is Read's translation of Buber's *Urhebertrieb*.
[67] Jones 1959, p. 149.

say) of a making which is determined neither by the technique of copying what has been made before nor by the technique of making something for a purpose. Origination thus implies the surpassing of technique by virtuosity; it implies the *otium* of not being bound to make something, or not only having to make something. How difficult it would be to make a chair *merely* with sitting in mind. In this perspective, tradition is not the contradiction of origination, but one of its conditions. Tradition is not just a formal restraint. It is one of the materials with which origination works; a part of the resistance which prevents a mere excess of facility, the decline of spontaneity into haphazard wandering. Sacrament, like art, is never only a matter of observance, subservience, adherence. It is a matter of making.

David Jones wrote his essay 'Art and Sacrament', which I have tried to follow here, to show that between sacrament and art there was the kinship of the maker, but also to show that man was somehow by his nature a maker, and a maker of sacraments. Is there not an echo here of that other definition of man, as 'made in the image of God'? And is not the 'Gratuity Ness' of man's making the only possible response to the arbitrariness of the first making?

BERENGAR AND LANFRANC: WHOLE AND FRAGMENT

Lanfranc's letter to Berengar, which was also a treatise against him, the 'Book on the Body and Blood of Our Lord', reminds us in its tenor of some of the miracles of eucharistic change – those sudden transformations of bread and wine into flesh and blood on the altar.[68] It has some of the same power to shock. Berengar, on his side, could not see how a bit of bread could, physically, become the body of Christ, who was, after all, lodged in heaven and had been for a thousand years. To this Lanfranc replied in strong language:

There is the sacrament (*sacramentum*) and there is the 'thing of the sacrament' (*res sacramenti*). The thing, or reality, of sacrament, is the body of Christ. Christ however, 'rising from the dead does not die; death has no more power over him' [Rom. 6:9]. But while ... the [pieces of] his flesh (*carnes*), are truly eaten, his blood truly drunk, he himself continues whole (*integer*) in the heavens at the right hand of the

---

[68] For these miracles, Browe 1938.

Father, till the time when all will be restored. He lives. If you ask me how this can happen, I say only this in brief for now: it is a mystery of faith. To believe it is a part of being saved. To enquire into it is futile.[69]

The consecration of the elements of bread and wine is therefore a shock to the natural order and to the normal expectancies of perception.[70] It breaks the pact of nature, ignoring the usual conditions of change in the world, to make bread and wine into the historical body and blood of the Christ who had lived in Jerusalem: into the *corpus ex Virgine*, the body born of the Virgin; into the 'body which hung from the cross, and ... the blood which flowed from the side of him who hung from the cross'.[71] The priest's words are a prodigy, invoking the same power – or something closely analogous – which at Creation had made the world from nothing. The words are *praeter naturam*, in the expression of Ambrose.[72] In the face of this, the 'philosophical' formulation provided by Lanfranc, and whose terms are borrowed from Aristotle – the explanation that after the consecration the bread and wine are *species* and the body and blood *essentia* or *substantia* – is negligible.[73] It is doubtful whether Lanfranc even meant it as an explanation: it is better seen as another way of putting across the inexplicable *sacratio* of metamorphosis.[74]

[69] *De corpore*, p. 167: 'Est igitur sacramentum, et res sacramenti, id est, corpus Christi. Christus tamen, "resurgens ex mortuis iam non moritur, mors illi ultra non dominabitur". Sed sicut dicit Andreas apostolus, cum uere in terris carnes eius sint comestae, et uere sanguis eius sit bibitus; ipse tamen usque in tempora restitutionis omnium in coelestibus ad dexteram Patris integer perseuerat, et uiuus. Si quaeris modum quo id fieri possit, breuiter ad praesens respondeo: mysterium est fidei: credi salubriter potest, uestigari utiliter non potest.' There is a fair sized literature on the debate between Berengar and Lanfranc: see esp. Gibson 1978, pp. 63–97; Macy 1984, pp. 35ff, 149ff. Chadwick 1989 places the dispute in the context of its development in the twelfth century and then in the Reformation; Chadwick 1990 in the context of Patristic writings and Reformation.

[70] *De corpore*, p. 164: 'Quis enim compos sui credat rem aliquam conuerti in aliam, nec tamen in ea parte desinere esse quod erat?'

[71] Ibid., p. 177.

[72] Ibid., p. 165, quoting Ambrose, *De mysteriis* 9.53 'Quid hic quaeris naturae ordinem in Christi corpore, cum praeter naturam sit ipse dominus Iesus partus ex Virgine?'

[73] *De corpore*, p. 165 (*uisibilis species/interior essentia*), p. 163: 'sed inter sacrandum incomprehensibiliter, et ineffabiliter in substantiam carnis, et sanguinis commutari'. On Lanfranc's debt to Aristotle's *Categories*, de Montclos 1971, pp. 373ff. Lanfranc is not using – and not intending to use – Aristotle's distinction between 'substance' and 'accidents' in a precise philosophical way, but is rather borrowing the language as one of the means of expressing the rift between invisible and visible, *figmentum* and *ueritas*. Later, Guitmund of Aversa will take over the language of substance and accidents to convey not the rift but the continuity between inner reality and outward sign: *De corporis et sang. Chr. ueritate* 1, cols. 1443–4.

[74] *De corpore*, p. 169.

Species and *essentia*, although they point the way to the later distinction between accidents and substance and therefore to the teaching of transubstantiation, are in Lanfranc an abdication of the philosophical, not a real use of it. But in the passage above, Lanfranc is talking about a second shock to the senses: the body of Christ is eaten now, as 'bits of flesh', *carnes*, and yet Christ remains whole, *integer*, in heaven. Christ, the historical Christ, was broken, literally in crucifixion and figuratively by death; and so he is eaten not as one flesh but as 'fleshes'. He has been scattered, like shards, by death. The shock of broken/whole: the body *fractum/ integrum*, is perhaps greater than that of metamorphosis. Some, says Lanfranc, have found it a hard saying.[75] There was even a certain violence about it, and this again is repeated in the miracles of eucharistic change – and in Cardinal Humbert's infamous insistence that the flesh of Christ was 'chewed';[76] but in what Lanfranc writes about it, the violence is put into the form of argument.

De Lubac, in his remarkable study of the *corpus mysticum* in the early Middle Ages, stressed the change undergone by the sense of the word *mysterium* in the eleventh and twelfth centuries.[77] Lanfranc's flat statement *mysterium est fidei* – from the canon of the Mass – to convey the impossibility of understanding how the whole and the broken bodies stood to one another is an example of the shift in sense. Before the eleventh century, the content of 'secret' in *mysterium* was greatly modified by the idea of something concealed which might be revealed. *Mysterium* therefore denoted not only the thing hidden, but the process of hiding, or the difficulty of finding which resulted from obscurity. It referred to an action. This content of the word came about partly through contact with the word *sacramentum*, which had often been used to translate the Biblical Greek *mysterion*. Again, *sacramentum* carried with it into the Middle Ages not only the notion of a 'holy thing', a *sacrum*, as Isidore of Seville had emphasized, but also that of a *signum* and of the action of sacrifice – senses preferred by Augustine. If *sacramentum* gave the edge to the motion in the mind as it followed the path from 'sign' to 'thing', so *mysterium* gave more room to the hidden thing itself; but whether alone or as a twosome, the words tended to give weight to the *relation* of sign to

---

[75] Ibid., p. 167.   [76] See above, p. 223 n. 7.
[77] De Lubac 1949, pp. 55ff, for this and what follows.

thing, over the hidden thing: over the *sacrum*. *Mysterium*, says de Lubac,

porte moins sur le signe apparent ou au contraire sur la réalité cachée que sur l'un et l'autre à la fois: sur leur rapport, sur leur union, sur leur implication mutuelle, sur le passage de l'un dans l'autre ou la pénétration de l'un par l'autre ... ce qui est proprement et d'abord *mystique*, c'est ainsi le lien secret et mouvant de l'*allusio*, de la *significatio: mystica figuratio, mystica similitudo, significationis internae mysterium*.[78]

The eucharist of the early Middle Ages is under the sign of this *mysterium*. It is not Lanfranc's shock-*mysterium*, the awful oxymoron of *corpus fractum/corpus integrum*; but the recovery of the original whole in the broken pieces of flesh; the recovery of the hidden, the lost, the *quondam* body *ex Virgine*, the dead body, in the fragment of this *corpus in altare*.

The power to 'resurrect the fragment' – as Candidus of Fulda (d. 845) put it talking about the eucharist[79] – recalls what Hanns Swarzenski said about the smallness of many of the 'monuments' of Romanesque art. To those who looked on these monuments, it seems, smallness was no obstacle:

the monumental quality of the art of this period is in no sense determined by size. There are frescoes and stone reliefs that have the minute subtlety and precision of miniatures, ivory carvings, and metal engravings; and there are book-paintings, statuettes, ivories, and metal engravings which show the broad summary handling of wall-paintings and stone sculptures ... These works, no matter how tiny they may be, stand enlargement to many times their size without distortion. In fact, it is often only through such enlargements that their whole hidden artistic richness and the fulness of their imaginative world can be revealed.[80]

The *small* work of art was not a reduction, a toy, but as expressive as the big, and this was in part because of the preciousness of the materials used, in part because of the attention given to techniques of 'delicate work', *opus subtile* – metalwork, enamelling, the

[78] Ibid., pp. 62–3 (*mystica figuratio*: Amalarius, *Liber offic.* 3.3.4, p. 267 (quoting Augustine, *De ciu. Dei* 17.14, p. 578); *mystica similitudo*: Pseudo-Haimo, *In Psalmum* 132, *PL* CXVI, cols. 650–1; *significationis internae mysterium*: Peter Damian, *De contemptu saec.*, *PL* CXLV, col. 282C).
[79] *De passione domini* 5, *PL* CVI, cols. 68–9. The same idea in Ivo, *Dec.* 2.1, col. 135A–B; Gratian, *Decretum, De consec.*, dist. 2, c. 36, p. 1326. Cf. de Lubac 1949, pp. 34–5. On Candidus, Manitius 1911–31, I, pp. 661–3.
[80] Swarzenski 1974, pp. 12–13.

working of gold, jewels, filigree.[81] Smallness is thus, in a sense, indistinguishable from great size, because it expresses the same intensity.

Smallness is not fragmentedness; but there is a similar failure to tell apart the fragment from the whole – or an ability, rather, to find the same intensity in both. In the eucharist, broken flesh, under the appearance of bread, was indistinguishable (in a sense: the sense of *mysterium-sacramentum*) from the whole body. This continuity between 'this body' on the altar and that other body, either the historical body *ex Virgine* or the perfect celestial body, is the continuity between head and members or between body and flesh:

That we may be in his body, beneath his very head, in his members, eating his flesh.

Ut simus in eius corpore, sub ipso capite, in membris eius, edentes carnem eius.[82]

The body which was persists in the flesh which is; the head in the members. This is not a playing with words,[83] but a real persistence of 'that body' in 'this body'; whole in fragment. It is a *persistence*, a going on through time, because the intensity of the whole body, although it is celestial and outside the reach of time, is always thought of in association with the historical body that was:

That which he took from the mass of humankind, broke in the passion, and, having broken, resurrected.

Quod enim ex illa massa generis humani assumpsit, passione fregit, et fractum resuscitauit.[84]

The whole persists in the fragment. This is not so alien in the end. The past, we naturally feel, is lost: it has gone by. Yet it is a common, even banal, experience to feel its substance returning to us. This is what happens when we look at a ruin. The ruin stands half-way between myth, which treats time as though it were not gone by, and history, which affirms the lostness of the past. The

[81] Suger had a taste for the grandness of precious things and intricate workmanship: *De admin.*, p. 46.
[82] Augustine, *In Ioh. euang. tr.* 27.1, p. 270 (see de Lubac 1949, p. 52).
[83] De Lubac 1949, p. 33.
[84] Candidus of Fulda, *De passione domini* 5, *PL* CVI, col. 68D.

ruin provokes a double-take: it causes us to think two things at the same time, or almost. Abandoned and broken, it confirms our suspicion that the past is not recoverable. But equally, being still there – it has survived – it stimulates in us a reflection on this past which can only be done in the present. Together, these two operations – one of losing, the other of re-possessing – give to time its familiar density: the knowledge that it consists neither in contingent events which peter out, nor in ideas living only in the mind, but in both. It is this conflict of senses which forms the 'sense of the past'. In central Australia, the Aranda treasure small pieces of polished stone or carved wood which link them with their ancestors: *churinga*.[85] As individuals, the ancestors have long been forgotten, because this is a society which wastes little effort on distinguishing what was from what has come to be. This is a society of 'synchronists'. But on the *churinga* is conferred all the sense of a once-was which perseveres into the now-is. The *churinga* compensates for what is otherwise a weak historical memory. The little piece of stone is charged with the persistence of a genealogy. It is as if the sense of the past is itself given a body: a body sufficiently small to suggest that it has been lost; but a body which is still here. In a similar way, the body of Christ *ex Virgine* perseveres in the body *in altare* because these two bodies are related to a third body – the body of a persistent genealogy – the body *quod est ecclesia*, the church:

'Take up and eat.' That is, people, make my body, which you now are. This is the body which is given over for you. This he took from the mass of human kind, broke in the passion, and, broken, resurrected ... This he took from us, gave over for us. And you are to 'eat' it, that is, make whole (*perficite*) the body of the church, that it become the whole, perfect, one, bread, whose head is Christ.[86]

Neither Lanfranc nor Berengar is capable of reintegrating the bones which have been flung apart. Their perspective is historical: the body *ex Virgine* is a thing of the past, the *corpus* in opposition to the *carnes*. The *quondam*-body may be imitated, but not 'done': *imitatur non operatur*.[87] The presence of this body on the altar (in the bread), the *uerum corpus* as it was increasingly called after this

---

[85] Lévi-Strauss 1962, pp. 315–23 – whose interpretation of the *churinga* I have used.
[86] Candidus of Fulda, *De passione domini* 5, PL CVI, cols. 68–9.
[87] Lanfranc, *De corpore*, p. 171. On the new importance attached to history in the twelfth century, Chenu 1976, pp. 62–89 ('Conscience de l'histoire'); and Southern 1970, 1971.

controversy, comes about not by imitation – which confirms its loss – but by the pure *mysterium* of metamorphosis (*mutatio materialis*).[88] Sacrament has been divided into a history play which *imitates* its subject in order to lead its audience to compunction, and a miracle which shocks, and which occurs with or wihout the assistance of the *corpus quod est ecclesia*, by the 'accession of the word to the element'.[89] It is divided into *imitatio* and *opus*. Berengar, for his part, appears to have held that sacrament (he is talking of both baptism and the eucharist) is a metaphor. That is, it happens in the mind (*intellectualiter*) and not in physical matter (*sensualiter*). The words spoken by Christ at the Last Supper, 'This is my body', are to be taken in the sense of the statement: 'Christ is the cornerstone', and not in the light of the episode when Moses' staff turned into a snake – or of any other transformation of one thing into another.[90] The thrust behind this is in two statements of Augustine: first, that sacrament depends on a connection of *likeness* between the sacrament as mere physical element (*sacramentum*) and the truth to which the *sacramentum* points;[91] second, that

sign is a thing which, out of itself, causes something to come into the mind other than that which has effect on the senses.

signum enim est res praeter speciem quam ingerit sensibus, aliud aliquid ex se faciens in cogitationem uenire.[92]

Metaphor – the modern usage which seems best adapted to this – is, as Berengar knew, a fictional association 'made up' in order to bring home more firmly a truth. Christ is not a cornerstone, but

---

[88] Ibid., p. 157.
[89] Augustine, *In Ioh. euang. tr.* 80.3, p. 529, lines 5ff: 'Detrahe uerbum, et quid est aqua nisi aqua? Accedit uerbum ad elementum, et fit sacramentum.' On the eucharist: 'Tolle ergo uerbum, panis est et uinum. Adde uerbum, et iam aliud est. Et ipsum aliud quid est? Corpus Christi et sanguis Christi. Tolle ergo uerbum, panis est et uinum. Adde uerbum, et fit sacramentum' (*Sermones inediti* 6.2, *PL* XLVI, col. 836; cf. Foulquié 1927).
[90] *Rescriptum* 1, pp. 68ff. Here the difference between two kinds of change is established: change by 'corruption' of one subject and 'generation' of another (*corruptio subiecti – generatio subiecti*), that is, the displacement of one subject by another, as in the change from snow to crystal over thousands of years (*sic*), or Lot's wife turned into salt; and change of the kind involved in 'figurative speech' or metaphor, where there is no displacement of one thing by another. For different views from the one expressed here on Berengar's 'realism', de Montclos 1971; Chadwick 1989.
[91] *Ep.* 98, col. 364: 'Si sacramenta rerum quarum sacramenta sunt similitudinem non haberent, omnino sacramenta non essent.'
[92] *De doctrina christiana* 2.1.1, p. 32.

to think of Christ and a cornerstone at once is to see better the firmness of Christ. The likeness in Berengar's *tropica locutio* (as he calls this kind of sign) is thus quite different from the likeness of the whole and the fragment – or the likeness of liturgical symbol generally. Berengar's likeness, and the likeness at work in Lanfranc's history play, do not arise from an intrinsic sympathy of sign and thing – the persistence of whole in fragment, or, the ultimate basis of such thinking, the intrinsic likeness of the Creator and his Creation. Likeness is not now this deep sympathy which man is privileged to perceive. It is an incidental and temporary connection. The frailty of this metaphoric or theatrical likeness, this mere imitation of one thing by another, is the problem faced by both Berengar and Lanfranc. Lanfranc answers it with the brute realism of *mutatio materialis*. There is likeness or *imitatio*; but there is also a *sacratio* which has nothing to do with likeness. Berengar answers it with his own brand of realism: instead of a material realism, an 'intellectual' realism, which anticipates – though feebly – the idea adopted later in his life by Abelard, that the concepts of the mind, through the affinity of the reasoning mind with the Creator, reflected the fundamental truths of things as laid down at the Creation, and were thus not properties of the mind alone.[93] Abelard's theory concerns language as a whole, but for Berengar, metaphor at least is fiction bearing truth; but the consecration in the eucharist brings about the one-off of a metaphor which is true. This, it seems, is what he has in mind when he talks of *conversio intelligibilis*.[94] The eucharist does involve a change (*conversio*): not the change of Moses' rod *into* a snake, by which the rod ceased to be and the snake began to be; but the 'change' which happens to something when it is pictured in a metaphor, when it has something else *added* to it:

the bread and wine at the Lord's table undergo a change (*converti*), not sensually, but intellectually, not by the removal [of bread and wine] but by their assumption (*non per absumptionem sed per assumptionem*); and not a change into a small portion (*portiuncula*) of flesh, which would be against Scripture, but into the whole body and blood of Christ, in agreement with Scripture.[95]

---

[93] Cf. Luscombe 1988.   [94] *Rescriptum* 2, p. 142.
[95] Letter to Adelmann, p. 534.

In the letter to Adelmann, Berengar is quite clear about the reality of the body added to bread: it is unquestionably, he says, the *uerum corpus*.[96]

The fragility of a likeness not rooted in the original likeness of Creation and Creator causes – throughout the twelfth century – a fear of fiction. Berengar, Lanfranc felt, ran dangerously close to the wind of fiction by bringing in metaphor and dissociating sacrament from the miracle of metamorphosis.[97] This is the reason for his urgency against Berengar. The time of the so-called Gregorian Reform was peculiarly susceptible to the threat of fiction. The concept of 'reform' depended on a purification of the priest from his attachment to the world: he was to take no wife or concubine, and to receive his office without exchange of money and without investment by a layman.[98] Having been made 'pure' in these ways, the priest was distanced from society by a difference of kind, not degree. He was not more holy, but absolutely holy. His separation was accompanied by the development of a separate language: the technical languages of law and of theology. In the debate between Berengar and Lanfranc, we see how the techniques of language – especially grammar and dialectic – are applied to the 'body' of the eucharist, and how the solidity of sacrament, its corporality, tends to be assumed into the techniques of language themselves – into Berengar's metaphor, or into the dialectic of Lanfranc, and his 'explanation' of the eucharist by *species* and *essence*.[99] Another symptom of the same tendency, a tendency for sacrament to become bloodless, appears in the use of dialectic – and the question and answer techniques –

[96] Ibid., p. 531; *Rescriptum* I, pp. 78–9: 'non ergo caro Christi, quae per mille iam annos tota constat inmortalitate nec potest usquequaque nunc incipere esse, fit de pane per generationem subiecti sui et corruptionem subiecti ipsius panis, quia caro illa nec absumi potest, quia immortalis et incorruptibilis est, ut destructa et restituta iterum esse incipiat, sed panis altaris, qui numquam caro fuerat ante consecrationem, fit non per corruptionem, sed per consecrationem caro Christi, quia non potest non superesse materialiter quod consecretur'.

[97] Lanfranc, *De corpore*, p. 158: 'Unde apparet peruersorem, ac subuersorem te esse diuinarum litterarum, et ex deprauatis, fictisque sententiis erroris nebulas spargere imperitis, falsumque esse quod ex falso principio constiterit emanare.' And see p. 165: 'fraude fingis non inuenta', etc.

[98] Fliche 1924 on the Reform in general; Moore 1980 on the connection between Reform and purification.

[99] Southern 1949 shows Berengar to have been more a grammarian, Lanfranc more a logician. On the development of legal method and language, Fournier and Le Bras 1931–2.

to define what is and is not sacrament, and what is and what is not a particular sacrament. Wherein lies its special efficacy?

In the mid-twelfth century, Peter the Lombard produced the following definition of baptism:

> Baptism is to be called a dipping (*tinctio*), that is an outer cleansing of the body done according to the prescribed form of words. Consequently, if the cleansing is done without the word, there is no sacrament. But whenever the word accedes to the element, there is sacrament. It is not the element which makes a sacrament, but rather the washing done in the element.[100]

The definition has been reached by a reconciliation of Augustine's notion of likeness (the exterior washing is *like* the washing of sin) and his notion of sacrament as 'word acceding to element'. And just as the process of reconciliation is the formal one of discovering the harmony in apparently conflicting *dicta* of authorities (Bible, Fathers, Councils), so its product is a form of words rather than the persistence of a tradition. The separateness of the priest is echoed in the language he speaks.

This formal language, however, is not quite to be trusted. It is a language arising from the methodical criticism of texts and which is itself committed to texts.[101] Like the text in which it is written down, it lacks solidity. For the text, although it might be a text of an *auctoritas*, and in this period was itself increasingly seen as having authority over the spoken word – the authority of fixity, and separateness or 'purity' from the fluidity of the oral – was also deceptive. There was always something fictitious about a written text, because, being a fixed form of words, and being, as it were, flat – having none of the physical substance of the voice, with its moods, registers, tones – it was even more likely than the voice to fail to convey what Augustine called the *ictus intelligentiae*: the thought as it leapt from the mind. The text was, as Abelard noted in the prologue to the *Sic et non*, treacherous:

---

[100] *Sent.* 4.3.1, p. 243. The literature of early scholasticism is, at least in appearances, a literature of definitions. See also the *Sententie diuine pagine* (school of Anselm of Laon – d. 1117), p. 42, distinguishing sacrament from ornament; and for other examples, Landgraf 1955, pp. 7–46. The tendency to bring baptism down to its bare essentials, and thus to make its operation, and its effect, more objective, is shown in William of Malmesbury's no-nonsense approach to the elaborate Amalarius of Metz: *Abbreuiatio Amalarii*, ed. Pfaff 1980 and 1981.

[101] On the increasing importance attached to texts in this period, and the implications of this change, Stock 1983.

The fact that in so great a multitude of words some of the sayings of the saints not only differ from one another but seem to contradict one another, does not mean we are to sit in judgement on [those saints] . . . or call them liars . . . Why should it surprise us if we fall short in our understanding of things said and written through the Spirit, and intimated to the writers by the Spirit, when the same Spirit is not with us? We are hindered greatly in coming to an understanding by unfamiliar manners of speech, and often by the diversity of meanings of the same words – for a word may be used now with this meaning, now with that.[102]

Fearing the fiction of the text, and of the dialectic whose job it is to reconcile conflicting texts, Lanfranc plumps for the solidity of the word. To get closer to the word, and so give body to the thin, flat text, he deliberately withdraws from formal argument into the looser speech of rhetoric.[103] He blunts his power of argument, to avoid the *phantasma* which it risks falling into: 'I would rather be a peasant among the crowd, a Catholic idiot, than be a courtly and facetious heretic with you.'[104]

Christianity begins from the loss of body. Again and again, it makes the effort to recover the body: in the body of the eucharist, the body of the crowd – thus the rejection of body by the anchorite in the desert implies his fusion with the body of the impoverished crowd in the city[105] – in the corporality of the woman, and thus in the fecundity of Christ on the cross,[106] in the city of Jerusalem: 'We shall worship in the place where his feet have trod' (Psalm 131:7) sang the crusaders as they set out on the first crusade – and the crusade was the pilgrimage to end pilgrimages, the return of the prodigal son to his *patriam*, the place from which (in theory) there could be no return.[107] But the land which the crusaders found, or at least the kingdom they set up there, was a fragile kingdom;[108] and what the crusaders found was

[102] *PL* CLXXVIII, col. 1339.
[103] *De corpore*, p. 160: 'in quantum possum per aequipollentias propositionum tego artem, ne uidear magis arte, quam ueritate, sanctorumque Patrum auctoritate confidere'.
[104] Ibid., p. 156. On Berengar as a 'courtly' writer, Gibson 1990.
[105] Brown 1988.   [106] Bynum 1987.
[107] Fulcher of Chartres, *Expedition to Jerusalem*, p. 74. Dupront 1987, pp. 239–63, resurrects for us this will to *parousia* in one of his astonishing essays ('La spiritualité des croisés et des pèlerins').
[108] Mayer 1972, pp. 63ff; and see Fulcher's depiction of the Latin kingdom, surrounded by hostile armies. It is a mystery – a miracle – he concludes, that 'a hundred times a hundred thousand fighters' did not advance on Jerusalem from Egypt, Persia, Mesopotamia, Syria (*Expedition to Jerusalem* 2.6, pp. 148ff).

not the body in its tomb, but no-body. Instead of body, there was the miracle of the lighting of the Easter fire each year.[109] And the *uerum corpus* on the altar, for all Lanfranc's efforts, became increasingly distant and frail: not the flesh *in terris*, but the *caro spiritualis*.[110] A body resembling the text in its insubstantiality; a fragment which, although it is body, defies reintegration.

BAPTISM AGAIN

Baptism, being the 'making good' of man (whether infant or adult, it hardly matters) who is not good enough except insofar as he is 'like' God (*capax dei* as Augustine put it), was peculiarly apt to express that sense of inadequacy which came over the crusaders when they found that the grave, after all, was empty. But while the question of the eucharist put stress on the body itself and the sense in which it could be said to be present in the Mass bread, the question of baptism tended to concentrate on the inward consciousness, or perception, of the body. This was not surprising, because baptism – even the rushed *quamprimum* baptism which happened too quickly to benefit from the rich associations of the 'Feasts of Idea' of Easter and Pentecost – still carried with it the meaning it had originally had, of a personal conversion, a *conversio cordis*.

In the end, though, the 'outward' and the 'inner' (as would be expected) answered to one another. The sight of the empty tomb threw the crusaders, and those to whom they returned with their message, back on to their own inward resources. Finding that the body was gone – that it was an historical body which had done no more than *pause* in the corrosion of time[111] – they were forced to see it in the mind's eye. The embodiment of God, as Hegel put it with enthusiasm, was not now external but a product of 'Subjective Consciousness':

---

[109] Thus Peter the Venerable, in his sermon *De laude dominici sepulchri*, recapitulates the initial enthusiasm of the crusaders, and then their disappointment, and finally consoles them with the universal, uncorrupted body, which he associates with the lighting of the Easter fire. The literal search for the 'filius hominis in corde terrae' (Matt. 12:40) turns out to be the moral search for the *uitale sepulchrum* within the self (see p. 238 and p. 242).

[110] On these developments, Lubac 1949, pp. 89ff and *passim*. For a remarkable presentation of the *corpus spirituale*, see the eucharistic miracle told by Peter the Venerable, *De miraculis* 1.1, pp. 7–8, where the language and the story combine to give an impression not of the physicality of the host, as in many eucharistic miracles, but of its strangeness, or uncanniness, and its proneness to disappear.

[111] Peter the Venerable, *De laude*, p. 243.

Thus the world attains the conviction that man must look within himself for that *definite embodiment* of being which is of a divine nature: subjectivity thereby receives absolute authorization, and claims to determine for itself the relation [of all that exists] to the Divine. This then was the absolute result of the crusades, and from them we may date the commencement of self-reliance and spontaneous activity. The West bade an eternal farewell to the East at the Holy Sepulchre, and gained a comprehension of its own principle of subjective infinite Freedom.[112]

The problem of presence, or embodiment, which had itself arisen out of the more supple conception of the *mysterium-sacramentum* as a making, and therefore a repeating under another form of its object, was resolved all of a sudden by recourse to *conscientia*: *conscientia* both as consciousness and as moral conscience. But Hegel's picture only shows a part of what happened. The West did not quite bid its farewell to the East; its subjective consciousness – and all the artistic, ethical and political freedom that it allowed – remained aware in everything it did of its own origins in the episode at the grave-side. For all its appearance of certainty, it did not forget that it had itself come from a *failure* to find what was sought – a failure anticipated in the story of Mary Magdalene in John 20:1–18, and a failure which stands for the incapacity of man as man to see things as they are.

The story, however, did not end with an empty tomb, but with the angel's, 'He has arisen, he is not here' (Mark 16:6). In the same way, for the crusader – and this is the message of Peter the Venerable's *Sermon in Praise of the Holy Sepulchre* – it did not end with the disappointment of arrival, but with the fable of a 'sublime' Jerusalem. Had it been a symbol, the physical existence of this city, drenched in its Biblical past and staked out with the ritual topography of Christ's sayings and doings, could not have been told apart from its significance: the one was 'made' from the other, and neither was prior. But Peter the Venerable's Jerusalem was a fable. Its appearance, and even its history, was deceptive. Not an outright deception, a deliberate attempt to cause misunderstanding, but a 'seeming' which was not itself the truth, but only a suggestion of it – and a suggestion which presented to the observer such beauty, such fulness, that it tempted him to think he had already seen the truth. How does this differ from the old sense

[112] Hegel 1956, p. 393. And so in Peter the Venerable, *De laude*, p. 242: 'Si uis ergo aliquid retribuere sepulto domino, quia pro te iacuit mortuus in sepulchro, esto et tu sepulchrum eius, ut in te non tantum triduo, sed perpetuo maneat et uigeat memoria eius.'

of *mysterium* and *sacramentum*, so marvellously paraphrased by de Lubac? Perhaps it is only a matter of degree. The art is still to see the thing in the sign; but in this fable there has intervened a melancholy, and a scepticism. The inspired movement between thing and sign, sign and thing, is stopped at a certain point, so that the viewer is left, unsatisfactorily, with a picture which is neither one nor the other. He is like the light sleeper whom restlessness awakes again and again, so that his dreams become distant memories. They are neither real nor false. They merely come from somewhere else. They pose riddles.[113]

We could put this slightly differently. In fable, the sign, instead of offering the 'stuff' out of which the thing is made, is made to stand for the thing, but in an attenuated form. The fable thus tells us two things – that there is some truth behind it (perhaps only *just* behind it, almost within grasp); and that this truth cannot be seen. This is also the new sense of *mysterium*: the condescension to appearances of what cannot be perceived – cannot be perceived even in faith, and faith, warned not to reach above its station, now has in it more of suspension of disbelief than active believing. The failure, then, is not only in the perception, but in the representations which are its objects; not only in faith, but in the fable faith looks at.

The fable which holds sway, not just in Peter's Jerusalem, but in the first half (or so) of the twelfth century, is that of completion. What is especially sublime about the Jerusalem which *conscientia* now holds up for admiration is that it is the *end* of the long travail of history. The pallid quiet of the grave has brought to an end the 'labour of restoration'; the dead Christ has 'completed' his thirty-three years of 'being born, preaching, working, suffering, and dying'.[114] Death, which in the perspective of symbol is both an end and a passing over, a *transitus* – an action

---

[113] Ibid., p. 241: 'Haec est igitur sublimis et omnem terrenam altitudinem excedens gloria sepulchri domini, quia in ipso mortuus saluator quiescens, et tartarum, in quem omnes populi terrarum more ualidi torrentis assidue ac certatim ruebant, clausit et facilem omnibus ad caelos ascensum parauit.' On *fabula* in the twelfth century, see Dronke 1974. The image of the light sleeper was suggested to me by David Medalie. He knew it from an essay by Virginia Woolf which takes E. M. Forster to task for being a light sleeper (Woolf 1943, pp. 104–12). The image has helped me a great deal and I would like to thank David Medalie for it.

[114] Peter the Venerable, *De laude*, p. 241: 'septimo die in hoc sepulchro quieuit, quia laborem restaurationis humanae quem per triginta et tres annos nascendo, praedicando, laborando, patiendo, moriendo, exercuit, septima die in sepulchro mortuus quiescendo compleuit'.

and not just an end to action – has become here an enigma of closure, which happens, like all that is finished, elsewhere. In this new perspective, Old and New Testament history, rather than being analogous to the development and education of man – a progression of enlightenment over the seven ages from Creation to the anticipated hour of rest, the 'breast–feeding' of man[115] – as it was for Ivo of Chartres and Hugh of St Victor, was itself a series of deceptive episodes in which the invisible *opus diuinum* might be guessed at, but only guessed at, and whose centre of gravity was not in the mud and the blood of the world but somewhere in the ether – suspended, in other words, between here and there. What is worth knowing about Jonah and the whale, for example, is not that Jonah was swallowed by a whale and taken *down* into the sea and the whale's belly, but that he was, arbitrarily, spewed up intact, and a better man for it.[116]

John of Salisbury said something interesting about the fictional nature of endings: 'Art was established as a kind of finite science of the infinite.'[117] By art he meant the liberal arts of the *triuium* and *quadriuium*: grammar, rhetoric, dialectic, and arithmetic, astronomy, geometry, music. It was almost a commonplace of twelfth-century philosophical thinkers (from William of Conches to Alan of Lille) that the method laid down by the combined discipline of these arts was insufficient to describe its chosen object, namely God. Any exercise in the arts would fall short of the *perfectio cogitationis* to which (nonetheless) they aspired.

The philosopher, said Abelard (after Socrates), did not find wisdom, but looked for it. He would remain a seeker, bent in an attitude of *inuestigatio*. Once, the certainty of miracle had shut the mouth of the garrulous sophist who mistook his own subtlety for the truth (shades of James Joyce's don, whose lawn-mower whispers 'Clever, clever, clever, clever' as it turns across the grass). But miracles are a thing of the past, and the philosopher has only words left with which to defend truth. 'Art' is the philosopher's reticence in the face of the loose talker who mistakes words for the things they are about; and the job of the philosopher is to restrict what he does with words and ideas and images not only by observing the rules of the various arts – although this is of the

---

[115] Ivo of Chartres, *Sermo de sac. neophyt.*, col. 506: 'ille populus tamquam paruulus est lactatus'.
[116] Peter the Venerable, *De laude*, p. 237.
[117] *Metalogicon* 1.11, p. 29. On fictions and endings, Kermode 1967.

utmost importance too – but by observing the general rule which governs them all: that they are what John of Salisbury called a 'finite science of the infinite', a fiction whose bearing on the truth is determined not from within themselves but from the spirit in which they are used – from the 'intention of the users'.[118] The pattern of thinking resembles the intellectual journey by which Abelard denied the existence of universals outside the nouns which named them, but then came to believe that the understanding of universals, resulting as it did from a direct knowledge, through reason, of the created world, could be *related* to the world by acts of interpretation.[119] The arts, and language with its dependency on universals, were for Abelard themselves fables: fictions which appeared from their completeness to be true, but whose truth was deceptive, consisting only in a relation to truth. The philosopher, then, must be wary. For all his good intentions, he will never *quite* say anything true. He must always, like Socrates, mock not only others, but himself – and the *Historia Calamitatum* was surely written to show us (among other things) the philosopher in the act of self-mockery. At the same time, philosophy to Abelard is less the *result* of the philosopher's work than the very capacity for self-mockery – or at least for an ever-vigilant awareness of self-limitation.

Was Abelard entirely out on a limb in this hesitancy? This is a question hard to answer in a word. But we might take Peter the Lombard – no self-mocker to be sure – as an obvious example of apparently straightforward scholastic conduct. This will give us the chance to get back to baptism while we are at it.

A consideration of the fourth book of the Lombard's *Sentences*, distinctions 1–7 (the *Sentences* were written between about 1155 and 1158), shows us a text *about* baptism. Peter distinguishes rigorously intention, in either minister or candidate, from the objective efficacy of baptism. The effect of baptism is to bring remedy to original and personal sin, and to increase the will's resistance to subsequent sinfulness (this increase in the will is *gratia adiutrix*). The grounds of all that the Lombard says on baptism is in a still more basic distinction between *sign* and *cause*. Sacrament is sign, and by this – after Augustine's 'sign is a thing which, out of itself, causes something to come into the mind other than that

[118] Abelard, *Theol. Christ.* 3.3–5, pp. 195–6.   [119] Luscombe 1988.

258

which has effect on the senses'[120] – is meant principally the intellectual operation of seeing a temporary, not a necessary or intrinsic, likeness, between one thing and another. But sacrament is also *sanctificatio*, a making holy. As sanctification, sacrament works by cause and effect. It is a machinery for making holy, or, put a little more gently, a good Samaritan who 'bandages the wounds of original and actual sin'.[121] Everything in the Lombard builds up the sense of an objective efficacy – which can only be spoken *about*, not understood. Circumcision provided a remedy to original sin, but it could not increase strength against sinfulness; it could not make a 'new man', but only brush down the old one. It was insufficient, leaving the just men and women who died before Christ dangling in the 'bosom of Abraham', waiting for his appearance.[122] Reading this, we realize that the entire Old Testament has been drained of that power of ambiguity lent it by the concept of *figura* – no longer is its insufficiency or sufficiency bound up with the perspective of the viewer (the exegete), who because of his privileged position in time knows that the insufficiency is superficial, and that below it lies the constant presence of the *logos*: in the crossing of the Red Sea, said Ivo of Chartres, in an extreme version of the principle of repetition, 'the sanctification of baptism is repeated'.[123] In a way, the Lombard is taking history more seriously, or at any rate treating the passing of time more objectively – something St Bernard also did in this connection.[124]

Attempting to see the past more objectively, St Bernard and

[120] *De doctrina christiana* 2.1.1, p. 32; Peter the Lombard, *Sent.* 4.1.3, p. 233.

[121] Ibid. 4.1.1, p. 231.

[122] Ibid. 4.1.7, p. 236.

[123] Ivo of Chartres, *Sermo de sac. neophyt.*, col. 507: 'et hic repetita est baptismi, per lignum salutiferum consecuti, sanctificatio, nam rubet mare rubrum, rubet et baptismus, Christi sanguine consecratus'.

[124] It would 'shorten the hand of God', writes Bernard in *c.* 1127–8 to Hugh of St Victor, to suppose that God only saved those few among the ancient just who had 'prescience' of Christ (even if one admits that this select band existed). God saved those who were just before he sent his son simply because he had it in his power to do so (Letter 77). Bernard wrote this letter in reply to Hugh, who was concerned about the opinions of 'a certain man'. It is possible that this certain man was Abelard, and section 3 of Bernard's letter (pp. 192–6), denying 'prescience of future things' in the ancients, does seem to attack an Abelardian view. The other opinions attacked (that none of the ancient just are saved, nor those who were ignorant of baptism after the conversation with Nicodemus in John 3), if they were ever thought by Hugh to be Abelard's, are certainly distortions of what he said. See below, pp. 263–6. On this letter and its relation to Abelard, Luscombe 1969, pp. 26 and 184–6.

Peter the Lombard lost the perception that what is known in a later period may already be known beforehand, but differently, less clearly perhaps, or less consciously; and they have replaced this not only with the 'common sense' view (the one familiar to us, that is), that knowledge grows with time – 'the knowledge of spiritual things in the Fathers grew with the growth of times', says Bernard[125] – but more radically with the absoluteness with which they conceive Christ's descent into history. The efficacy of baptism, the power which enables it to do more than just point, but to make holy, coincides with the manner of Christ's coming, which is a coming from *outside* history into history: not a concentration of history into a moment, not even a consummation of history, but a visitation which alters the course of history. It brings 'newness' – something which no one had known before. It carries with it a *completeness* which 'makes good' – that is, it completes man who had until now been incomplete. So, Christ waited as long as he did before coming to 'finish' man, that man should have time to find out for himself that the law, and the mere signs of the Old Testament, were not enough.[126] It was not a new thing to talk about man's incompleteness. A part of the teaching of the equilibrium of man was that to be what he is (in other words, fully man), he must be aware of his own limitations. To be like God, he must know that likeness is not sameness. But now the stress put on the 'break' of Christ's coming by its estrangement from the propaedeutic of Old Testament history – and the derivation of baptism from this 'break' – made man not so much a participant in his own completing, as a witness to it. The sign by which he understood it, and in a sense did it for himself, shrank back (though did not disappear) before the course of cause and effect by which it happened anyway – whatever he thought of it, or intended it to mean.

Yet we might still ask of the Lombard whether his words were meant, or were taken, principally to describe a process of cause and effect, or whether they did not arrogate to themselves the efficacy of sacrament – whether there was not some slippage between the language 'of' sacrament, and language 'about' sacrament, in such a way that the force of sacrament came to lie in the priest's discussion of it rather than only in the doing of it. After all,

---

[125] Letter 77.3.14, p. 195.
[126] *Sent.* 4.2.2, p. 240: 'Christus autem uenire noluit antequam homo de lege naturali et scripta conuinceretur quod neutra iuuare posset.'

the 'cause' at work in baptism – and the other sacraments – is beyond comprehension, and yet it is represented within the confines of the arts, and thus made to seem comprehensible. This ambiguity runs right through the attempt in canon law and the early Sentence literature to make a 'harmonious dissonance' – to arrange the polyphony of 'authorities' who have uttered different, often conflicting statements on a subject in such a way that they speak together in harmony. The skill of this musical exercise tended to draw attention not only to the solutions of these conflicts, but equally if not more to the art of polyphony – to the beauty of the music. So the notion of divine law in Gratian's *Decretum* is tied closely to the harmonious arrangement of the many different laws or 'authorities' which makes up this *concordia discordantium*, to the principle within the discourse. Much the same holds for the Lombard's attempt to 'score' the two conflicting propositions that 'No one who has not been born again in water and the Holy Spirit can enter the kingdom of heaven' (John 3:5), and that 'The heart has only to believe, if we are to be justified; the lips have only to make confession, if we are to be saved' (Rom. 10:10).[127] The *determinatio*, or solution, to this crux, is a simple distinction between the *uirtus sacramenti*, for which the outward form of baptism is not required, but may be fulfilled by martyrdom or desire to be baptized, and outward baptism in water. So far so good; but the question is then raised, what does baptism do for those who are already justified by their will to be baptized? What does it add that the will does not have? Committed as he is to the principle of *cause*, the Lombard cannot answer that baptism in water is an expression of the will that precedes it. Nothing if not honest, he declares obscurely that baptism in water is the cause of the will that precedes it. This is justified by an appeal to the interdependence of sign and cause: 'For [the sacrament] is the sign of everything of which it is the cause.'[128] But this seems difficult to reconcile with the earlier separation of sign and cause, made in order to protect baptism from those who would see it as no more than sign, or as no more than an expression of *conuersio cordis*.

---

[127] Ibid. 4.4.3ff, pp. 255ff. On this crux in other scholastic writings of the twelfth century, Landgraf 1928.

[128] *Sent.* 4.4.7, p. 261. I would like to express my thanks to Prof Marcia Colish, who was kind enough to send me a very full letter on the Lombard's views of baptism, in advance of the publication of her study of his life and thought.

I give this example not to pick a quarrel, but to suggest what is not easy to convey – that the language of the *Sentences* is inadequate to its object, and even that those who used this language were aware of its shortcomings. In this sense, it too is a kind of fable, which is only to say, with John of Salisbury, that it is a 'finite science of the infinite'.

Liturgical symbol is man doing what he is: a making in response to making. He yields to what is there, and makes from it. In baptism, this yielding and making is the yielding will and the active will: the fluency with which Roland accepts what will become of him – a fluency which is neither passive obedience nor personal choice, but both. In this way, liturgy does not set out to tell us anything, but is a doing. The Sentence-writer stood outside this doing, and tried to tell himself what it was. But his words were like photographs, and all he could see were the successive states of a movement, not the movement itself, as in those serial photographs of athletes running which give so poor an impression of what it is to run.

There were some who found a way through the fable of the arts to something like the old robustness – who overcame the disappointment of loss:

> Incomprehensıbilis erat (Deus)
> et inaccessibilis,
> inuisibilis
> et inexcogitabilis omnino
> nunc uero
> comprehendi uoluit
> uideri uoluit,
> cogitari uoluit,
> Quonam modo, inquis?
> Nimirum
> iacens in praesepio
> in uirginali gremio cubans,
> in monte praedicans,
> in oratione pernoctans;
> aut in cruce pendens,
> in morte pallens,
> liber inter mortuos
> et in inferno imperans,
> seu etiam tertia die resurgens
> et apostolis loca clauorum,
> uictoriae signa demonstrans,

nouissime coram eis
caeli secreta conscendens.
Quid horum non uere,
non pie, non sancte cogitatur?
Quicquid horum cogito,
Deum cogito,
et per omnia ipse est Deus meus.

God was beyond my understanding then, inaccessible, invisible, quite unthinkable. But now, He wanted to be understood, wanted to be seen, wanted to be thought. How, you ask. This way, lying in the crib, sleeping in the virgin's lap, preaching on the mountain, praying through the night; or, hanging on the cross, flagging in death, free among the dead and ruling hell, or again, rising on the third day and showing the signs of His victory to the apostles, the holes made by nails, and finally, still among them, climbing the unseen sky. Which of these is not truly thought, respectfully, holily? Whichever of them I think, I think God, and through all things He is my God.[129]

The rhythm of yielding to epiphanies – all of which is contained in the 'through' of this last line – recalls the sleep of the paralytic who since ancient times had passed the night, sometimes many nights, by a shrine of Asclepius or by the tomb of a holy man, and waited for the god or saint to put his bones back in place. It was a deep sleep, untroubled by restlessness.[130]

There were others, though, who slept lightly. Rather than yield, they listened, knowing there was something there, but separated from it by a thin wall.

Abelard, the mocker whose keenness never gave him much peace of mind, unable to stay with anything finished, worked his way backwards, against the swim, from the truth of Incarnation to the shadow not only of the Old Testament, but of all· Antiquity, all those who did not yet know, yet almost knew:

we do not promise to teach the truth, to which, we believe, neither do we suffice nor any mortal, but rather to put forward some resemblance, something nearby human reason but not against holy faith.[131]

[129] Bernard of Clairvaux, *In nat. BMV*, ed., and set out like this in Leclercq 1969, p. 189.
[130] On this practice of incubation, see the examples given in Mallardo 1949. Also, Gessler 1946.
[131] *Theol. Christ.* 3.54, p. 217.

Or:

Whatever we may say of that highest philosophy, we declare to be shadow (*umbra*), not truth (*ueritas*), and a likeness of some kind, not the thing itself.[132]

His preference for likeness over thing is the source of Abelard's compassion for the ancients. This is not the compassion of certainty for those that still have only uncertain knowledge – as, for example, was Bernard's for those souls who did not happen to hear Christ's 'whispering' by night to Nicodemus ('No one who has not been born again of water . . . '), and had the misfortune to die before this message was widely heard.[133] It is the compassion of like for like. Abelard, who comes after the 'successful symbol' of Incarnation, refuses this success, and continues, rigorously, to regard the fable of theology as a fable, as a failure of sight. The shadow in which the ancient philosophers lived was the shadow in which he too lived, and in this way, their truth, which had not yet been completed by revelation, seemed closer to truth than the complacency of his own times.[134]

So it is with the suicide of Diogenes the Cynic – the wittiest and saddest of Abelard's anti-heroes.[135] Diogenes was on his way to the Olympic Games with some friends, when he fell ill with a fever. He lay down at the side of the road. His friends tried to get him on to the back of a mule or a wagon, but he wouldn't let them, and found himself a bit of shade under a tree. 'You go to the Games', he said, 'Tonight either I'll do for the fever or it'll do for me. One way I'll come, the other I'll go to hell.' That night he cut his throat. 'It wasn't quite that I died', says Diogenes in Jerome's version of it, 'more that I got death to see the fever off.' With his theologian's hat on, Abelard disapproves of this, on the grounds that Diogenes has allowed contempt for the world, which must be without passion, to become a passion against the world. Diogenes' mistake, like that of Theobrotus who threw himself off a wall as soon as he read in Plato that the soul was immortal, was that he sought an end where an end was not due. It is not within man's power to make an end. Plotinus had developed this point in a very subtle way. You should not kill yourself, he had said, while life affords you the possibility of bettering yourself. But does it then follow that someone who has purified himself should end his

[132] Ibid. 3.57, p. 218. [133] Letter 77.1.5, pp. 187–8.
[134] On Abelard's 'partial failures, each unique in the way it fails', Dronke 1985, p. 67.
[135] *Theol. Christ.* 2.81–6, pp. 167–70.

life, since there is no room for improvement in him? The answer must be no, because this would be to act out of *hope* for a life of endless perfection, and hope, as much as fear, is a passion. Again, the end is false if it is self-imposed. Man is not sufficient to himself. And yet Abelard's knowledge of God is in the unrelenting demonstration of this inadequacy; and because his knowledge is of this kind, it is those who also fall short whom he most admires and loves. Was Diogenes wrong to do what he did? In its inadequacy it was a noble deed – and was there not, when it comes down to it, the detached humour of *contemptus mundi* in it? – however much it was the theologian's task to *say* that it was inadequate.

Baptism, meanwhile, provided Abelard with a no less apt image of unresolved compassion. Both Bernard and Peter the Lombard point to Ambrose's speech of consolation before the sisters of the dead emperor Valentinian.[136] To them, it is proof of the efficacy of the personal will without physical baptism, for Valentinian had died after sending a message to Ambrose that he wished to be baptized, but before Ambrose got to him. Ambrose had felt able to console the sisters that their brother was safe, but Abelard selected from the words of the speech so as to keep up the possibility that he was not: he stops with the anguish of Valentinian himself, and the grief of Ambrose who is at this point unsure whether he can console:

You thought I would rescue you from dangers. You did more than love me as a parent. You hoped I would redeem you and make you free. You said, 'Do you think I will see my father?' This will you expressed of me had a beauty in it – but anticipation is not good enough. Oh vain hope in man! Woe! Woe is me! Why did I not know this will sooner? Lord, no one has more to give than he wants for himself: do not part me after death from those I have dearest in life. Lord, I ask that 'Where I shall be they shall be with me' [John 17:24]. I ask this, high God, that you breathe life back into these youths [Ambrose is now remembering Gratian, Valentinian's older brother, who had died some years before], raise them up with a mature resurrection, that you make good with this mature resurrection the immature course of this life.[137]

Abelard, on the fate of Valentinian and on that of the pagan philosophers, was 'compelled to diffidence'.[138] But he was diffi-

[136] *Sent.* 4.4.5, p. 256; Bernard, Letter 77.2.7, p. 189.
[137] *Theol. Christ.* 2.114, pp. 183–4; quoting *De obitu Valentiniani* 51–2, PL xvi, col. 1435AB.
[138] *Theol. Christ.* 2.115, p. 184: 'diffidere cogamur'.

dent about them because he was diffident about himself. In his diffidence, precisely because it is so nearly confidence, there is a kind of awe:

> Ich horche immer. Gieb ein kleines Zeichen.
> Ich bin ganz nah.

> Nur eine schmale Wand ist zwischen uns,
> durch Zufall . . .
> (Rilke, *Vom mönchischen Leben*)

> I listen all the time. Give a little sign.
> I am so near.

> Only a thin wall is between us,
> by chance . . .

Excursus I

BAPTISTERY, LITURGY, CITY

In the first excursus, I will try to give some answer to the question why the baptistery remained such an important building in the townscapes of Languedoc, and especially northern Italy, in the twelfth century and after, when in northern Europe most baptisteries had been removed to make way for larger cathedrals. The answer has to do with the relation between liturgical ritual and city ritual. In the second, I will offer an hypothesis of what the inspiration behind a cycle of frescoes in one baptistery might have been. The baptistery is in the small town, once a Roman frontier colony, of Concordia Sagittaria, in Friuli, and a few miles east of Venice. I would like to suggest, in this attempt to trace an inspiration, that the art of this period (of any period, no doubt) is neither principally didactic, nor iconographic.

THE SHAPE OF THE BAPTISTERY

Corpore nam tumulum, mente superna tenet
(Bede, *Hist. Eccles.* 5.7)

It is not known how many baptisteries once stood in or beside the cathedrals of northern Europe. There is archaeological evidence of a baptistery on the Ile de la Cité in Paris, the church of St-Jean-le-Rond a few hundred yards west of Nôtre-Dame; and of others in Nantes, Angers, Nevers and Rouen. All were destroyed to make way for Gothic cathedrals. Only the baptistery at Poitiers, 'a palimpsest of building stages' dating probably from the sixth century onwards, still stands.[1] In the north, the eleventh and

---

[1] On fonts and baptisteries generally, Davies 1962. Khatchatrian 1962 gives groundplans, dates, bibliography for Nantes, Angers, Nevers. All three are sixth or seventh century; Nevers, after restorations in the ninth, tenth and eleventh centuries, was only pulled down in the thirteenth (p. 113, fig. 336). On Rouen, mentioned in the eleventh century, Lasteyrie 1929, p. 697. On St-Jean-le-Rond in Paris, Friedmann 1959, p. 55. On Poitiers,

especially the twelfth centuries were the great period of the creation of parishes. For all the authority of the bishops, religious life was spread over the countryside and, within the town (London is an extreme example), divided into a large number of private or local chapels. Here the history of baptism is the history of fonts, their size reflecting the small scale of the parishes they served.[2]

Things were very different in Italy and Provence. Not only did baptisteries continue to stand; many were restored or built in the eleventh and twelfth centuries. In Provence, baptisteries were rebuilt in this period in Mélas, Riez, Aix-en-Provence, and the baptistery at Fréjus restored in the ninth century. In Italy, the cities of Ascoli Piceno, Asti, Bari in the south, Cremona, Florence, Novara, Padua, Parma, Pisa, Treviso, Verona and Ventimiglia all erected, or restored, baptisteries in the eleventh or twelfth centuries.[3]

Why did old baptisteries stand, and why were new ones built, in Provence and north Italy in the eleventh and twelfth centuries and later? Why did the baptistery matter so much in this Mediterranean hinterland, so little in the north?[4]

To begin with, a simple answer. The baptistery, a centrally planned building forming part of the *campo santo* of the city, situated usually with the cathedral – in Milan there were two cathedrals and two baptisteries until the vast Gothic cathedral was built over all four in the fourteenth century[5] – near the centre of the city, and, more than the cathedral, reminiscent of the architecture of ancient Rome, was the place in which the city in its conflicting parts was resolved into one; it could come to rest in the harmonizing memory of Rome. It was the place where the factions out of which these cities were made, each adhering to its *gentilice* church and withdrawing in the stress of open conflict into its quarter and its defensive tower, found their unifying principle.[6] The baptistery in the city is the white in the middle of the

Claude 1960, p. 10, and endpiece map (the palimpsest is Christopher Brooke's analogy, Brooke 1977, p. 465).

[2] Brooke 1977. On fonts, Bond 1908; Pudelko 1932; and the magnificent colour-plate of the sculpted stone font at Castle Frome (Herefordshire) in Zarnecki, Holt and Holland 1984, p. 65, no. 139.

[3] Cattaneo 1970, on Italy; and for Provence, Février 1954 (with bibliographies). Also Khatchatrian 1962, *passim*.

[4] See n. 40 below.   [5] Angelis d'Ossat 1969.

[6] On the *gentilice* churches and the whole question of clans and factions in Italy and elsewhere, Heers 1974, esp. pp. 225–60.

colour chart in which the grades and sects of colour add up to an absence of colour, or return to the light they began from. In the south, apparently in Provence as well as Italy, the baptistery is a phenomenon of towns, and of a religious culture based on towns.

But this power to resolve did not rest only on the baptistery as an abbreviation of Roman civic architecture. Inscriptions in the baptistery of the Lateran in Rome and the baptistery of Santa Thecla in Milan, as well as the established idea that the baptistery (like other buildings such as Charlemagne's chapel in the palace at Aachen) was a 'copy' of the church of the Holy Sepulchre in Jerusalem, make it clear that the baptistery also bore a liturgical sense of death-and-resurrection and rebirth. The baptistery, we might say, was a reminder of the civic (Roman) past, but a performance of baptismal themes. At this time when the city-commune was struggling to undo itself from the episcopal clench, and so to manoeuvre from an ecclesiastical to a secular polity, it is not hard to see how the baptistery, with this double memory of the secular-Roman and liturgical, might hold centre-stage in the self-conscious topography of the nascent city-state.

In Cremona (admittedly an unusual example), baptistery and cathedral face *palazzo comunale* across the same square:[7] bishop faces commune in a dialectic of the religious and the secular: the dialectic, in fact, from which the communes came into being. In the *exiguum punctum*, the tiny drop, or point,[8] of the baptistery, the same dialectic is resumed in a single structure. Small wonder baptisteries went on being built.

The baptistery is reminiscent of, and may originally have borrowed from, a gamut of Roman buildings.[9] It is the *thermae*, with which it shares the associations of water and bathing: the baptistery at Ostia was built over *thermae*, its font an adapted bath. It is the *fons uitae*, the fountain of life set in a garden, a *locus amoenus* recalling the verdure of a Roman paradise with its abundance of plants, shrubs and birds: this is borne out admirably in the fifth-century baptistery of San Giovanni in fonte in Naples.[10] The baptistery is the triumphal building, the Pantheon. It preserves the association of the dome with the starred sky and

---

[7] On Cremona, Coleman 1987. In Todi, *palazzo comunale* faces the cathedral; on this and other examples, Reggiori 1971.

[8] From the inscription in the baptistery of Sta. Thecla in Milan, given in *DACL* I, col. 1386: for the text, below, n. 15.

[9] For what follows, Khatchatrian 1982.   [10] See Maier 1964.

therefore with military and political power: the *triclinium* (dining hall) of Nero's palace, in which guests were sprinkled with fake rain at dinner, is re-iterated in the gold stars and blue skies of baptistery domes in Naples and Albenga, or of the mausoleum of Galla Placidia in Ravenna.[11] But while these senses had their 'fittingness', recourse to the domed octagon, the circle or the *triconchos* (square or near-square with apses on three sides) for the baptistery from the fourth century onwards seems to have been intended more deliberately as a carrying-over of the Roman mausoleum, the circular, domed burial-chamber typified by the mausoleum of Diocletian at Spalato.[12] It may at the same time have owed something to the Greek *tholos*, another round building, given to the cult of earth and water, and to the possibilities of rebirth which those elements suggested.[13]

So much for the Roman inheritance, of which the effect was probably in the end an unspecified residue in the city's mind of *romanitas*, rather than a catalogue of exact senses. Beside it are the liturgical ideas held fast in the baptistery, above all the two great liturgical ideas of death-and-resurrection and rebirth. The first is already hinted at by the shadow of the mausoleum. Not infrequently, the temporal continuum between pagan place of death and Christian place of birth was concentrated into a single architectural proposition by the use of the *martyrium* – the burial place of the martyr – as a baptistery.[14] In the inscription ascribed by an eighth-century pilgrim to Ambrose, in the baptistery of Santa Thecla in Milan, the perception that birth is a resurrection from death is linked to the eight-sidedness of the baptistery:

He put up the eight-walled temple and set it to holy use. In this gift of eight sides it was only right to put an eight-sided font: and so the hall of the baptized was built in eights, because in it salvation itself made full circle back to its own people, making its way by the light of resurgent Christ, who scatters the cloister of death and lifts from the grave those who have breathed their last breath, and, resolving the repentant guilty

---

[11] Lehmann 1945 argues that the baptistery in this way takes up the ancient tradition, going back at least to the Etruscans, which saw in the dome an image of heaven, and therefore used it to indicate power. Lavin 1962 believes the *triconchos* (central plan with three radiating apses), a form used in the *triclinium* of Maximianus' palace in Piazza Armerina in Sicily (early fourth century) and re-appearing in the west in the Lateran palace and in the chapel of Charlemagne's palace at Ingelheim (eighth century), is associated with imperial power too.

[12] Cf. Krautheimer 1942.   [13] Robert 1939.   [14] Grabar 1946.

of the stain which is their wrongdoing, has washed it to nothing in the irrigation of the clean-streaming fountain. Here, anyone who wants to lay down the wrongs of a misspent life washes his heart. He makes a clean breast. To this place come the zealous; the ungodly ventures too and then turns away whiter than snow. Here hasten saints, and in these waters every saint has been. In them is the kingdom of God's glory and the counsel of his justice. Show me an act more divine than this: that the guilt of a people falls in this tiny drop.[15]

If the baptistery is a relic of the Roman past, it is also, according to this inscription, a place where something happens in the present. It encloses two distinct mental procedures. It 'calls back into the mind' (as Augustine would have put it)[16] the past happening of Rome, but equally it repeats the liturgical idea it signifies. It is a sacrament. The octagon, if we are to take Ambrose (or whoever this is) seriously, is not just a form held in the mind, a geometrical reduction of the city, say, but a shape repeatedly made, in that its sense is re-enacted at each liturgical occasion. Eight is the number of return to the beginning of last week which is also the beginning of the next; as this week is at once the same and more than last week, so resurrection is more than and the same as life.[17] Eight can therefore be used to underwrite, not to say absorb into itself, the theology of Romans 6.3ff, that in baptism resurrection surpasses life by returning to it by way of death. In the inscription this theology is given not in the more abrupt Pauline manner (baptism is burial with Christ, and thus resurrection with him), but by means of the story of Christ's descent into hell to rescue the

---

[15]   Octachorum sanctos templum surrexit in usus,
            octagonus fons est munere dignus eo.
        Hoc numero decuit sacri baptismatis aulam
            surgere, quo populis uera salus rediit
        luce resurgentis Christi, qui claustra resoluit
            mortis et e tumulis suscitat exanimes
        confessosque reos maculoso crimine soluens
            fontis puriflui diluit inriguo.
        Hic, quicumque uolent probrosae crimina uitae
            ponere, corda lauent, pectora munda gerant.
        Huc ueniant alacres: quamuis tenebrosus adire
            audeat, abscedet candidior niuibus.
        Huc sancti properent: non expers ullus aquarum
            sanctus; in his regnum est consiliumque Dei,
        gloriae iustitiae: nam quid diuinius isto,
            ut puncto exiguo culpa cadat populi.
                            (*DACL* I, col. 1386; cf. Dölger 1934)

[16] *Ep.* 55.1, cols. 204–5: 'in memoriam reuocari'. See above, p. 90 and ff.
[17] Talley 1986 on this principle in the formation of the Christian week.

just (the *confessos reos*, the penitent guilty) from death – the story which in Byzantine art was by this time the usual idiom for the resurrection.[18] The story makes an interlude of narrative between the imponderables of death and resurrection. It is a relief to know what was going on in the three days between, and something about how the first is connected with the third. But the story is the occasion of a pun too. The *tumulus* of the grave, out of which the dead are lifted, is the sepulchre of the baptistery itself. The shape of the baptistery, its *mira rotunditas*, is a fulness. But it has this shape because it is built in the same gesture as the gesture with which Christ pulls out the dead – and the gestures are brought together in another pun: the *templum surrexit* of the first line ('He raised up the temple') is the resurrection of the later *resurgens Christus*, and of the raising of the dead, *suscitat exanimes*. The neophyte is the beneficiary of this gesture. Standing in the 'tiny drop' of the font, he is pulled out of the grave. But the gesture is also the 'gesture' of building: *templum surrexit*.

The inscription in Santa Thecla is thus composed round an analogy between sacrament and building. In it, the building becomes a sacrament. Another prelate of Milan, Benedictus Crispus, wrote this inscription for the tomb of Caedwalla, King of the West Saxons (d. 689):

Corpore nam tumulum, mente superna tenet.

With his body he holds a burial mound, with his mind eternity.[19]

It is Caedwalla who is stretched between the chthonic and the astral in this way; but could the same not be said of the building he lies in? The inscription, like the building, is not as inactive as it looks. Its surface is smooth, but beneath it, as beneath the 'face' of the baptismal water (which is no longer the 'living water') or beneath the 'veil' which covers the bones of a saint, a lot is going on. In about 403, Paulinus of Nola suggested this inscription for the baptistery which Sulpicius Severus had recently completed near Agen in south-west France:

HIC REPARANDARVM GENERATOR FONS ANIMARVM
VIVVM DIVINO LVMINE AGIT

---

[18] Kartsonis 1986.
[19] Bede, *Hist. Eccles.* 5.7, p. 472. Also see Plummer's commentary in his edition, II, pp. 278ff.

SANCTVS IN HVNC CAELO DESCENDIT SPIRITVS AMNEM
  CAELESTIQVE SACRAS FONTE MARITAT AQVAS
CONCIPIT VNDA DEVM SANCTAMQVE LIQVORIBVS ALMIS
  EDIT AB AETERNO SEMINE PROGENIEM
MIRA DEI PIETAS PECCATOR MERGITVR VNDIS
  MOX EADEM EMERGIT IVSTIFICATVS AQVA
SIC HOMO ET OCCASV FELICI FVNCTVS ET ORTV
  TERRENIS MORITVR PERPETVIS ORITVR
CVLPA PERIT SED VITA REDIT VETVS INTERIT ADAM
  ET NOVVS AETERNIS NASCITVR IMPERIIS.[20]

Here the birth-giving spring of souls to be restored pushes the river alive with divine light. Down into the pool comes the Holy Spirit from heaven and marries the holy waters to the heavenly spring. The flow conceives God and in these maternal waters God's beneficence brings forth a holy progeny from the eternal seed. Wonderful is the goodness of God. The sinner is immersed in the waves, and soon emerges from the same water justified. So it is that man undergoes a happy fall and rises from it; dies to the things of the world, and rises to things everlasting. Blame perishes, but life returns; the old Adam is buried and the new is born to eternal empires.

One has only to pick out the rapid succession of verbs describing present action to see just how much is going on: the flowing out and back, the rushing down and joining, the conceiving, immersing, emerging, dying, rising, perishing, returning, burying, being born (*agit–descendit–maritat–concipit–mergitur–emergit–moritur–oritur–perit–redit–interit–nascitur*), all of them things done in the water or by the water. The assonance of the verbs is accompanied by a kind of assonance of the 'many waters' in this eulogy (*fons–amnis–aqua–unda–liquores*), and an assonance of theologies – which are, however, centred on the stunning affirmation: *Concipit unda deum*, the water conceives God, in other words the theology (also Leo's and that of the inscription in the Lateran baptistery) of baptism stemming from the Nativity. Under the placid face of the inscription, there is a turbulence of ideas and water.

  Like the inscription on its facade, the baptistery is itself active. It is not an idea, a product of the mind – *cosa mentale* – carried over into a physical substance. It is not a temporary 'victory of Idea

---

[20] Le Blant 1865, p. 390. For the notion of the altar holding relics as a 'veil', see ibid., p. 394: 'Pignora sanctorum diuinae gloria mensae / Velat apostolicis edita corporibus.'

over matter', as Plotinus might have thought of it, a rupture in the normal state of things in which the world of forms briefly and uncharacteristically overcomes its antipathy for the material world.[21] It is rather an inter-penetration of idea, or the thought which sees idea, and matter, or the perception which apprehends matter. Death-and-resurrection is not on the one hand an abstraction from past happening, or on the other a mere recognition that an event did happen; it is equally an idea of the happening and what happened. Liturgy bears this out by being at once word and thing, the abstractness of form and the concreteness of bread and water and body; a reflection on bread and water or on the body of a child, as well as an eating, a drinking, a nurturing. This complicity of word and thing, by which liturgy is always doing something and not just saying it, is what is meant by performance. The baptistery performs because in the same way it binds thought with perception (by perception here I mean direct apprehension of a thing), idea with thing. It is this too which makes it a shape and not a form: instead of being a form (an octagon, a hexagon, a circle) which matter has been made to obey, it is a coincidence of form and matter which addresses the senses as much as the mind, or addresses that part of the mind which is caught up in the senses, its power of intuition.[22] The difference between this way of seeing and that of the Greeks, or at least of the Platonic tradition, is that its energy is engaged in bringing together the poles of idea and matter, not in pushing them apart; and yet the conception that they are two poles is essential to the whole exercise of epiclesis:

Show me an act more divine than this: that the guilt of a people falls in this tiny drop (*exiguum punctum*).[23]

The baptistery is big with grace. If this is distinct from Plotinus' view of what the artist could do (make matter momentarily obey form), it is different too from the Renaissance objectification of Nature, which was the first step in the Renaissance project to idealize Nature.[24]

We get a closer look at the baptistery as shape if we think again how mausolea were not infrequently used as baptisteries, so that the 'idea' of death-and-resurrection was performed in the physical

---

[21] Panofsky 1968, pp. 25ff.   [22] See above, pp. 155ff.
[23] *DACL* I, col. 1386.   [24] Panofsky 1968, pp. 47ff.

fact of the saint's remains; the eternity of his existence brought into line with the perishable bone he left behind. The baptistery, from this aspect, is an oversize reliquary, and with the same regenerative power. We see the compulsion of shape again in the phenomenon remarked by Richard Krautheimer in his study of architectural 'copies' in the early Middle Ages: the baptistery – as well as many other centrally planned buildings – can in certain cases be shown to have been a copy of the basilica of the Holy Sepulchre in Jerusalem (built in the early seventh century and then again in the eleventh, over the rock-cave which was the supposed site of Christ's tomb).[25] The early twelfth-century baptistery in Pisa, for example, copied the Holy Sepulchre, but not in the obvious sense that it had the same size, form, ornament and so on; the same measurements and proportions. It repeated the shape not exactly (which would have been to draw attention only to the outward appearance of the building), but with reference to what the building did, as an embodiment of death-and-resurrection; to the effect the building had both as a tomb generally, and as the particular tomb of the God-man; and to the abiding perception, fed by pilgrimage and then crusade, of the centrality of Jerusalem. In the art which depicts Jerusalem – a genre unto itself – the effort to state the psychological force of this central place towards which all other places must be bent is apparent: in its representations, Jerusalem is the place of ultimate Judgement, of apostolic authority, of fertility and, perhaps more than anything, of preciousness.[26] From the outside, this is what is visible, as in the reliquary; often in the art of this time, the artist and the patron attempt to translate the presence of the holy into the preciousness of gems, an impulse which quickens to something like an obsession in Suger.[27] It was in this spirit of the vagueness of forms, or of shapes, that Gregory of Nyssa could call an octagon a 'circle with eight angles'.[28] He knew the difference between an octagon and a circle, but he was more interested in their shared sense of eternal return. So it did not matter at all (for example) that a copy of the Holy Sepulchre in Paderborn, made in 1036, was octagonal while the Holy Sepulchre itself was at this time

[25] Krautheimer 1942.
[26] Rev. 21:2ff: 'et ciuitatem sanctam Hierusalem nouam uidi descendentem de caelo a deo paratum sicut sponsam ornatam uiro suo et audiui uocem magnam de throno dicentem ecce tabernaculum Dei cum hominibus'.
[27] *De admin.*, passim.   [28] Cited by Krautheimer 1942, p. 119.

circular.[29] Their performance was the same. As the Chinese painter said, 'it is not given to everyone to achieve an absence of likeness'.

The baptistery, however, did more than one thing. It was more than the place of death-and-resurrection. The inscription of the Lateran baptistery in Rome, put there by Sixtus III (432–40) but expressing the theology of Leo the Great, rehearses with a solemn economy which anticipates the later documents of the Roman liturgy the notion that baptism is a rebirth. Implied in the wording are two further precisions: that this rebirth is also the birth of Christ of the Virgin (baptism is Christmas, to put it bluntly); and that the 'font of life' (*fons uitae*) which is the source of all this fecundity (Christmas-birth and baptism-birth) is the water issuing from Christ's side at the crucifixion:

[They are] conceived by the breath of God, and born, fruit of a virgin, when birth-giving Church brings them from her waters [fourth distich]. This is the font of life, which has washed the world, taking its beginning from Christ's wound [seventh distich].[30]

Rebirth and death/resurrection might seem too close to quibble over; yet the Lateran inscription (twelve distichs altogether) has a quite different emphasis from the one in Milan. Instead of the circularity of the octagon, it is the theme of the river and its source which dominates; instead of repetition of a seminal event (Christ's death/resurrection), continuity from a seminal event (Christ's birth of a Virgin). In the north, two Carolingian manuscripts, the Godescalc Lectionary and the Gospel Book of St Médard de Soissons, in order to depict the *fons uitae*, simply show the structure – eight columns linked by arches and supporting a canopy – which surrounds the font of the Lateran Baptistery.[31] Invoking the Lateran in this way, they invoke (in the Godescalc Lectionary explicitly, by direct reference to the passage in Matt.

---

[29] Ibid., pp. 117ff.
[30] Dölger 1930, p. 253:

> Virgineo faetu genitrix ecclesia natos,
> quos spirante deo concipit, amne parit ...
> Fons hic est uitae, qui totum diluit orbem
> sumens de Christi uulnere principium.

See Dölger's comments on pp. 252–7 for attribution to Leo, etc.
[31] For what follows, Underwood 1950.

1:18–21 mentioning the virgin conception of Christ) the theology of the inscription in the Lateran: that is, the idea that baptism stems from the conception and birth of Christ. Both these Carolingian manuscripts place this illustration of the *fons uitae* at the opening, before the canon tables which denote the correspondence between passages of the four Gospels according to subject-matter. This arrangement makes the book itself into a miniature performance of idea: the twofold idea (as Rabanus Maurus, Abbot of Fulda, put it) that: 'The river issuing from paradise [cf. Gen. 2:4–17; esp. 2:6; 2:10] carries the image of Christ flowing from the Father his source, irrigating his church with the word of his preaching and with the gift of baptism . . . Again, allegorically [that] the four rivers of paradise are the four Gospels sent out to preach to all peoples.'[32] By introducing the canon tables with the 'fountain of life', these books suggest that the four Gospels (conceived of as a symphony of corresponding parts) are at the head of the rivers of preaching just as Christ's birth is the headwater of baptism.

I have gone into this because the Carolingian manuscripts offer a clear interpretation of the Lateran and its theology, and therefore illustrate another possible enactment performed by the baptistery. The baptistery is the source, a measured space like the temple of Solomon or the canon tables themselves, from which all else devolves. In liturgy as in music, however, themes intertwine. The seventh distich of the Lateran inscription sees the 'beginning' not as the Virgin Birth but as the water flowing from Christ's pierced side:

This is the font of life, which has washed the world, taking its beginning from Christ's wound.

I have discussed above, in the context of martyrdom, the psychological inter-dependency of death/resurrection and

---

[32] *Comm. in Genesim, PL* cvii, col. 479C, quoted by Underwood 1950, p. 48. It is tempting in the light of this passage to see Christ as the river and the river as Christ in the miniature of the Baptism of Christ in the *Fulda Sacramentary*, fo. 19r: the Jordan sweeps past the naked Christ, running from top right to bottom left of the frame, with a vigour which gives it as much life as the two figures (Christ and John). Also see Bede, *Expositio Actuum apostolorum* 1.16, pp. 11–12, on baptism as the out-flowing from the plenitude which is Christ; and it is worth noting in this context that the fonts of Castle Frome in Herefordshire, and Cividale (Friuli, Italy), bear sculpted depictions of the eagle, the lion, the bull, the man, to denote the evangelists (Castle Frome: illustration in Zarnecki, Holt and Holland 1984, p. 65; Cividale, description in De Rubeis 1754, pp. 377–8).

rebirth.[33] The Lateran inscription, and the rather intricate use it is put to by the Carolingian manuscripts, demonstrate something different. They suggest how the performance of the two themes, their arrangement in a 'musical' counterpoint, is integral to their combined effect. As in music, two 'melodies' (or more) can be heard at once, in such a way that although they are not the same, they have become inseparable. As the interwoven melodies of a piece of music catch to themselves the ear of the listener, so the themes of liturgy come together in a single sound, and invite their audience to make what they can of them. What music does with sound, liturgy does with its themes. They each, in their way, draw in their audiences by putting before them a puzzling combination; and this power of liturgy to draw into itself becomes clearer with the study of the paintings which accompany it. In this, liturgy is like music; but it also is music, for liturgy is, itself, sound. It is the word and song which can be heard (and all liturgical prayer is song, regulated by modulations of the voice, chanted in fact), as well as the gesture which can be seen. As sound and sight, music and theatre, liturgy again weaves themes together. Now it draws in its congregation by appealing less to the mind than to the senses. Addressing the eye and ear (like opera which is a parody of liturgy), liturgy never quite articulates its thought. It is never *logos*, but remains a texture in the fabric of the senses. It is thought constantly pulled back towards its beginning in sensation. The result, at least at this level of perception, is a *vagueness* in the themes; they are sentiments more than hard-edged thoughts. But there is a third level, neither music-like nor musical, at which themes are bound together, this time not over a duration as in the musical and theatrical and story-telling aspect of the rite, but by being refined into a small space and into an instant, into the *exiguum punctum*. The many themes (I have mentioned two here, but there are always more) come together in the ambiguity of a single thing, in this case the baptistery, but equally the matter of water, say, or – perhaps most of all – the figure of a saint, immobile and quiet, but resounding with the senses it has absorbed from the gaze of the one who looks at it. To get the impression of the multiplicity of sense resting in one limited place, there is perhaps nothing better than leafing through the undergrowth of benedictions in Franz's *Die kirchlichen Benediktionen* where, in example

---

[33] Above, pp. 78ff.

1 The woman, the dragon and the child (Rev. 12:1ff); wall-painting,
baptistery, Novara

after example, grace descends into wells, fields, houses, beds,
cheeses, wines, animal carcases, and so on.[34] This sudden convul-
sion of the spirit is what epiclesis is.

The baptistery is the octagon of death and beyond death, and
the fertile flood emanating from the Virgin Birth: tomb and
womb. These are the *leitmotifs*. The origins of the baptistery in
Greek and Roman architecture, the iconography of baptistery art,
as well as inscriptions in baptisteries, are evidence of other, minor
themes. In the baptistery of Novara, on the Lombard plain, a
series of eight scenes was painted, in the tenth century, on the
octagonal drum (the section between the domed roof and the
lower structure of the building).[35] There is one painting on each
face of the drum. Seven of the frescoes depict the lethal effects

[34] Franz 1909.   [35] Wettstein 1971, pp. 3–56, with plates.

which follow the seven trumpet-blasts of the angels of the Apocalypse (Rev. 8:3–9:14): the devastation of hail, and fire mingled with blood; a mountain in flames falling into the sea; a star falling from heaven and embittering the waters of the earth; the cursing of a third part of the heavens with darkness; a second falling star which splits open the abyss and lets out a swarm of stinging locusts; the four horsemen with their murdering armies; and the passing of the power of judgement to 'the Lord of us all, and to Christ his anointed'. On the eighth panel is the 'woman that wore the sun for her mantle' (cf. Rev. 12:1ff) (see Ill. 1). She gives birth, in great pain, to a male child who is 'caught up to God' and snatched away from the dragon which threatens to swallow him. There is a resonance in the woman who gives birth of the Lateran motif of rebirth. Commentaries on the Apocalypse made the assumption that the child was the Christ-child, and the woman the Virgin, so that this apocalyptic birth was the birth of the baptized from the womb of the church, which happens not once but (as the tenth-century commentary of Berengaudius puts it) daily, in other words, again and again in baptism.[36] But the accent in these frescoes is elsewhere. What is brought to the fore is the context of birth in danger, the drama of threat to the child. What is being performed – in a manner obvious to anyone, not just the theologians – is the threat involved in passing from birth to rebirth; the precariousness of this snatching up in the nick of time; the idea that judgement is not so much a segregation of souls to heaven and hell, but more a passage, which must be undergone, from pain and punishment to bliss, or perhaps from sin to grace. What do the frescoes *mean*? That in baptism as in the Apocalypse, the neophyte undergoes a painful passage. But the iconography, the explicit meaning which is supposed to make pictures the means of teaching those who cannot understand the written or spoken word of Latin, is less important than the emotional effect, here the prevailing mood of threat; and it is this which makes the pictures in Novara baptismal. A similar mood, a mingling of fear and relief, is painted not as a *transitus* but as a single moment in the Anastasis at Torcello (late tenth/early eleventh century);[37] the

---

[36] The source for these paintings is more likely to have been the presence of Revelation in the liturgy (see below, pp. 310–19) than any particular commentary; but see Mauck 1975, maintaining that the pictures come from a reading of the commentary of Berengaudius.

[37] Kartsonis 1986, pp. 221ff.

Anastasis (resurrection) here combines the rescue of the just from hell with the Last Judgement. This great painting of the end of time when judgement is made conveys finality by freezing the turbulence of the event – the division once and for all between heaven and hell – on to the one flat plane of the west wall of the church as though photographically. On the other side of this wall, it seems, was the baptistery of Torcello, so that here again, baptism is juxtaposed with judgement. Whether it appears as a process from one state to another, a rite of passage, or as a single instant, the mood of these paintings does away with the distinction between what is represented and the perception which gives it force. What is seen 'up there' on the wall is what is already known from experience. Its effect is from mood as much as from what is depicted.

This power to address, whereby a picture or a building involves an onlooker in its sense – and is not content only to inform – is a feature of all great works of art, and many not so great. In painting, this power, although it may be enhanced by the subject-matter, is at root a power of abstraction, having more to do with colour, tone, line, form, than with the identity or the particular narrative progression of the figures. Architecture, as is often said, is already abstract in its nature. It would be possible to compare the moods, in this sense, of the mosaic or fresco cycles in other baptisteries: the wide open spaces, suggesting the absence which follows Christ's apotheosis, in the baptisteries of the Arians and Orthodox in Ravenna;[38] or the astonishing conflict, in the late fifth-century baptistery of San Giovanni in fonte in Naples (attached to the cathedral of San Gennaro), between the abstraction of the pervasive blue – the colour of the last things – and the almost ponderous corporeal presence, typical in Late Antique mosaic, of the figures in the episodes in the dome: the Samaritan woman at the well; Peter on the water; the miraculous catch of fish, and others.[39]

The meaning of the mosaics in Naples, the ground-bass as it were, is the saving works of Christ in relation to baptism (most of the scenes involve water). But the meaning is enacted, and taken inward, in the antinomy of weightless colour (the blue of distant heaven), and the heavy Biblical figures. The ambiguity of mood

[38] Deichmann 1958.   [39] Maier 1964.

goes on somewhere beneath the level of straight meaning, making meaning itself secondary, an initial stage of less potency.

THE BAPTISTERY IN THE CITY

The conception of the baptistery as the place where liturgical senses are concentrated in an *exiguum punctum* would have been sustained in northern Italy and Provence by the custom that the people of the city and the *contado* (the surrounding country) should come together for the baptism of children at Easter and Pentecost. In England and the continent from Carolingian times, the tendency had been to make children safe by having them baptized shortly after birth. Thereby hangs a history all its own: the short delay before baptism was no doubt partly a result of the multiplication of small parishes in northern Europe, which made seasonal baptism by the bishop seem an unnecessary pomp, and one which given the size of dioceses would have been difficult for most people to get to. It was practical that baptism should be done by a priest locally, and that the bishop's part should be reserved to confirmation.[40] Was it also a greater feeling of urgency in Germanic and Frankish Christendom which made for early baptism, an urgency grown out of a darker religious consciousness? Did the religion of fear for which the Catholic Middle Ages has been notorious strike less deep among those who lived by the Mediterranean, whose paganism had been less thunderous and nihilistic and who were more given to melancholy than fear? Whatever they had in their heads, the people of Provence and north Italy persisted in their baptismal descent on the city at the appointed seasons, and for this they needed their baptisteries.[41]

But there was something else too. The convergence was also a

[40] Fisher 1965 for these developments.

[41] Février 1954, concerned mainly with the possible baptistery at Venasque, gives evidence from archaeological excavation and from liturgical manuscripts of continuing seasonal baptism in Provence. But M. Février (to whom I am grateful for his readiness to help in this), tells me in a letter (about 1982), that he no longer thinks this four-lobed building in Venasque can safely be called a baptistery. The 'font', it turns out, is an addition of the nineteenth century. The evidence for a liturgical type, again with a tendency towards seasonal baptism into the thirteenth century, stretching from the diocese of Narbonne into Catalonia, is given very fully by Gros 1975. For north Italy, see the collection of services of the eleventh century edited by Lambot, which he associates with Grado, Pavia, or Brescia. For the rite of Aquileia, Quarino 1967; De Rubeis 1754, pp. 236ff. For Milan, Cattaneo 1954.

convergence of citizens. From the vagueness and psychological depth of liturgy there began to emerge an outward and civic ritual. It was as if the *palazzo comunale* in Cremona, instead of being just another building across the square, had somehow detached itself from the liturgical complex of cathedral and baptistery opposite, but without being able to free itself entirely. The baptistery, however, contains this ambiguity in itself: for it makes unmistakable reference, in the centre of the city, to Ancient Rome, and so to the source of *ciuilitas humana*.

Very often, it was by a recollection of Ancient Rome that the burgeoning cities of Europe in this age defined themselves. But the fact that they also depicted Jerusalem on their seals suggests it was not only the pagan political past they were remembering. The truly creative step taken in the development of a town is not the conglomeration of buildings, the density of population or the draughting of an urban charter, but rather the idea among its citizens that what they live in is indeed a town;[42] that they are not just a group of people, but a certain group of people within certain walls, with certain customs consciously ratified, and above all distinct from the population of the surrounding countryside. When they see themselves on their seals or in paintings, or simply think of themselves as inhabitants in a second Rome or Jerusalem, they express their urbanity through an objective ideal of the town: Rome or Jerusalem. The same process occurs time and again in Trecento and Quattrocento painting, where the city is an organized assembly of planes and corners, a measured and gracious space, divided by its outer walls from what sometimes looks like a most unruly *contado*. Nothing brings out this theme like the tale of John the Baptist going out (from the town) into the wilderness. A painting by Giovanni di Paolo (active 1420) in the National Gallery in London shows him making off into a landscape of twisted, angry mountains, leaving behind a city of obedient angles. The striking thing in all this is its self-consciousness. In such representations, the town-dwellers made an object of their own unity by making it small enough to be seen at a glance, and by exaggerating its geometry and confinement.[43]

In the crucial time of the foundation of the city-states, the eleventh and twelfth centuries, the baptistery was well placed to act as an architectural reduction and objectification along the same

[42] Rosser 1990.   [43] Puppi 1982.

lines. A theological myth, it gave the elements of a myth of *civiltà*. It was in the centre of the town, or near enough, at a time when the topography of a town reflected accurately its interests. We must see the baptistery as part of this history of 'placing and dedication', *ubicazione e dedicazione*, in the Italian town, which is much more than a history of town-planning.[44] Even in the city, which has erected a *piazza* over rock and spring, memories of an older sense of place can break to the surface. The *Liber Pergaminus*, a celebration of the city of Bergamo probably written in the 1130s by Mosè de Brolo, devotes a long digression to the praise of the water-springs on which the city stands.[45] Especially clear and fresh is the spring of Vasine, whose water, instead of becoming wine, will 'correct' the taste of any wine to which it is added. Over the spring a colonnade and arches have been built. The elegant verses make their panegyric to this hidden source of the city, trembling beneath the marble. The baptistery is another such *fons uitae*, around which the whole city is built. Naturally, the effect of this is the greater when the patron of the city – that other half-hidden source of *civiltà* – is also the patron of the baptistery, as at Florence. Here in Florence, the movement by which the saint becomes a figure of civic *virtù*, as it were, takes place in the baptistery – 'il mio bel San Giovanni', as Dante called it.

Civiltà is an abstraction – though none the less forceful for that. It is an abstraction of attitude and, as we know later from Castiglione, of gesture and posture. It is an art made possible by an idealizing conception of the city. The perfection of the civic form was for Vitruvius the octagon, each of its sides facing one of the eight winds, its streets along the axial lines.[46] Whether or not we should trace some connecting thread in the conscious or unconscious architectural mind between Vitruvius and the Middle Ages (copies of Vitruvius' plans are not rare in the early Middle Ages), there can be no doubt of the idealism vested in the baptistery by its recollection of the 'startling rotundity' of the Holy

---

[44] Violante and Fonseca 1964; and Brooke 1977.

[45] Lines 209–62. At lines 213ff: 'Fons erat in medio gelidus uisuque uenustus, / nec lune radiis nec lampade solis adustus; / marmoreis igitur scalis per concaua jactis / fornicibusque super firmis summopere tractis, / tramite cliuoso fontem traxere per ima / uallis, ad Arctoum rugoso frigore clima.'

[46] See Rosenau 1983, pp. 16ff. It is Arculf who calls the Holy Sepulchre *mira rotunditas*: Adamnanus, *De locis sanctis* 1.2, pp. 42–3.

Sepulchre in Jerusalem. But the liturgical memory (of death and resurrection, rebirth, and so forth), has now been appropriated by the spirit of *civiltà*, and transmuted into a civic memorial.

Nowhere is this clearer than in Pisa, where the new cathedral, baptistery and (late in the twelfth century) the *torre pendente*, the leaning tower, and then later still a cloister and other buildings, were all built on the same divine complex.[47] This Piazza de' Miracoli commemorated the victory at sea, in the 1060s, of a Pisan over a Muslim fleet, to which the citizens dated the beginning of their prosperity. As the building went on, supervised by a *capitolo* of twelve canons of the cathedral and a lay *operaio* elected by them to oversee the work on the ground, other events occurred, and, naturally, stuck to the buildings as memories. The *capitolo*, meanwhile, was vigorously independent of the bishop – when they refused him membership, he excommunicated them all – and turned its face towards the lay population by way of a society formed from those who made regular contributions to the *opera*: the *conuersi* as they were called. Civic memory took over liturgical memory: the baptistery, a repetition (as Richard Krautheimer has shown)[48] of the Holy Sepulchre, served, besides other things, to recall the part of Pisa in the sack of Jerusalem in the first crusade.

When Pisa made its *campo santo*, it had two distinct things in mind. It was building a shape, in the case of the baptistery the womb-tomb where God was buried and returned to life; and it was building the ideal, objective form in which the city could regard itself. As a shape, it was cavernous and vague, in the way of tombs and wombs. The memory it called up was one which when put into words had a way of sinking back to where it had come from. As a form, it presented a definite outline attached to the happy recollection of successes in commerce and battle. The accessibility of this second memory made it a kind of liberation from the vagueness of shape; in Dante, this movement of liberation is brought about by a resolute separation of the civic from the ecclesiastical. *Imperiatus*, he maintained, the government of man-in-the-world, is to be independent of *papatus*, the rule of man in his capacity for eternity. It was not just political pragma-

47 For what follows, Smith 1975.
48 Krautheimer 1942, pp. 139–40 and *passim*.

285

tism which lay behind this kind of thinking, a need to find some way out of the quarrel between emperor and pope which so divided the cities of Dante's day. *Imperiatus* and *papatus* were to lead man in the journey towards two goals, to the earthly perfection which lay within reach of man as man, man in his civic capacity; and to the eternal perfection which he could only reach with the help of grace. With some exaggeration (admittedly), Ernst Kantorowicz urges that Dante, in his *Purgatorio*, expressed this separation of the humanist from the divine potential in man by an allegory; and the allegory, he thought, was drawn mainly from the rite of baptism.[49] By this reading, there lies beneath Dante's account of purgatory – beneath purgatory in the accepted sense of a purification which makes possible entry into celestial paradise – a 'civic' purgatory whose purification is the education of man in the moral, rather than the theological, virtues. This purgatory leads man not to the celestial paradise, which would require grace, but back to the earthly paradise of Eden. Instead of charting the gradual ascent from human to Christ's justice, Dante's intention is to depict the return of man to his first innocence, and to show how this is the innocence of the good humanist; and he turns (says Kantorowicz) to the Lenten rites of baptism – the seasonal baptism still practised in north Italy in Dante's time – for the content of this process of a purifying education. The seven terraces of purgatory at each of which one of the seven deadly sins is scoured away and replaced by its contrary virtue – pride, envy, anger, sloth, avarice, gluttony and lust, by humility, kindness, gentleness, zeal, generosity, temperance and chastity – would thus be founded on the seven scrutinies by which the candidate is prepared for baptism (and these, indeed, went back to those tests of moral probity which were the basis for education towards baptism in Hippolytus).[50] The structure of Dante's *Purgatory* is, in other words, baptismal, and so – to put it rather crudely – the poet has made the liturgy into an allegory of *civiltà*: the innocence of the baptized child stands for the order of the well-governed city.

This is neat, all too neat. Dante began as an allegorist, parading ideas in costumes to show their beauty; but when he came to write the *Comedy*, he had turned to the use of symbol: Vergil, for

[49] Kantorowicz 1957, pp. 451–95. See Dante, *De Mon.* 3. 11. .10–12.
[50] Above, pp. 9–20.

example, is a symbol; not a fiction made to personify human reason or paganism, but a character in history and with his own history.[51] In this usage, which allows idea and thing to inhere in one another – as we have said for the very different use of symbol in sacrament – grace and human will (or human reason, or virtue) run together. There is no separation by which one is used to mean the other, but a concomitance in which one is always discovered in the other. Against this background, if baptism makes an appearance in Dante's *Purgatory*, as a means to express the structure of purification, it is because baptism is at once the return to Eden which lies within man's own grasp, and the ascent to God's heaven which does not. If baptism is there – and it is certainly there in some form, as we know from the opening *canto* of the *Purgatory*, where the association of purifying dew and dawn-light on Easter Sunday morning make it unmistakable – it is there like everything else in the *Comedy*, to re-connect grace with the life of virtue. This optimist's purgatory depicts both the education of man's innate faculties and the shaping of him in God's fingers; it is the ascent from one to the other which this *both-and* makes possible.

Does not the *piazza* at Cremona, where cathedral and baptistery face *palazzo comunale* from opposite sides, teach the same lesson of connectedness rather than separation? Do not the buildings of the *campo santo* and those of the commune, once they have been separated, begin to lean towards one another? The rituals of the city – the processions which were no doubt as important as the architecture itself in enabling the citizens to define the limits of their city, to emphasize the importance of some parts over others, even to make something like a moving picture of the city – continued, after all, to be liturgical rituals. And if we say that in the twelfth century the city became a city by drawing back from the church, should we not also say that, conversely, the piety of the thirteenth and fourteenth centuries found its purest expression in a predominantly secular art: secular not in subject-matter so much as in method, in its reliance on the civic accomplishments of measurement, proportion, perspective and of 'problem-solving'?[52]

---

[51] On this, Foster 1957, pp. 15ff, where the shift from allegory to symbol is located very precisely within Dante's *Canzone, Le Tre Donne*.
[52] See Baxandall 1972. On problem-solving as the drive behind the Renaissance idea of progress in art, and even behind art generally, Gombrich 1966.

Liturgy makes the 'once upon a time' of Old Testament and New Testament into the 'now' of performance because it is anchored in the timeless experiences of death-and-resurrection and rebirth (among others). It is not to say that all intimation of this is lost to observe that the commune borrows from liturgy its superficial features: the performance which involves all of man, all his capacity for understanding, becomes a show; a *spectacle* to behold. The report given by Beroldus of Milan, which tells us how baptism would have been celebrated in Milan in the twelfth century, with its inter-leaving of spectacle and symbol, might make us wonder how much that work of art which was the Italian city-state owed to liturgy:[53] on the afternoon of Easter Saturday, after the Easter candle had been lit by the new fire in the summer church of Santa Thecla, Beroldus tells us, and carried by a priest of San Sepolcro to the winter church of Santa Maria Maggiore, and when the *Exultet* blessing of the wax had been read from its roll over a second candle, the archbishop, the deacons, and the subdeacons retired to put on their ceremonial vestments, before leaving in procession for the 'baptismal church', the baptistery of San Giovanni, next to the winter church of Santa Thecla. The archbishop walked behind two deacons who carried two candelabra, the candles lit from the wax blessed a few minutes earlier. They in turn walked behind two subdeacons, one carrying a thurible with incense, the other a burning lamp. Singing the antiphon *Exsurge, quare obdormis*, the procession arrived at the baptistery, where the bishop removed his dalmatic and stole, and put on a 'baptismal cloak',[54] and round his midriff a towel and belt, knotted so that part of it hung down like a sword. The knots of the leather straps on his sandals he then tied into a shape which made them resemble spurs. His mitre was still on his head, and the effect of it all, says Beroldus, was to make the archbishop seem both a king and a pontiff. In the procession from the summer to the winter church and then on to the baptistery, this priest-king thus led a people come together from city and country, to the source of renewal. At the font, he intoned the benediction of the waters, poured chrism into the water from a silver spoon with a

---

[53] Beroldus, *Kalendarium et ordines*, pp. 108–14. On the two baptisteries of Milan (that of San Giovanni, by the church of Santa Thecla, and that of Santo Stefano, by the church of Santa Maria Maggiore), Angelis d'Ossat 1969.

[54] '. . . induit se paludamentum baptismale': the *paludamentum* was originally a military cloak, often worn by a general (Lewis and Short, pp. 1294–5).

motion of the hand which formed the sign of the cross; when he had done this three times, he moved round to the east of the font, while three unbaptized boys were found from among those that had been brought. If possible, one was to be called Peter, one Paul, one John. This first little group of three would have represented the inception of all baptisms in the mission of the disciples (Matt. 28:19: 'Go out, making disciples of all the nations, baptizing them in the name of the Father, and of the Son, and of the Holy Ghost'), in the mission of the apostles, and, no doubt, in the composite 'John' of John the Evangelist (cf. John 3:5, the conversation with Nicodemus), and John the Baptist. These first three boys – one can imagine the jostle of competitive parents pushing forward their Peters, Pauls and Johns, in their ambition for the holy – were held up by three minor deacons, as the archbishop asked what they sought: 'To be baptized', they replied, in the mouths of the deacons. 'Do you believe in God the Father, creator of heaven and earth?' 'We believe', they replied. The archbishop asked two more such questions, drawn from the Creed, and then – just as Christ had commanded the disciples – he ordered the deacons to baptize: 'Baptize them in the name of the Father, and of the Son, and of the Holy Ghost.' The deacons began by baptizing the three boys, with triple immersion, in the form *Baptizo te*, saying the name of the child.[55] After the litanies, genuflecting towards the east, the archbishop anointed the boys with chrism on the forehead, and, finally, as had been the custom in the rite of Milan and Aquileia since at least the fourth century, he washed their feet, wiped their feet with the towel that hung from his belt, kissed the feet and raised the heels on to his head. With this he mimed the humility with which Christ had washed the feet of the disciples, and, according to a certain tradition, had in this way baptized them (for they had not otherwise been baptized, or apparently not).[56] From liturgy, there has thus

---

[55] On the form of baptism in Beroldus, Paredi 1935: the command to baptize is a feature of the rite of Milan.

[56] Kantorowicz 1956. The washing of the feet is given sacramental (not just exemplary) significance by Ambrose, *De sac.* 3.4–7, pp. 72–4; *De mysteriis* 31–3 (he gives two different accounts of the effect of the rite); and by Chromatius of Aquileia, in the fourth century: *Sermo* 15, pp. 66–70, who considers it an act of humility associated with the crucifixion, as well as a sacramental washing of the sin of Adam. For another episode of liturgical theatre in Beroldus, see *Kalendarium et ordines*, pp. 98ff.: on the Monday before Easter, three lepers, supposedly descendants of those healed by St. Ambrose, were ritually purified. Cattaneo 1954 suggests that this may also refer to the leper in whose

developed at least the fragment of a play, a show in which the archbishop, besides being as always the medium of benediction, has taken a part among other parts. He apparently plays himself, the ruler-priest, as well as Christ, sending forth his disciples into the world. To ritual efficacy has been added a spectacle with political implications. The kind of awareness which a scene like this evokes is very much that of the citizens of Pisa building their baptistery. The celebration of the liturgy has become, also, the celebration of the city.

Beroldus ends his account of this day with the masses said in both winter and summer churches, this being the season when winter passes over into summer.[57] The resurrection is announced, and there begins a jubilant feast.

If we were to go on with the history of spectacle in Italy, of the indulgence of outward forms and that great theatrical production observed by Burckhardt, the city-state as a work of art, we would have to ask ourselves how it was that in the thirteenth century there grew from this elegance of surfaces a new religion of sentiment; how *civiltà* gave rise not only to Dante (who in the *Divine Comedy* finds an equilibrium between the city and its theological destiny), but also to the broken mystical poetry of Jacopone da Todi, and the lyrical devotion of Cimabue.

house Jesus was anointed before the Passover; Cattaneo thinks the rite of Milan is inclined to lay stress on this kind of miniature 'history play', and so to give less attention than the Roman rite to the 'Feasts of Idea'.

[57] Beroldus, *Kalendarium et ordines*, p. 113. The alternation between summer and winter churches is to go on through the octave of Easter.

THE WALL-PAINTINGS IN THE BAPTISTERY
OF CONCORDIA SAGITTARIA

The small town of Concordia Sagittaria lies on the site of the
Roman frontier colony of Iulia Concordia, towards the eastern
boundary of the Veneto, near Portogruaro. In the time of reprieve
after the Hungarian invasions, Otto III confirmed Concordia as
one of the six suffragan sees of Aquileia.[1] The *triconchos* of the
baptistery stands to the north-east of the apse of the present
cathedral. Immediately beyond it is the site of an earlier building
of the same ground-plan, probably built in the fourth century,
and, possibly, the very building made to house the relics of SS.
Hermagoras and Fortunatus, and consecrated by Chromatius of
Aquileia in a homily which survives.[2] The baptistery, according
to an inscription in the *atrium*, was put there by Bishop Reginpoto
(1089–1105), and the work on it completed perhaps around
1100.[3] Beside it, the fourth-century building is an exposed
excavation.

The baptistery is a squat, red-brick temple, its simplicity
belonging to the early Christian style of building still practised at
this time in the exarchate of Aquileia, and which had largely
resisted the newer forms of Byzantine and Romanesque architecture. On the walls inside are three phases of fresco-painting.[4]

The first is almost contemporary with the building. It consists
of the scenes in the cupola: Christ in Majesty within mandorla,
flanked by two seraphim, their wings studded with eyes, and
accompanied by a St Michael, who holds an orb surmounted with

[1] Zovatto 1947a, p. 172; Degani 1922; and the verses of Paulinus of Aquileia on the
destruction of Aquileia during the Hungarian invasions, *MGH Poet. lat. aevi Carol.*, pp.
142–4.
[2] On the baptistery, Zovatto 1947a and 1947b. On the early Christian church, Paschini
1911; Khatchatrian 1962, fig. 313 (plan), p. 77 (bibliography).
[3] Zovatto 1947a, pp. 173–6.
[4] Zovatto 1947b sees only two phases of painting, late twelfth or early thirteenth century;
and fourteenth. Zovatto and Brusin 1960, comparing the earlier phase with the frescoes
of the nearby abbey of Summaga, places this group of paintings in the late eleventh or
early twelfth century. This is more convincing, and is seconded by Demus 1970, p. 292.

2 View of interior of the baptistery in Concordia Sagittaria, showing
Maiestas domini with St Michael and seraphim and dove in the cupola;
prophets and lamb in the drum

3 St Matthew the Evangelist; baptistery, Concordia

4 St Mark the Evangelist; baptistery, Concordia

5 Baptism of Christ; baptistery, Concordia

a cross in his left hand; above the head of the *Maiestas* the dove; the figures in the drum (the band running beneath the cupola), seven of which are prophets, each holding a scroll, and the eighth the lamb of God (see Ill. 2); then in the pendentives (the concave triangles which make the transition from the dome to the arches below) the four evangelists with their symbols, the eagle, bull, lion and man (see Ills. 3 and 4); and finally, the paintings of the main apse and on the arch of the recess leading into the apse. In the conch of the apse, the Baptism of Christ, badly damaged, shows Christ standing in the Jordan up to his waist, his legs cut off at the knee by the curvature of the window below, his disproportion-ately long arms spread out almost to the surface of the water, and his palms turned outward (see Ill. 5). Fishes swim towards him from either side. From the empty semi-circle above his head, a shaft of light descends on to his nimbus. To his right the taller figure of John the Baptist, who wears the garment of a priest under his coat of camel's hair, lays his right hand on Christ's head, a gesture not in the New Testament accounts of the Baptism, but which had become a commonplace in the art of both East and West.[5] Beyond John, an angel waits with a towel held in outstretched hands, and to the left of Christ, two more angels,

[5] Walter 1982, p. 127.

295

6 Moses receiving the tablets; baptistery, Concordia

7 Abraham and Isaac; baptistery, Concordia (the sword can be seen at
the very top of picture)

8 Melchisedech offering; baptistery, Concordia

9 St Peter; baptistery, Concordia

10 St Paul; baptistery, Concordia

11 St George and the dragon; baptistery, Concordia

with their towels, give the composition an inexact symmetry.[6] On the upper limb of the arch leading into the apse, to the left, Moses receives the tablets of the law (see Ill. 6). Opposite him, the corresponding scene has left almost no trace. It no doubt showed another event in the life of Moses, or from the life of a different prophet: perhaps Moses taking off his sandals, as in San Vitale, Ravenna (see Ill. 14), or even the water issuing from the rock at Mara.[7] In the main apse, on the wall between the entry into the apse and the first of its niches, one on each side of the apse, are the figures of Abraham and Melchisedech, communicating with one another across the mouth of the apse. On the left (see Ill. 7), Abraham holds Isaac by a tuft of hair, raising a great sword above his head (Gen. 22). On the right (see Ill. 8), Melchisedech makes his offering to Abraham (Gen. 14:18–24). A solitary figure, he holds out his amphora of wine, eyes lifted towards a receptive and benedictory hand in the top of the panel. His own hands are veiled as was customary in the act of offering.[8]

Four figures, painted into the rounded niches cut away from the wall of the main apse, complete the message of revelation

---

[6] Ibid., p. 128; cf. Chromatius of Aquileia, *Sermo* 14.4, p. 63.
[7] See plates 5 and 11 of Muratori 1945.   [8] *DACL* x, cols. 1209ff.

12 St Mary Magdalene; baptistery, Concordia

working downward from above; but in style they belong to a later date, probably in the mid-twelfth century. The two niches at the back of the apse are shorter, reaching up to a point about two feet beneath the conch, while those on either side of the mouth of the apse extend some two feet above the base of the conch. In the shorter niches are SS. Peter and Paul (see Ills. 9 and 10), one with his keys, the other with his rolled epistle; in the longer SS. Hermagoras and Fortunatus, the first bishop of Aquileia and his deacon, legendary martyrs whose cult was appropriated in this period by Venice as a part of its founding myth.[9]

The style of the niche paintings belongs to the movement of Byzantinizing art back to the stockier figures and thicker lines of fifth- and sixth-century Ravenna or Rome. The St Paul of Concordia is comparable with the mosaic of Paul in the Palatine chapel at Palermo (mid-twelfth-century).[10] It shares the same deliberate clarity. Very similar to the apostles of Concordia are the late eleventh-century mosaics of apostles and saints in the main porch of St Mark's, Venice.[11] This style, Byzantinizing yet identifiably Western, travels north into Germany: among the illustrations of the Prayer Book of Erentrud (1180–90), from a Salzburg scriptorium, are full-length portraits of Peter and Paul remarkably close to those in the baptistery.[12] These four apostolic figures come from an art already found in St Mark's, and handed on from this part of Italy northward across the Alps.

In the right-hand of the two smaller apses are two paintings on different parts of the wall, less easy to date. They represent St George fighting the dragon, and – at least according to the legend running down one side of the painting – 'Maria Magdalena' (see Ills. 11 and 12). The daubs of red paint on the cheeks, and a stiffness in the handling of the figures and (in the case of George) their action, the roundedness of the heads and the look of steady wonderment in the eyes – all of which make visible the effect of

[9] See Kaftal 1978, fig. 505, for the fresco of 1031 in the apse of the basilica of Aquileia showing Hermagoras presenting Conrad II to the Virgin and Child, Fortunatus looking on, a book in his hand, as at Concordia.
[10] Demus 1949, pl. 16a (mosaic showing the apostle Paul).
[11] Demus 1984, I, pls. 4, 14–15; and Demus 1970, p. 292.
[12] Swarzenski 1908, figs. 430, 432, 443. On the date, Swarzenski 1913, p. 147. On communications between the Veneto and Bavaria, Zovatto and Brusin 1960, pp. 152–62, where he argues that the chapel of All Saints at Regensburg is derived from the baptistery at Concordia. Also, Demus 1970, p. 192, on the stylistic derivation of the paintings in the Stiftskirche, Lambach (Upper Austria), from the paintings at Concordia.

innocent fable conveyed especially in the earliest Latin version of George's life – carry a faint recollection of the monastic cycle of wall-paintings in Sant' Angelo in Formis (near Capua), finished shortly before 1100.[13] Many panels in this Benedictine cycle, despite their skilled use of space for the purpose of story-telling, have some of the same simple emotional force. But the very comparison with Sant' Angelo in Formis indicates that St George and Mary Magdalene at Concordia are a good deal later. The legend of George and the dragon appears in Latin literature quite early in the twelfth century, and in Italian and French art in the 1130s or 1140s;[14] but the first depictions have about them a reserve which is foreign to the stylized exuberance of the St George of the baptistery. The naivety of touch, the attention to detail in the accoutrements of horse and rider, and a general confusion in the composition, lead to a date towards the middle of the thirteenth century.[15]

Why should George and the dragon and Mary Magdalene be painted in a baptistery, together or alone? Were these pictures, rather crude in execution, put there as objects of devotion, a focus of personal anxieties or wishes outside the public cult? Were they in some sense icons? The Mary Magdalene, a full-length portrait, has the frontal stance of many icons, and the same sense of silent watching. Were these pictures in some way relics, embodying the saints' power to intercede and protect, as if they were the real dust and blood? Or were they somehow related to the ritual of the baptistery? Without digressing too much, we can say something about how both the George and the Mary could have grown out of the Easter liturgy. The theology which prevails throughout the celebration of Easter Sunday in Milan (whose rite is close to that of Aquileia), is that of salvation by the cross. The Gospel lection for this day is John 20, the story of Mary Magdalene at the empty tomb, where she meets the gardener who turns out to be Christ risen. So we need go no further than the liturgy to find why the Magdalene should be here in the baptistery – but also to explain the otherwise puzzling detail that instead of her usual flask of ointment she is carrying a cross. A collect said before communion on the same day makes a correspondence between the sacrifice

[13] Morisani 1962, for illustrations and comments.
[14] Aufhauser 1911, pp. 231ff. The Latin is a translation from Greek.
[15] The St George and dragon here might be compared with that of MS Verona, Biblioteca civica, MS 1853 (Kaftal 1978, col. 350, fig. 412), of the late thirteenth century.

of the lamb and the sacrifice of penitence made by the communicants:

Come, peoples. Now is the time when we enact, with fear and with faith, this immortal and holy thing, this mystery poured down. We come to it with clean hands, and we communicate the gift of penitence: for the lamb of God has proposed a sacrifice to the Father on our behalf . . .[16]

Is Mary Magdalene not making an offering of her penitence, *cum timore, et fide*, in the appropriate form of a cross? As for George, he is the knight of exorcism, comrade-in-arms to St Michael accompanying the *Maiestas* in the earlier group of paintings; like Michael, George is associated with the slaying of the dragon of the Book of Revelation. The story of George and the dragon, as it was told in the Latin version of the early twelfth century and then in the version of Jacob of Voragine in the second half of the thirteenth, is at least in part a story about bad water (the *stagnum* of the Book of Revelation) against good water. It ends with George baptizing the people of the city afflicted by the dragon, and miraculously founding a spring in the city square. But the story is also about saving a child (the king's daughter) from the dragon, and transferring her, as it were, from the bad water which is her fate, to the good water of baptism.[17] The fascinating implications of all this – that saints and saints' lives are so closely related to the liturgy – makes another subject.

Three further paintings, of the mid-fourteenth century, show three bishops, seating or standing. They stare out, offices more than persons, two in the main apse, the third in the right-hand apse. One of them raises his hand in blessing, the others remain aloof beneath mitres, croziers in hand. The paintings represent the dignity of the church in its higher functionaries.[18]

The first phase of painting, of about 1100, is closest to the liturgy of baptism in its subject-matter, and says most about the visual element in liturgy. Like much painting of this period in Italy, the style is somewhere between the solemn, almost mathematically

[16] *Missale duplex*, p. 253: 'Venite, populi: sacrum immortale, mysterium illibatum agendum cum timore, et fide. Accedamus manibus mundis, poenitentiae munus communicemus: quoniam agnus dei propter nos patri sacrificium propositus est . . .'.

[17] Aufhauser 1911, p. 184: 'Domine mi, in hac aqua natus est draco inmanis, qui pene totum huius ciuitatis populum interficiebat.' The words echo Rev. 13:1–2.

[18] Zovatto and Brusin 1960, p. 150.

balanced harmonies of Byzantine contemplative art, and the heavier, more solid representations of Romanesque.[19] Of this meeting of Greek and Latin art comes a great suggestive power. In Sant' Angelo in Formis, near Capua in Campania, a naive realism in the handling of narrative scenes, an innocent roundness in the features, sit side by side with the attempt to transfigure the ingenuous into the pure beauty of formal rhythm.[20] Nor were Latin and Greek always so far apart. Within this Greek art of the contemplative, in the sixth-century mosaics of St Catherine's below Mt Sinai, for example, or in the wall-paintings in Nerezi (Yugoslav Macedonia) of about 1270, a strain of realism inhabits the pattern of forms.[21] Peter stretches sleepily beneath the Transfiguration at St Catherine's, Sinai; and in the Descent from the Cross in the church of Saint Panteleimon, Nerezi, a crouching helper (Nicodemus) pulls the nails from Christ's feet – an earth-bound figure getting on with his work, his basket of tools on the ground by his side – while Christ's mother takes the limp body from Joseph of Arimathea and leans to kiss the head. Rather as in Rogier Van der Weyden's Descent, the lines of the body held in death mime the living movement in the other figures, and narrative goes together with the more abstract considerations of form to make a dance of the quick and the dead.

In Concordia, the action of the dance has been interrupted; the paintings induce an acute awareness that something about to happen has been stopped. Any picture stops the action it depicts, unable to do otherwise. However hard it tries, being incapable of following the motion itself, it picks out an instant in the motion. But while some pictures invite the onlooker to make good this failing – the line-drawings of the Utrecht Psalter would be one example from the Middle Ages – and restore the movement by the force of his own imagination, others do all they can to prevent him from intruding in this way. In the history of art, such standoffishness is rare: landscapes do not usually refuse movement in this way, even if they seem to at a glance, and nor do portraits. The majority of paintings invoke movement and change. It is the icon, the image of a saint in some way holy in itself, which tends

[19] Cf. Ancona 1935, pp. 14–15.

[20] Morisani 1962: the prophets on the north side of the nave, especially Malachy and Moses (pls. 57 and 58), and the disciple on the left in the scene of the meeting on the road to Emmaus (pl. 52), have a sober elegance which distinguishes them from the other figures.

[21] Forsyth and Weitzmann 1973 for St Catherine's, Sinai; Grabar 1968, pp. 52–3, and pl. on p. 53, for the Descent at Nerezi.

to refuse it most flatly, or at least to throw back the possibility of movement most directly on to the powers of the beholder. The wall-paintings of Concordia, with many other images of this period, fall into a third group. Depicting an action in mid-flow, instead of doing the obvious thing and letting the onlooker finish it off for them – bring down Abraham's sword on Isaac's twisting neck for example – they wish him to remain with the action in its unfinished state. They restrain themselves from accomplishment, from the 'It is done' (Rev. 21:6), preferring the 'time [which] is at hand' (Rev. 1:3). Here Luke waits on his bull, John on his eagle, before they write anything down; in the drum, the prophets wait on the *Maiestas* of the cupola; Moses has taken the tablets of the law, but remains locked in a posture of astonishment, gazing into God's hand above him; Melchisedech extends the amphora in a gesture of offering.

All these scenes had already appeared in the early sixth century in the mosaics of the *presbyterium* of San Vitale, Ravenna. The painters of Concordia have relied on the mosaics as a source, in some cases, as that of Abraham and Isaac, staying very close to the model (see Ills. 13 and 14). But although the art of Ravenna, partly because of the richness of the material – the highly coloured cut glass *tesserae* whose surfaces are set at slightly different angles, so that each piece of glass has its own luminosity, one piece catching the light more than the next – is an idealizing art, this same sumptuousness gives it a certain solidity. However much they are made up of light, the figures of Abraham and Melchisedech are sturdy figures. Their idealism is an heroic one, and in this sense, it remains a thing of flesh and blood.[22]

Not so in the frescoes of Concordia. The paintings in the baptistery show the hesitancy which occurs in the split second between certainties. Making use of the discrepancy between the motionless picture itself and the action it depicts, they ask the onlooker to consider what it is like to be caught in the midst of an action. Abraham must kill his son with his own hand, and then hears the command to kill a ram instead. Abraham, as Kierkegaard said, was at once obedient to God's command to sacrifice his 'single-born, beloved' son, and certain that he would not be called upon to do so. This was the twofold content of his faith, or at least so runs Kierkegaard's understanding of what Abraham said to his

---

[22] Muratori 1945, pls. 5 and 8.

13 Below, Abraham receives the three angels, Abraham and Isaac; above, right, Moses with the tablets; above, left, the prophet Jeremiah; San Vitale, Ravenna, mosaic

14 Below, Abel and Melchisedech; above, Moses taking off his sandals, the prophet Isaiah; San Vitale, Ravenna, mosaic

son: 'My son, God will provide a victim for his holocaust' (Gen. 22:8).[23] But the painter is less interested in this feat of obedience than in the switch, the turn, from one certainty to another, from obedience to relief; and it is the switch itself that matters to him. What he has suggested in this simple figure of Abraham with his sword raised, above all in the eyes lifted to the voice of the angel (the place of the sacrifice is 'the place of seeing': Gen. 22:2), is something like that instant of not quite understanding which falls between two talkers, who are closer in their awkwardness than at all the other times when they are defended from one another by their agreements. The awkwardness is there in the eyes of the prophets and evangelists too, turned upward, in puzzlement, towards the *Maiestas* in the roof, with a turn of the head not at all unlike the sideways glance of the two talkers. It is in the spareness of the content of the paintings, which provides nothing not relevant to the simple gesture they depict; nothing to take the mind off this one instant to ideas of what might have gone before or might come after it.

The ram in the thicket is absent from the scene of Abraham's sacrifice. The river Jordan in Christ's Baptism has its fishes, and the evangelists sit against a backcloth of city buildings; but the props are at a minimum, everything conspiring to suppress a movement that has begun. In keeping with this design, the body of each figure has been muted by the weightless, linear play of folds over the joints, bones and flesh which ought to be there. In some of the figures – the Abraham and the Melchisedech more than the Christ of the Baptism – there is the effect of a certain kind of Byzantine painting where the folds fall in such a way over the body – not with it but against its natural shapes – as to make its presence doubtful, so that the body itself 'lacks body'.[24] In the case of the naked Isaac, it is the precarious geometry of the draughtsmanship, not folds, which achieves this effect.

High up, the brown and purple 'seated one' in the roof, the one figure whose eyes look out straight, not sidelong or up, is uncomfortably at odds with all the weaker tones and frail bodies below, so that these lower scenes are affected by something baleful and fearsome, a presentiment of judgement.

The presentiment of judgement is an effect of style – of the use of colour, tone, line and form. It is abstract. But it has a material

---

[23] Kierkegaard 1939.   [24] Grabar 1951, pp. 127ff.

source in the Book of Revelation. The paintings are an interpretation of Revelation, but one which instead of dwelling on the grimness of judgement – on the punishment or fear of being punished against which innocence delineates itself, the subject-matter of the frescoes at Novara – has chosen to refine from all the shouting and blood the exquisite sensation (which is indeed a great theme of Revelation) of the instant before judgement, or even the instant of judging, but before the impact of judgement has struck. Out of the fear and trembling of God's vengeance, expressed by magnitude, number, the heaping of dead on dead, loudness, and all the reckless confusion of disaster, the baptistery painters have found (or tried to find, for these are admittedly not the finest works of art) the moment's pause just before the noise starts. They have singled out the calm of the 'silence in heaven' which falls after the opening of the seventh seal and before the blowing of the seven trumpets (Rev. 8:1); or of the prophet glimpsed standing at the sea's edge (*stetit super harenam maris*) after the dragon's attempt on the child but before his re-appearance from the water (Rev. 12:18). The organization of the Book of Revelation is not easy to make out, but perhaps the most important thing about it is that it concerns a resolution or a series of resolutions of the war between good and evil, which has not yet happened; for all its imagery of a final violence and a final peace, it looks forward.

The grave God in the roof of the baptistery is dark enough to be part of the threatening atmosphere of Revelation, and his lieutenant Michael is with him, to remind us of the great war in heaven, after which Satan – in the form of the dragon or serpent – is plunged for a thousand years into the abyss, in a defeat which at least anticipates his annihilation; and the seraphim are on the ceiling to recall the heavenly court singing day and night, 'Holy, holy, holy'; and the seven prophets in the drum surely represent the twenty-four elders of the court, as well as the principle of prophecy (seven is half the number of the Old Testament prophets). With them is the lamb – the 'lamb standing as though slain' of Rev. 5:6 – and beneath, in the pendentives, the four animals and the Gospel-writers, all of it as shown to John, or at any rate, easily recognized:

After these things, I saw a door in heaven, standing open, ... and there was a seat placed in heaven, and on the seat one sitting, ... and around the seat twenty-four stools, and on these, twenty-four elders, shrouded in white clothes, ... and where the seat was and around the seat were four animals filled with eyes front and back; the first animal like a lion, the second like a bull-calf; the third had the face of a man; the fourth animal was like an eagle in flight. (Rev. 4:1–7)

In the cupola, drum and pendentives, the baptistery follows Revelation straightforwardly.

But the Apocalypse looks forward to a happy ending, in which the powers of good will prevail. The 'earth and the sky flee back before the face of the seated one' (20:11), as though the film-reel is running backward at double speed, and all of a sudden everything begins again:

ecce noua facio omnia: Behold, I make all things new. (21:5)

Rather than the pathos of destruction after a real battle, the fantasy of vision substitutes light straightaway for horror, the water of life for the stagnant lake of the dragon. It is an exorcism, and, in a sense, a baptism. In this time, Jerusalem will come down from heaven, 'having the clarity of God' (21:11), and with it the temple, measured out according to the plan given in Ezechiel 48; there will be 'no more death, nor battle, nor shouting, nor pain' (21:4). The imagery is tangled and dense, but it is dominated in these last chapters of Revelation by the final vision of clarity, light, peace, water and washing. It is the end of an ordeal:

And he said to me, it is done. I am Alpha, I am Omega, the beginning and the end. I will give to the thirsty one from the font of living water; it is my free gift. (21:6)

The second death, in the form of the stagnant lake, threatens once more, but fades before the clarity of Jerusalem and the temple. Then,

he showed me the river of the water of life shining like crystal coming from the seat of God and of the lamb. (22:1)

At the end of the book, John hears the voice of God:

I am Alpha, I am Omega, I am before all, I am at the end of all, the beginning of all things and their end. Blessed are those who wash their garments, that their power may be in the wood of life. (22:13–14)

And then again,

Come, you who are thirsty, take, you who will, the water of life; it is my free gift. (22:17)

Hence, I think, the Baptism of Christ in the main apse at Concordia; and hence the emotional unease felt in contemplating these two scenes together: the baleful 'seated one', and the Baptism of Christ. The judging God above, and the Immanuel – the youthful 'God-with-us' – below, seem to contradict one another. One frightens, the other reassures. This is indeed a part of their effect; it is a combined effect, as when the calm sea anticipates with certainty the storm. In one perspective, the Book of Revelation, and the frescoes of the baptistery, might at first be seen as a sequence of scenes (from top to bottom in the baptistery), putting before us the progressive revelation of truth. They show light coming out of the dark; clarity from judgement; the threat and then the promise in the prophet's voice. In a different perspective, each scene is an instant suspended between ignorance and understanding. We have seen this in the case of Abraham and Isaac. It is true too of the *Maiestas*, which is not a picture of judgement extended, in time, as suffering (this is the subject of the paintings of Novara), but of the very instant of judgement. It is for this reason that the judgement does not merely frighten; being unfinished, it accuses. The Baptism of Christ is another instant; it cannot quite be made distinct from the mood of judgement to which everything in the baptistery must partly refer; but in itself it is a picture not of the story of Christ's Baptism, but of the Baptism as the moment – half-angelic and half of this earth – when the sky opened (cf. Luke 3:21).

The Book of Revelation itself looks forward, through the visions given to John, to the horrible events which will in the end bring a resolution; but its unyielding insistence on the events themselves might make us forget that they are given in a vision, and that the vision is a vision of what is about to happen (or possibly what is still happening), not what has happened:

He said to me, Do not seal up the words of prophecy of this book. The time is at hand. The one who does harm will go on doing his damage; and the one who is in filth will go on spreading it. (Rev. 22:10–11)

The baptistery painters have restored the 'thinness' of John's vision – they have recognized that vision is close to illusion – and with it the sense of a time which is at hand. They have caught, not the desire for an end – the will to get it over, to reach the other shore; or the yearning for what will be – nor the capacity of repetition to raise past time and time future up to a no-time where all is the same (despite having coming up out of difference); but the lull where eternity is instinct in time, because, taking place in the infinitely thin space between before and after, it is an absence of time which can only be seen from the passage of time from which it is absent.[25]

Other paintings do something similar: the liturgical act of offering often appears in illuminations as an opposition between the hand of God in the ceiling and the hands of offering below, their fingers spread towards the almost empty space above them. In the illumination of the charter of a lay brotherhood attached to the Pyrenean monastery of Saint-Martin-du-Canigou, drawn up about 1195, the suspense before the offering is accepted – the offering which must cross so much empty space – is caught less in the general upward and downward rhythm of folds and pointing fingers by which the two horizontal sections of the picture communicate, the upper containing Christ in mandorla (the Virgin and St Martin on his right and left both point down to the offerers with a long index finger), the lower the members of the brotherhood at Mass, than in the detail of one of the members, a woman, who half-kneels, half gets up, her hands still veiled after giving up her oblation to the priest.[26] What these pictures catch is the awful hesitation before the epiclesis takes effect, before the finger of God touches the finger of Adam; when the prophet (like Abraham in Concordia) hears a voice, and turns to see what it is:

And I turned to see the voice which spoke to me. (Rev. 1:12)

In a tenth-century liturgical roll from the Casanatense Library in Rome, containing the text of the *Benedictio fontis* – the roll would have been unrolled by a deacon as the blessing was intoned, so that the images on it could be seen by the congregation – the first image shows the magnitude, even the arbitrariness, of the joining of sky and earth in benediction, by showing what things were like just before they were joined.[27] From Christ in aureola at the top of the frame appears a dove holding a crown, not brooding suggestively over the waters, but held a long away above them, and with nothing in between. In the twelfth century, especially in the second half, increasing interest in the narrative details of Christ's

[25] Thus Eliot's *Little Gidding*: 'Suspended in time, between pole and tropic'; and above p. 172 n. 110.
[26] Paris, Cabinet de Beaux-Arts, Cabinet Jean Masson, I. Text of charter in *Bibliothèque de l'école des chartes* 42 (1881), pp. 6–7.
[27] 724 BI 13: see Avery 1936, pls. ciii–cxvii, esp. cx.

life provide many examples of another version of this hesitancy, as in the Descent from the Cross at Nerezi, where it is the narrative flow of this action which has been stopped.[28] In Concordia, liturgical action is held up; but the Abraham and Isaac – this more than the other scenes – show how a liturgical episode (ultimately the descent of the roof into the font) and a narrative episode might be used in tandem.

THE BAPTISM OF CHRIST

If liturgy had a tendency to turn into narrative – the use of the saints' lives in liturgy, and in this baptistery the appearance of SS. George and Mary Magdalene, are an example of this tendency – it had always been adept at taking scenes from stories and giving them theological significance. Maximus of Turin (d. 408/23) had a taste for this kind of metamorphosis, and indeed for metamorphosis generally. One day he compared Christ on the cross with Ulysses lashed to the mast of his ship;[29] on another, when he heard the crowd outside baying at the waning moon to help it back to fulness, he used this drunken outburst as the starting-point for a short, essay-like, address on the freedom of the will by which man, unlike the moon, can become 'as a moon full to eternity' (Ps. 88: 38).[30] He took pleasure from whatever ran against the grain in this way, in the little conceits of grace, and one wonders if his audience (which had clearly not forgotten its pagan past) was not a bit bemused.

The whole business of baptism he regarded in this manner, and the Baptism of Christ, when Christ who had already been born pure, was, oddly, born again, was to him the most piquant of events. He relished the difficulty in Christ's being baptized at all, turning it in his hand to consider it from every angle.

What he liked most, was that in the Baptism of Christ – in the Turin of Maximus, both the Baptism of Christ and baptism generally still took place on the day of Epiphany[31] – we can see with utter clarity the power of eternity over time. It is tempting to say: the shattering effect of eternity on time. But this would not

[28] On the development of narrative in twelfth-century illumination, Pächt 1962.
[29] Sermo 37, pp. 145–7.
[30] Sermo 30, pp. 117–19.
[31] Botte 1932, plays down the importance of Epiphany as the season of baptism in Maximus (pp. 40ff); Maximus, however, devotes three sermons to this connection.

be right. Maximus rejects melodrama in favour of delicate cameo-scenes depicting reversal: benediction, for him, runs against nature – 'benediction runs more subtle than the flow of water', as he put it in one of his sermons for Epiphany.[32] Why was Christ baptized in the Jordan, when he was more pure than the water which was to purify him?[33] Because Christ's Baptism was not a washing of Christ but a washing of water; by it, the merciful water was provided by which the 'whore of the world', whose body absorbs everything it touches and pollutes it, could herself be cleaned.[34] This is a powerful image. Maximus associates the whore with idolatry, but we can make out in her the general principle of the mother-goddesses of Antiquity, who survived as 'Tellus', or Nature, into the Middle Ages.[35] It is an image which puts emphasis not on continuity from paganism to Christianity, or from before baptism to after, but on Christianity, or baptism, as oblivion.

This is the whore who after her washing says she has done nothing wrong; . . . a whore has been made a virgin, and has forgotten the crimes she did before . . .[36]

But in the end the effect of Maximus' preoccupation with such reversals of the past is to fascinate us with the instant of turning back. A whore becomes a virgin. We are not asked to consider the progression involved; there is no sentimental confrontation, nor psychological credibility, nor sequence of episodes to suggest the sprouting of one condition out of another – as there is in the story of Mary Magdalene for example – but only the metamorphosis on its own, and so we are led back to the peculiarity of that slice out of time, fragile as egg-shell and psychologically not even a possibility, when there is neither a whore nor a virgin. The same goes for another image of what happened at Christ's Baptism, taken from Psalm 113:

[32] *Sermo* 13 b, p. 49: 'Subtilior enim est benedictionum cursus quam aquarum meatus.'
[33] *Sermo* 13 a, p. 45: 'Quale hoc est baptismum, ubi purior ipso est fonte ille qui mergitur?'
[34] *Sermo* 22 a, p. 87.
[35] Augustine, *De ciu. Dei* 7.24, pp. 205–7; *Tellus* appears in the *Exultet*, now purified: 'Gaudeat se tellus inradiatam fulgoribus, et aeterni regis splendore lustrata, totius orbis se sentiat amisisse caliginem' (*Hadrianum Supplement*, no. 1021, p. 360).
[36] *Sermo* 22 a, pp. 87–8: 'Haec, inquam, illa est meretrix, quae posteaquam lota est, nihil dicit fecisse se prauum. Posteaquam enim ecclesia baptismi nitore purgata est, diabolicae inpietatis non meminit, religione ueritatis exultat, factaque de meretrice uirgo non recordatur priorum scelerum, sed gloriatur in integritate uirtutum.'

In a marvellous way, when Christ was put in the Jordan, the river glided but the stream of benediction ran . . . and – amazing though it seems – the Jordan was turned back to its origin by the consecration of baptism, the river of benediction pulling against the river of water. This is surely what David had in mind when he said, The Jordan was turned back.[37] (Ps. 113:3)

It is not easy to say whether Maximus meant this as a hyperbole. Certainly he thought of sacrament as against nature, the eye of the needle dangled in the world, only to be brought up again immediately; and this would have set him apart from the usual understanding of sacrament as a fusion of benediction with nature.

In Maximus, the Baptism of Christ, instead of making the body clean, makes the water clean. In the words of an inscription on the font from the baptistery of Cividale (eighth century, first half), a few miles from Concordia, this image is put with that of Christ's Baptism as an opening in the sky:

When Christ, coming brilliant into the Jordan, made this river holy by mystic baptism, he opened the kingdom of the pious.[38]

So had said Luke (3:21):

When Jesus had been baptized, and was at prayer, the sky opened.

The baptistery, as a piece of architecture, is nothing other than an opening in the sky. This, as the words of the inscription convey, is why the covering (*tegurium*) of the font – the canopy held over it by an arcade, making the font a baptistery within a baptistery – is made of 'trembling marble' (*uibrante marmorum scema*).[39] The wall-painters of the baptistery at Concordia have represented this

---

[37] *Sermo* 13 b, p. 49: 'Mirum enim in modum Christo in Iordane posito aquarum quidem flumina labebantur, sed et benedictionum fluenta currebant; inde aluei gurges turbidior ferebatur, hinc fons saluatoris purissimus emanabat; et stupore quodam retrorsum ad Iordanis originem consecratio baptismatis ascendebat, et contra aquarum fluuium benedictionum fluuius ferebatur, unde Dauid sanctum arbitror dixisse: Iordanes conversus est retrorsum. In baptismate enim Christi retrorsum Iordanes non aquis conversus est sed sacramentis, et in naturae sui originem benedictione magis quam substantia remeauit.' Cf. Ambrose, *De mysteriis* 51, p. 124: 'Iordanis retrorsum conuersus contra naturam in sui fontis reuertit exordium.'

[38] De Rubeis 1754, pp. 376–7: 'Cum Christus, ueniens in Iordanem, hoc [flumen] sacrabit mystico baptismate; nitens piorum regnum patuit.' Quarino 1967 gives a photograph of the font, facing p. 65. Cf. *Missale duplex* (rite of Milan), prayer for Epiphany, p. 82: 'Baptizat miles regem, seruus dominum suum, Johannes saluatorem. Aqua Jordanis stupuit . . .'

[39] De Rubeis 1754, pp. 376–7: 'Cernites tegurium beati Callisti, quod (ipse) ornabit uibrante marmorum scema.'

opening of the sky by the Baptism of Christ in the main apse; by the Abraham and Isaac, Melchisedech, Moses, and the general reference to prophecy; but at the same time by taking up the repeated sky-openings with which Revelation punctuates its story of disclosure:

After I had seen these things, behold, a door was opened in heaven (*ecce ostium apertum in caelo*). (4:1)

And the temple of God was opened in the sky . . . (*apertum est templum dei in caelo*) (11:19)

And I saw the sky open. (*et uidi caelum apertum*). (19:11)

The Abraham and Isaac, Melchisedech, Moses, the evangelists and prophets, see this opening. Juxtaposed with it is the opening of the book of seven seals which cannot be opened other than by the lamb:

I saw in the right hand of the one seated on the throne a book with writing inside and out, and sealed with seven seals. I saw a strong angel crying out with a great voice, Who is worthy to open the book and break its seals? No one in heaven, or on earth, or under the earth, was able to open the book and look at it. I was all in tears, that none should be found worthy to open the scroll or look on it; until one of the elders said to me, There is no need for tears. Here is one who has gained the right to open the book, by breaking its seven seals, the lion that comes from the tribe of Judah, from the stock of David (Rev.5:1–5).

The lion, it turns out, is the lamb, who stands as if slain (5:6) in the middle, where the throne is, among the four animals and the twenty-four elders. In Concordia, the lamb, bearing the standard of victory, stands in the drum immediately beneath the feet of the *Maiestas*, who holds an open book (in his left hand), surrounded by the seven prophets, each of whom holds a book. *Maiestas* and lamb are in line with the Baptism of Christ below.

This theme of opening, and the interest in moments of disclosure – the essence of which the artists in the baptistery have tried to catch – is characteristic, in the liturgy of north Italy, not so much of Easter as of the season of Christmas and Epiphany. The opening of the book (Rev. 5) is the pericope for the feast of John the Evangelist on 27 December, whose dominant motif is the annunciation of the word;[40] while the opening of the sky, at the Baptism of Christ, is the ruling idea at Epiphany, when the three

---

[40] *Missale duplex*, pp. 54ff.

disclosures of the Baptism, the coming of the Magi and the wedding at Cana (the three first signs of Christ) are brought together into one.[41] What the painters have done, and no doubt this would have been second nature to them – it is second nature to the liturgy – is to borrow the liturgical ideas of one group of feasts, and import them to another. They have looked to the time of Nativity and Epiphany to illuminate baptism at Easter.

[41] Ibid., pp. 78ff. Preface on p. 80: 'Caelos aperuisti, aerem benedixisti, fontem purificasti, et tuum unicum filium per speciem columbae sancto spiritu declarasti.' For the linking of the three events: 'Hodie caelesti sponso iuncta est ecclesia: quoniam in Jordane lauit eius crimina. Currunt cum munere Magi ad regales nuptias: et, ex aqua facto uino, laetantur conuiuia' (p. 81). On this prayer, Casel 1925.

BIBLIOGRAPHY

PRIMARY SOURCES

Authors living before 1600
(Saints' lives under name of saint)

Abelard, Peter, *Capitula heresum Petri Abaelardi*, ed. N. M. Häring, 'Die vierzehn Capitula heresum Petri Abaelardi', in *Cîteaux* 31 (1980), pp. 35–52 (at pp. 43–52).

  Ethics, ed. and transl. D. E. Luscombe, Oxford Medieval Texts (Oxford 1971).

  Historia Calamitatum, ed. J. T. Muckle, in *Mediaeval Studies* 12 (1950), pp. 175–211.

  Theologia Christiana, ed. E. M. Buytaert, *CCM* CXXI (Turnhout 1969).

Acts of Paul, in Hennecke–Schneemelcher 1965, pp. 252–90.

Acts of Thomas, in Hennecke–Schneemelcher 1965, pp. 442–531.

Adamnanus, *De locis sanctis*, ed. D. Meehan, Scriptores latini Hiberniae 3 (Dublin 1958).

Ad Nouationem, ed. G. F. Diercks, *CCSL* IV (Turnhout 1972), pp. 137–52.

Aelius Aristides, *Sacred Tales I*, ed. and transl. C. A. Behr, *Aelius Aristides, the Complete Works*, II (Leiden 1981), pp. 278–91.

Life of St Æthelwold: Wulfstan of Winchester. The Life of Æthelwold, ed. M. Lapidge and M. Winterbottom, Oxford Medieval Texts (Oxford 1991).

Alcuin, *Letters*, ed. E. Dümmler, *MGH Epist. Karol. aevi* II, pp. 1–481.

Life of St Willibrord [*see* Willibrord], in Talbot 1954, pp. 1–22.

Amalarius of Metz, *Liber officialis*, ed. I. M. Hanssens, *Amalarii episcopi opera liturgica omnia*, 3 vols., Studi e Testi 138–40 (Vatican 1948–50), II.

Ambrose of Milan, *De Abraham, PL* XIV, cols. 442–524.

  De mysteriis, ed. B. Botte, *Ambroise de Milan. Des sacraments, Des mystères, SC* XXV (Paris 1949), pp. 108–28.

  De sacramentis, ibid., pp. 54–107.

  Exameron, ed. C. Schenkl, *Sancti Ambrosii Opera*, part I (Vienna etc. 1896), pp. 1–261.

  Explanatio symboli, ed. R. H. Connolly, *The Explanatio Symboli ad Initiandos – a Work of St. Ambrose*, A Provisionally Reconstructed Text Edited with Introduction, Notes and a Translation by the Late Dom R. H. Connolly, Texts and Studies 10 (Cambridge 1952).

Ambrosiaster, *Commentary on Romans*, ed. H. Vogel, *Ambrosiastri qui dicitur commentarius in epistulas Paulinas*, 3 vols., *CSEL* LXXXI (Vienna 1966–9), I.

Bibliography

Andreas, in *Anglo-Saxon Poetry*, selected and transl. by R. K. Gordon (London etc. 1954).

Anselm of Canterbury, *Cur deus homo*, ed. R. Roques, *SC* XCI (Paris 1963).

S. *Anselmi Cantuariensis archiepiscopi opera omnia*, ed. F. S. Schmitt, 6 vols. (Edinburgh 1946–61).

Anselm of Laon, school of, *Sententie diuine pagine*, ed. F. P. Bliemetzrieder, *Anselms von Laon systematische Sentenzen*, I, Beiträge zur Geschichte der Philosophie des Mittelalters 18, parts 2–3 (Münster-in-Westfalen 1919), pp. 1–46.

Aristotle, *The Nicomachean Ethics*, ed. H. G. Apostle (Dordrecht and Boston 1975).

Arno of Salzburg, *Ordo de catecizandis rudibus uel quid sint singula quae geruntur in sacramento baptismatis: ex diuersis sanctorum dictis patrum excerpta testimonia*, ed. Bouhot 1980, pp. 205–30.

Asclepius I, ed. Scott 1924, pp. 286–377.

Asser, *Life of Alfred*, ed. W. H. Stevenson (Oxford 1904).

Augustine, *Confessions*, ed. L. Verheijen, *CCSL* XXVII (Turnhout 1981).

De baptismo contra Donatistos, ed. M. Petschenig, *CSEL* LI, i (Vienna and Leipzig, 1908), pp. 143–375.

De catechizandis rudibus liber unus, ed. and transl. with introduction by J. P. Christopher, The Catholic University of America, Patristic Studies, vol. 8 (Washington DC 1926).

De ciuitate Dei, ed. B. Dombart, A. Kalb, 2 vols., *CCSL* XLVII–XLVIII (Turnhout 1955).

De diuersis quaestionibus ad Simplicianum ed. A. Mutzenbecher, *CCSL* XLIV (Turnhout 1970).

De doctrina christiana libri iv, ed. J. Martin, *CCSL* XXXII (Turnhout 1962), pp. 1–167.

De libero arbitrio, ed. W. M. Green, *CCSL* XXIX (Turnhout 1970), pp. 211–321.

De natura et origine animae libri iv, ed. C. F. Urba and I. Zycha, *CSEL* LX (Vienna and Leipzig 1913), pp. 303–419.

De nuptiis et concupiscentia, ed. C. F. Urba and J. Zycha, *CSEL* XLII (Vienna etc. 1902), pp. 211–319.

De peccatorum meritis et remissione et de baptismo paruulorum, ed. C. F. Urba and J. Zycha, *CSEL* XLII (Vienna etc. 1902), pp. 3–151.

De quantitate animae, *PL* XXII, cols. 1035–80.

De sermone domini in monte, *PL* XXXIV, cols. 1229–1308.

De trinitate libri xv, ed. W. J. Mountain, 2 vols., *CCSL* L (1–12) and LA (13–15) (Turnhout 1968).

Enarrationes in psalmos, ed. E. Dekkers and J. Fraipont, 3 vols., *CCSL* XXXVIII–XL (Turnhout 1956).

Ep. 54 (*ad inquisitiones Januarii liber primus*), *PL* XXXIII, 199–204.

Ep. 55 (*ad inquisitiones Januarii liber secundus*), *PL* XXXIII, cols. 204–23.

Ep. 98 (*ad Bonifacium*), *PL* XXXIII, cols. 359–64.

In Iohannis euangelium tractatus, ed. A. Mayer, *CCSL* XXXVI (Turnhout 1954).

Sermo 26, *PL* XXXVIII, cols. 171–8.

Sermo 58, *PL* xxxviii, cols. 393–400.

Sermo 225, *PL* xxxviii, cols. 1095–8.

Sermo 294, *PL* xxxviii, cols. 335–48.

Sermo 363, *PL* xxxix, cols. 1634–8.

Sermones ex collectione Guelferbytana, ed. G. Morin, *Sancti Augustini Sermones post Maurinos reperti, Miscellanea Agostiniana* i (Rome 1930), pp. 439–585.

Barnabas, *Letter of*, ed. P. Prigent, *L'Epître de Barnabé, SC* clxxii (Paris 1971).

Bede, *De temporum ratione*, ed. C. W. Jones, *Bedae Uenerabilis opera de temporibus* (Cambridge, Mass., 1943), pp. 175–291.

Expositio Actuum apostolorum, ed. M. L. W. Laistner, *CCSL* cxxi (Turnhout 1983), pp. 1–104.

Historia Ecclesiastica, ed. B. Colgrave and R. A. B. Mynors, *Bede's Ecclesiastical History of the English Peoples* (Oxford 1969); another edition by C. Plummer, 2 vols. (Oxford 1896).

Homilies, ed. D. Hurst, *Bedae Uenerabilis homiliarum euangelii, CCSL* cxxii (Turnhout 1955).

In Canticum canticorum, ed. D. Hurst, *CCSL* cxixb (Turnhout 1983), pp. 165–375.

Beowulf, transl. in Clark Hall 1911.

Berengar of Tours, *Letter to Adelmann of Liège (Purgatoria epistola contra Almannum)*, ed. de Montclos 1971, pp. 531–8.

Rescriptum contra Lanfrannum, ed. R. B. C. Huygens, *CCCM* lxxxiv (Turnhout 1988).

Bernard of Clairvaux, *Breuis commentatio in canticum canticorum, PL* clxxxiv, cols 407–36.

Letter 77, ed. J. Leclercq, *S. Bernardi opera*, vii (Rome 1974), pp. 184–200.

Bernardus Silvestris, *Cosmographia*, ed. with introd. and notes by P. Dronke, Textus minores in usum academicum, 53 (Leiden 1978).

Beroldus, *see under* 'Liturgical sources and rituals'.

Life of Boniface, in Talbot 1954, pp. 23–62.

Boniface II, Pope, *Letter to Caesarius of Arles*, Mansi viii, cols. 735–7.

Caesarius of Arles, *Sermo* 225, ed. G. Morin, *CCSL* civ (Turnhout 1953) pp. 888–92.

Sermo 229, ibid., pp. 905–10.

Christ and Satan, in *Anglo-Saxon Poetry*, selected and transl. by R. K. Gordon (London etc. 1954).

Chromatius of Aquileia, *Sermo* 14, ed. R. Etaix and J. Lemarié, *Chromatii Aquileiensis opera, CCSL* ixa (Turnhout 1974), pp. 62–4.

Sermo 15, ibid., pp. 66–70.

Community Rule, transl. G. Vermes, in *The Dead Sea Scrolls in English*, pp. 71–94.

Corpus Hermeticum IV, ed. Scott 1924, pp. 157–65.

Corpus Praefationum, ed. E. Moeller, *Etude préliminaire, CCCM* clxi (Turnhout 1981).

Crispin, Gilbert, *De altaris sacramento*, ed. A. S. Abulafia and G. R. Evans, Auctores Britannici Medii Aevi, 8 (London and Oxford 1986), pp. 124–42.

Cyprian of Carthage, *Ad Donatum*, ed. M. Simonetti, *CCSL* iiia (Turnhout 1976) pp. 3–13.

Bibliography

De lapsis, ed. M. Bévenot, *CCSL* III (Turnhout 1972), pp. 220–42.

Letters, ed. G. Hartel, *S. Thasci Caecilii Cypriani opera omnia, CSEL* III (Vienna 1868), pp. 464–842.

Pseudo-Cyprian, *De xii abusiuis saeculi*, ed. S. Hellmann, *Texte und Untersuchungen zur Geschichte der altchristlichen Literatur*, ed. A. von Harnack and C. Schmidt, XXXIV (Leipzig 1910), pp. 32–60.

Cyril of Jerusalem, *Mystagogic Catecheses*, ed. A. Piedagnel, *SC* CXXVI (Paris 1966).

The Dead Sea Scrolls in English, ed. and transl. G. Vermes (London 1975).

Dhuoda, *Manuale*, ed. P. Riché, transl. into French by B. de Vregille and C. Mondésert, *Manuel pour mon fils, SC* CCXXV (Paris 1975).

Didache, ed. and transl. C. Bigg and A. J. Maclean (London 1912).

Diogenes Laertius, *Lives of the Eminent Philosophers*, ed. and transl. R. D. Hicks, 2 vols., Loeb Classical Library (Harvard and London 1925).

Diognetus, Letter to, transl. by M. Stanforth in *Early Christian Writings. The Apostolic Fathers* (Harmondsworth 1968), pp. 173–85.

Einhard, *Life of Charlemagne*, ed. and transl. L. Halphen, *Eginhard, Vie de Charlemagne*, Classiques de l'histoire de France au moyen âge (Paris 1967).

Eusebius of Caesarea, *De uita Constantini, PG* XX, cols. 909–1230.

Exegesis on the Soul, ed. and transl. W. Förster in *Gnosis. A Selection of Gnostic Texts*. Engl. edn and transl. by R. M. Wilson, 2 vols. (Oxford 1972 and 1974), II, pp. 102–9.

Faustus of Riez, *Homilia de Pentecosten*, ed. Buchem 1967, pp. 40–4.

Firmicus Maternus, Julius, *De errore profanarum religionum*, ed. and transl. G. Heuten, Travaux de la Faculté de Philosophie et Lettres de l'Université de Bruxelles, 8 (Brussels 1938).

Fulcher of Chartres, *Expedition to Jerusalem*, in H. S. Fink (ed.), *Fulcher of Chartres. A History of the Expedition to Jerusalem 1095–1127*, transl. from the Latin by F. R. Ryan (Knoxville, Tenn., 1969).

Gospel of Philip, ed., transl. W. Förster in *Gnosis. A Selection of Gnostic Texts*, Engl. edn and transl. by R. M. Wilson, 2 vols. (Oxford 1972 and 1974), II, pp. 76–101.

Gospel of Thomas, ed. and transl. from Coptic by A. Guillaumont and others, *The Gospel according to Thomas* (Leiden and London 1959).

Gottschalk of Orbais, *De praedestinatione*, in *Œuvres théologiques et grammaticales de Gottschalk d'Orbais*, ed. D. C. Lambot, Spicilegium sacrum Lovaniense, Études et documents, 20 (Louvain 1945), pp. 180–258.

Gratian, *Decretum*, ed. E. Friedberg, *Decretum Magistri Gratiani*, in *Corpus Juris Canonici*, I (1879).

Gregory the Great, *Letter to Augustine of Canterbury (Liber Responsionum)*, in Bede, *Historia Ecclesiastica*, 1.27, pp. 78–103.

Registrum epistularum libri xiv, ed. D. Norberg, *CCSL* CXL (1–7), CXLA (7–14) (Turnhout 1982).

Gregory of Tours, *The History of the Franks*, transl. L. Thorpe (Harmondsworth 1974).

Guibert de Nogent, *De bucella Iudae data, et de ueritate dominici corporis, PL* CLVI, cols. 527–38.

Bibliography

Monodiae, ed. E. R. Labande, *Guibert de Nogent, Autobiographie*, Classiques de l'histoire de France au moyen âge, 34 (Paris 1984).

Guitmund of Aversa, *De corporis et sanguinis Christi ueritate in eucharistia*, PL CXLIX, cols. 1427–94.

Herbord, *Vita Ottonis* (*see under* Otto)

Hildefonsus of Toledo, *Liber de cognitione baptismi*, PL XCVI, cols. 111–72.

Liber de itinere deserti quo pergitur post baptismum, PL XCVI, cols. 171–92.

Hippolytus of Rome, *Commentary on Daniel*, ed. and transl. G. Bardy, SC XIV (Paris 1947).

Apostolic Tradition (*see under* 'Liturgical sources and rituals')

The Hymn of the Pearl, in Hennecke-Schneemelcher 1965, pp. 498–504.

Hymns Scrolls, transl. G. Vermes, in *The Dead Sea Scrolls in English*, pp. 149–201.

Isidore of Seville, *Etymologiae*, ed. W. M. Lindsay, *Isidori Hispalensis Episcopi Etymologiarum sive originum libri xx*, Scriptorum classicorum bibliotheca Oxoniensis, 2 vols. (Oxford 1911).

Ivo of Chartres, *Decretum*, PL CLXI, cols. 47–1022.

Sermo de sacramentis neophytorum, PL CLXII, cols. 505–12.

Jerome, *De uiris illustribus*, PL XXIII, cols. 601–720.

In psalmos, ed. G. Morin, CCSL LXXVIII (Turnhout 1958), pp. 3–447.

Jesse of Amiens, *Epistola de baptismo*, PL CV, cols. 781–96.

John of Salisbury, *Metalogicon*, ed. C. C. J. Webb (Oxford 1929).

John the Deacon, *Epistola ad Senarium*, in Wilmart 1933, pp. 170–9.

Jonas of Orléans, *De institutione laicali*, PL CVI, cols. 121–278.

De institutione regia, PL CVI, cols. 279–306.

Lactantius, *Diuinae institutiones*, PL VI, cols. 111–322.

Lanfranc of Bec, *Liber de corpore et sanguine domini nostri aduersus Berengarium*, ed. J. A. Giles, *Beati Lanfranci archiepiscopi Cantuariensis opera quae supersunt omnia*, 2 vols. (Oxford 1844), II, pp. 147–99.

Leidrad of Lyon, *Liber de sacramento baptismi*, PL XCIX, cols. 853–72.

Leo the Great, *Sermo 62*, PL LIV, cols. 349–52.

Lucretius, *De rerum natura*, ed. and transl. into French by A. Ernout, 2 vols. (Paris 1924).

Magnus of Sens, *Libellus de mysterio baptismatis*, PL CII, cols. 981–4.

Life of St Martin, ed. J. Fontaine, *Sulpice Sévère, Vie de Saint Martin*, 3 vols., SC CXXXIII–CXXXV (Paris 1967–9).

Maximus of Turin, *Sermons*, ed. A. Mutzenbecher, *Maximi Episcopi Taurinensis Collectio Sermonum antiqua nonnullis sermonibus extrauagantibus adiectis*, CCSL XXIII (Turnhout 1962).

Melito of Sardis, *Fragment on Baptism*, in Grant 1957, pp. 73–4.

Homily on the Passion, ed. and transl. C. Bonner, *Melito, Bishop of Sardis, The Homily of the Passion, with some Fragments of the Apocryphal Ezekiel*, Studies and Documents, 12 (London and Philadelphia 1940).

Minucius Felix, *Octauius*, ed. B. Krytzler, Bibliotheca Scriptorum graecorum et romanorum Teubneriana (Leipzig 1982).

Montaigne, Michel Eyquem de, *Essais*, ed. M. Rat, 2 vols. (Paris 1962).

Mosè de Brolo, *Liber Pergaminus*, ed. G. Gorni, 'Il "Liber Pergaminus" di Mosè di Brolo', in *Studi Medievali*, 3rd ser., 11 (1970), pp. 409–60.

Bibliography

The Nag-Hammadi Library in English, transl. by members of the Coptic Gnostic Library Project of the Institute for Antiquity and Christianity, director J. M. Robinson (Leiden 1977).

Odes of Solomon, ed. and transl. Bernard 1912; ed. and transl. Harris and Mingana 1920.

Life of St Odo of Cluny, PL cxxxIII, cols. 43–86.

Optatus of Milevum, *Homily on Mary Magdalen*, in Saxer 1970.

Oratio sancti Brandani, in *Testimonia orationis christianae antiquioris*, ed. P. Salmon, C. Coeburgh and P. de Puniet, *CCCM* xlvii (Turnhout 1977).

Origen, *Contra Celsum*, transl. with an introduction and notes by H. Chadwick (Cambridge 1953).

Life of St Otto of Bamberg: Herbordi vita Ottonis episcopi, ed. R. Köpke, *MGH Script.* xii, pp. 746–822.

Passio SS. Perpetuae et Felicitatis, ed. and transl. H. Musurillo, *The Acts of the Christian Martyrs* (Oxford 1972), pp. 106–31.

Peter the Lombard, *Sentences, Magistri Petri Lombardi Parisiensis Episcopi Sententiae in IV Libris distinctae*, 2 vols., Spicilegium Bonaventurianum, 4–5 (3d edn, Grottaferrata 1971 and 1981).

Peter the Venerable, *De miraculis*, ed. D. Bouthillier, *CCCM* lxxxiii (Turnhout 1988).

   De laude dominici sepulchri, ed. G. Constable, 'Petri Venerabilis sermones tres', in *RB* 64 (1954), pp. 224–72, on pp. 232–54.

Physiologus B, ed. F. J. Carmody, *Physiologus latinus, versio B* (Paris 1939).

Plato, *Meno*, ed. W. R. M. Lamb, Loeb Classical Library (London and Cambridge, Mass., 1952).

   Republic, trans. F. M. Cornford (Oxford 1941).

Polycarp, Martyrdom of, ed. T. Camelot, *SC* x (Paris 1969).

Quodvultdeus of Carthage, *De tempore barbarico*, ed. R. Braun, *Opera Quoduultdeo Carthaginiensi episcopo tributa*, *CCSL* lx (Turnhout 1976), pp. 422–37.

Rabanus Maurus, *De institutione clericorum*, PL cvii, cols. 293–420.

Ratramnus of Corbie, *De corpore et sanguine domini*, PL cxxi, cols. 125–222.

Regularis Concordia, ed. and transl. Dom Thomas Symons, Nelson's Medieval Classics (London etc. 1953).

Life of St Rumwold: Vita Rumwoldi confessoris, ed. C. De Smet and others, in *Acta Sanctorum*, Nov. iii (Paris 1887), pp. 685–90.

Rupert of Deutz, *De diuinis officiis*, ed. H. Haacke, *CCCM* vii (Turnhout 1967).

Siricius, Pope, *Letter to Himerius of Tarragona*, PL xiii, cols. 1131–48.

Suger of St-Denis, *De administratione*, ed. E. Panofsky, *Abbot Suger on the Abbey Church of St.-Denis and its Art Treasures* (Princeton 1946), pp. 40–81.

Sulpicius Severus, *Vita sancti Martini* (*see under* Martin)

Miraculi S. Swithuni, PL clv, cols. 65–80.

Tatian, *Oratio ad Graecos*, ed. and transl. M. Whittaker (Oxford 1982).

Tertullian, *Aduersus Hermogenem*, ed. A. Kroymann, *Tertulliani opera pars i: Opera Catholica, Aduersus Marcionem*, *CCSL* i (Turnhout 1954), pp. 395–435.

   Aduersus Iudaeos, ed. A. Kroymann, *Tertulliani opera pars ii: Opera Montanistica*, *CSL* ii (Turnhout 1954), pp. 1339–96.

Bibliography

Aduersus Marcionem, ed. and transl. E. Evans (Oxford 1972).

Apologeticum, ed. E. Dekkers, *CCSL* I, pp. 85–171.

De anima, ed. J. H. Waszink, *CCSL* II, pp. 780–869.

De baptismo, ed. J. G. P. Borleffs, *CCSL* I, pp. 276–95.

De corona, ed. A. Kroymann, *CCSL* II, pp. 1039–65.

De fuga in persecutione, ed. J. J. Thierry, *CCSL* II, pp. 1135–55.

De oratione, ed. G. P. Diercks, *CCSL* I, pp. 257–74.

De resurrectione mortuorum, ed. J. G. P. Borleffs, *CCSL* II, pp. 920–1012.

De testimonio animae, ed. R. Willems, *CCSL* I, pp. 175–83.

De uirginibus uelandis, ed. E. Dekkers, *CCSL* II, pp. 1207–26.

Scorpiace, ed. A. Reifferscheid and G. Wissowa, *CCSL* II, pp. 1069–97.

Theodoret of Cyrus, *Haereticarum fabularum compendium*, *PG* LXXXIII, cols. 439–556.

Theodulph of Orléans, *Liber de ordine baptismi*, *PL* CV, cols. 223–40.

Treatises of Cyprian, The Treatises of S. Caecilius Cyprian, Bishop of Carthage, and Martyr, Library of Christian Fathers, 3 (Oxford 1839).

Vincent of Lérins, *Commonitorium*, ed. R. S. Moxon (Cambridge 1915).

Walafrid Strabo, *De exordiis et incrementis rerum ecclesiasticarum*, *MGH Capit. reg. Franc.* II, pp. 473–516.

Walter of Honnecourt, *Letter to Roscelin of Compiègne*, ed. G. Morin, in *RB* 22 (1905), pp. 172–5.

William of Conches, *Glosae super Platonem*, ed. E. Jeauneau, Textes philosophiques du moyen âge, 13 (Paris 1965).

William of Malmesbury, *Abbreviatio Amalarii*, in Pfaff 1981.

Life of St Willibrord (by Alcuin), in Talbot 1954, pp. 1–22.

Wulfstan of Winchester, *see under* Æthelwold

Zeno of Verona, *Tractatus*, ed. B. Löfstedt, *CCSL* XXII (Turnhout 1971).

Liturgical sources and rituals

Antiphonary of Bangor: An Early Irish Manuscript in the Ambrosian Library at Milan, ed. F. E. Warren, 2 vols., HBS 4 and 10 (London 1893 and 1895).

Beroldus, *Beroldus sive ecclesiae Ambrosianae Mediolanensis kalendarium et ordines saeculi xii, ex codice Ambrosiano I. 152. Inf.*, ed. M. Magistretti (Milan 1894).

Bobbio Missal, ed. E. A. Lowe, HBS 58 (London 1920).

Fulda Sacramentary, ed. G. Richter and A. Schönfelder, *Sacramentarium Fuldense saeculi x* (Fulda 1912, reprinted HBS 101, London 1980).

Gelasian Sacramentary, ed. L. C. Mohlberg (with L. Eizenhöfer, P. Siffrin), *Liber Sacramentorum Romanae Aecclesiae ordinis anni circuli (Cod. Vat. Reg. Lat. 316/Paris Bibl. Nat. 7193, 41/56)*, Rerum ecclesiasticarum documenta, fontes, 4 (Rome 1960).

Hadrianum, ed. J. Deshusses, *Le Sacramentaire Grégorien. Ses principales formes d'après les plus anciens manuscrits*, Edition comparative, I: 'Le Sacramentaire, le Supplément d'Aniane', Spicilegium Friburgense 16 (Fribourg-en-Suisse 1971), pp. 85–348.

Hadrianum Supplement, ibid., pp. 351–605.

Hippolytus of Rome, *The Apostolic Tradition*, ed. B. Botte, *La Tradition*

Bibliography

Apostolique de saint Hippolyte, Essai de reconstitution, Liturgiewissenschaftliche Quellen und Forschungen, 39 (Münster-in-Westfalen 1963).

Leonine Sacramentary, see under Sacramentarium Veronense

Liber Ordinum, ed. M. Férotin, *Le Liber Ordinum en usage dans l'Eglise Wisigothique et Mozarabe d'Espagne* (Paris 1904).

Liber Sacramentorum Gellonensis, ed. A. Dumas, *CCSL* CLIX (Turnhout 1981).

Manuale Ambrosianum, Manuale Ambrosianum ex codice saeculi XI, ed. M. Magistretti, *Monumenta ueteris Liturgiae Ambrosianae*, III (Milan 1904).

Missale duplex, Missale Ambrosianum duplex . . . ex manuscriptis schedis A. M. Ceriani, ed. A. Ratti and M. Magistretti (Milan 1913).

Missale Francorum, ed. L. C. Mohlberg, L. Eizenhöfer and P. Siffrin, Rerum ecclesiasticarum documenta, Series major, fontes, 2 (Rome 1957).

Missale Gallicanum Vetus, ed. L. C. Mohlberg, L. Eizenhöfer and P. Siffrin, Rerum ecclesiasticarum documenta, Series major, fontes, 3 (Rome 1958).

Missale Gothicum, ed. L. C. Mohlberg, Rerum ecclesiasticarum documenta, Series major, fontes, 5 (Rome 1961).

North Italian Services of the Eleventh Century. Recueil d' 'Ordines' du XIe siècle de la Haute-Italie (Milan Bibl. Ambrosiana T. 27 Suppl.), ed. C. Lambot, HBS 67 (London 1931).

Ordo XI, ed. M. Andrieu, *Les Ordines Romani du haut moyen âge*, II Spicilegium sacrum Lovaniense, 23 (Louvain 1948), pp. 417–47.

Ordo XV, ed. M. Andrieu, ibid., III Spicilegium sacrum Lovaniense, 24 (Louvain 1951), pp. 95–125.

Le Pontifical Romain du haut moyen âge, ed. M. Andrieu, 2 vols., Studi e Testi 86 (Vatican 1938).

Rituel cathare, ed. L. Clédat, in idem, *Le Nouveau Testament traduit au xiiie siècle en Langue provençale, suivi d'un rituel cathare*, Bibliothèque de la Faculté de Lettres de Lyon (Paris 1881), pp. ix–xxvi.

The Romano-Germanic Pontifical of the Tenth Century, ed. R. Elze and C. Vogel, 3 vols., Studi e Testi 226, 227, 269 (Vatican 1963, 1972).

Sacramentarium Veronense, ed. L. C. Mohlberg, with L. Eizenhöfer and P. Siffrin, Rerum Ecclesiasticarum Documenta, Series major, fontes, 1 (Rome 1956).

Sacramentary of Angoulême, Liber Sacramentorum Engolismensis. MS. B.N. lat. 816, Le Sacramentaire Gélasien d'Angoulême, ed. P. S. Roch, *CCSL* CLIXC (Turnhout 1987).

SECONDARY WORKS

Adam, K. 1932. *St. Augustine. The Odyssey of his Soul*, transl. from the German by Dom J. McCann (London).

Aland, K. 1963. *Did the Early Church Baptize Infants ?*, transl. from the German by G. R. Beasley-Murray and J. F. Jansen (London).

Amimann, H. 1962. Review of Russell 1958 in *Historische Zeitschrift* 194, pp. 678–82.

Ancona, P. d' 1935. *Les Primitifs Italiens du XIe au XIIIe siècle* (Paris).

Angelis d'Ossat, G. de 1969. 'Origine e fortuna dei battisteri Ambrosiani', in *Arte Lombarda* 14, pp. 1–20.

Bibliography

Angenendt, A. 1973. 'Taufe und Politik im frühen Mittelalter', in *Frühmittelalterliche Studien* 7, pp. 143–68.

  1984. 'Theologie und Liturgie der mittelalterlichen Toten-Memoria', in K. Schmid and J. Wollasch (eds.), *Memoria. Der geschichtliche Zeugniswert des liturgischen Gedenkens im Mittelalter* (Munich).

  1987. 'Der Taufritus im frühen Mittelalter', in *Segni e Riti nella Chiesa altomedievale occidentale*, Settimane di Studio del Centro Italiano di Studi sull'alto Medioevo, XXXIII, 1985 (Spoleto), pp. 275–336.

Ariès, P. 1960. *L'Enfant et sa famille sous l'Ancien Régime* (Paris).

Arnold, N. 1980. *Kind und Gesellschaft im Mittelalter und Renaissance*, Beiträge und Texte zur Geschichte der Kindheit, Sammlung Zebra B/2 (Paderborn and Munich).

Audet, J.-P. 1958. *La Didachè, Instruction des Apôtres*, Etudes Bibliques (Paris).

Auerbach, E. 1959. 'Figura', in idem, *Scenes from the Drama of European Literature* (New York), pp. 11–76.

  1965. *Literary Language and its Public in Late Antiquity and in the Middle Ages*, transl. R. Mannheim (London).

Auf der Maur, H. J., and Waldram, J. 1981. 'Illuminatio verbi divini – confessio fidei – gratia baptismi. Wort, Glaube und Sakrament in Katechumenat und Taufliturgie bei Origenes', in H. J. Auf der Maur and others (eds.), *Fides sacramenti. Sacramentum fidei, Studies in Honour of P. Smulders* (Assen), pp. 41–95.

Aufhauser, S. 1911. 'Das Drachenwunder des heiligen Georg in der griechischen und lateinischen Uberleiferung', *Byzantinisches Archiv*, 5.

Avery, M. 1936. *The Exultet Rolls of South Italy* (Princeton).

Barnes, T. D. 1971. *Tertullian. A Historical and Literary Study* (Oxford).

Barthes, R. 1987. *Michelet*, transl. from the French by R. Howard (Oxford).

Bartlett, R. 1986. *Trial by Fire and Water, the Medieval Judicial Ordeal* (Oxford).

Barton S. C., and Horsley, G. H. R. 1981. 'A Hellenistic Cult Group and the New Testament Churches', in *Jahrbuch für Antike und Christentum* 24 (Münster-in-Westfalen), pp. 7–41.

Baumstark, A. 1958. *Comparative Liturgy*, revised by B. Botte, English transl. by F. L. Cross (London).

Baxandall, M. 1972. *Painting and Experience in Fifteenth Century Italy. A Primer in the History of Pictorial Style* (Oxford).

Beasley-Murray, G. R. 1962. *Baptism in the New Testament* (London).

Beatrice, P. F. 1978. *Tradux peccati. Alle fonti della dottrina Agostiniana del peccato originale*, Studia Patristica Mediolanensia 8 (Milan).

Beckwith, J. 1972. *Ivory Carvings in Early Medieval England* (London).

Benoit, P. 1965. *Le Baptême chrétien au second siècle. La théologie des Pères*, Etudes d'Histoire et de Philosophie Religieuses de l'Université de Strasbourg 43 (Paris).

Benton, J. F. (ed.) 1970. *Self and Society in Medieval France. The Memoirs of Guibert of Nogent (1064?–c.1125), with Revised Translation of C. C. Swinton Bland* (New York and Evanston).

Bernard, J. H. 1912. *The Odes of Solomon*, Texts and Studies 8.3 (Cambridge).

Bibliography

Bieler, L. 1935 and 1936. *Theios aner, das Bild des 'göttlichen Menschen' in Spätantike und Frühchristentum*, 2 vols. (Vienna).

Blomme, R. 1958. *La Doctrine du péché dans les écoles théologiques du xiie siècle* (Louvain).

Bloomfield, M. W. 1952. *The Seven Deadly Sins: An Introduction to the History of a Religious Concept, with Special Reference to Medieval English Literature* (East Lansing).

Blumenthal, U.-R. (ed.) *Carolingian Essays, Andrew Mellon Lectures in Early Christian Studies* (Washington).

Boas, G. 1948. *Essays in Primitivism and Related Ideas in the Middle Ages* (Baltimore).

Boismard, M.-E. 1956. 'Une liturgie baptismale dans la Prima Petri', in *Revue Biblique* 63, pp. 182ff.

Bond, F. 1908. *Fonts and Font Covers* (London).

Bonner, G. 1986. 'Augustine's Conception of Deification', in *JTS* 37, pp. 369–86.

Borst, A. 1953. *Die Katharer*, Schriften der Monumenta Germaniae Historica, XII (Stuttgart).

Botte, B. 1932. *Les Origines de la Noël et de l'Epiphanie. Etude historique*, Textes et études liturgiques, 1 (Abbaye du Mont César, Louvain).

—— 1951. 'Note sur le symbole baptismal de saint Hippolyte', in *Mélanges J. de Ghellinck* 1 (Gembloux), pp. 189–200.

Botte, B., and Mohrmann, C. 1953. *L'Ordinaire de la Messe, texte critique, traduction et études*, Etudes liturgiques publiées sous la direction du Centre Pastorale Liturgique et l'Abbaye du Mont César 2 (Paris and Louvain).

Bouhot, J.-P. 1978. 'Explications du rituel baptismal à l'époque Carolingienne', in *Revue des études Augustiniennes* 24, pp. 278–301.

—— 1980. 'Alcuin et le "De catechizandis rudibus" de saint Augustin', in *Recherches augustiniennes* 15, pp. 176–240.

Bourque, E. 1948. *Etude sur les sacramentaires romains*, 1, Studi di Antichità Cristiana 20 (Vatican).

Bradley, S. A. J. 1982. *Anglo-Saxon Poetry. An Anthology of Old English Poems in Prose Translation* (London).

Bremond, H. 1967–8. *Histoire littéraire du sentiment religieux en France depuis la fin des guerres de religion jusqu'à nos jours*, 11 vols. (2nd edn, Paris).

British Museum 1923. *British Museum: Reproductions from Illustrated Manuscripts*, ser. 1 (3rd edn, London).

Brooke, C. N. L. 1969. *The Twelfth Century Renaissance* (London).

—— 1977. 'The Medieval Town as an Ecclesiastical Centre: General Survey', in M. W. Barley (ed.), *European Towns, their Archaeology and Early History* (London), pp. 459–74.

Browe, P. 1938. *Die Eucharistischen Wunder des Mittelalters*, Breslauer Studien zur historischen Theologie, NF, 4 (Breslau).

Brown, P. 1969. *Augustine of Hippo. A Biography* (2nd edn, London).

—— 1981. *The Cult of the Saints. Its Rise and Function in Latin Christianity* (Chicago).

—— 1988. *The Body and Society. Men, Women and Sexual Renunciation in Early Christianity* (New York).

Bibliography

Brown, R. E., and others (eds.) 1968. *The Jerome Biblical Commentary*, 2 vols. (London).

Buber, M. 1955. *I and Thou*, transl. from the German by R. G. Smith (Edinburgh).

Buchem, L. A. van 1967. *L'Homélie pseudo-Eusébienne de Pentecôte. L'Origine de la 'confirmatio' en Gaule Méridionale et l'interprétation de ce rite par Fauste de Riez* (Nijmegen).

Büchler, A. 1928. *Studies in Sin and Atonement in the Rabbinic Literature of the First Century*, Jews' College Publications 11 (London).

Bullough, D. 1983. 'Alcuin and the Kingdom of Heaven', in Blumenthal 1983, pp. 1–69.

Bultmann, R. 1972. 'New Testament and Mythology', in H.-W. Bartsch (ed.), *Kerygma and Myth. A Theological Debate*, transl. R. H. Fuller (London), pp. 1–44.

Bynum, C. W. 1980. 'Did the Twelfth Century Discover the Individual?', in *JEH*, 31, pp. 1–17.

   1982. 'The Spirituality of the Regular Canons in the Twelfth Century', in idem, *Jesus as Mother. Studies in the Spirituality of the High Middle Ages* (Berkeley), pp. 22–58.

   1987. *Holy Feast and Holy Fast. The Religious Significance of Food to Medieval Women* (Berkeley and London).

Camelot, P. T. 1978. 'Profession de foi baptismale et symbole des apôtres', in *La Maison-Dieu* 134, pp. 19–30.

Campbell, J. 1973. 'Observations on the Conversion of England', in *Ampleforth Journal* 78, pp. 12–26; reprinted in idem, *Essays in Anglo-Saxon History* (London 1986), pp. 69–84.

Capelle, B. 1930, 'Les Origines du Symbole Romain', in *RTAM* 2, pp. 5–20.

   1933. 'L'Introduction du catéchumenat à Rome', in *RTAM* 5, pp. 129–54.

Cappuyns, M. 1934. 'L'Origine des "Capitula" d'Orange 529', in *RTAM* 6, pp. 121–42.

Casel, O. 1925. 'Der Taufe als Brautbad der Kirche', in *JLW* 5, pp. 144–7.

   1926. 'Das Mysteriumgedächtnis der Messliturgie im Lichte der Tradition', in *Jahrbuch für Liturgiewissenschaft* 6, pp. 113–204.

Cassirer, E. 1963. *Individual and Cosmos in Renaissance Philosophy* (Oxford).

Cattaneo, E. 1954. 'Particolarità del rito Ambrosiano', in *Storia di Milano*, Fondazione Treccani degli Alfieri per la Storia di Milano, vol. 3, part 8, pp. 804–37.

   1970. 'Il battistero in Italia dopo il Mille', in *Miscellanea G. G. Meersseman, Italia Sacra*, 15–16, 2 vols. (Padua), 1, pp. 171–5.

Chadwick, H. 1980. 'The Domestication of Gnosis', in Laynton 1980, pp. 3–16.

   1989. 'Ego Berengarius', in *JTS* 40, pp. 414–45.

   1990. 'Symbol and Reality: Berengar and the Appeal to the Fathers', in *Auctoritas und Ratio. Studien zu Berengar von Tours*, Wolfenbütteler Mittelalter Studien, 2, ed. P. Ganz and others (Wiesbaden), pp. 25–45.

Chavasse, A. 1958. *Le Sacramentaire gélasien (Vaticanus Reginensis 316), sacramentaire presbytéral en usage dans les titres romains au viie siècle*, Bibliothèque de théologie, ser. 4, histoire de théologie, 1 (Tournai).

Bibliography

Chenu, M.-D. 1976. *La Théologie au douzième siècle*, Etudes de philosophie médiévale, 45 (3d edn, Paris).

Clanchy, M. T. 1990. 'Abelard's Mockery of St. Anselm', in *JEH* 41, pp. 1–23.

Clark Hall, J. R. (ed.) 1911. *Beowulf and the Finnesburg Fragment*, a translation into modern English prose, revised by C. L. Wrenn, introd. by J. R. R. Tolkien (London).

Claude, D. 1960. *Topographie und Verfassung der Städte Bourges und Poitiers bis in das 11. Jahrhundert*, Historische Studien, 380 (Lübeck and Hamburg).

Coleman, E. F. 1987. 'Cremona. City and Civic Identity 996–1128', (DPhil Oxford).

Colgrave, B. 1958. 'The Earliest Saints' Lives Written in England', in *Proceedings of the British Academy* 44, pp. 35–60.

Congar, Y. 1968. *L'Ecclésiologie du haut moyen âge* (Paris).

Connolly, R. H. 1916. *The So-Called Egyptian Church Order and Derived Documents* (Cambridge).

　　1924. 'On the Text of the Baptismal Creed of Hippolytus', in *JTS* 35, pp. 131–9.

Courcelle, P. 1953. 'L'Enfant et les sorts bibliques', in *Vigiliae Christianae* 7, pp. 194–220.

Cullmann, O. 1948. *Le Baptême des enfants et la doctrine biblique du baptême*, Cahiers théologiques de l'actualité protestante 19/20 (Neuchâtel and Paris).

　　1951. *Christ and Time*, transl. from the French by F. V. Filson (London).

　　1966. *Early Christian Worship* (London).

Cumont, F. 1929. *Les Religions orientales dans le paganisme romain* (Paris).

Curtius, E. R. 1953. *European Literature and the Latin Middle Ages* (London).

Dalton, O. M. 1909. *Catalogue of the Ivory Carvings of the Christian Era in the Department of British and Mediaeval Antiquities and Ethnography of the British Museum* (London).

Daniélou, J. 1950. *Sacramentum Futuri. Etudes sur les origines de la typologie biblique* (Paris).

　　1964. *The Theology of Jewish-Christianity. The Development of Christian Doctrine before the Council of Nicaea*, 1 ed. and transl. J. A. Baker (London).

Davies, J. G. 1962. *The Architectural Setting of Baptism* (London).

Davies, W. O. 1955. *Paul and Rabbinic Judaism* (London).

Degani, E. 1922. *La diocesi di Concordia* (Udine).

Deichmann, F. W. 1958. *Frühchristliche Bauten und Mosaiken von Ravenna* (Baden-Baden).

de Labriolle, P. 1913. *Les Sources de l'histoire du Montanisme, textes grecs, latins, syriaques* (Fribourg-en-Suisse).

Delbono, F. 1967. 'La letteratura catechetica di lingua tedesca (il problema della lingua nell'evangelizzazione)', in *La Conversione al Cristianesimo nell'Europa dell'alto Medioevo*, Settimane di studio del centro Italiano di Studi sull'alto Medioevo XIV, 1966 (Spoleto), pp. 697–741.

de Lubac, H. 1949. *Corpus mysticum, l'eucharistie et l'Eglise au moyen âge* (2nd edn, Paris).

331

Bibliography

de Montclos, M. 1971. *Lanfranc et Bérenger. La controverse eucharistique du xie siècle*, Spicilegium sacrum Lovaniense, études et documents, 37 (Louvain).

Demus, O. 1949. *The Mosaics of Norman Sicily* (London).

1970. *Romanesque Mural Painting*, transl. from the German by M. Whittall (London).

1984. *The Mosaics of San Marco in Venice*, 4 vols. (Chicago).

De Rubeis, G. F. 1754. *Dissertationes duae: prima de Turranio, seu Tyrannio Rufo … altera de vetustis liturgicis aliisque sacris ritibus, qui vigebant olim in aliquibus Forojuliensis provinciae ecclesiis* (Venice).

Dibelius, M. 1956. 'Paul on the Areopagus', in idem, *Studies in the Acts of the Apostles*, ed. H. Greeven (London), pp. 26–77.

Didier, J.-C. 1959. *Le Baptême des enfants dans la tradition de L'Eglise*, Monumenta Christiana Selecta, 7 (Tournai etc.).

Dix, G. 1945. *The Shape of the Liturgy* (London).

1953. *Jew and Greek. A Study in the Primitive Church* (London).

Dodd, C. H. 1953. *The Interpretation of the Fourth Gospel* (Cambridge).

Dodds, E. R. 1951. *The Greeks and the Irrational* (Berkeley).

1965. *Pagan and Christian in an Age of Anxiety* (Cambridge).

Dölger, F. J. 1909. *Der Exorcismus in altchristlichen Taufritual*, Studien zur Geschichte und Kultur des Altertums, 3 (Paderborn).

Sphragis. Eine altchristliche Taufbezeichnung in ihren Beziehung zur profan und religiöse Kultur des Altertums, Studien zur Geschichte und Kultur des Altertums, 5, part 3/4 (Paderborn).

1930. *Antike und Christentum. Kultur- und Religionsgeschichtliche Studien* (Münster-in-Westfalen), II, pp. 1–40: 'Antike Parallelen zum leidenden Dinocrates in der Passio Perpetuae'; II, pp. 117–141: 'Tertullian über die Bluttaufe. Tertullian De baptismo 16'; II pp. 252–7: 'Die Inschrift im Baptisterium S. Giovanni in Fonte an der Lateranensischen Basilika aus der Zeit Xystus' III (432–40) und die Symbolik des Taufbrunnens bei Leo dem Grossen'.

1934. *Antike und Christentum*, IV pp. 153–87: 'Zur Symbolik des altchristlichen Taufhauses, I, Das Oktogon und die Symbolik der Achtzahl. Die Inschrift des hl. Ambrosius im Baptisterium der Theklakirche von Mailand'.

1950. *Antike und Christentum*, VI, pp. 70–1: '*Iuppiter omnipotens* – Allmächtiger Gott!'.

Doob, P. R. 1990. *The Idea of the Labyrinth from Classical Antiquity through the Middle Ages* (Cornell).

Doresse, J. 1960. *The Secret Books of the Egyptian Gnostics* (London).

Driscoll, M. S. 1986. 'Alcuin et la pénitence à l'époque Carolingienne', thèse présentée pour l'obtention du doctorat du IIIe cycle en sciences des religions, Université de Paris, Sorbonne-Institut Catholique, Paris.

Dronke, P. 1974. *Fabula. Explorations into the Uses of Myth in Medieval Platonism* (Leiden and Cologne).

1984. *Women Writers of the Middle Ages* (Cambridge).

1986. *Poetic Individuality in the Middle Ages. New Departures in Poetry 1000–1150*, Westfield Publications in Medieval Studies, 1 (2nd edn, London).

Bibliography

Duby, G. 1964. 'Au douzième siècles: les "jeunes" dans la société aristocratique', in *Annales, Economies, Sociétés, Civilisations* 19, pp. 835–46.

Dujarier, M. 1962. *Le Parrainage des adultes aux trois premiers siècles de l'Eglise. Recherches historiques sur l'évolution des garanties et des étapes catéchumenales avant 313* (Paris).

Dumont, L. 1983. *Essais sur l'individualisme. Une perspective anthropologique sur l'idéologie moderne* (Paris).

Dupont-Sommer, A. 1961. *The Essene Writings from Qumran*, transl. G. Vermes (Oxford).

Dupront, A. 1987. *Du sacré. Croisades et pèlerinages, images et langages* (Paris).

Edsman, C.-M. 1940. *Le Baptême de feu*, Acta Seminarii neotestamentici upsaliensis 9 (Leipzig and Uppsala).

Eliot, T. S. 1934. 'Tradition and the Individual Talent', in *Selected Essays* (2d edn, London), pp. 13–22.

Erdmann, C. 1977. *The Origin of the Idea of Crusade*, transl. from the German by M. W. Baldwin and W. Goffart (Princeton).

Evans, E. (ed.) 1964. *Tertullian's Homily on Baptism* (London).

Evans-Pritchard, E. E. 1965. *Theories of Primitive Religion* (Oxford).

Ferluga, J., Hellmann, M., and Ludat, H. (eds.) 1977. *Glossar zur frühmittelalterlichen Geschichte im Ostlichen Europa*, series A: 'Lateinische Namen bis 900', 1 (Wiesbaden).

Festugière, A. J. 1932. *L'Idéal religieux des Grecs et L'Evangile*, Etudes Bibliques (Paris).

1938. 'Hermetica, I. Le baptême dans le cratère (C.H. IV. 3–4)', in *Harvard Theological Review* 31, pp. 1–12.

1967. *Hermétisme et mystique païenne* (Paris).

Février, P.-A. 1954. 'Les Baptistères de Provençe pendant le moyen âge', in *Actes du Ve Congrès International d'archéologie chrétienne* (Vatican and Paris).

Fischer, H. 1926. *Mittelalterliche Miniaturen aus der Staatlichen Bibliothek Bamberg* (Bamberg).

Fisher, J. D. C. 1965. *Christian Initiation: Baptism in the Medieval West. A Study in the Disintegration of the Primitive Rite of Initiation*, Alcuin Club Collection 47 (London).

Fliche, A. 1924. *La Réforme Grégorienne*, 1, *La Formation des idées Grégoriennes*, Spicilegium sacrum Lovaniense, Etudes et documents, 6 (Louvain and Paris).

Focillon, H. 1964. *Vie des formes* (5th edn, Paris).

Forsyth, G. H., and Weitzmann K. 1973. *The Monastery of St. Catherine at Mt. Sinai*, vol. of plates (Ann Arbor, Mich.).

Foster, K. 1957. *God's Tree, Essays on Dante and Other Matters* (London).

1977. *The Two Dantes* (London).

Foulquié, P. 1927. 'Un texte de s. Augustin sur la matière et la forme des sacrements', in *Recherches de science religieuse* 17, p. 146.

Fournier, P. and Le Bras, G. 1931–2. *Histoire des collections canoniques en Occident depuis les fausses décrétales jusqu'au décret de Gratien*, 2 vols. (Paris).

Franz, A. 1909. *Die kirchlichen Benediktionen im Mittelalter*, 2 vols. (Freiburg-in-Breisgau).

Franz, M.-L. von 1951. '*Die Passio Perpetuae*. Versuch einer psychologischen

Deutung', in C. G. Jung, *Aion. Untersuchungen zur Symbolgeschichte* (Zurich), pp. 387–496.

Frazer, J. G. 1922. *The Golden Bough. A Study in Magic and Religion* (abridged edn, London).

Fredouille, J.-C. 1972. *Tertullien et la conversion de la culture antique*, Etudes Augustiniennes (Paris).

Frend, W. H. C. 1952. *The Donatist Church. A Movement of Protest in Roman North Africa* (Oxford).

Freud, S. 1986. *The Essentials of Psycho-analysis*, selected, with an introduction and commentaries, by Anna Freud, transl. from the German by James Strachey (Harmondsworth).

Fridh, Å 1968. *Le Problème de la Passion des saintes Perpétue et Félicité*, Studia Graeca et Latina Gothoburgensia 26 (Göteborg).

Friedmann, A. 1959. *Paris, ses rues, ses paroisses, du moyen âge à la révolution: origine et évolution des circonscriptions paroissiales* (Paris).

Garrigou-Lagrange, R. 1954. 'La Grâce efficace et la grâce suffisante selon saint Augustin', in *Angelicum* 31, pp. 243–51.

Geertz, C. 1973. *The Interpretation of Cultures. Selected Essays* (New York).

Gessler, J. 1946. 'Notes sur l'incubation et ses survivances', in *Le Muséon* 59, pp. 661–70.

Ghellinck, J. de 1949. *Patristique et Moyen Age. Etudes d'histoire littéraire et doctrinale*, I, *Les Recherches sur les origines du symbole des Apôtres* (Gembloux, Brussels and Paris).

Gibson, M. T. 1978. *Lanfranc of Bec* (Oxford).

1990. 'Letters and Charters Relating to Berengar of Tours', in P. Ganz and others (eds.), *Auctoritas und Ratio. Studien zu Berengar von Tours* (Wiesbaden), pp. 5–23.

Giet, S. 1970. *L'Enigme de la Didachè*, Publications de la Faculté des Lettres, Université de Strasbourg, 149.

Gilson, E. 1944. *L'Esprit de la philosophie médiévale*, Etudes de philosophie médiévale, 33 (2nd edn, Paris).

Godman, P. 1985. *Poetry of the Carolingian Renaissance* (London).

Golb, N. 1985. 'Les Manuscrits de la Mer Morte: une nouvelle approche du problème de leur origine', in *Annales, Economies, Sociétés, Civilisations*, 40, pp. 1133–49.

Gombrich, E. H. 1966. 'The Renaissance Conception of Artistic Progress and its Consequences', in idem, *Norm and Form* (London), pp. 1–10.

Gougaud, L. 1911, 1912. 'Etude sur les loricae celtiques et sur les prières qui s'en rapprochent', in *Bulletin d'ancienne littérature et d'archéologie chrétienne* (1911), pp. 265–81; (1912), pp. 33–41, 101–27.

Grabar, A. 1946. *Martyrium. Recherches sur le culte des reliques et l'art chrétien antique*, 2 vols. (Paris).

1951. 'La Représentation de l'intelligible dans l'art byzantin du moyen âge', in *Actes du VIe Congrès International d'Etudes Byzantines* 2 (Paris), pp. 127–43.

1953. *Byzantine Painting* (Lausanne).

1968. *L'Art du Moyen Age en Europe Orientale* (Paris).

1969. *Christian Art. A Study of its Origins* (London).

Bibliography

Grant, R. M. 1949. 'Melito of Sardis on Baptism', in *Vigiliae Christianae* 3, pp. 33–6.

1957. *Second Century Christianity: A Collection of Fragments* (London).

Gregory, T. 1955. *Anima mundi, la filosofia di Guglielmo di Conches e la scuola di Chartres*, Pubblicazioni del Istituto di filosofia, Università di Roma, 3 (Florence).

Grimm, J., and Grimm, W. 1854 (1984). *Deutsches Wörterbuch* (Leipzig; reprinted in 33 vols., Munich).

Gros, M. S. 1975. 'El antiguo ordo bautismal catalono-Narbonense', in *Hispania Sacra, Revista de Historia Eclesiastica* 38, pp. 37–101.

Gross, J. 1960. *Entstehungsgeschichte des Erbsündendogmas*, 2 vols. (Munich and Basel).

Guiraud, J. 1904. 'Le "Consolamentum" Cathare', in *Revue des questions historiques* 75, pp. 74–112.

Gy, P.-M. 1978. 'Quand et pourquoi la communion dans la bouche a-t-elle remplacé la communion dans la main dans l'église latine?', in *Gestes et paroles dans les diverses familles liturgiques*, Conférences Saint-Serge, XXIVe semaine d'études liturgiques, Paris, 28 juin – 1 juillet 1977 (Rome), pp. 117–21.

1982. 'La Formule "je te baptise" (et ego te baptizo)', in *Communio sanctorum. Mélanges offerts à J. J. von Allmen* (Geneva), pp. 65–72.

1987. 'La Doctrine eucharistique dans la liturgie romaine du haut moyen-âge', in *Segni e Riti nella Chiesa altomedievale occidentale*, Settimane di studio del Centro Italiano di studi sull'alto Medioevo, 33, Spoleto, 1985, pp. 533–54.

Hall, J. R. 1976. 'The Old English Epic of Redemption: The Theological Unity of MS Junius 11' in *Traditio* 32, pp. 185–208.

Halphen, L. 1921. *Etudes critiques sur l'histoire de Charlemagne* (Paris).

Hanning, R. W. 1979. ' "Mony Turned Tyme": The Cycle of the Year as a Religious Symbol in Two Medieval Texts', in King and Stevens 1979, pp. 281–98.

Hanssens, J.-M. 1959. *La Littérature d'Hippolyte: ses documents, son titulaire, ses origines et son caractère*, Orientalia Christiana Analecta, 155 (Rome).

Harnack, A. von 1904. *The Expansion of Christianity in the First Three Centuries*, transl. from the German by J. Moffatt, 2 vols. (London and New York).

1924. *Marcion: das Evangelium vom fremden Gott* (2nd edn, Leipzig).

Harris, M., and Mingana, A. 1920. *The Odes and Psalms of Solomon*, 2 vols. (Manchester etc.).

Heaney, S. 1983. *Sweeney Astray* (London).

Heers, J. 1974. *Le Clan familial au moyen âge* (Paris).

Hegel, G. W. F. 1956. *The Philosophy of History*, transl. from the German by J. Sibree (New York).

Hill, R. 1976. 'Bede and the Boors', in G. Bonner (ed.), *Famulus Christi. Essays in Commemoration of the Thirteenth Centenary of the Birth of the Venerable Bede* (London), pp. 93–105.

Hoffmann, K. 1968. *Taufsymbolik im mittelalterlichen Herrscherbild*, Bonner Beiträge zur Kunstwissenschaft, 9 (Dusseldorf).

Hubert, H. 1972. *Der Streit um die Kindertaufe. Eine Darstellung der von Karl Barth*

Bibliography

1943 ausgelösten Diskussion um die Kindertaufe und ihre Bedeutung für die heutige Tauffrage (Frankfurt-am-Main).

Hubert, H. and Mauss, M. 1899 (1968). 'Essai sur la fonction et la nature du sacrifice', in *Année Sociologique* 2, pp. 29–138; reprinted in M. Mauss, *Oeuvres*, I, *Les Fonctions sociales du sacré* (Paris).

Hyams, P. 1981. 'Trial by Ordeal: The Key to Proof in Early Common Law', in M. S. Arnold and others (eds.), *On the Laws and Customs of England: Essays in Honor of Samuel E. Thorne* (Chapel Hill).

Jaeger, W. 1962. *Early Christianity and Greek Paideia*, Carl Newell Jackson Lectures 1960 (Cambridge Mass.).

James, W. 1960. *The Varieties of Religious Experience* (London).

Jeanmaire, H. 1952. 'Sexualité et mysticisme dans les anciennes sociétés hélléniques', in *Mystique et Continence*, Etudes Carmélitaines (Paris and Bruges), pp. 51–60.

Jeremias, J. 1967. *Le Baptême des enfants dans les quatre premiers siècles*, transl. from the German by B. Hübsch and F. Stoessel (Le Puy and Lyon).

1972. *The Parables of Jesus* (London).

Jonas, H. 1958. *The Gnostic Religion. The Message of the Alien God and the Beginnings of Christianity* (2nd edn, Boston).

Jones, C., Wainwright, G. and Yarnold, E. 1978. *The Study of the Liturgy* (London).

Jones, David. 1959. *Epoch and Artist*, ed. H. Grisewood (London).

1974. *The Sleeping Lord and Other Fragments* (London).

Jung, C. G. 1923. *Psychological Types, or, The Psychology of Individuation*, transl. from the German by H. G. Baynes, International Library of Psychology (London and New York).

1967. *Alchemical Studies*, transl. from the German by R. F. C. Hull, in *The Collected Works of C. G. Jung*, XIII (London).

Kaftal, G. 1978. *Iconography of the Saints in the Painting of North East Italy* (Florence).

Kantorowicz, E. 1952. 'Deus per naturam, deus per gratiam', in *Harvard Theological Review* 45, pp. 253–77.

1956. 'The Baptism of the Apostles', in *Dumbarton Oaks Papers* 9–10, pp. 203–51.

1957. *The King's Two Bodies. A Study in Mediaeval Political Theology* (Princeton).

1965. 'Puer exoriens', in *Selected Studies* (Locust Valley, New York), pp. 25–36.

Kartsonis, A. 1986. *Anastasis. The Making of an Image* (Princeton).

Keefe, S. 1984. 'Carolingian Baptismal Expositions: A Handlist of Tracts and Manuscripts', in Blumenthal 1983, pp. 169–237.

Kelly, J. N. D. 1975. *Jerome. His Life, Writings and Controversies* (London).

Kendall, C. B. 1979. 'Imitation and the Venerable Bede's *Historia Ecclesiastica*', in King and Stevens 1979, pp. 161–90.

Kermode, F. 1967. *The Sense of an Ending. Studies in the Theory of Fiction* (Oxford).

Bibliography

Khatchatrian, A. 1962. *Les Baptistères paléochrétiens: plans, notices et bibliographie* (Paris).

1982. *Origine et typologie des baptistères paléochrétiens* (Mulhouse).

Kierkegaard, S. 1939. *Fear and Trembling. A Dialectical Lyric by Johannes de Silentio*, transl. from the Danish by R. Payne (Oxford).

1985. *Johannes Climacus*, in *Philosophical Fragments, Johannes Climacus*, transl. from the Danish by H. V. and E. H. Hong (Princeton).

Kilian. 1989. *Kilian. Mönch aus Irland – aller Franken Patron, 689–1989, Katalog der Sonder-Ausstellung zur 1300-Jahr-Feier des Kiliansmartyriums*, 1 July 1989–1 October 1989, Mainfrankisches Museum, Würzburg (Würzburg).

King, M. H., and Stevens, W. M. (eds.) 1979. *Saints, Scholars and Heroes. Studies in Medieval Culture in Honour of Charles W. Jones*, 2 vols. (Collegeville, Minn.).

Klauser, T. 1939. 'Taufet in lebendigem wasser', in T. Klauser and A. Rücker (eds.), *Pisciculi. Studien zur Religion und Kultur des Altertums*, F. J. Dölger zum sechzigsten Geburtstage dargeboten, Antike und Christentum Ergänzungsband, 1 (Münster-in-Westfalen), pp. 157–64.

Klee, P. 1966. *On Modern Art*, with an introduction by Herbert Read, transl. into Eng. by Paul Findlay (2nd edn, London).

Klibansky, R., Panofsky, E., and Saxl, F. 1964. *Saturn and Melancholy. Studies of Natural Philosophy, Religion and Art* (London).

Knox, R. 1950. *Enthusiasm. A Chapter in the History of Religion, with Special Reference to the XVII and XVIII Centuries* (Oxford).

Krautheimer, R. 1942. 'Introduction to an "Iconography of Medieval Architecture" ', in *Journal of the Warburg and Courtauld Institutes* 5, pp. 1–33.

Kümmel, W. G. 1975. *Introduction to the New Testament* (London).

Ladner, G. B. 1959. *The Idea of Reform. Its Impact on Christian Thought and Action in the Age of the Fathers* (Cambridge, Mass.).

1983. *Images and Ideas in the Middle Ages. Selected Studies in History and Art*, 2 vols., Storia e Letteratura, Raccolti di Studi e Testi 155–6 (Rome).

Lampe, G. W. H. 1961. *A Patristic Greek Lexicon* (Oxford).

1967. *The Seal of the Spirit. A Study in the Doctrine of Baptism and Confirmation in the New Testament and the Fathers* (2nd edn, London).

Landgraf, A. M. 1928. 'Kindertaufe und Glaube in der Frühscholastik', in *Gregorianum* 9, pp. 337–72, 497–543.

1955. *Dogmengeschichte der Frühscholastik*, II, part 3 (Regensburg).

Lasteyrie, R. de 1929. *L'Architecture religieuse en France à l'époque roman* (2nd edn, Paris).

Lavin, I. 1962. 'The House of the Lord. Aspects of the Role of Palace Triclinia in the Architecture of Late Antiquity and the Early Middle Ages', in *Art Bulletin* 44, pp. 1–27.

Laynton, B. L. (ed.) 1980. *The Rediscovery of Gnosticism*, 1, *The School of Valentinus* (Leiden).

Leach, E. 1967. 'Genesis as Myth', in J. Middleton (ed.), *Myth and Cosmos* (New York), pp. 1–13.

Le Blant 1856. *Inscriptions chrétiennes de la Gaule antérieures au viiie siècle*, 1 (Paris).

Bibliography

Leclercq, J. 1953. *Recueil d'études sur saint Bernard et le texte de ses écrits*, Analecta sacri ordinis Cisterciensis, 9.1–2 (Rome).

1968. 'La Tradition: baptême et profession, génèse et évolution de la vie consacrée', in idem, *Aspects du monachisme hier et aujourd'hui* (Paris), pp. 69–97.

1969. *Recueil d'études sur saint Bernard et ses écrits*, III, Storia e letteratura 114 (Rome).

Le Goff, J. 1973. 'Petits enfants de la littérature des XIIe–XIII siècles', in *Enfants et Sociétés* (special issue of *Annales de démographie historique*) (Paris), pp. 29–32.

1981. *La Naissance du Purgatoire* (Paris).

1988. *The Medieval Imagination*, transl. from the French by A. Goldhammer (Chicago and London), pp. 193–231: 'Christianity and Dreams (Second to Seventh Century)'; pp. 47–59: 'The Wilderness in the Medieval West'.

Lehmann, K. 1945. 'The Dome of Heaven', in *Art Bulletin* 27, pp. 1–27.

Levison, W. 1946. *England and the Continent in the Eighth Century*, The Ford Lectures, 1943 (Oxford).

Lévi-Strauss, C. 1962. *La Pensée sauvage* (Paris).

Lévy-Bruhl, L. 1951. *Les Fonctions mentales dans les sociétés inférieures* (9th edn, Paris).

Löfstedt, B. 1959. *Late Latin*, Institut for Sammenlignende Kulturforskining, Serie A: Forelesninger, 25 (Oslo etc.)

Louth, A. 1981. *The Origins of the Christian Mystical Tradition: From Plato to Denys* (Oxford).

1986. 'Pagan Theurgy and Christian Sacramentalism in Denys the Areopagite', in *JTS* 37, pp. 432–8.

Lundberg, P. 1942. *La Typologie baptismale dans l'ancienne église*, Acta seminarii neotestamentaci Upsaliensis, 10 (Leipzig and Uppsala).

Luscombe, D. E. 1969. *The School of Peter Abelard. The Influence of Abelard's Thought in the Early Scholastic Period*, Cambridge Studies in Medieval Life and Thought, n.s. 14 (Cambridge).

1988. 'Peter Abelard', in P. Dronke (ed.), *A History of Twelfth-Century Western Philosophy* (Cambridge).

forthcoming. Paper on Abelard's 'mockery' of St Anselm, Proceedings of the Conference on St Anselm held in Paris under the auspices of the International Anselm Studies Committee, 1990, 'S. Anselme, penseur d'hier et d'aujourd'hui'.

Lynch, J. H. 1986. *Godparenthood and Kinship in Early Medieval Europe* (Princeton).

McKitterick, R. 1977. *The Frankish Church and the Carolingian Reforms 789–895* (London).

Macy, G. 1984. *The Theologies of the Eucharist in the Early Scholastic Period: A Study of the Salvific Function of the Sacrament according to the Theologians, 1080–1220* (Oxford).

Maier, J.-L. 1964. *Le Baptistère de Naples et ses mosaïques. Etude historique et iconographique* (Fribourg-en-Suisse).

Mallardo, D. 1949. 'L'incubazione nella Cristianità medievale napoletana', in *Analecta Bollandiana* 67 (Mélanges Paul Peeters, 1), pp. 465–98.

Bibliography

Manitius, M. 1911–31. *Geschichte der lateinischen Literatur des Mittelalters*, 3 vols. (Munich).

Marett, R. R. 1933. *Sacraments of Simple Folk* (Oxford).

Markus, R. A. 1964. ' "Imago-similitudo" in Augustine', *Revue des études augustiniennes* 10, pp. 125–43.

1970. 'Gregory the Great and a Papal Missionary Strategy', in G. J. Cuming (ed.), *The Mission of the Church and the Propagation of the Faith, Studies in Church History* 6 (Cambridge), pp. 29–38.

Marouzeau, J. 1949. *Quelques aspects de la formation du latin littéraire*, Collection linguistique publiée par la Société de Linguistique de Paris, 53 (Paris).

Marrou, H.-I. 1938. *S. Augustin et la fin de la culture antique*, Bibliothèque des écoles françaises d'Athènes et de Rome (Paris).

1956. *A History of Education in Antiquity*, transl. from the French by A. Lamb (London).

Martimort, A. G. 1949. 'L'Iconographie des catacombes et la catéchèse antique', in *Rivista di archeologia cristiana* 25, pp. 105–14.

Mauck, M. 1975. 'The Apocalypse Frescoes of the Baptistery in Novara, Italy' (PhD, Tulane University), pp. 73–99.

Mauss, M. 1966. 'Une catégorie de l'esprit humain: la notion de la personne, celle du moi', in idem, *Sociologie et anthropologie* (3rd edn, Paris).

Mayer, H. E. 1972. *The Crusades*, transl. J. Gillingham (Oxford).

Mayr-Harting, H. 1972. *The Coming of Christianity to Anglo-Saxon England* (London).

1991. *Ottonian Book Illumination: An Historical Study*, II (London).

Meyer-Baer, K. 1970. *Music of the Spheres and the Dance of Death. Studies in Musical Iconology* (Princeton).

Michaélides, D. 1970. *Sacramentum chez Tertullien* (Paris).

Mitchell, L. L. 1966. *Baptismal Anointing*, Alcuin Club Collection, 48 (London).

Mohrmann, C. 1957. *Liturgical Latin: Its Origins and Character* (London).

1958. *Etudes sur le latin des chrétiens*, I, Storia e letteratura, Raccolta di Studi e Testi, 65 (Rome), pp. 179–87: 'Rationabilis-logikos'; pp. 205–22: 'Pascha, Passio, Transitus'; pp. 233–44: 'Sacramentum chez les plus anciens textes chrétiens'.

1961. Ibid., II, 87, pp. 81–92: 'Locus refrigerii'; pp. 135–53: 'Les former du Latin dit "Vulgaire"'; pp. 235–46: 'Observations sur la langue et le style de Tertullien'.

1965. Ibid., III, 103, pp. 171–96: 'Linguistic Problems in the Early Christian Church'.

1973. 'Sacramentum chez Tertullien', in W. den Boer and others (eds.), *Romanitas et Christianitas: Studia I. Waszink . . . oblata* (Amsterdam and London), pp. 233–42.

Monceaux, P. 1912, 1920, 1922, 1923. *Histoire littéraire de l'Afrique chrétienne depuis les origines jusqu'à l'invasion arabe*, 7 vols, IV, V, VI, VII (Paris).

Moore, R. I. 1980. 'Family, Community and Cult on the Eve of the Gregorian Reform', in *TRHS* 5th ser., 30, pp. 49–69.

1985. 'Guibert de Nogent and his World', in H. Mayr-Harting and R. I.

Moore (eds.), *Studies presented to R. H. C. Davis* (London and Ronceverte), pp. 107–17.

Morghen, R. 1968. 'Problèmes sur l'origine de l'hérésie au moyen âge', in *Hérésies et Sociétés dans l'Europe pré-industrielle, 11e–18e siècles*, Communications et débats du Colloque du Royaumont, Civilisations et Sociétés, 10 (Paris), pp. 121–34.

Morisani, O. 1962. *Gli Affreschi di S. Angelo in Formis* (Naples).

Muratori, S. 1945. *I Mosaici Ravennati della Chiesa di S. Vitale* (2nd edn, Bergamo).

Murray, A. 1978. *Reason and Society in the Middle Ages* (London).

Nardi, B. 1930. *Saggi di Filosofia Dantesca*, Biblioteca Pedagogica Antica e Moderna Italiana e Straniera, 57 (Milan etc.).

Nocent, A. 1967. 'Un fragment de sacramentaire de Sens au Xe siècle. La liturgie baptismale de la province ecclésiastique de Sens dans les manuscrits du IXe au XVIe siècles', in *Miscellanea Liturgica in onore di sua eminenza il Cardinale G. Lercaro* (Rome), pp. 649–794.

Nock, A. D. 1925. 'Studies in Graeco-Roman Beliefs of the Empire', in *Journal of Hellenic Studies* 45, pp. 84–101.

　　1928. *Early Gentile Christianity and its Hellenistic Background* (London).

Norden, E. 1913. *Agnostos Theos. Untersuchungen zur Formengeschichte religiöser Rede* (Leipzig).

Norris, R. 1979. 'The Transcendence and Freedom of God: Irenaeus, the Greek Tradition and Gnosticism', in Schoedel and Wilken 1979, pp. 87–100.

Ohly, F. 1958. *Hohelied-Studien, Grundzüge einer Geschichte der Hohliedauslegung des Abendlandes bis um 1200*, Schriften, Wissenschaftlichen Gesellschaft an der Johann Wolfgang Goethe-Institute, Geisteswissenschaftliche Reihe, 1 (Wiesbaden).

Pächt, O. 1962. *The Rise of Pictorial Narrative in Twelfth-Century England* (Oxford).

Panofsky, E. 1968. *Idea. A Concept in Art History* (New York etc.).

Paredi, E. 1935. 'Formulari battesimali Ambrosiani', in *La Scuola Cattolica* 63, pp. 3–14.

Paschini, P. 1911. 'Note sull'origine della chiesa di Concordia nella Venezia e sul culto agli apostoli nell'Italia settentrionale alla fine del secolo IV', in *Memorie Storiche Forogiuliensi* 7, pp. 9ff.

Pfaff, R. W. 1980. 'The Abbreviatio Amalarii of William of Malmesbury', in *RTAM* 47, pp. 77–113.

　　1981. 'The Abbreviatio Amalarii of William of Malmesbury', in *RTAM* 48, pp. 128–71.

Pierce, M. 1984. 'Themes in the "Odes of Solomon" and Other Early Christian Writings and their Baptismal Character', in *Ephemerides Liturgicae* 98, pp. 35–59.

Plinval, G. de 1958. 'Prosper d'Aquitaine interprète de saint Augustin', in *Recherches Augustiniennes* 1, pp. 339ff.

Pound, Ezra. 1975. *Selected Poems* (London).

Pranger, B. 1984. ' "Studium sacrae scripturae". Comparaison entre les méthodes dialectiques et méditatives dans les œuvres systématiques et dans la

Bibliography

première méditation d'Anselme', in *Les Mutations socio-culturelles au tournant des xie-xiie siècles*, Etudes Anselmiennes (IVe session), Colloques internationaux du CNRS, Abbaye Notre-Dame du Bec, Le Bec-Hellouin, 11–16 juillet 1982 (Paris), pp. 469–90.

Pudelko, M. 1932. *Romanische Taufsteine* (Berlin).

Puech, H.-C. 1949a. 'Le Cerf et le serpent. Note sur le symbolisme de la mosaïque découverte au baptistère de l'Henchir Messaouda', in *Cahiers Archéologiques* 4, pp. 17–60.

1949b. *Le Manichéisme* (Paris).

1978. 'Une collection de paroles de Jésus récemment retrouvée: *L'Evangile selon Thomas*', in idem, *En quête de la Gnose*, 2 vols., Bibliothèque des sciences humaines (Paris), II, pp. 33–57.

1979. 'La Conception manichéene de salut', in idem, *Sur le manichéisme et autres essais* (Paris),. pp. 5–101.

Puppi, L. 1982. *Verso Gerusalemme, Immagini e temi di urbanistica e di architettura simboliche fra il XIV e il XVIII secolo* (Rome).

Quarino, L. 1967. *Il battesimo nel rito aquileiese* (Udine).

Quasten, J. 1939. 'Das Bild des Guten Hirten in der altchristlichen Baptisterien und in den Taufliturgien des Ostens und Westens. Das Siegel der Gottesherde', in T. Klauser and A. Rücker (eds.), *Pisciculi. Studien zur Religion und Kultur des Altertums*, F. J. Dölger zum sechzigsten Geburtstage dargeboten, Antike und Christentum Ergänzungsband, 1 (Münster-in-Westfalen).

1947. 'The Painting of the Good Shepherd at Doura-Europos', in *Mediaeval Studies* 9, pp. 1–18.

1950. *Patrology*, 1 (Utrecht and Brussels).

Quispel, G. 1951. 'L'Inscription de Flavia Sophé', in *Mélanges J. de Ghellinck*, 2 vols. (Gembloux), I, pp. 201–14.

1974. *Gnostic Studies*, Uitgaven van het Nederlands Historisch–Archaeologisch Instituut te Istanbul, 34.1, I (Istanbul), pp. 140–57: 'Das ewige Ebenbild des Menschen zur Begegnung mit dem Selbst in der Gnosis'; pp. 196–212: 'Gnosticism and the New Testament'; pp. 221–39: 'The Birth of the Child. Some Gnostic and Jewish Aspects'.

Read, H. 1943. *Education through Art* (London).

Reggiori, F. 1971. 'Aspetti urbanistici ed architettonici della civiltà communale', in C. D. Fonseca (ed.), *I Problemi della civiltà comunale* (Bergamo), pp. 97–110.

Rice, D. G., and Stambaugh, J. E. 1979. *Sources for the Study of Greek Religion*, Society of Biblical Literature, Sources for Biblical Study, 14 (Missoula, Mont.).

Riché, P. 1976. *Education and Culture in the Barbarian West from the Sixth through the Eighth Century*, transl. from the French by J. J. Contreni (Columbia, S.C.).

Ricoeur, P. 1960. *La Symbolique du mal* (Philosophie de la volonté: finitude et culpabilité, II; Paris).

Riedlinger, H. 1958. *Die Makellosigkeit der Kirche in den lateinischen Hoheliedkommentaren des Mittelalters*, Beiträge zur Geschichte der Philosophie und Theologie des Mittelalters, 38 (Münster-in-Westfalen).

Rivière, J. 1928. 'Le Marché avec le démon chez les Pères antérieurs à Saint Augustin', in *Revue des sciences religieuses* 8, pp. 257–70.

1930. 'Mort et démon chez les pères', in *Revue des sciences religieuses* 10, pp. 577–621.

1933. *Le Dogme de la rédemption chez Saint Augustin* (3rd edn, Paris).

1934. *Le Dogme de la rédemption au début du moyen âge*, Bibliothèque thomiste, Section historique, 16 (Paris).

Robert, F. 1939. *Thymélè: recherches sur la signification et la destination des monuments circulaires dans l'architecture religieuse de la Grèce*, Bibliothèque des écoles françaises d'Athènes et de Rome, 147 (Paris).

Rordorf, R. 1972. 'Un chapitre d'éthique judéo-chrétienne: les deux voies', in *Judéo-christianisme, recherches historiques et théologiques offertes en hommage à Cardinal Jean Daniélou* (Paris), pp. 109ff.

Rosenau, H. 1983. *The Ideal City, its Architectural Evolution in Europe* (London and New York).

Rosser, G. 1990. 'The Essence of Medieval Urban Communities: The Vill of Westminster 1200–1540', in R. Holt and G. Rosser (eds.), *A Reader in English Urban History 1200–1540* (London and New York), pp. 216–37.

Russell, J. C. 1958. 'Late Ancient and Medieval Population', in *Transactions of the American Philosophical Society*, n.s. 48 (Philadelphia), pp. 1–152.

1965. 'Recent Advances in Medieval Demography', in *Speculum* 40, pp. 84–101.

Ryle, G. 1949. *The Concept of Mind* (London).

Sage, A. 1967. 'Péché originel. Naissance d'un dogme', in *Revue des Etudes Augustiniennes* 13, pp. 211–48.

Sagnard, F. M. 1947. *La Gnose Valentinienne et le témoignage de Saint Irénée* (Paris).

Saintyves, P. 1931. *En marge de la légende dorée* (Paris).

Saxer, V. 1970. 'Un sermon médiéval sur la Madeleine, reprise d'une homélie antique attribuable à Optat de Milève (d. 392)', in *RB* 80, pp. 17–50.

Schapiro, M. 1977. 'On Geometrical Schematism in Romanesque Art', in *Romanesque Art, Selected Papers*, 1 (London), pp. 265–84.

Schiel, H. (ed.) 1960. *Codex Egberti der Stadtbibliothek Trier, voll-Faksimile Ausgabe*, 2 vols., Textband, Facsimile (Basel).

Schiller, G. 1971 and 1972. *Iconography of Christian Art*, 2 vols. (London).

Schmitt, J.-C. *The Holy Greyhound. Guinefort, Healer of Children since the Thirteenth Century*, Cambridge Studies in Oral and Literate Culture, 6 (Cambridge and Paris).

Schoedel, W. R. 1979. 'Enclosing, not Enclosed: The Early Christian Doctrine of God', in Schoedel and Wilken 1979, pp. 75–86.

Schoedel, W. R., and Wilken, R. L. (eds.) 1979. *Early Christian Literature and the Classical Intellectual Tradition*, in honorem Robert M. Grant, Collection Théologie Historique, 54 (Paris).

Scholem, G. 1955. *Major Trends in Jewish Mysticism* (London).

Schürer, E. 1973, 1979, 1986. *The History of the Jewish People in the Age of Jesus Christ (175BC–AD 135)*, new English version revised and ed. by G. Vermes, F. Millar and M. Black, 3 vols. (Edinburgh).

Schwartz, E. 1910. *Uber die pseudoapostolischen Kirchenordnung*, Schriften der wissenschaftlichen Gesellschaft in Strassburg, 6 (Strasbourg).

Scott, W. (ed.) 1924. *Hermetica: The Ancient Greek and Latin Writings which*

Bibliography

Contain Religious or Philosophical Teachings Ascribed to Hermes Trismegistus, with English transl. and notes, I (Texts and translations) (Oxford).

Segelberg, E. 1962. 'The Baptismal Rite According to Some of the Coptic-Gnostic Texts of Nag-Hammadi', in *Studia Patristica* 5.3 (Berlin), pp. 117–28.

Sider, R. D. 1971. *Ancient Rhetoric and the Art of Tertullian* (Oxford).

Sinclair, J. D. 1961. *The Divine Comedy of Dante Alighieri*, with transl. and commentary by John D. Sinclair, 3 vols. (New York).

Smalley, B. 1964. *The Study of the Bible in the Middle Ages* (Notre Dame).

Smith, C. 1975. *The Baptistery of Pisa* (New York and London).

Sot, M. 1988. 'Hérédité royale et pouvoir sacré avant 987', in *Annales, Economies, Sociétés, Civilisations* 43, pp. 705–33.

Southern, R. W. 1948. 'Lanfranc of Bec and Berengar of Tours', in R. W. Hunt, W. A. Pantin and R. W. Southern (eds.), *Medieval Studies Presented to F. M. Powicke* (Oxford), pp. 27–48.

1970. 'Aspects of the European Tradition of Historical Writing', I, 'The Classical Tradition from Einhard to Geoffrey of Monmouth', in *TRHS* 5th ser., 20, pp. 173–96.

1971. 'Aspects of the European Tradition of Historical Writing', II, 'Hugh of St. Victor and the Idea of Historical Development', ibid., 21, pp. 159–79.

Spanneut, M. 1957. *Le Stoïcisme des Pères de l'Eglise de Clément de Rome à Clément d'Alexandrie*, préface de H.-I. Marrou, Patristica Sorboniensa, I (Paris).

Steiner, G. 1975. *After Babel. Aspects of Language and Translation* (Oxford).

Stevenson, J. 1987. *The Liturgy and Ritual of the Celtic Church*, by F. E. Warren, 2nd edn, introd. by J. Stevenson (Woodbridge).

Stock, B. 1983. *The Implications of Literacy: Written Language and Models of Interpretation in the Eleventh and Twelfth Centuries* (Princeton).

Stroumsa, G. G. 1982. Review of Louth 1981, in *Numen* 29.2, pp. 278–82.

Swarzenski, G. 1908, 1913. *Die Salzburger Malerei von den ersten Anfängen bis zur Blütezeit des romanischen Stils*, Denkmaler der Süddeutschen Malerei des frühen Mittelalters, 2.1–2, 2 vols. (Leipzig).

Swarzenski, H. 1974. *Monuments of Romanesque Art. The Art of Church Treasures in North-Western Europe* (2d edn, London).

Tafel, S. 1925. 'The Lyons Scriptorium', in W. M. Lindsay (ed.), *Palaeographia latina* 4, St Andrew's University Publications, 20, pp. 40–70.

Talbot, C. 1954. *Anglo-Saxon Missionaries in Germany* (London).

Talley, T. J. 1986. *The Origins of the Liturgical Year* (New York).

Taviani, H. 1979. 'Du refus au défi. Essai sur la psychologie hérétique au début du xie siècle', in *Actes du 102e Congrès National des sociétés savantes*, Limoges 1977, II (Paris), pp. 175–86.

TeSelle, E. 1970. *Augustine the Theologian* (London).

Theis, L. 1976. 'Saints sans famille? Quelques remarques sur la famille dans le monde franc à travers les sources hagiographiques', in *Revue historique* 255, pp. 3–20.

Thouzellier, C. 1969. *Catharisme et Valdéisme en Languedoc à la fin du xiie et au début du xiiie siècle. Politique pontificale – controverses*, Publications de la Faculté des Lettres et sciences humaines de Paris, série recherches, 26 (Paris).

343

Bibliography

Thwaites, R. G. (ed.) 1897. *The Jesuit Relations and Allied Documents. Travels and Explorations of the Jesuit Missionaries in New France 1610–1791*, v (Cleveland).

Turner, V. 1967. *The Forest of Symbols* (Ithaca and London).

Underwood, P. 1950. 'The Fountain of Life in Manuscripts of the Gospels', in *Dumbarton Oaks Papers* 5, pp. 41–138.

Van der Lof, L. J. 1962. 'The Date of the *De catechizandis rudibus*', in *Vigiliae Christianae* 16, pp. 198–204.

  1964. 'Présence réelle selon saint Augustin', in *Revue des Etudes Augustiniennes* 10, pp. 295–304.

Van der Meer, F. 1961. *Augustine the Bishop. The Life and Work of a Father of the Church*, transl. from the Dutch by B. Battershaw and E. R. Lamb (London and New York).

Van Gennep, A. 1960. *Rites of Passage*, transl. from the French by M. B. Vizedom and G. L. Caffee (London).

Van Werrecke, H. 1960. Review of Russell 1958, in *Le Moyen Age* 56, pp. 199–204.

Vaughan, Henry. 1914. *Works*, ed. L. C. Martin, 2 vols. (Oxford 1914).

Verheijen, L. 1957. 'Mysterion, sacramentum, et la synagogue', in *Recherches de science religieuse* 45, pp. 321–37.

Vermes, G. 1973. *Jesus the Jew. A Historian's Reading of the Gospels* (New York).

  1983. *Jesus and the World of Judaism* (Philadelphia).

Violante, C., and Fonseca, C. D. 1964. 'Ubicazione e dedicazione delle cattedrali dalle origini al periodo romanico nelle città dell'Italia centro-settentrionale', in *Il Romanico Pistoiese nei suoi rapporti con l'arte romanica dell'Occidente*, Atti del I Convegno internazionale di studi medioevale di storia e d'arte, Centro di Studi Storici, Pistoia, pp. 303–52.

Vogel, C. 1983. *Medieval Liturgy: An Introduction to the Sources*, revised and transl. by W. G. Storey and N. K. Rasmussen (Washington).

Von Simson, O. G. 1956. *The Gothic Cathedral* (London).

Walsh, M. M. 1977. 'The Baptismal Flood in the Old English Andreas: Liturgical and Typological Depths', in *Traditio* 33, pp. 137–58.

Walter, C. 1982. *Art and Ritual of the Byzantine Church* (London).

Warnock, M. 1976. *Imagination* (London).

Wedderburn, A. J. M. 1987. 'The Soteriology of the Mysteries and Pauline Baptismal Theology', in *Novum Testamentum* 39, pp. 53–72.

Weil, S. 1951. *Attente de Dieu* (Paris).

Wettstein, J. 1971. *La Fresque romane: Italie, France, Espagne. Etudes comparatives*, I, Bibliothèque de la Société française d'Archéologie, 2 (Geneva).

Wilmart, A. 1933. 'Un florilège carolingien sur le symbolisme du baptême, avec un appendice sur la lettre de Jean Diacre', in *Studi e Testi* 59 (Vatican), pp. 153–79.

Wood, C. T. 1981. 'The Doctors' Dilemma: Sin, Salvation, and the Menstrual Cycle in Medieval Thought', in *Speculum* 56, pp. 710–27.

Woolf, Virginia. 1943. *The Death of the Moth* (London).

Wormald, P. 1978. 'Bede and Beowulf', in R. T. Farrell (ed.), *Bede and Anglo-Saxon England*, papers in honour of the 1300th anniversary of the birth of

Bibliography

Bede, given at Cornell University in 1973 and 1974, British Archaeological Reports 46, pp. 32–69.

Ysebaert, J. 1962. *Greek Baptismal Terminology. Its Origins and Early Development*, Graecitas christianorum primaeva, 1 (Nijmegen).

Zarnecki, G., Holt, J. and Holland, J. (eds.) 1984. *English Romanesque Art 1066–1200, Catalogue of the Exhibition at the Hayward Gallery, London 5 April–8 July 1984* (London).

Zovatto, P. L. 1947a. 'Il battistero di Concordia Sagittaria', in *Arte Veneta* 1, pp. 171–84.

    1947b. 'Il battistero di Concordia Sagittaria', in *Arte Veneta* 1, pp. 243–50.

Zovatto, P. L. and Brusin, G. 1960. *Monumenti Romani e Cristiani di Iulia Concordia* (Pordenone).

Zwi Werblowsky, R. J. 1957. 'On the Baptismal Rite According to Saint Hippolytus', in *Studia Patristica* 2.2, pp. 93–105.

    1975. 'A Note on Purification and Proselyte Baptism', in J. Neusner (ed.), *Christianity, Judaism, and Other Greco-Roman cults*, III (Leiden), pp. 200–5.

INDEX

Aachen (chapel of Charlemagne), 269

Abelard, 7–8, 220; on authorities, 252–3; diffidence of, 257–66; and the philosophers of Antiquity, 263–6; on suicide, 264–5; *Ethics*, 227–8; *Historia Calamitatum*, 227–31; *Sic et non*, 252–3; *Theologia Christiana*, 263–6

Abraham, 168, 200; and Isaac, 297 (pl. 7), 301, 307–10, 308 (pl. 13)

Acts of the Apostles, 9, 10, 40–3, 49, 71

Adam, Karl, 98

Admonitio Generalis, 138 n. 22, 217

Adoptianism, 187, and n. 37

Ælfric of Winchester, 138 n. 21, 139 n. 24

Aelius Aristides, 56, 61, 82

Æthelwold of Winchester, St, 234 n. 42

Alan of Lille, 257

Albenga, *see* baptisteries

Alcuin, 1, 139; on anointing before baptism, 151; on baptism and conversion, 130; on the meaning of baptism, 157 n. 83; on penitence, 116, 184 n. 21; on persuasion and baptism, 186–90

allegory, 210–11, 217–19

Ambrose of Milan, 1, 2, 3, 7, 32, 47, 87, 102, 116, 121, 159; on death and resurrection, 69–71; the image of the fish, 69–71; on memory, 66–8; on Naaman the Syrian, 67; on original sin, 118–19; on sacrament 67–72; Ambrose the possible author of inscription in the baptistery of Santa Thecla, Milan, 270–1

Ambrosiaster, 120 n. 108

Anabaptism, 72

anamnesis, 15, 61, 104 n. 55, 108, 167–73, 170, 195, 203, 231

Anastasis, 281

Andreas, 6, 145, 189, 201–2

Andrew, Acts of, 202

androgyny, 27

anointing, 14, 41, 173; of chest and shoulders in baptism, 151; with chrism, 154–5, 208–9, 212; of priest's hands, 142

Anselm of Canterbury, 103 n. 49; *Cur deus homo*, 180–1; *Meditations*, 230 n. 31

Anselm of Laon, 252 n. 100

apertio aurium, 143, 164

Apuleius, 34, 54, 61

Aquileia, 291; *see also* liturgical types

Arians, 152

Aristotle, 17, 244–5

Arno of Salzburg, on catechizing, 188–93

Ascension, the, 33

Asclepius, 263

Asclepius I, 57 n. 42

Asser, *Life of Alfred*, 207

Athanasius, 16

Auerbach, Erich, 217

Augustine of Canterbury, St, 197

Augustine of Hippo, St, 1–5, 85, 136–7, 169–71, 229, 238, 249 nn. 89 and 91–2, 252, 258–9, 271; on catechizing, 94–109, 189–92; on *charitas*, 95–8, 101–9; and 'clinical baptism', 117–18; on the cross, 100–1; on *cultus dei*, 88, 92–100, 107, 110–12; and Donatism, 123, 127; on history, 95–8; on infant baptism, 113–29; on original sin, 109–29; on *peregrinatio*, 87–8, 91; on *renouatio*, 87–9, 92–4, 111; on sacrament and remembering, 89–98, 112; on the Two Cities, 101, 122, 128; on understanding signs, 89, 102–10

authorities, 1, 252–3, 261

autobiography, 226–36

Avars, 185–6, 191

baptism
   baptismal practices: 'clinical baptism',

347

Index

15–16, 117–18; baptism at Easter and Pentecost, *see under* Easter and Pentecost; baptism at Epiphany, 137, 315–19; baptism of immersion, 31, 53, 140, 151, 155 n. 76, 195 n. 65, 273; threefold immersion, 140–1, 187 n. 37; baptism in interrogatory form, 140–1; Jewish proselyte baptism, 11 and n. 9; baptism in 'living water', 10; repetition of baptism, 127; baptism in the Syrian rite, 26 n. 52

baptismal themes: baptism as burial, 32, 70, 91, 101, 155 n. 76; cosmic baptism, 57; the crossing of the Red Sea, 78, 167, 200–1, 259, *see also* Red Sea; as death and resurrection, 32, 34, 70–1, 78, 83, 101, 155 n. 76, 168, 173, 270–82, *see also* death and resurrection; and the descent of the Holy Spirit, 25, 211; the Flood, 78, 167, 200; and the imagery of marriage, 27, 72, 319 n. 41; as a mirror, 25, 183–4, 210; and the Nativity, 273–4, 276–80, 318–19; and the 'new man', 50, 145, 184, 259; baptism as offering, 42–3; Passover, 78; as purification, 9–20, 30, 47, 158; as rebirth, 3, 19, 27, 32, 50–2, 69, 70–1, 83, 156, 173, 232–5, 270–82, *see also* rebirth; baptism and resurrection, 27; as threat, 78–9, 279–80

themes associated with baptism; baptism and conceptions of time, 87–98, 181–2, 291–319, *see also* anamnesis; history; repetition; baptism and dream, 73–86; baptism and persuasion, 185–206; *see also* catechesis; conversion; dualism; eucharist; Harrowing of Hell; kingship; liturgy; passage; priesthood; repentance; sacrament; sacrifice; *similitudo*; symbol
see also exorcism; washing of feet

Baptism of Christ: as anointing of Christ, 41, 215; with Christ as child, 3, 149 and n. 57; and descent of Holy Spirit, 25, 41, 43; fresco in the baptistery of Concordia Sagittaria, 295, 310, 313, 315–19; in Maximus of Turin, 315–19; and river Jordan, 12 n. 11, 57, 158, 168, 172

baptism of fire, 79

baptism of infants, 3, 7, 10, 178, 242; and confirmation, 179–84; and the problem of moral intention, 125–9, 131–6, 188, 222, 231–5 (Guibert de Nogent), 236, 254–66 (Abelard); baptism *quamprimum* ('as soon as possible') 115–16, 125, 138, 254; and the religion of the Middle Ages, 136–55; as remedy for original sin, 87–8, 113–29; and Semipelagianism, 131–3

baptism in the theology of St John the Evangelist and St Paul, 32–5, 71

baptisteries: Albenga, 270; Cividale (Friuli), 277 n. 32; Concordia Sagittaria, 291–319; Cremona, 269, 283, 287; Dura-Europos, 41 n. 85; San Giovanni, Florence, 284; San Giovanni, Milan, 288; Santa Thecla, Milan, 121–2, 269, 270–2; San Giovanni, Naples, 41 n. 85, 269, 281–2; Lateran baptistery, Rome, 269; in Northern Europe, 267–8; Novara, 279–81, 312; Ostia, 269; Pisa, 275, 285–6; of the Arians and of the Orthodox, Ravenna, 12, 281; *see also* Venasque

baptistery: and *civiltà*, 282–90; and inscriptions, 270–6; as octagon, 270–2, 275–6; and Roman architecture, 268–70; as tomb, 69, 270–3; and urban topography 268–9; as womb, 271–3, 276–7; *see also martyrium*; *tholos*; *triclinium*; *triconchos*

Barnabas, Letter of, 18

Basil the Great, 58

Bede, 6, 152 n. 68, 192, 267; on Christ and time 172 n. 110; Bede's clear-sightedness, 207–10; on conversion, 194, 197–200; and the humility of King Oswin, 205–6; on the possibility of innocence, 153–5

bees, 4; eulogy of bees, 177–8

Benedict of Aniane, 1, 141, 188

Benedictio fontis (blessing of the waters), 167–73, 314–15

Benedictus Crispus, bishop of Milan, 272

Beowulf, 6, 174, 193–4, 198, 207

Berengar of Tours, 1, 157, 221–3, 243–54; *Rescriptum contra Lanfrannum*, 223, 249–54; *Letter to Adelmann*, 250–1

Berengaudius, 280

Bernard of Clairvaux, St, 225–6, 259–60, 262–3, 264, 265

Bernardus Silvestris, 163, 171

Beroldus of Milan, 288–90

Index

blessing of the waters, see *Benedictio fontis*
blindness, 40, 64–8
body, 13, 112, 221–3; *see also under* Christ
Boethius, 229
Boniface, St, bishop of Mainz, 139, 141, 185, 203–6
Boniface V, Pope, 193
Boniface, bishop of Carthage, 125–9
Botte, Dom Bernard, 64
brazen serpent, 33
bread, 13, 75, 100
Brendan, St, Prayer of, 174–5
Brooke, Christopher, 163
Brown, Peter, 39
Burchard of Worms, 149
Burckhardt, Jakob, 290
Byzantine art, 303–7

Caedmon, 200
Caedwalla, King of the West Saxons, 272
Caesarius of Arles, 136, 140, 155–6
Cainites, the, 60
Camelot, P. T., 48
Candidus of Fulda, 246
Candlemas, 134 n. 10, 150 n. 60, 242
canon law, 218, 251 and n. 99, 261
catechesis, 10, 15–16, 32, 58, 94–109, 116, 137, 142–4, 189–97
catechumens, 11, 14, 49, 98, 105, 151–2, 169, 187
Catharism, 235–6
Celsus, 58
charisma, 43
Charlemagne: letter on baptism, 151, 154, 187; war against the Saxons and Avars, 185–7
Chartres, 235
child, 3, 115, 131–6, 141–5, 148–52, 160, 173, 178, 195–6; and drawing lots, 150; ritual hair-cutting of, 149–50; *see also* baptism of infants; Christ-child
Christ, 168, 231; the body of Christ in the eucharist, 243–54; and the empty tomb, 254–5, 304–5; as Immanuel, 313; Nativity of, 4, 273, 276–7, 318–19
Christ and Satan, 147, 200–3
Christ-child, 3, 134, 149, 280
Christianity: as interpretation, 44; and language, 46; as rejection of society, 35–9, and the 'unknown God', 32, 39, 193ff; *see also* conversion; Gnosticism; Judaism; paganism
Christmas, 90, 94, 276, 318

Chromatius of Aquileia, 289 n. 56, 291
church, the, 125–8, 153–4
churching, 149 n. 56
Cicero, 54
Cimabue, 290
circumcision, 42, 47, 119, 259
Cividale, *see* baptisteries
Clement of Alexandria, 58
Clovis, King of the Franks, 198
Community Rule, 18–19
Concordia Sagittaria, 5, 6, 291–319; *see also* baptisteries; baptistery
confession, 235
confirmation, 179–84
conscientia, 206, 255ff
Constantine, Emperor, 16 n. 20
conversion, 3, 7; in the Acts of the Apostles, 40–3; and the Baptism of Christ, 315–17; and catechizing in Augustine, 98–109; and the *Confessions* of Augustine, 227; as 'crisis', 9–20, 28–35, 35–6, 46; and mission, 185–206; and polemic against paganism, 35–9; as progression into Christianity, 45–7; *see also* baptism; passage; repentance
coparenthood, 158
Cornelius, the centurion, 42–3
Corpus Hermeticum, 100
corpus mysticum, 245–7
Councils: Aix (836), 138 n. 22; on the banks of the Danube (796), 186; Girone (517), 138; Orange (529), 136–7; Paris (829), 138 n. 22
covenant, 32, 47
creatio ex nihilo, 35–8, 148, 161, 193, 196, 226
Creation, 3, 57, 157, 171–2; baptism as re-creation, 148–9; Creation in the blessing of the waters, 167; and the eucharistic change, 244; in the *Gelasian* blessing of the oil, 211–13; and likeness, 250; in Neoplatonism and liturgy, 161–3; and sacrament as making, 236; as a type of baptism, 200
Creed, 43, 48–9, 190; Apostles' Creed, 31, 140; Creed of Nicaea-Constantinople, 143
crusade, 253–5
Cyprian of Carthage, 59; baptism and conversion, 50–2, 87; the church as *hortus conclusus,* 69, 127–8; and original sin, 118–19
Pseudo-Cyprian, 184 n. 20, 197 and n. 71
Cyril of Jerusalem, 65 n. 68, 69

349

Index

Fulda, 140, 217
Fulda Sacramentary, see liturgies

Galla Placidia, mausoleum of (Ravenna), 270
Geertz, Clifford, 111
Gelasian Sacramentary, see liturgies
Genesis (Anglo-Saxon version) 200, 215
George, St, 301 (pl. 11), 303–5
Gilson, E. P., 223–6
Giovanni di Paolo, 283
Gnosticism, 20–35, 39, 40, 43, 146; and the absurd, 23; and antinomianism, 21; and the meeting with the self, 25; and myth, 21–3, 29; and twinship, 28 n. 58
godparenthood, 143, 158
Good Friday, 62
Good Shepherd, the, 75, 119 n. 107
Gothic architecture, 163–4, 166
Gottschalk of Orbais, 220
Gratian, *Decretum*, 261
Gregorian Reform, 251
Gregory the Great, 179 n. 2; *Homily on Ezechiel*, used indirectly for catechesis, 192; on humility and miracle, 205 and n. 93; on original sin, 132–3; on single and triple immersion in baptism, 187 n. 37
Gregory II, Pope, 105
Gregory Nazianzen, 58
Gregory of Nyssa, 58, 275
Gregory of Tours, 6, 198 n. 76, 217
Guibert de Nogent, 123, 175; autobiography and baptism, 231–5
Guinefort the holy greyhound, 233 n. 37

Hadrianum; *see* liturgies
Hadrianum Supplement, see liturgies
von Harnack, Adolf, 59
Harrowing of Hell, the, 25, 124, 146, 271; *see also* Anastasis
Hebrews, Letter to the, 49
Hegel, G. W. F., 254–5
heimarmenē, 21, 28, 29
Hellenistic religion, 17 and n. 23
heresy, 235–6
Hermagoras, St, first bishop of Aquileia, 291, 303
Hermas, 41
Hildefonsus of Toledo, 206
Hildegard of Bingen, 7, 71
Hippolytus of Rome, *Apostolic Tradition*, 2, 9–20, 22, 28, 30, 32–4, 35, 39, 75, 116, 142

history: and changes in liturgical practice, 218; and the death of Christ, 34; and the increase in religious understanding, 257, 260; Jerusalem the end of history, 256–7; as loss and permanence, 221, 247–9; and repetition, 167–73; and revelation, 31, 49–50; as sign, 66–8, 95–9, 104
holy man, 39, 263
Holy Saturday, 143, 180, 200, 210
Homer, 37, 57
honey, 13, 30, 75
Hugh of St Victor, 1, 257, 259 n. 124
Humbert of Silva-Candida, 223
humours of the body, 234 n. 43
hylē, 21
Hymn of the Pearl, 24–5

Ignatius, St, 240
illuminatio in the liturgy, 143–4
imago dei, 223–7
imitatio Christi, 112, 231; in Lanfranc's account of the eucharist, 249–50
incubation, 263 and n. 130
Ine, Laws of, 138 n. 21
Ingelheim (chapel in palace of Charlemagne) 270 n. 11
ingenium, 228
Innocents, the Feast of, 133–6, 142, 173
integumentum, 162, 171–2
Irenaeus of Lyon, 48–9
Isidore of Seville, 184
Italian communes, 268–9, 282–90
Ivo of Chartres, 257, 259

Jacopone da Todi, 290
James, William, on the 'sick soul', 28–9, 35–6, 46
Jerome, St, 52, 186, 264
Jerusalem, 283, 312; Council of, 42; and the crusaders, 253; and the Holy Sepulchre, 253, 255, 269, 275, 284 n. 46, 285
Jesse, Tree of, 170, 183, 214
Jesse of Amiens, 156 n. 80, 178
Jewish-Christianity, 18–19, 22, 26 n. 52, 29, 40, 41
John the Baptist, 12; and the baptism of repentance, 35; Cathars' opposition of John the Baptist and Christ, 236; as child-prophet, 149; in fresco of Concordia Sagittaria, 295; going out into the wilderness, 283
John Cassian, St, 132

351

Index

John of the Cross, St, 28
John the Deacon, 142–3, 151 n. 62, 187
John the Evangelist, 32–5, 64–5, 66; Feast of, in Rite of Milan on 27 December, 318–19
John of Salisbury, 257, 262
John Scot Eriugena, 163
Jonah, 34, 173, 257
Jonas of Orléans, 183–4
Jonas, Hans, 24
Jones, David, 236–43
Jordan river, 12, 67, 149 n. 57, 150, 167–8, 211, 277, 295, 317
Joshua, 159
Judaism, liking for allegory in Alexandrian Judaism, 39; association between water and the lower world in Judaism, 146 n. 45; Christianity and Gnosticism as developments from Judaism, 28; clean and unclean food, 42; clean and unclean water, 12–13; death as final repentance in rabbinic thinking, 34, 78; Jews included in a formula of exorcism, 152; original sin in rabbinic thought, 113 n. 84; see also circumcision
Julian of Eclanum, 114, 124, 154
Jung, Carl-Gustav, 55 n. 31, 79–80
Junius 11 (Bodley MS), 200–3
Juvenal, 59

Kantorowicz, Ernst, 155, 286–7
kerygma, 39, 42
Kierkegaard, Søren, 203 n. 86, 226, 307–8
Kilian, St (Irish missionary), 203–4
kingship, 30, 41, 155, 183–4, 206
Klee, Paul, 238
'Know Thyself', 223–7
Knox, Ronald, 52–3, 60
Krautheimer, Richard, 275–85

Lactantius, 37–8
Lampe, G. W. H., 41
Lanfranc of Bec, 1, 221–3, 243–54
Last Judgement, the, 124, 144, 281
laying on of hands, 11, 14, 19, 31, 154, 179 n. 2; see also confirmation; sphragis
Leidrad of Lyon, 5, 156 n. 76, 159–65, 167–70, 188 n. 39
Lent, 143, 176, 185, 195–6
Leo the Great, 215–17, 221, 225, 273, 276–7
Leonine or Verona Sacramentary: see Liturgies

Lévi-Strauss, Claude, 241–2
Lévy-Bruhl, Lucien, 239–41
likeness, see similitudo
litany, 225 n. 11
liturgical types: of Aquileia, 140 n. 27, 283 n. 41, 289, 304; of Catalonia-Narbonne, 140 n. 27, 283 n. 41; Eighth-Century Gelasian, 140; Gallican, 6; Gregorian, 6, 140 n. 27, 141–8 passim, 176, 188; Irish, 6, 108–9; Milanese, 140, 288–90, 304; Mozarabic, 6, 12, 162–6, 195
liturgies
  missals: Missale duplex, 305 n. 16, 317 n. 38, 318 and n. 40; Missale Gothicum, 135 n. 13, 141 n. 30
  sacramentaries: Sacramentary of Angoulême, 141 n. 30; Fulda Sacramentary, 12 n. 11, 134 n. 11, 195–6, 204, 242, 277 n. 32; Gelasian Sacramentary, 6, 140–8, 151, 160 n. 92, 172–7, 179–80, 195, 197, 200, 211–13, 215–17, 219–20; Liber Sacramentorum Gellonensis (Saint-Guilhem-le-Désert), 134 n. 11, 172 n. 112; Hadrianum, 115, 141–4, 150 n. 60; Hadrianum Supplement, 141–5, 151, 160 n. 92; Sacramentary of Marmoutier, 144 n. 37; Sacramentary of Saint Denis, 140 n. 27; Verona or Leonine Sacramentary, 133–6, 142, 149 n. 56, 165, 173
  various: Antiphonary of Bangor, 108; Benedictional of St Æthelwold, 149 n. 57; Godescalc Lectionary, 276; Liber Ordinum, 162–3; North-Italian Services (from Grado, Pavia, or Brescia), 151–2, 283 n. 41; Ordo XI, 43–5, 151; Ordo XV, 141 n. 30; Romano-Germanic Pontifical, 149–50
liturgy: and architecture 267–90; and the city 267–90; as cultus dei, 4, 88, 92–4, 107, 110–12; and efficacy, 157–8, 217, 260; and enlightenment, 143–4; and explanation, 217; and forms, 136–58, 234–5; and intuitio, 162–7, 176, 274; and painting, 279–81, 291–319; and presence, 165–7, 179–81, 184; and story, 200–3; and theatre, 160–1, 207–10, 250, 288–90; and vagueness, 278; see also anamnesis; history; repetition; sacrament
logos, 32–5
lorica, 175

352

Index

Index

Index

Cambridge studies in medieval life and thought
Fourth series

*Also published as a paperback.